HORI-san and MIYAMURA-kun

HORIMIYA

10

HERO
×
DAISUKE HAGIWARA

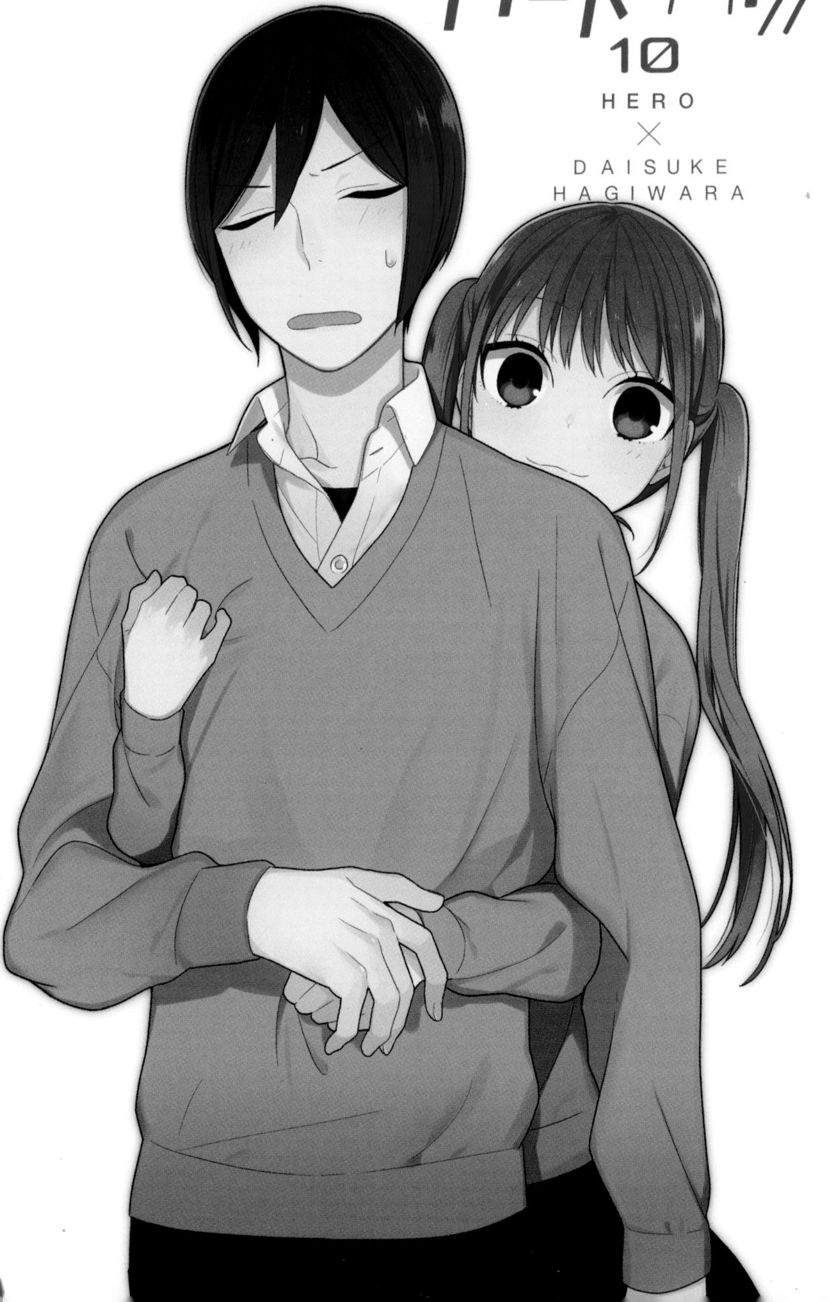

HORI-SAN AND
MIYAMURA-KUN

HORIMIYA
10

C O N T E N T S ★

page·64	3
page·65	35
page·66	49
page·67	63
page·68	89
page·69	107
page·70	117
page·71	147

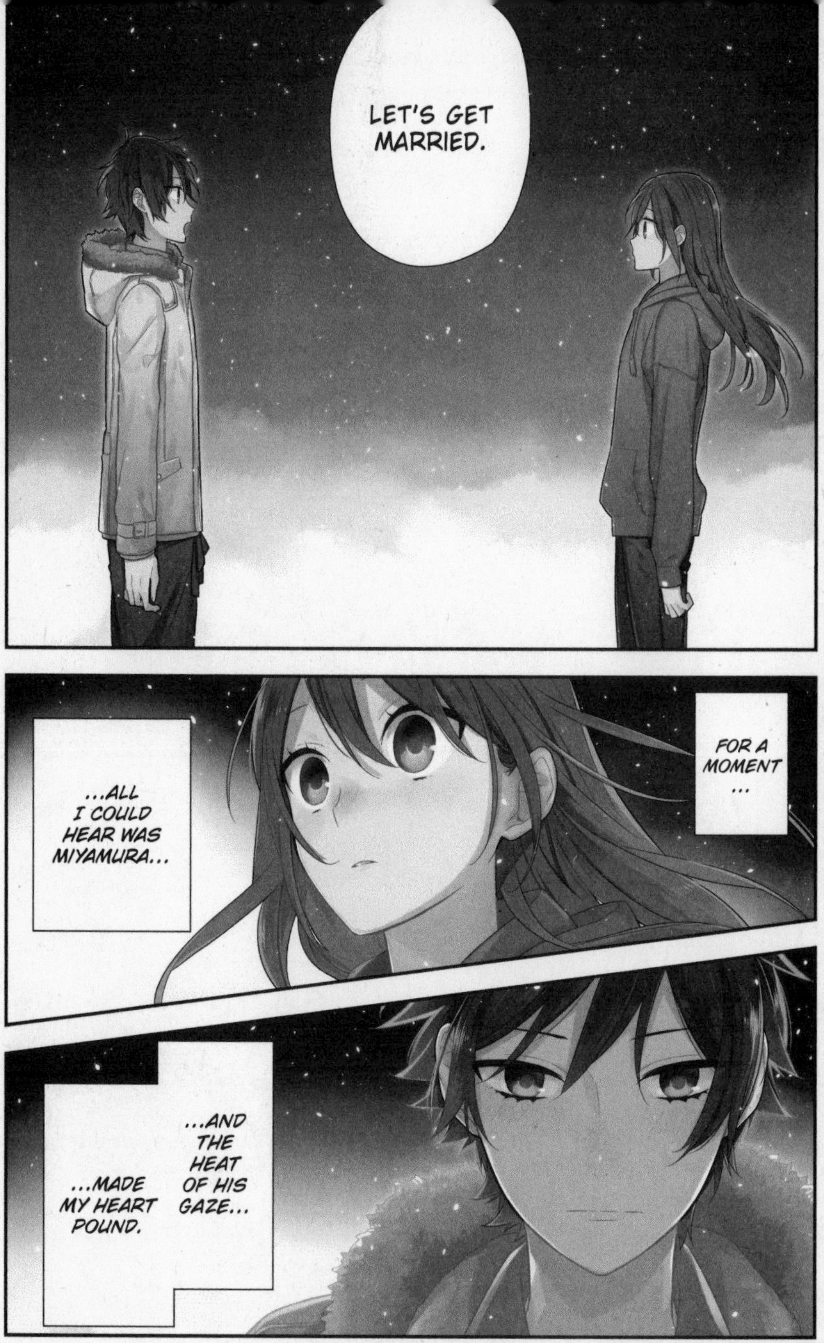
LET'S GET MARRIED.
FOR A MOMENT...
...ALL I COULD HEAR WAS MIYAMURA...
...AND THE HEAT OF HIS GAZE...
...MADE MY HEART POUND.

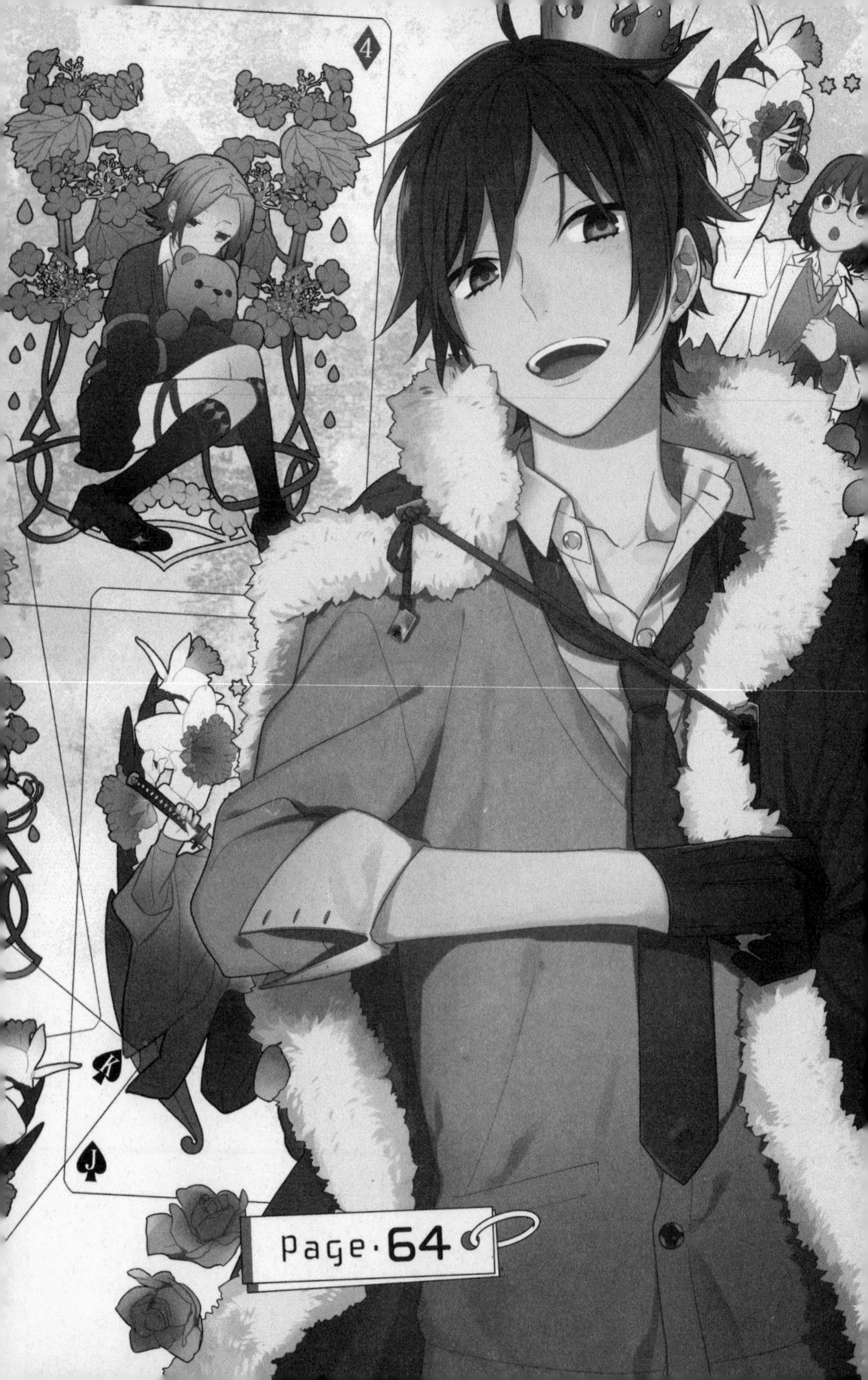
page.64

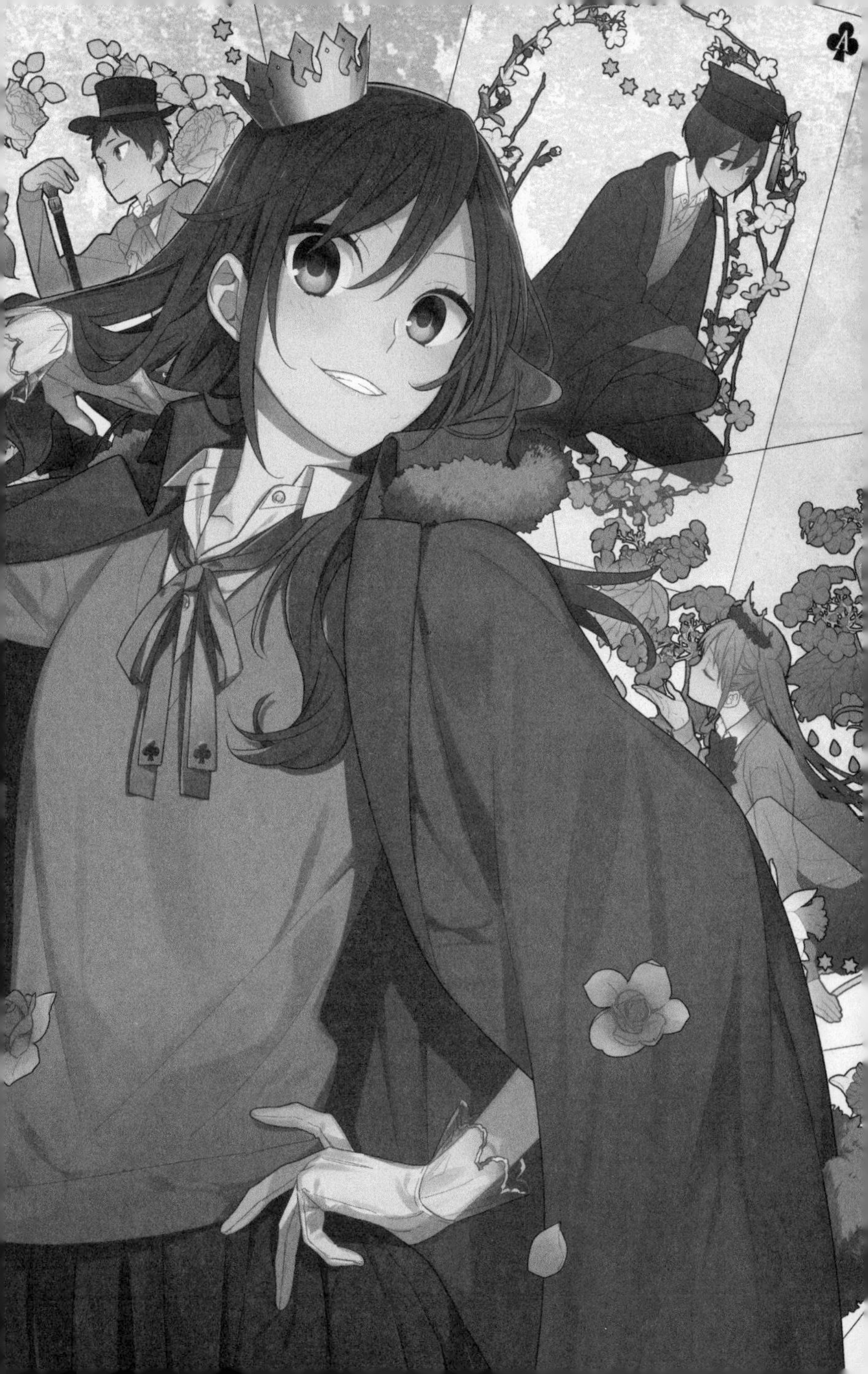

HORIMIYA

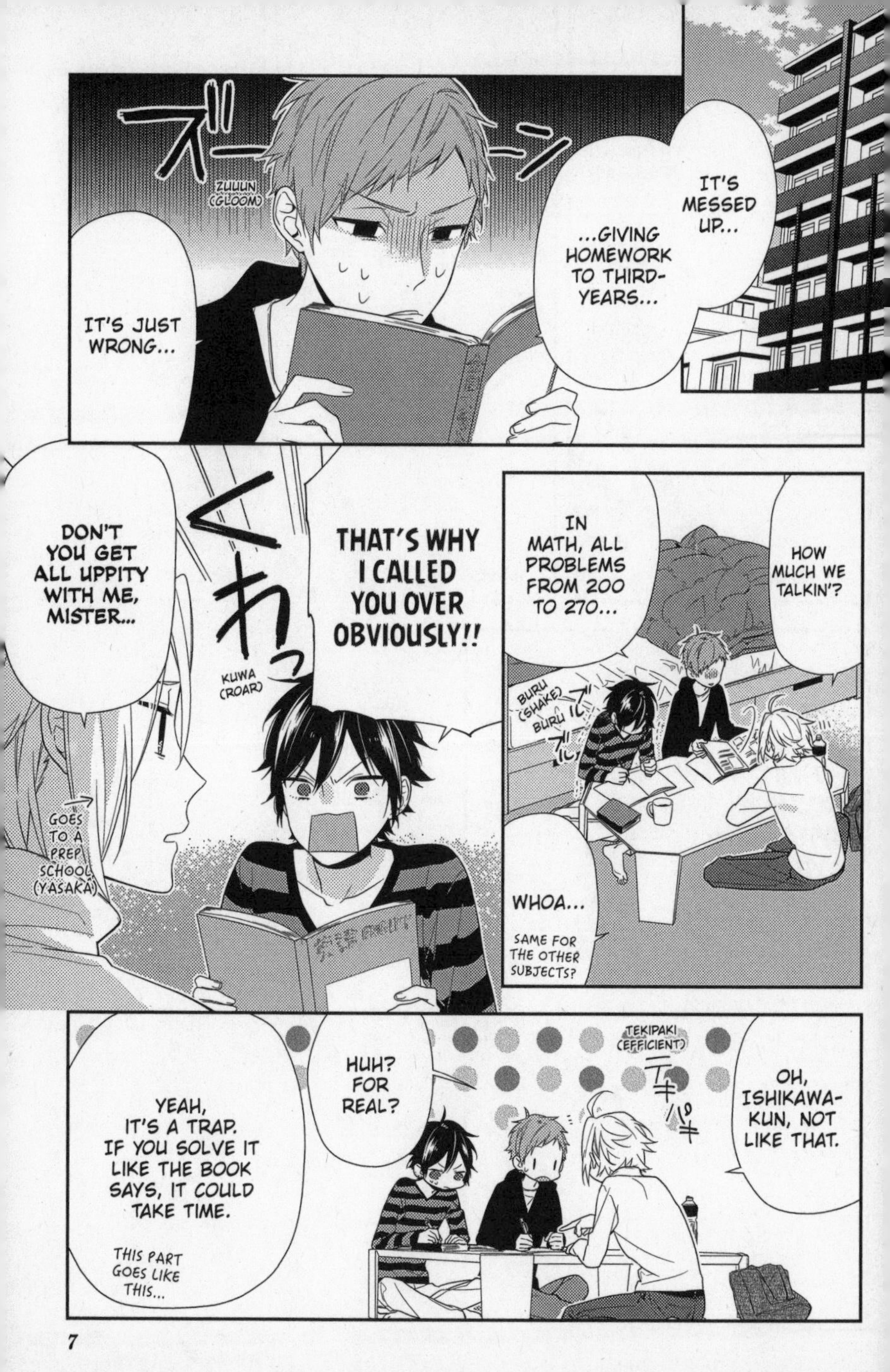
IT'S MESSED UP...
...GIVING HOMEWORK TO THIRD-YEARS...
ZUUUN (GLOOM)
IT'S JUST WRONG...
HOW MUCH WE TALKIN'?
IN MATH, ALL PROBLEMS FROM 200 TO 270...
BURU (SHAKE) BURU
WHOA...
SAME FOR THE OTHER SUBJECTS?
THAT'S WHY I CALLED YOU OVER OBVIOUSLY!!
KUWA (ROAR)
DON'T YOU GET ALL UPPITY WITH ME, MISTER...
GOES TO A PREP SCHOOL (YASAKA)
OH, ISHIKAWA-KUN, NOT LIKE THAT.
TEKIPAKI (EFFICIENT)
HUH? FOR REAL?
YEAH, IT'S A TRAP. IF YOU SOLVE IT LIKE THE BOOK SAYS, IT COULD TAKE TIME.
THIS PART GOES LIKE THIS...

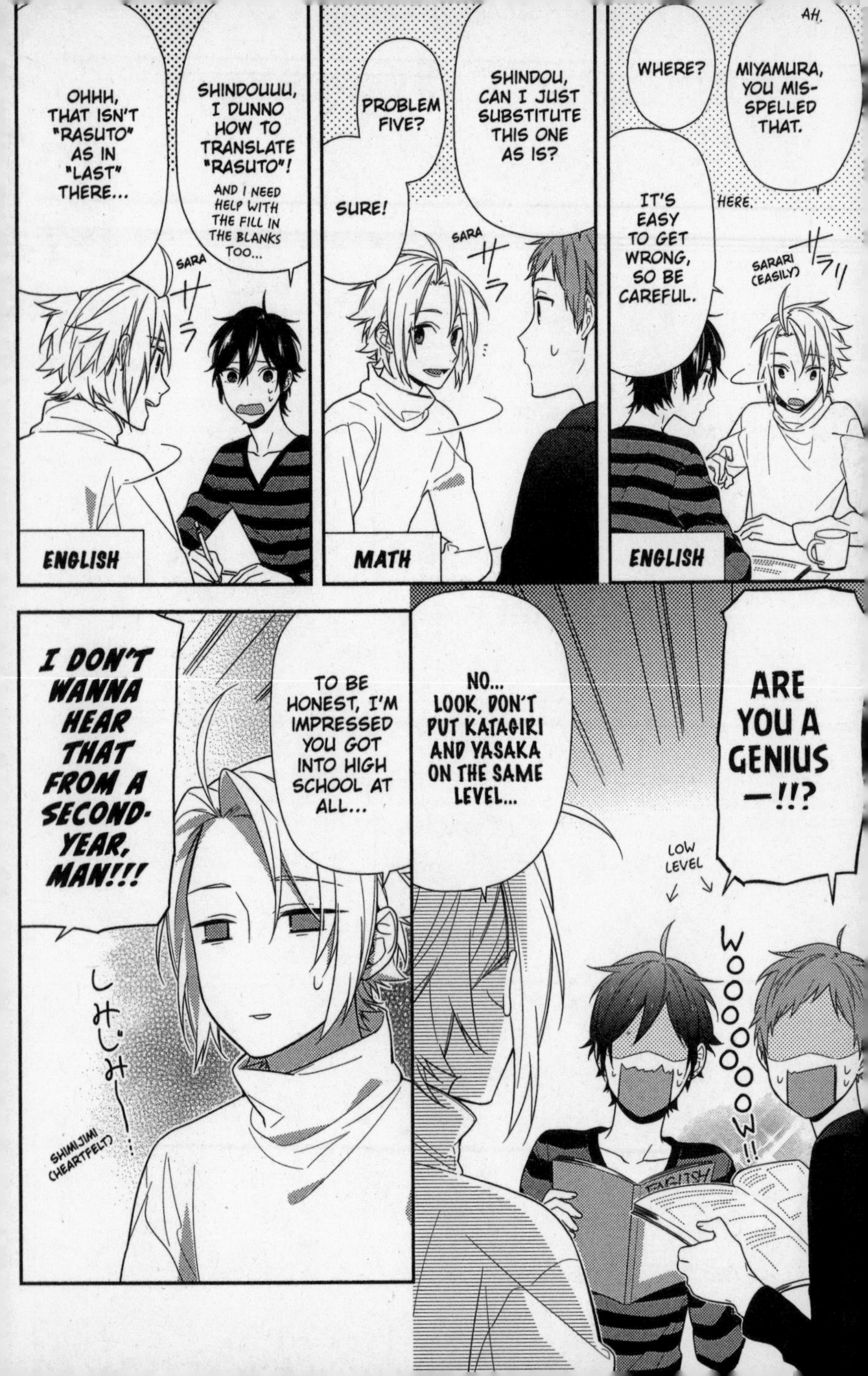
AH.
MIYAMURA, YOU MIS-SPELLED THAT.
WHERE?
HERE.
IT'S EASY TO GET WRONG, SO BE CAREFUL.
SARARI (EASILY)
ENGLISH
SHINDOU, CAN I JUST SUBSTITUTE THIS ONE AS IS?
PROBLEM FIVE?
SURE!
SARA
MATH
SHINDOUUU, I DUNNO HOW TO TRANSLATE "RASUTO"!
AND I NEED HELP WITH THE FILL IN THE BLANKS TOO...
OHHH, THAT ISN'T "RASUTO" AS IN "LAST" THERE...
SARA
ENGLISH
ARE YOU A GENIUS—!!?
LOW LEVEL
WOOOOOOOOW!!
NO... LOOK, DON'T PUT KATAGIRI AND YASAKA ON THE SAME LEVEL...
TO BE HONEST, I'M IMPRESSED YOU GOT INTO HIGH SCHOOL AT ALL...
I DON'T WANNA HEAR THAT FROM A SECOND-YEAR, MAN!!!
しみじみー…
SHIMIJIMI (HEARTFELT)

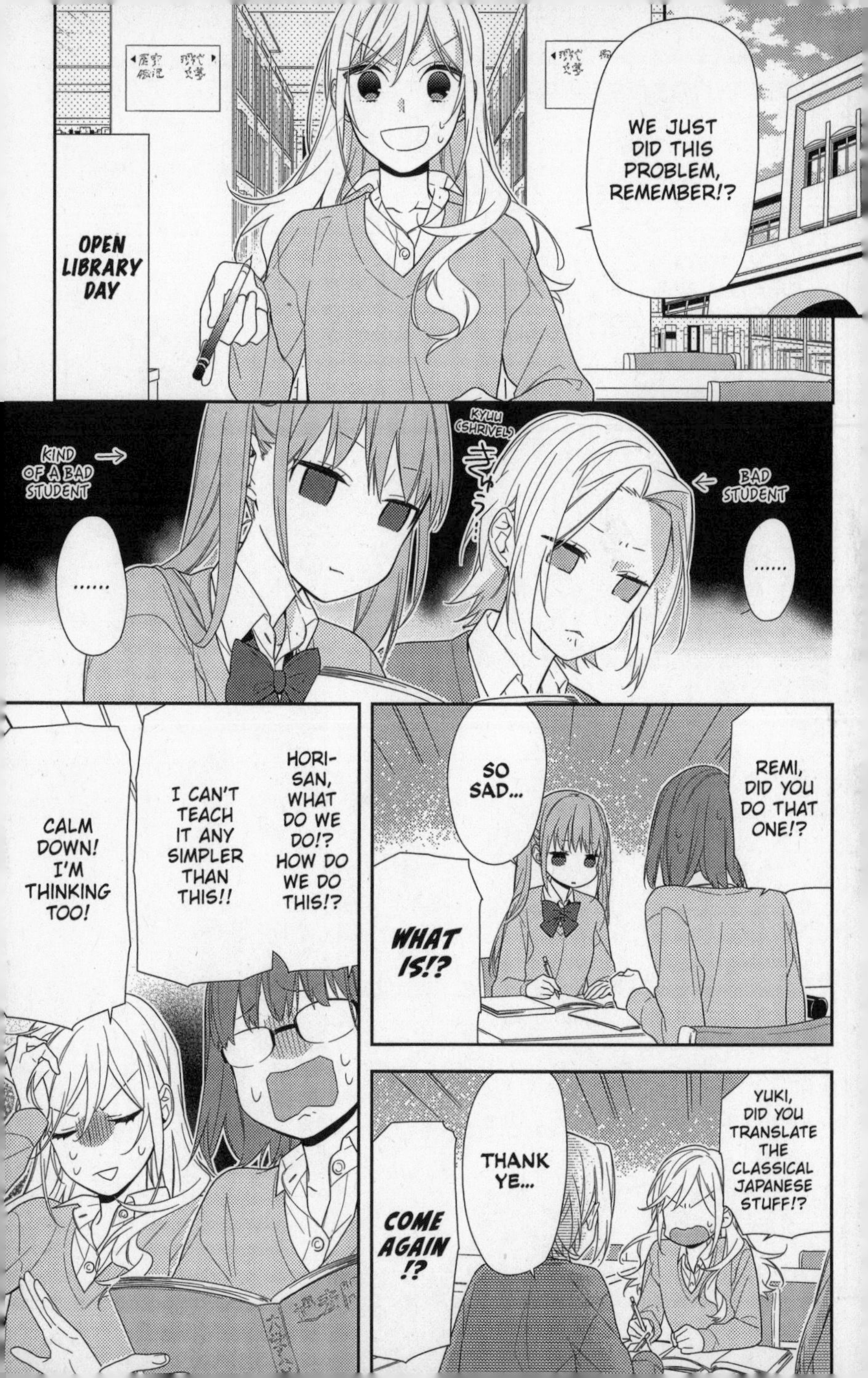
WE JUST DID THIS PROBLEM, REMEMBER!?
OPEN LIBRARY DAY
BAD STUDENT
......
KYUU (SHRIVEL)
きゅう…
KIND OF A BAD STUDENT
......
REMI, DID YOU DO THAT ONE!?
SO SAD...
WHAT IS!?
YUKI, DID YOU TRANSLATE THE CLASSICAL JAPANESE STUFF!?
THANK YE...
COME AGAIN!?
HORI-SAN, WHAT DO WE DO!? HOW DO WE DO THIS!?
I CAN'T TEACH IT ANY SIMPLER THAN THIS!!
CALM DOWN! I'M THINKING TOO!

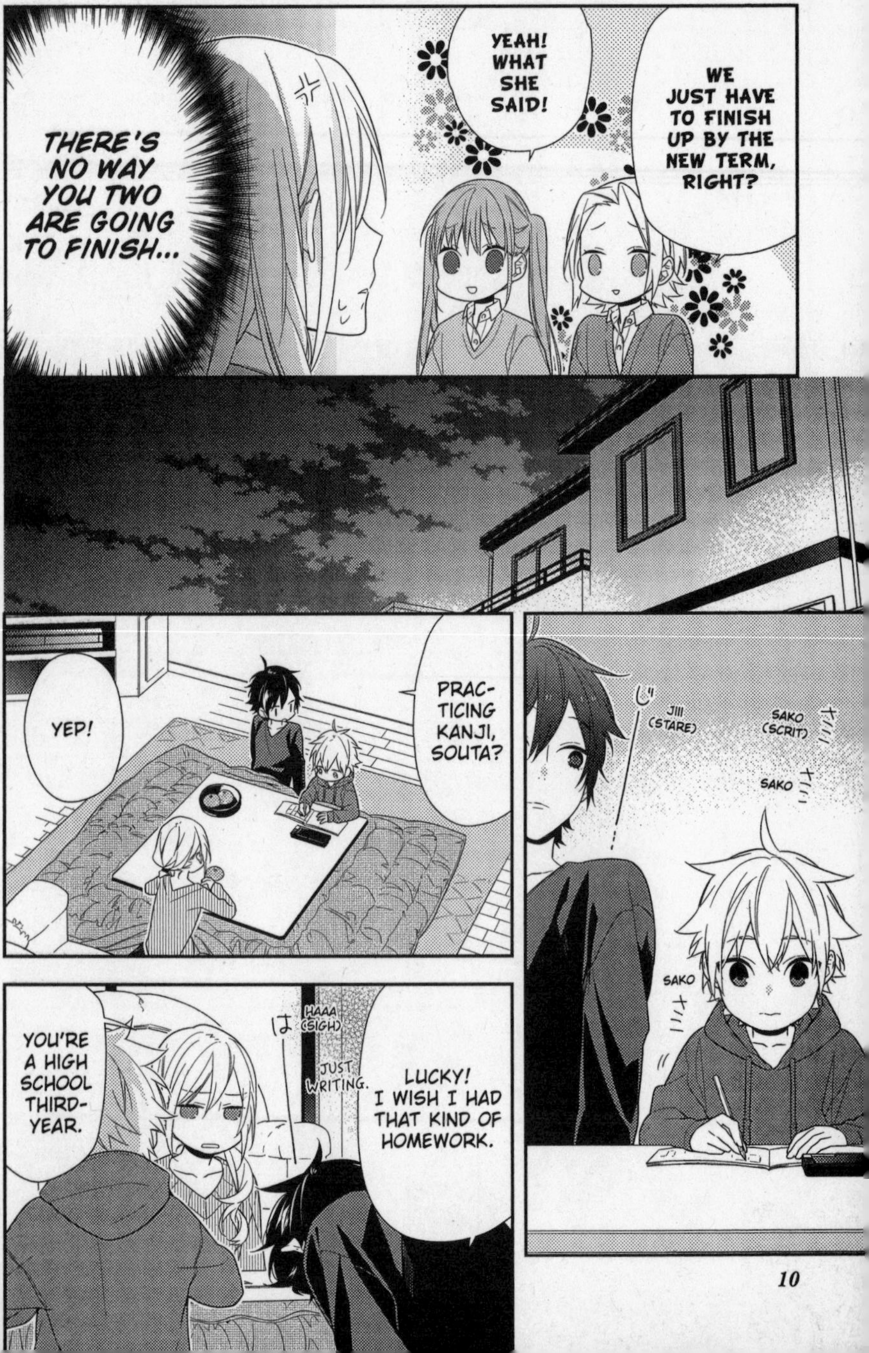
WE JUST HAVE TO FINISH UP BY THE NEW TERM, RIGHT?
YEAH! WHAT SHE SAID!
THERE'S NO WAY YOU TWO ARE GOING TO FINISH...
JIII (STARE)
SAKO (SCRIT)
SAKO
SAKO
PRACTICING KANJI, SOUTA?
YEP!
LUCKY! I WISH I HAD THAT KIND OF HOMEWORK.
JUST WRITING.
HAAA (SIGH)
YOU'RE A HIGH SCHOOL THIRD-YEAR.

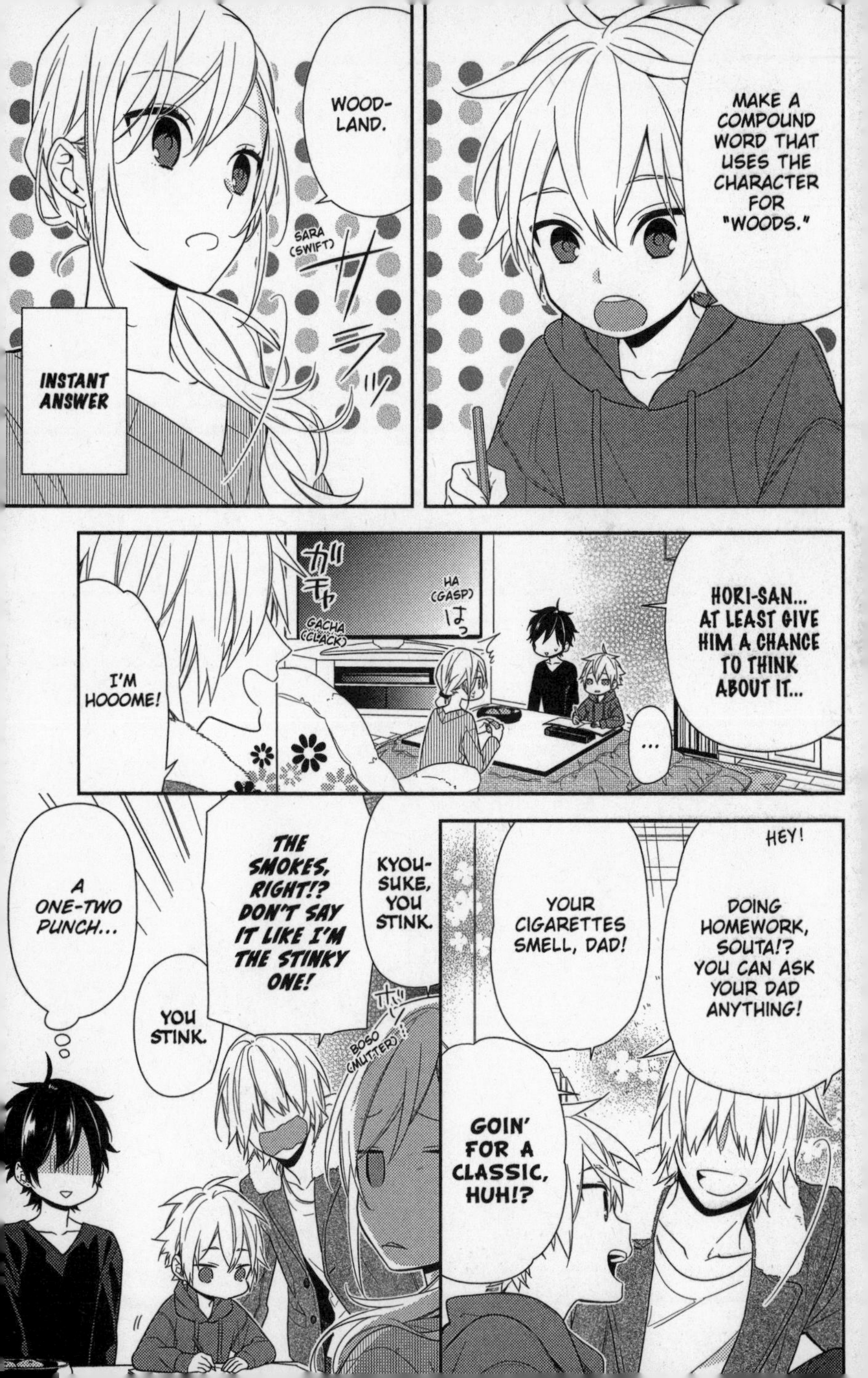
MAKE A COMPOUND WORD THAT USES THE CHARACTER FOR "WOODS."
WOOD-LAND.
SARA (SWIFT)
INSTANT ANSWER
HORI-SAN... AT LEAST GIVE HIM A CHANCE TO THINK ABOUT IT...
...
HA (GASP)
GACHA (CLACK)
I'M HOOOME!
HEY!
DOING HOMEWORK, SOUTA!? YOU CAN ASK YOUR DAD ANYTHING!
YOUR CIGARETTES SMELL, DAD!
GOIN' FOR A CLASSIC, HUH!?
KYOU-SUKE, YOU STINK.
THE SMOKES, RIGHT!? DON'T SAY IT LIKE I'M THE STINKY ONE!
BOSO (MUTTER)
YOU STINK.
A ONE-TWO PUNCH...

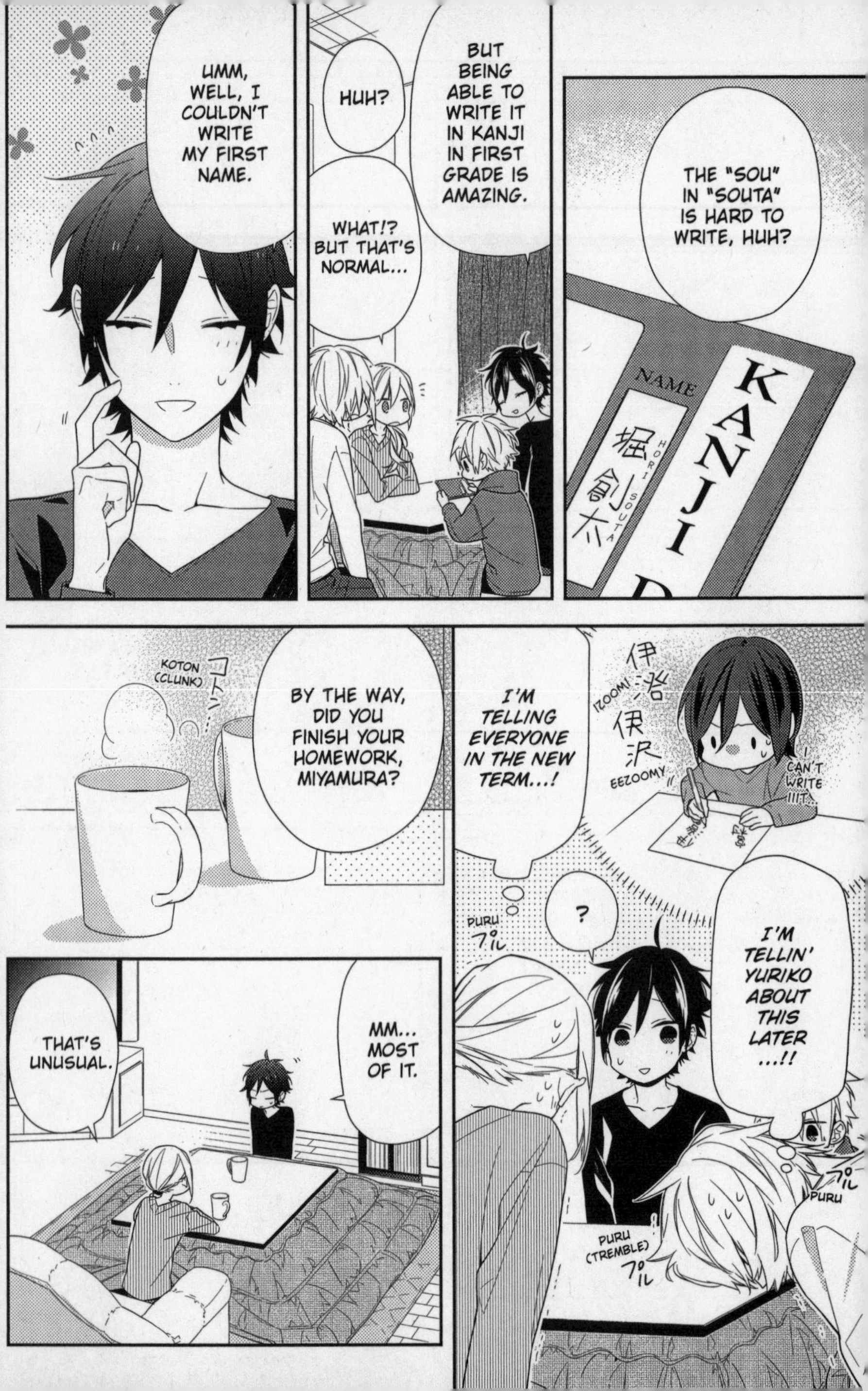
THE "SOU" IN "SOUTA" IS HARD TO WRITE, HUH?
KANJI D
NAME
HORI SOUTA
堀創太
BUT BEING ABLE TO WRITE IT IN KANJI IN FIRST GRADE IS AMAZING.
HUH?
WHAT!? BUT THAT'S NORMAL...
UMM, WELL, I COULDN'T WRITE MY FIRST NAME.
伊浴 IZOOMI
伊沢 EEZOOMY
I CAN'T WRITE IIIT...
I'M TELLING EVERYONE IN THE NEW TERM...!
?
I'M TELLIN' YURIKO ABOUT THIS LATER...!!
PURU プル
PURU プル
PURU (TREMBLE) プル
KOTON (CLUNK) コトン...
BY THE WAY, DID YOU FINISH YOUR HOMEWORK, MIYAMURA?
MM... MOST OF IT.
THAT'S UNUSUAL.

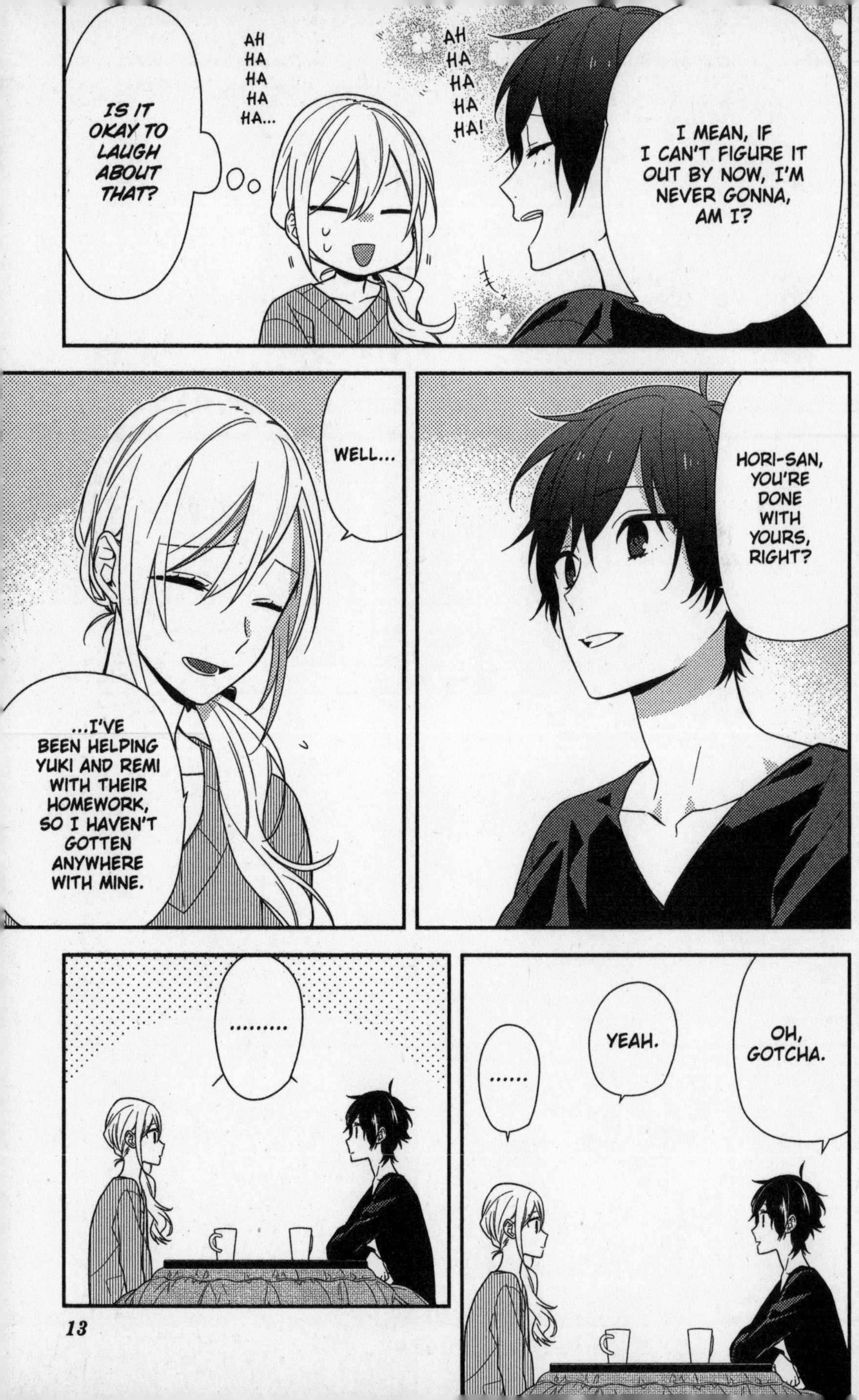
I MEAN, IF I CAN'T FIGURE IT OUT BY NOW, I'M NEVER GONNA, AM I?
AH HA HA HA HA!
AH HA HA HA HA...
IS IT OKAY TO LAUGH ABOUT THAT?
HORI-SAN, YOU'RE DONE WITH YOURS, RIGHT?
WELL...
...I'VE BEEN HELPING YUKI AND REMI WITH THEIR HOMEWORK, SO I HAVEN'T GOTTEN ANYWHERE WITH MINE.
OH, GOTCHA.
YEAH.
......
....

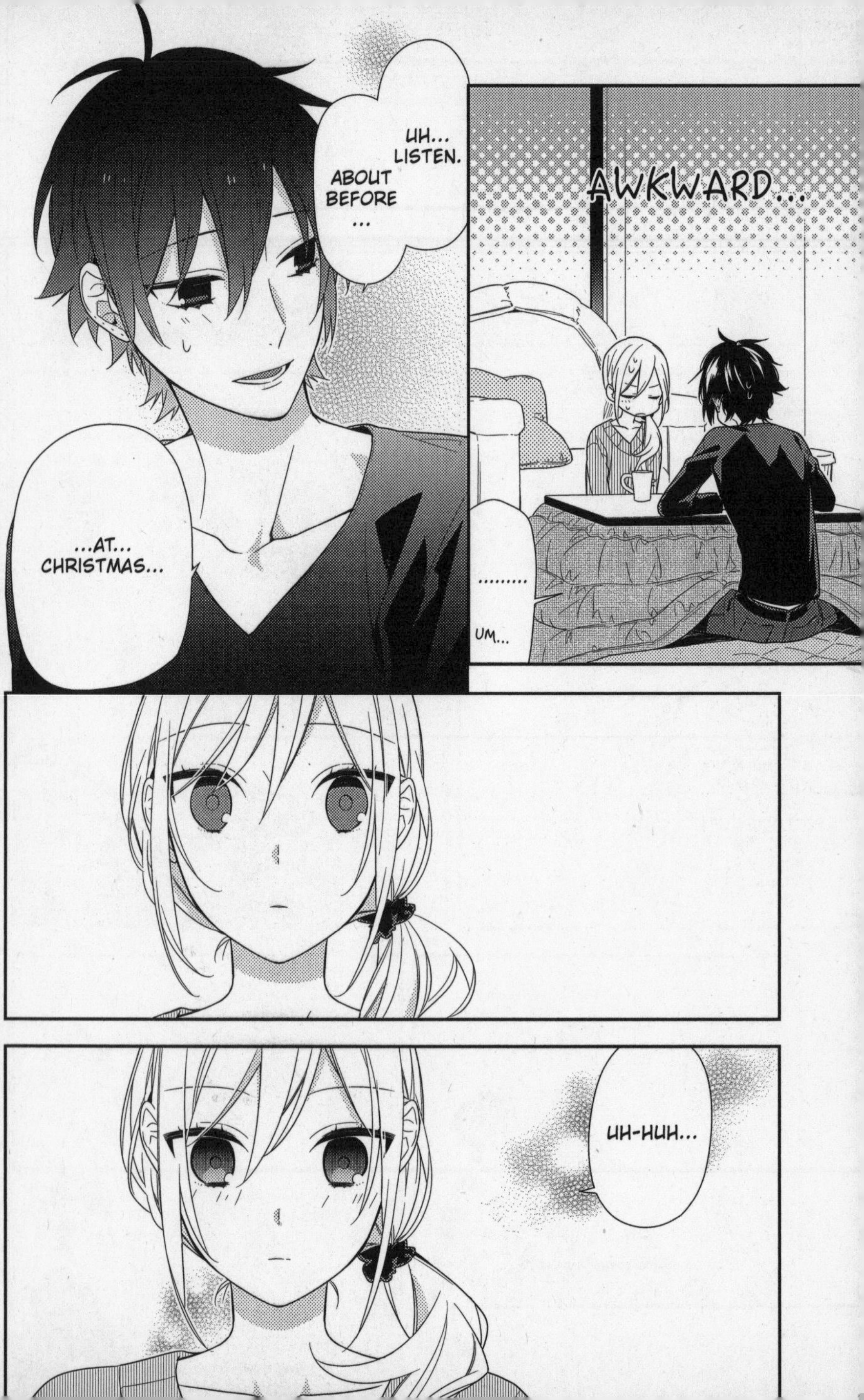
AWKWARD...
....
UM...
UH... LISTEN. ABOUT BEFORE ...
...AT... CHRISTMAS...
UH-HUH...

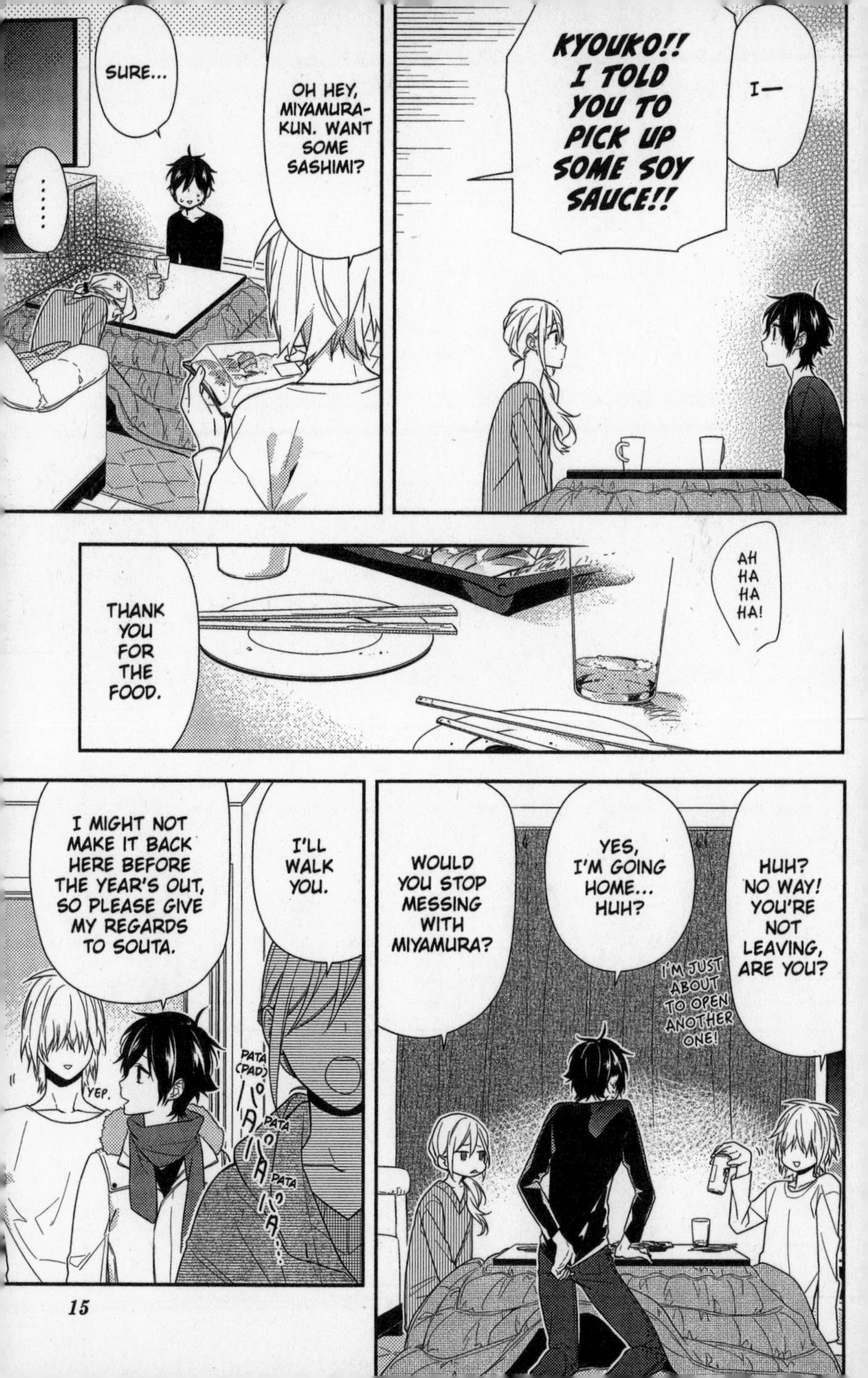
I—
KYOUKO!! I TOLD YOU TO PICK UP SOME SOY SAUCE!!
OH HEY, MIYAMURA-KUN. WANT SOME SASHIMI?
SURE...
......
AH HA HA HA!
THANK YOU FOR THE FOOD.
HUH? NO WAY! YOU'RE NOT LEAVING, ARE YOU?
I'M JUST ABOUT TO OPEN ANOTHER ONE!
YES, I'M GOING HOME... HUH?
WOULD YOU STOP MESSING WITH MIYAMURA?
I'LL WALK YOU.
PATA (PAD) PATA PATA
I MIGHT NOT MAKE IT BACK HERE BEFORE THE YEAR'S OUT, SO PLEASE GIVE MY REGARDS TO SOUTA.
YEP.

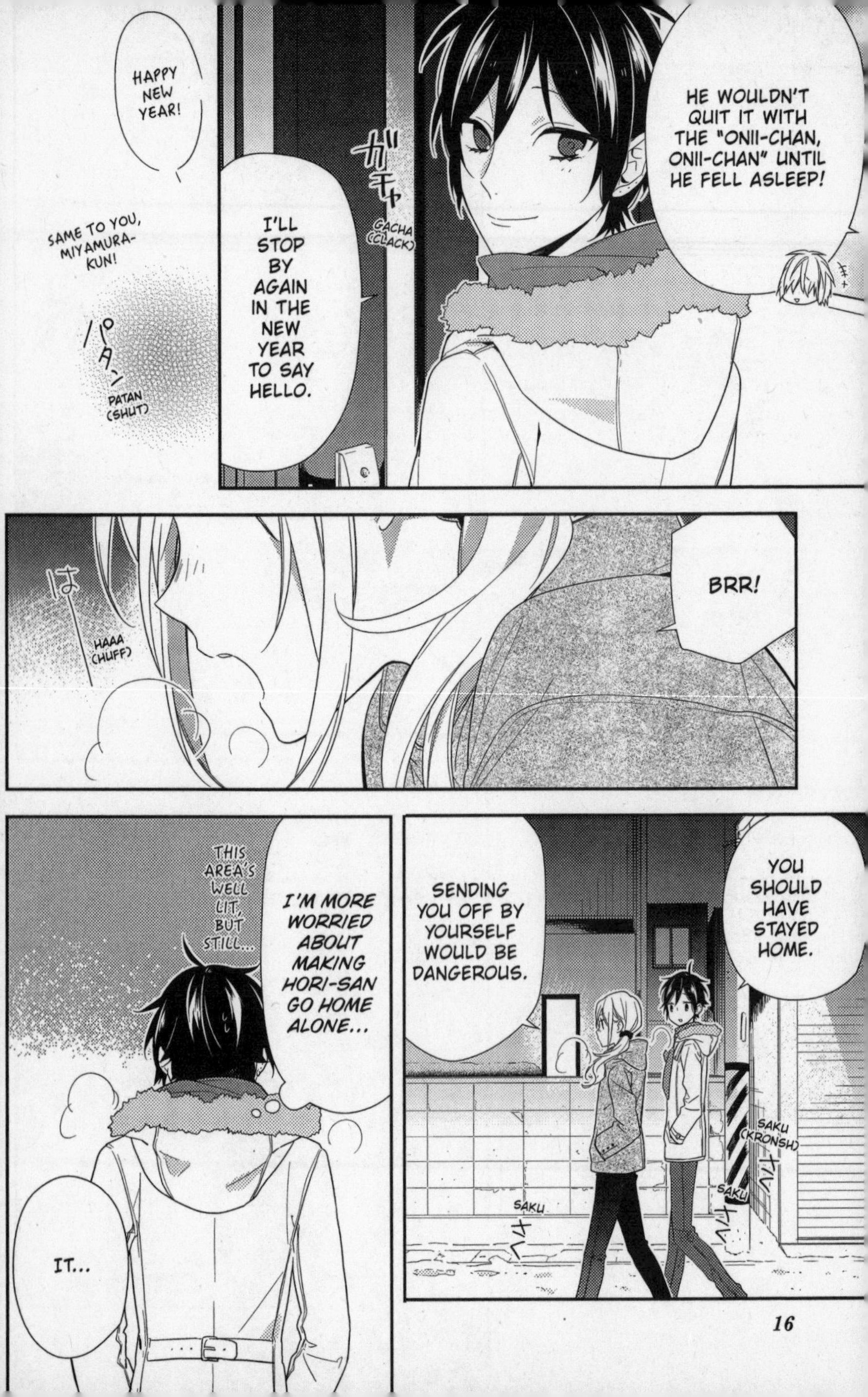

HE WOULDN'T QUIT IT WITH THE "ONII-CHAN, ONII-CHAN" UNTIL HE FELL ASLEEP!
I'LL STOP BY AGAIN IN THE NEW YEAR TO SAY HELLO.
GACHA (CLACK)
HAPPY NEW YEAR!
SAME TO YOU, MIYAMURA-KUN!
PATAN (SHUT)
BRR!
HAAA (HUFF)
YOU SHOULD HAVE STAYED HOME.
SENDING YOU OFF BY YOURSELF WOULD BE DANGEROUS.
SAKU (KRONSH)
SAKU
SAKU
I'M MORE WORRIED ABOUT MAKING HORI-SAN GO HOME ALONE...
THIS AREA'S WELL LIT, BUT STILL...
IT...

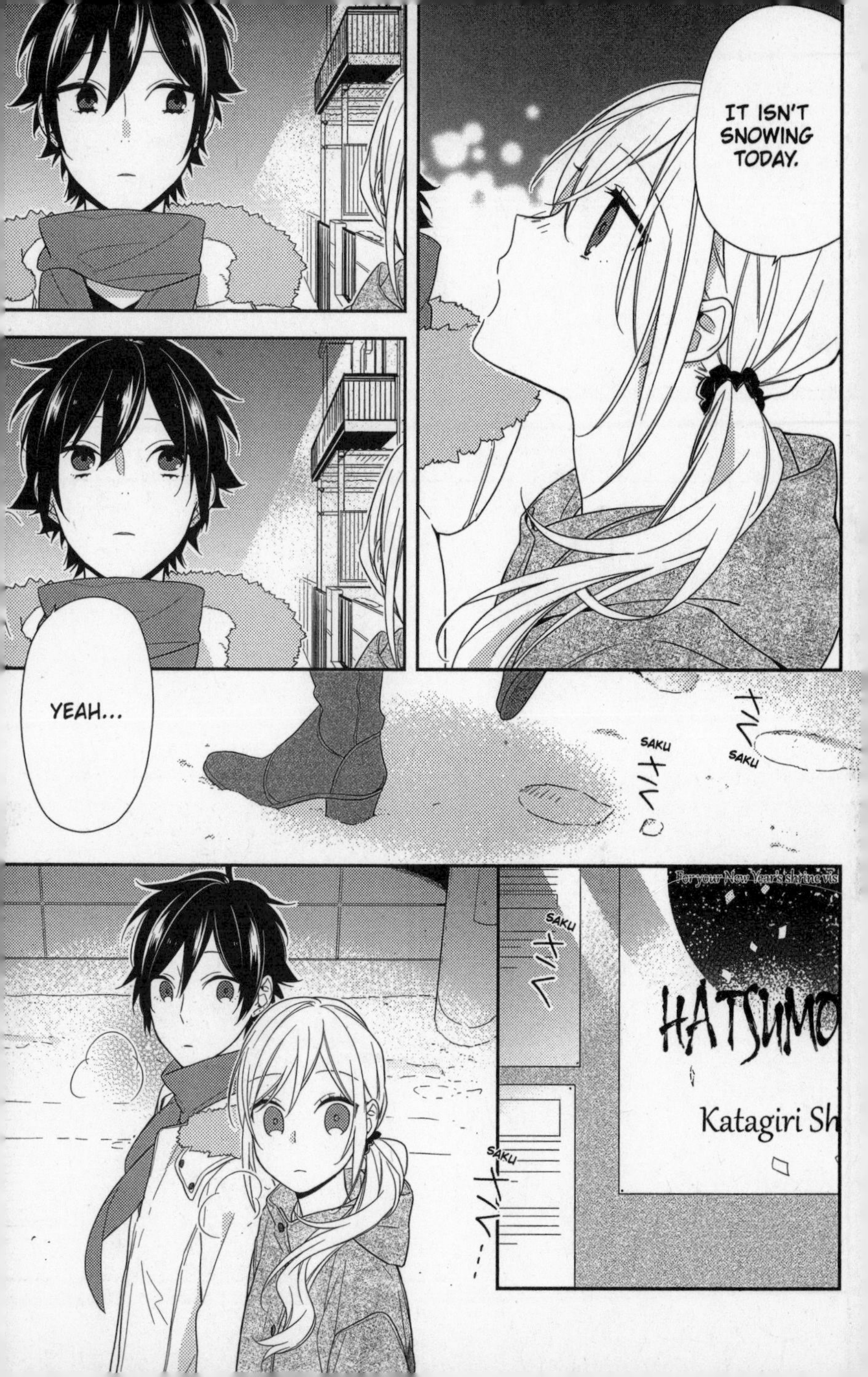
IT ISN'T SNOWING TODAY.
YEAH...
SAKU
SAKU
For your New Year's shrine visi
HATSUMO
Katagiri Sh
SAKU
SAKU

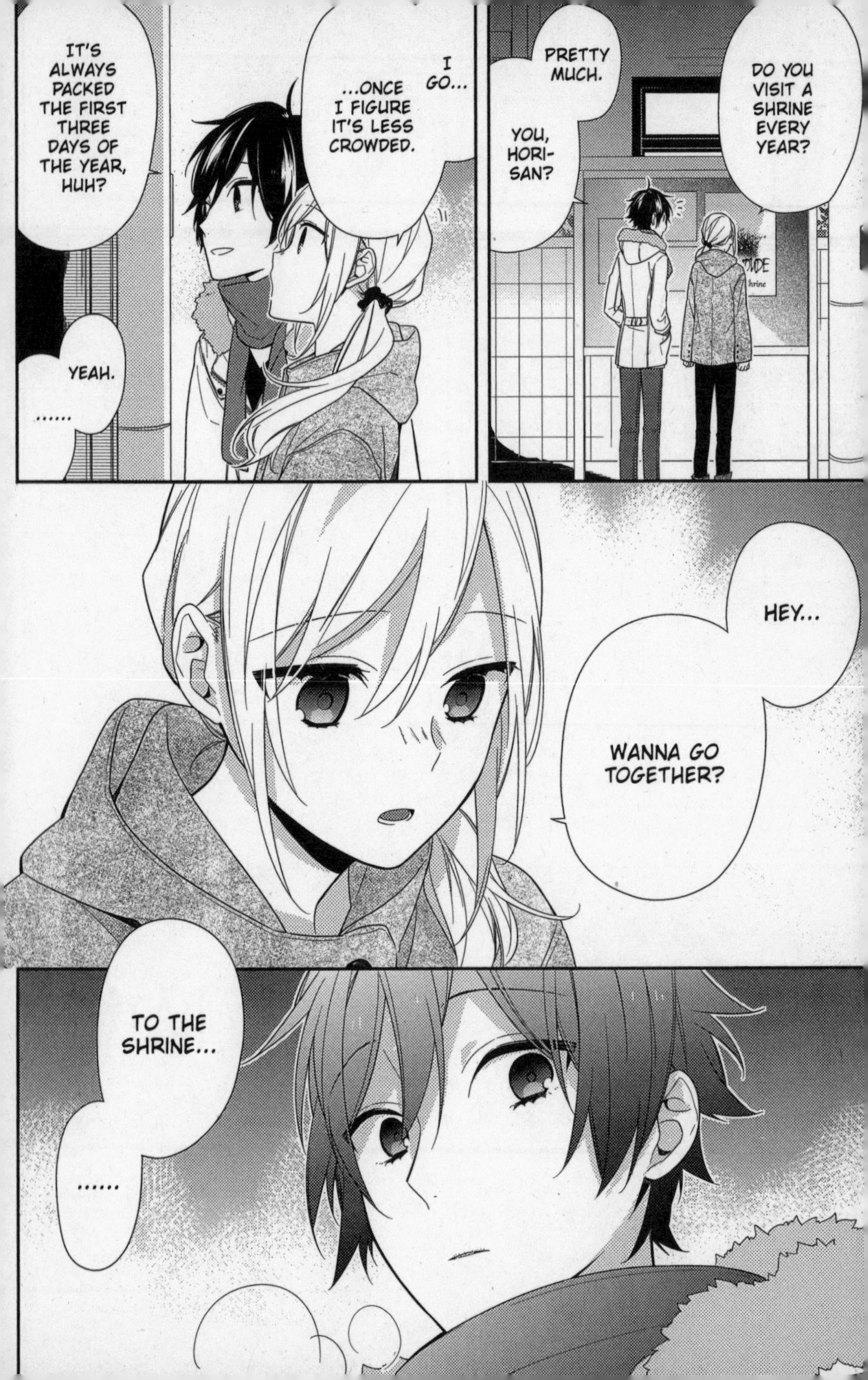
DO YOU VISIT A SHRINE EVERY YEAR?
PRETTY MUCH.
YOU, HORI-SAN?
I GO...
...ONCE I FIGURE IT'S LESS CROWDED.
IT'S ALWAYS PACKED THE FIRST THREE DAYS OF THE YEAR, HUH?
YEAH.
......
HEY...
WANNA GO TOGETHER?
TO THE SHRINE...
......

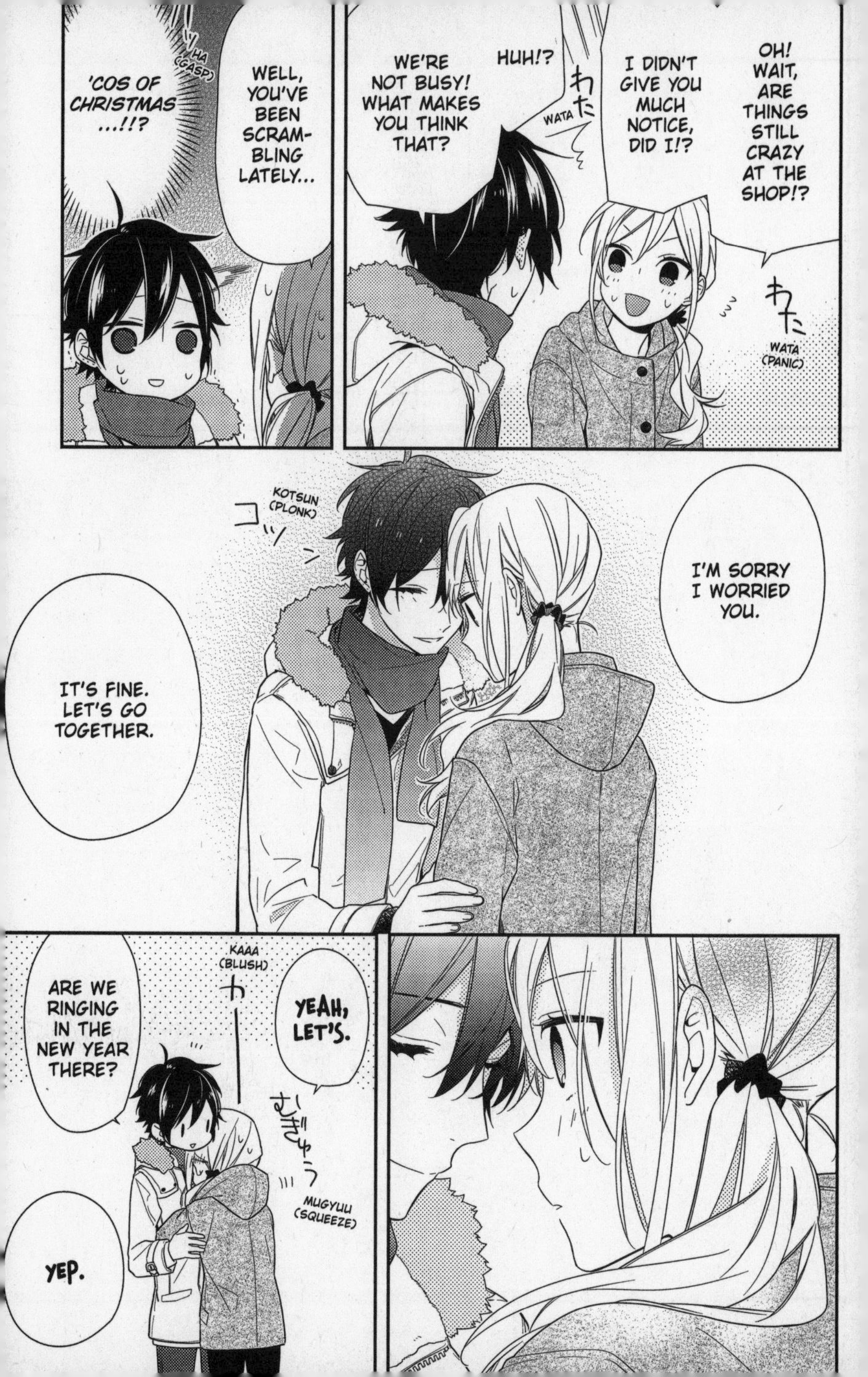
OH! WAIT, ARE THINGS STILL CRAZY AT THE SHOP!?
WATA (PANIC)
I DIDN'T GIVE YOU MUCH NOTICE, DID I!?
WATA
HUH!?
WE'RE NOT BUSY! WHAT MAKES YOU THINK THAT?
WELL, YOU'VE BEEN SCRAM-BLING LATELY...
HA (GASP)
'COS OF CHRISTMAS ...!!?
I'M SORRY I WORRIED YOU.
KOTSUN (PLONK)
IT'S FINE. LET'S GO TOGETHER.
YEAH, LET'S.
KAAA (BLUSH)
ARE WE RINGING IN THE NEW YEAR THERE?
MUGYUU (SQUEEZE)
YEP.

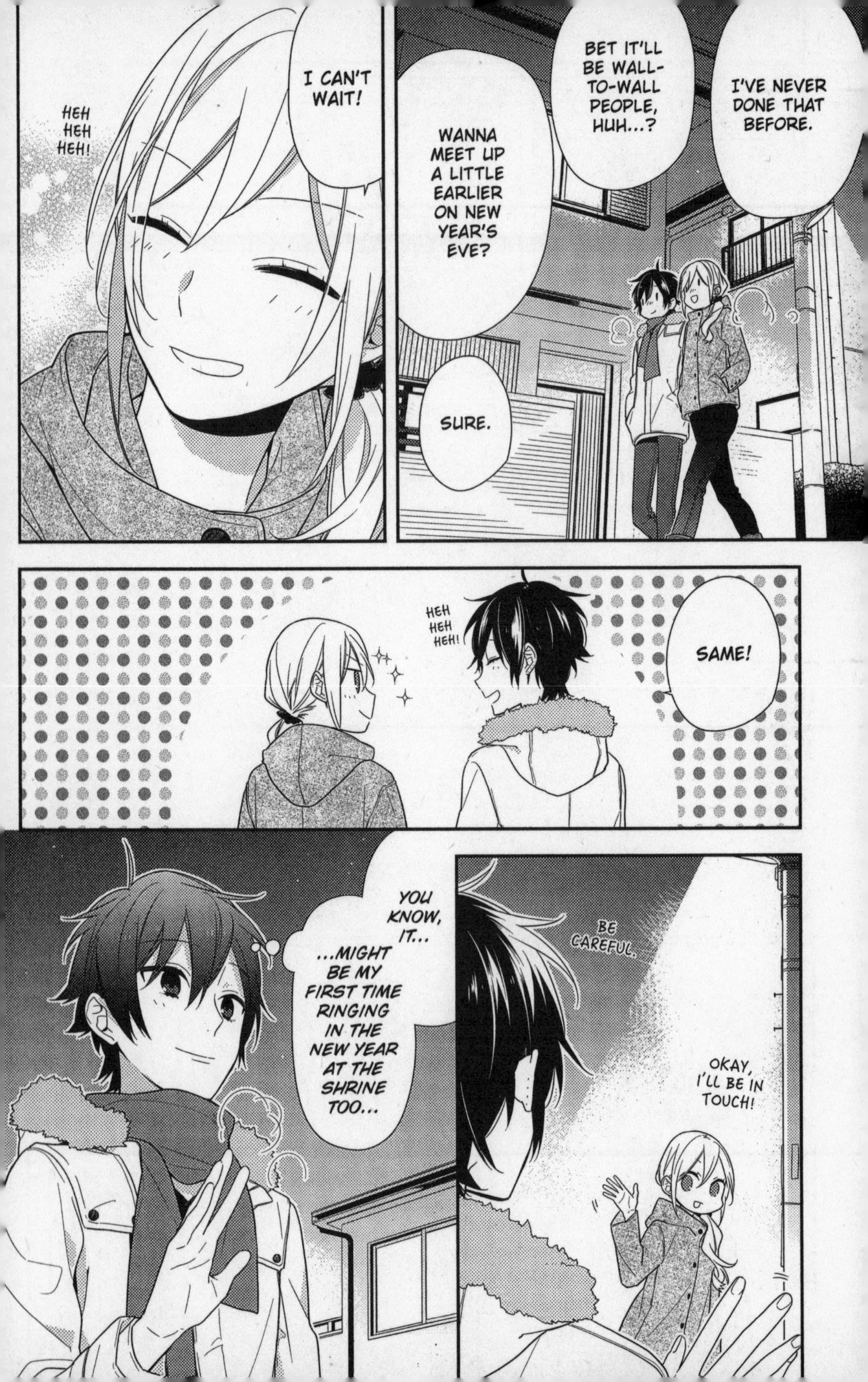
I'VE NEVER DONE THAT BEFORE.
BET IT'LL BE WALL-TO-WALL PEOPLE, HUH...?
WANNA MEET UP A LITTLE EARLIER ON NEW YEAR'S EVE?
SURE.
I CAN'T WAIT!
HEH HEH HEH!
SAME!
HEH HEH HEH!
BE CAREFUL.
OKAY, I'LL BE IN TOUCH!
YOU KNOW, IT...
...MIGHT BE MY FIRST TIME RINGING IN THE NEW YEAR AT THE SHRINE TOO...

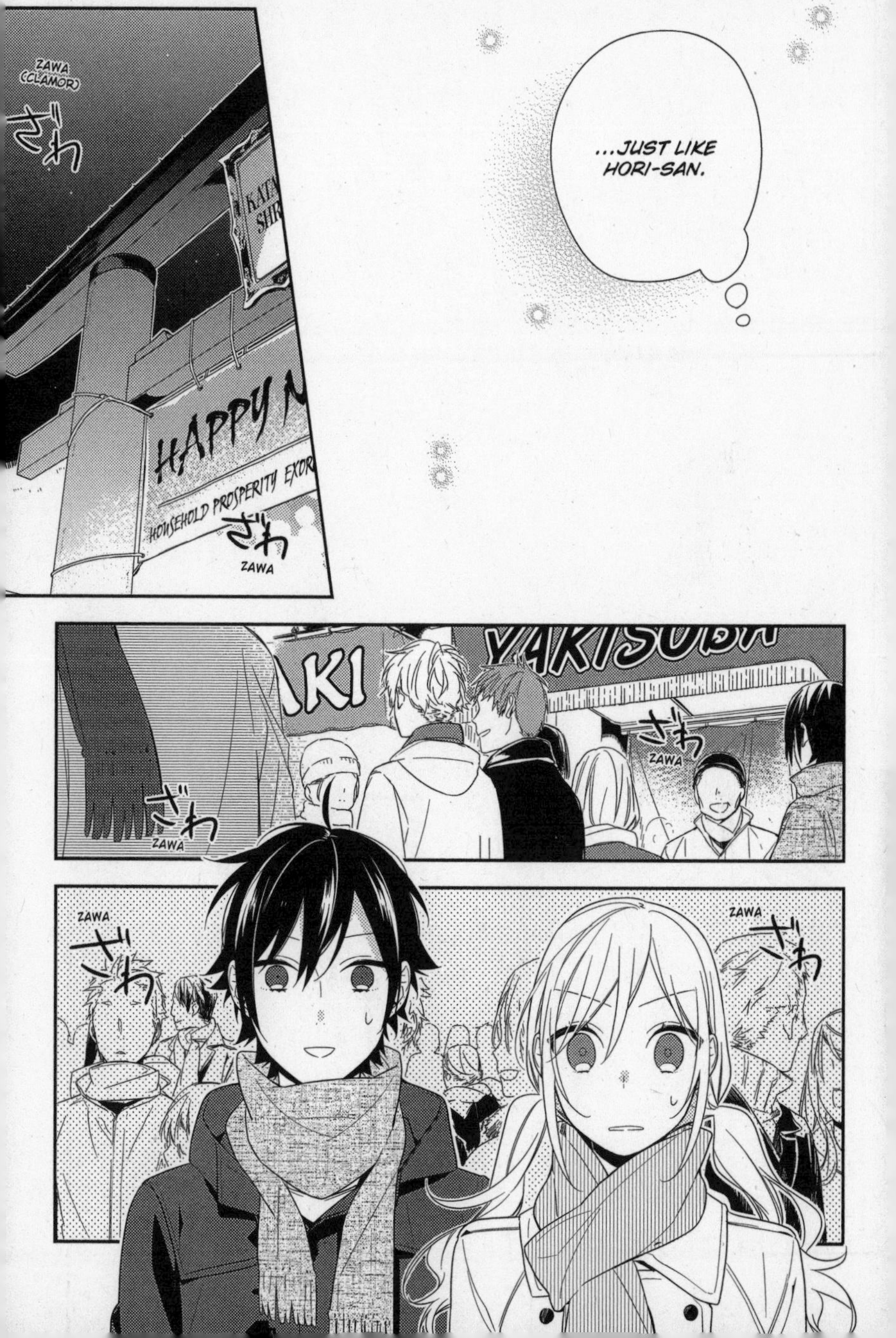
...JUST LIKE HORI-SAN.
ZAWA (CLAMOR)
ざわ
HAPPY
HOUSEHOLD PROSPERITY
ざわ
ZAWA
YAKISOBA
ざわ
ZAWA
ざわ
ZAWA
ZAWA
ざわ
ZAWA
ざわ

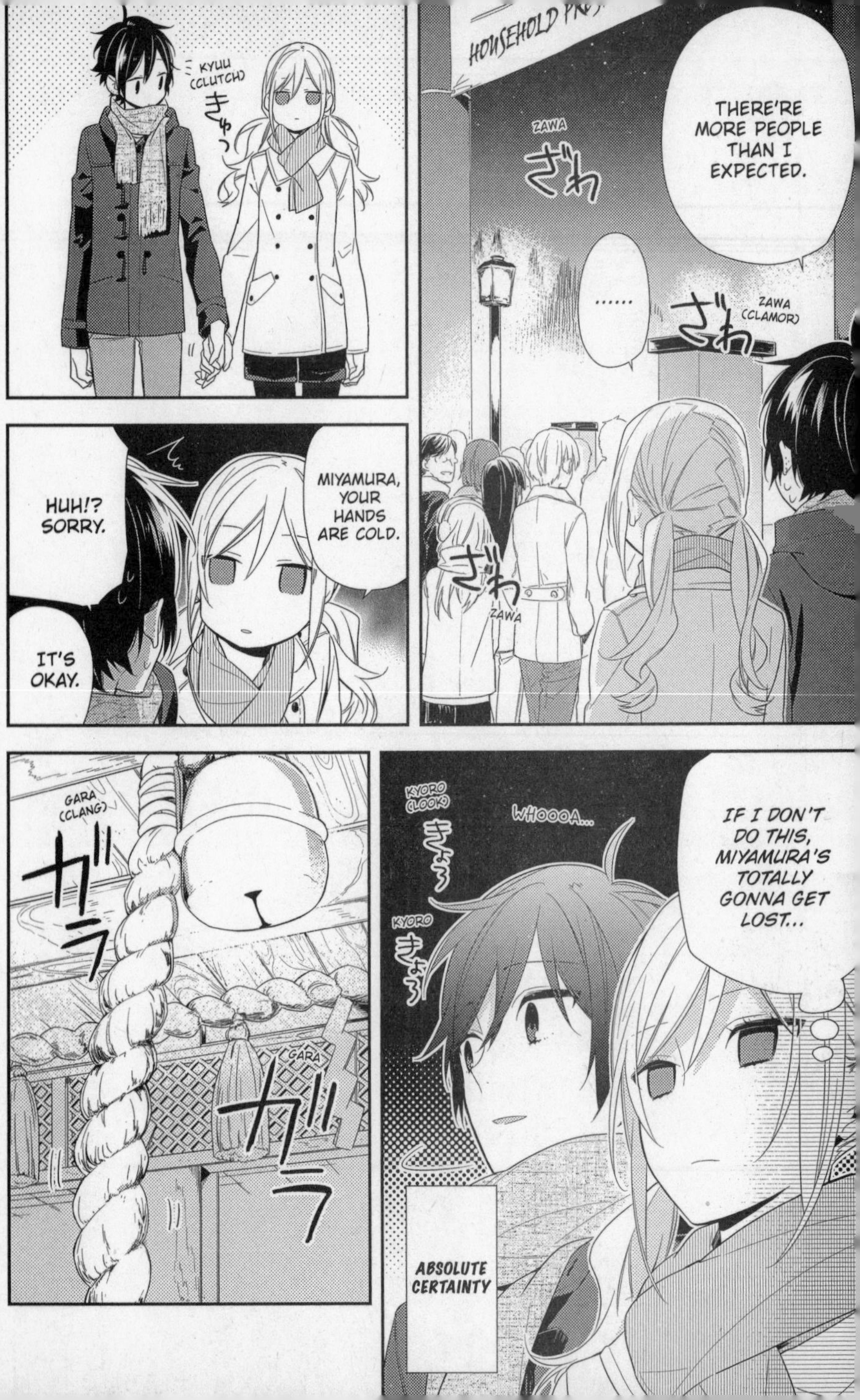
HOUSEHOLD PR
THERE'RE MORE PEOPLE THAN I EXPECTED.
ZAWA
ざわ
......
ZAWA (CLAMOR)
ざわ
ざわ
ZAWA
KYUU (CLUTCH)
きゅっ
MIYAMURA, YOUR HANDS ARE COLD.
HUH!? SORRY.
IT'S OKAY.
IF I DON'T DO THIS, MIYAMURA'S TOTALLY GONNA GET LOST...
WHOOOA...
KYORO (LOOK)
きょろ
KYORO
きょろ
ABSOLUTE CERTAINTY
GARA (CLANG)
ガラ
GARA
ガラ

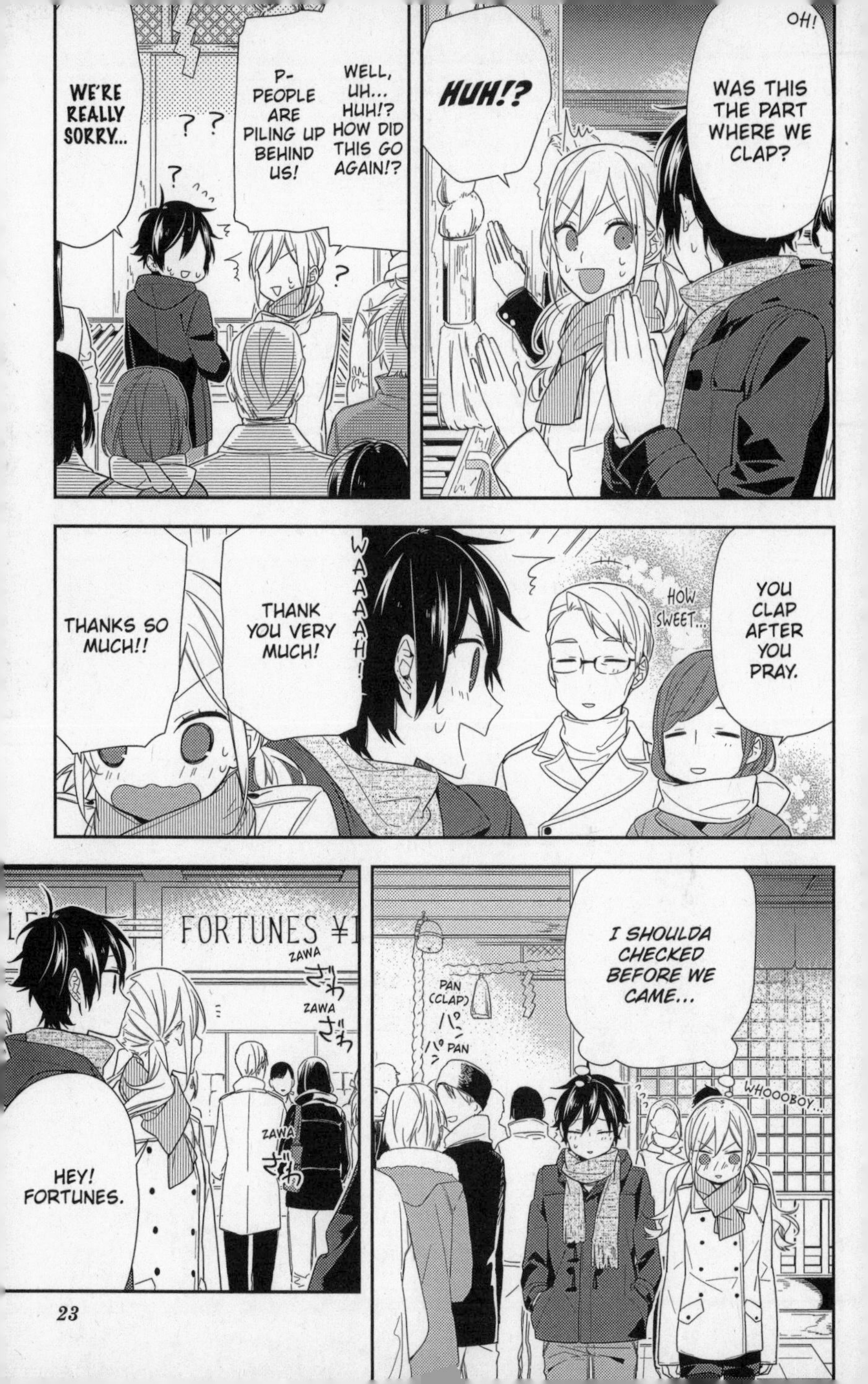
OH!
WAS THIS THE PART WHERE WE CLAP?
HUH!?
WELL, UH... HUH!? HOW DID THIS GO AGAIN!?
P-PEOPLE ARE PILING UP BEHIND US!
WE'RE REALLY SORRY...
YOU CLAP AFTER YOU PRAY.
HOW SWEET...
WAAAAAH!
THANK YOU VERY MUCH!
THANKS SO MUCH!!
I SHOULDA CHECKED BEFORE WE CAME...
WHOOOBOY...
PAN (CLAP)
PAN
FORTUNES ¥1
ZAWA
ZAWA
ZAWA
HEY! FORTUNES.

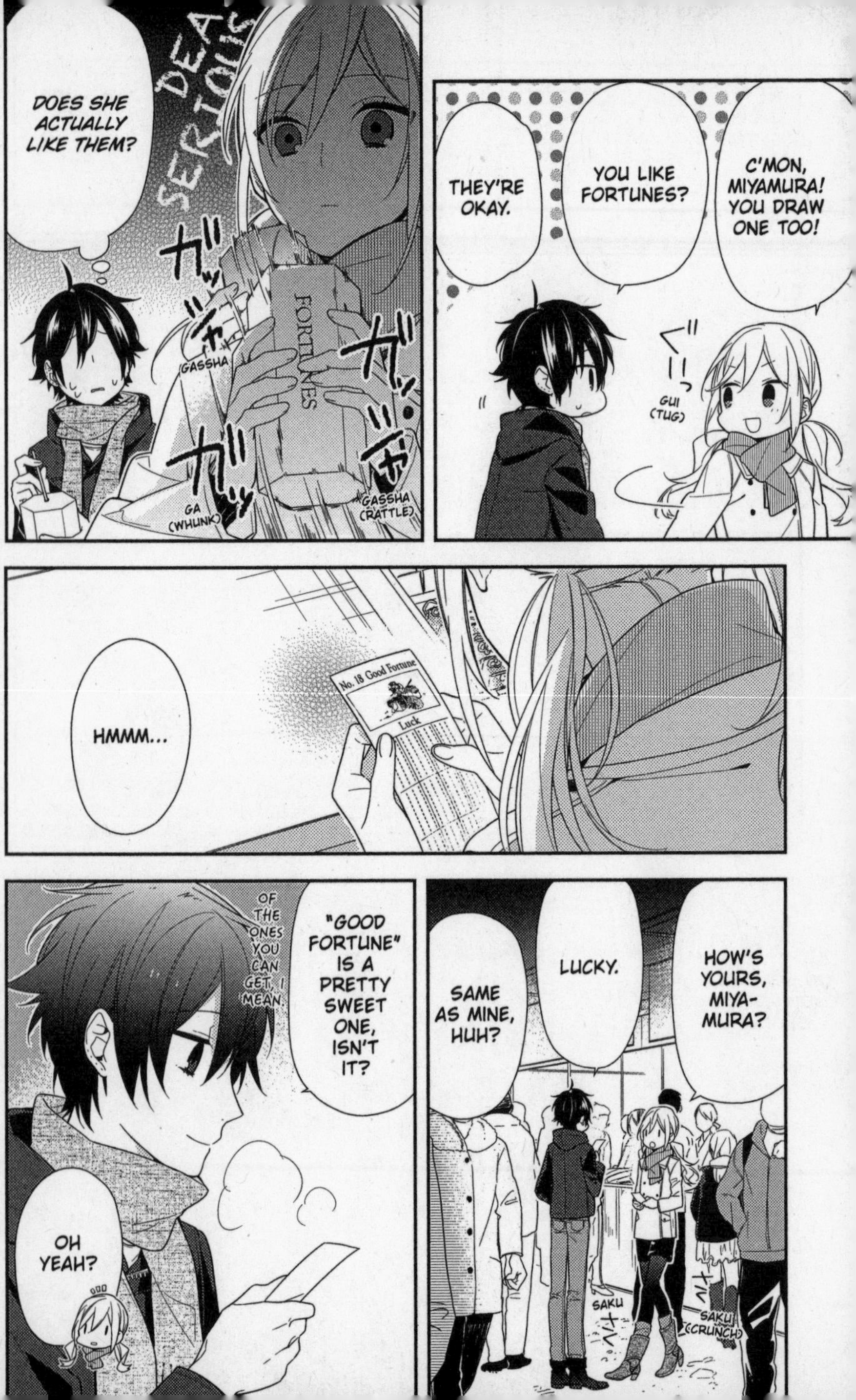
C'MON, MIYAMURA! YOU DRAW ONE TOO!
GUI (TUG)
YOU LIKE FORTUNES?
THEY'RE OKAY.
SERIOUS
FORTUNES
GASSHA
GASSHA (RATTLE)
GA (WHUNK)
DOES SHE ACTUALLY LIKE THEM?
No. 18 Good Fortune
Luck
HMMM...
HOW'S YOURS, MIYA-MURA?
LUCKY.
SAME AS MINE, HUH?
SAKU
SAKU (CRUNCH)
"GOOD FORTUNE" IS A PRETTY SWEET ONE, ISN'T IT?
OF THE ONES YOU CAN GET, I MEAN.
OH YEAH?

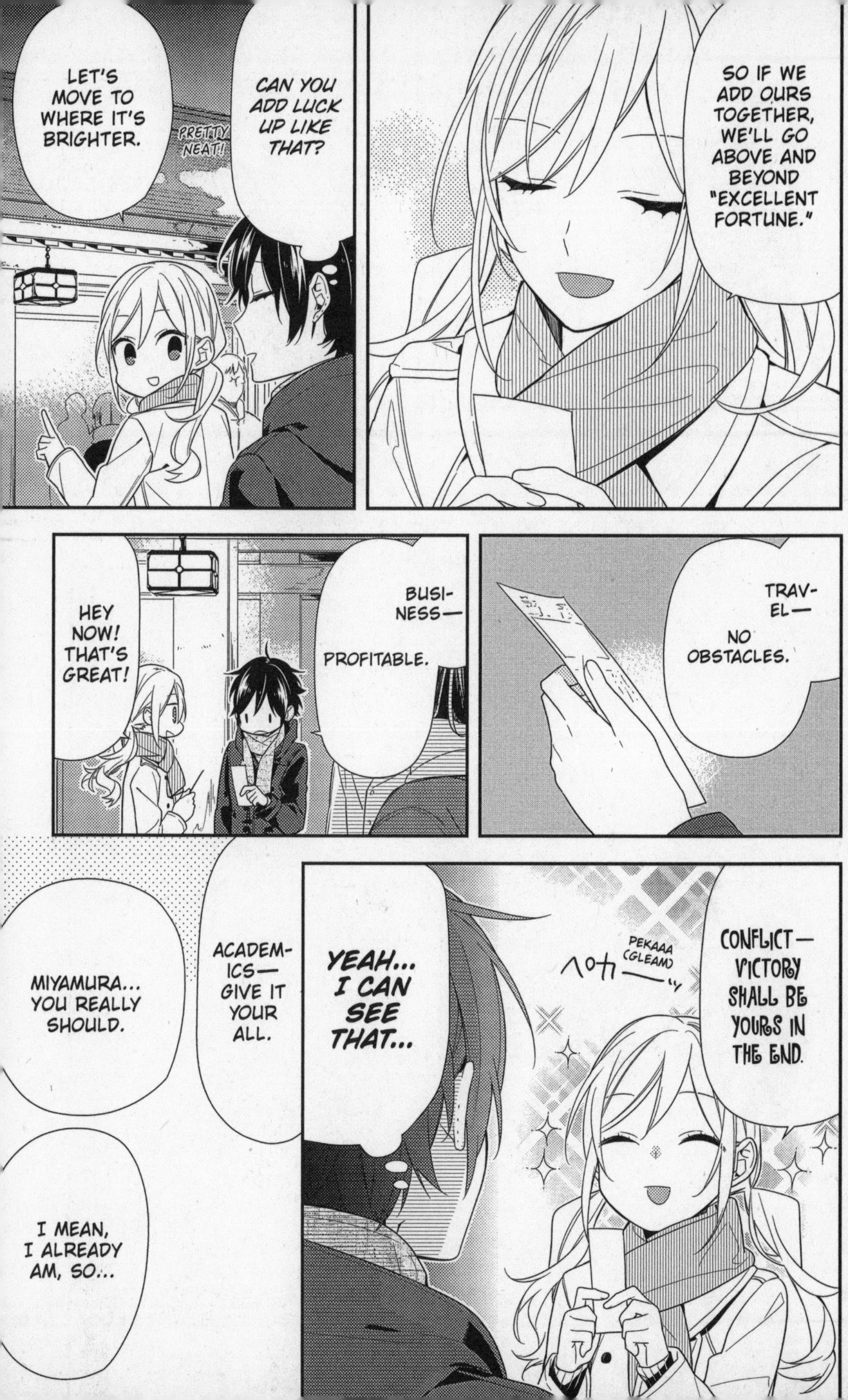
SO IF WE ADD OURS TOGETHER, WE'LL GO ABOVE AND BEYOND "EXCELLENT FORTUNE."
CAN YOU ADD LUCK UP LIKE THAT?
PRETTY NEAT!
LET'S MOVE TO WHERE IT'S BRIGHTER.
TRAV-EL—
NO OBSTACLES.
BUSI-NESS—
PROFITABLE.
HEY NOW! THAT'S GREAT!
CONFLICT— VICTORY SHALL BE YOURS IN THE END.
ペカーッ
PEKAAA (GLEAM)
YEAH... I CAN SEE THAT...
ACADEM-ICS— GIVE IT YOUR ALL.
MIYAMURA... YOU REALLY SHOULD.
I MEAN, I ALREADY AM, SO...

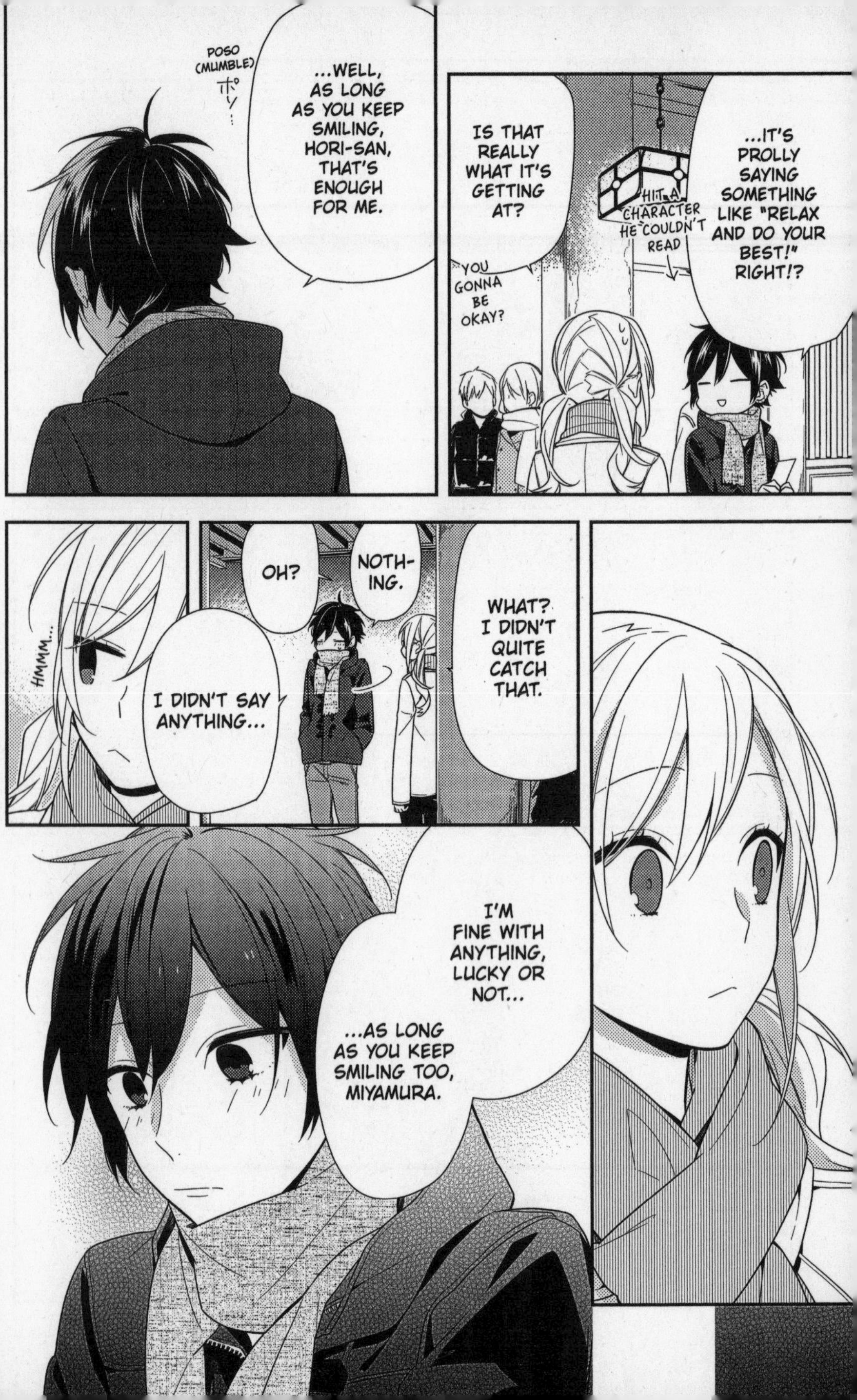
...IT'S PROLLY SAYING SOMETHING LIKE "RELAX AND DO YOUR BEST!" RIGHT!?
HIT A CHARACTER HE COULDN'T READ
IS THAT REALLY WHAT IT'S GETTING AT?
YOU GONNA BE OKAY?
...WELL, AS LONG AS YOU KEEP SMILING, HORI-SAN, THAT'S ENOUGH FOR ME.
POSO (MUMBLE)
ポソ…
WHAT? I DIDN'T QUITE CATCH THAT.
NOTH-ING.
OH?
I DIDN'T SAY ANYTHING...
HMMM...
I'M FINE WITH ANYTHING, LUCKY OR NOT...
...AS LONG AS YOU KEEP SMILING TOO, MIYAMURA.

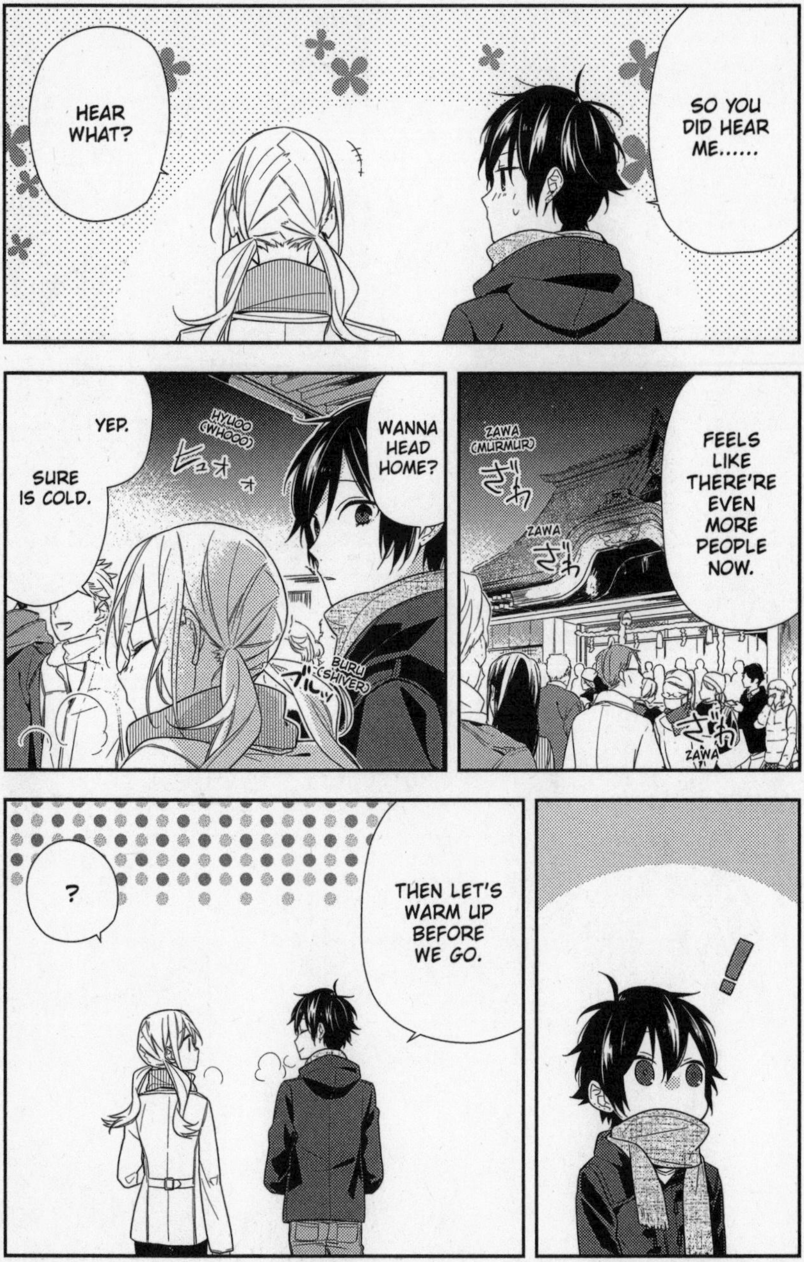
SO YOU DID HEAR ME......
HEAR WHAT?
FEELS LIKE THERE'RE EVEN MORE PEOPLE NOW.
ZAWA (MURMUR)
ZAWA
ZAWA
WANNA HEAD HOME?
HYUOO (WHOOO)
YEP.
SURE IS COLD.
BURU (SHIVER)
!
THEN LET'S WARM UP BEFORE WE GO.
?

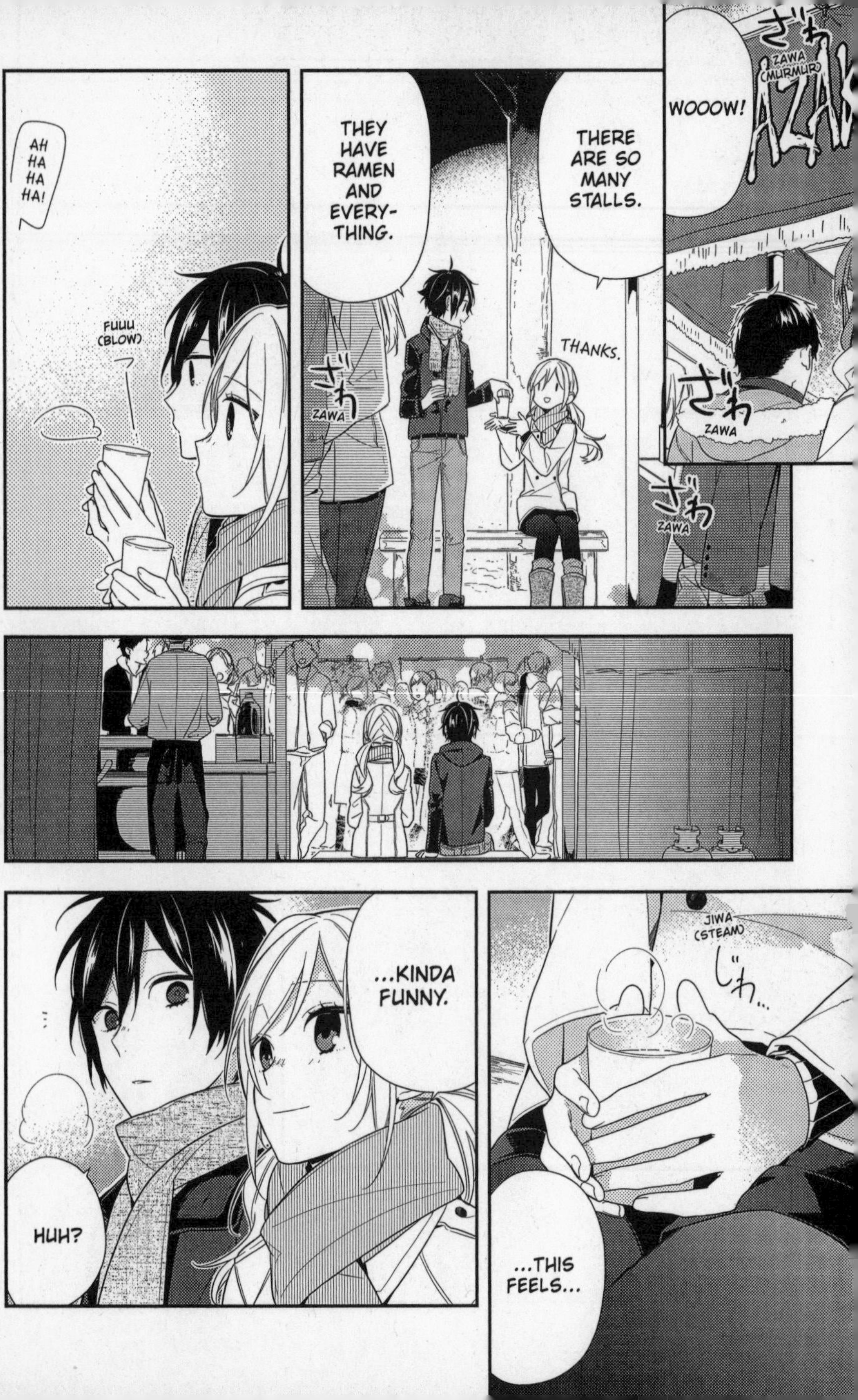

ざわ
ZAWA (MURMUR)
WOOOW!
ざわ
ZAWA
ざわ
ZAWA
THERE ARE SO MANY STALLS.
THEY HAVE RAMEN AND EVERYTHING.
THANKS.
ざわ
ZAWA
AH HA HA HA!
FUUU (BLOW)
JIWA (STEAM)
じわ...
...THIS FEELS...
...KINDA FUNNY.
HUH?

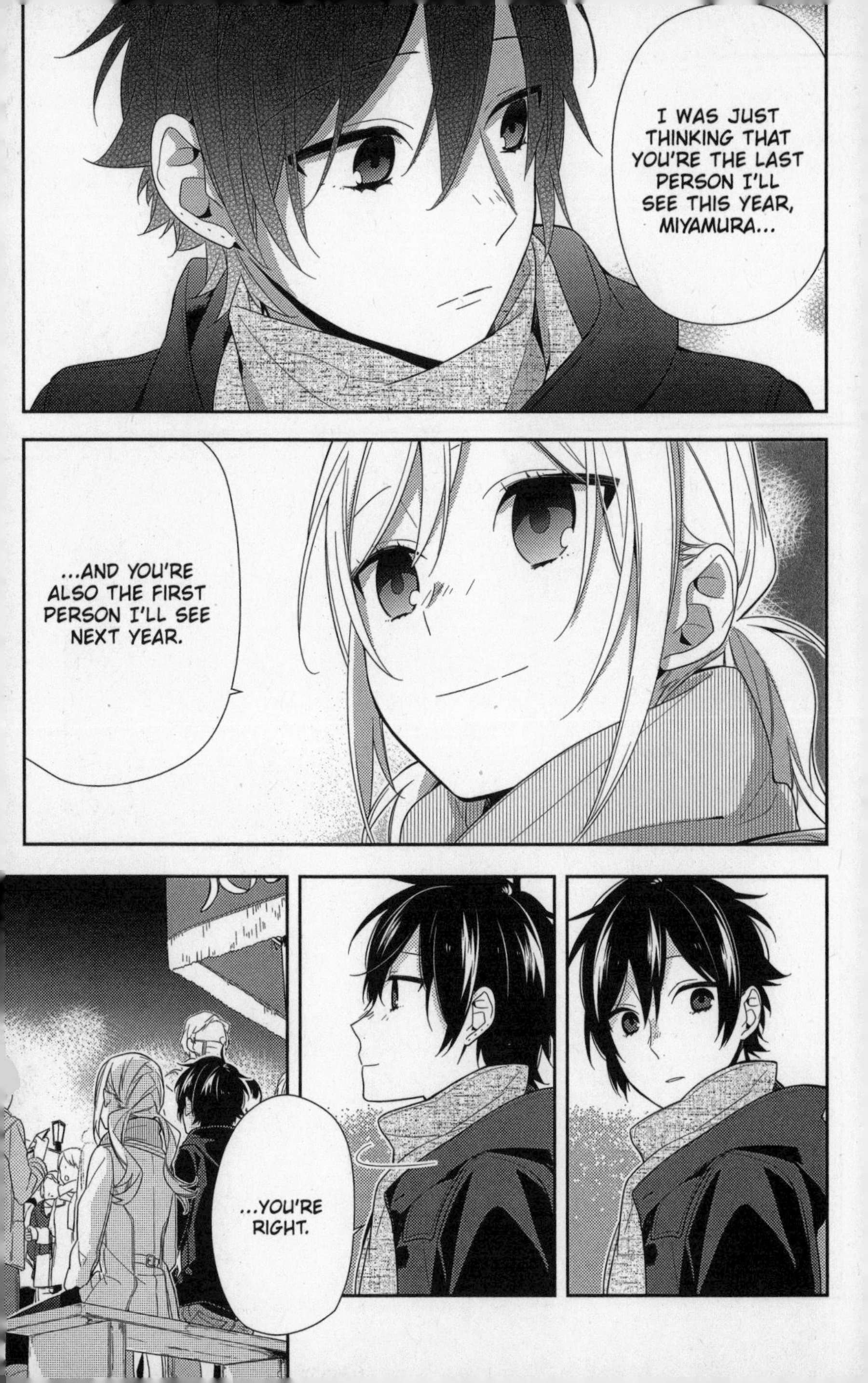
I WAS JUST THINKING THAT YOU'RE THE LAST PERSON I'LL SEE THIS YEAR, MIYAMURA...
...AND YOU'RE ALSO THE FIRST PERSON I'LL SEE NEXT YEAR.
...YOU'RE RIGHT.

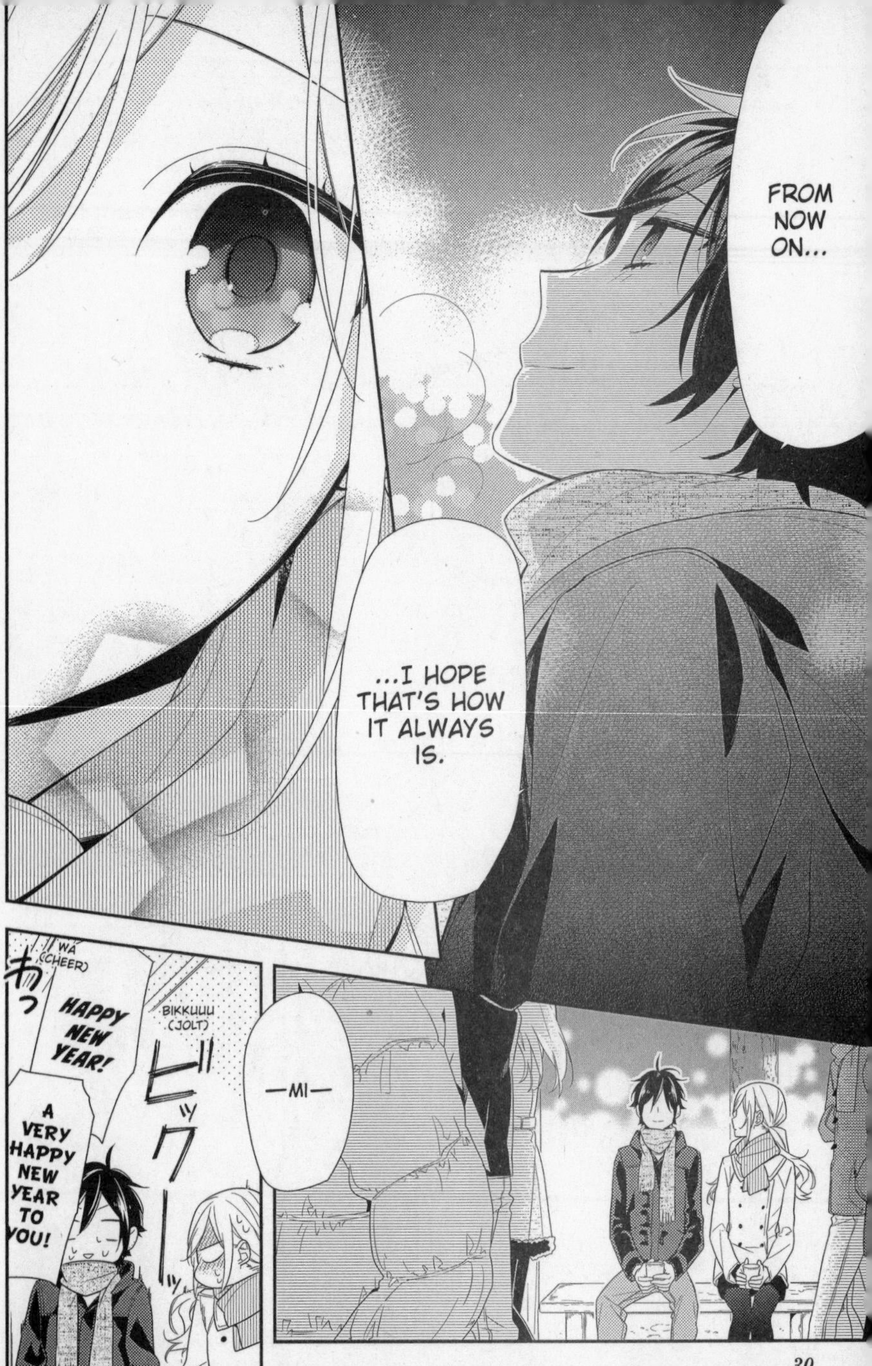
FROM NOW ON...
...I HOPE THAT'S HOW IT ALWAYS IS.
—MI—
WA (CHEER)
HAPPY NEW YEAR!
BIKKUUU (JOLT)
A VERY HAPPY NEW YEAR TO YOU!

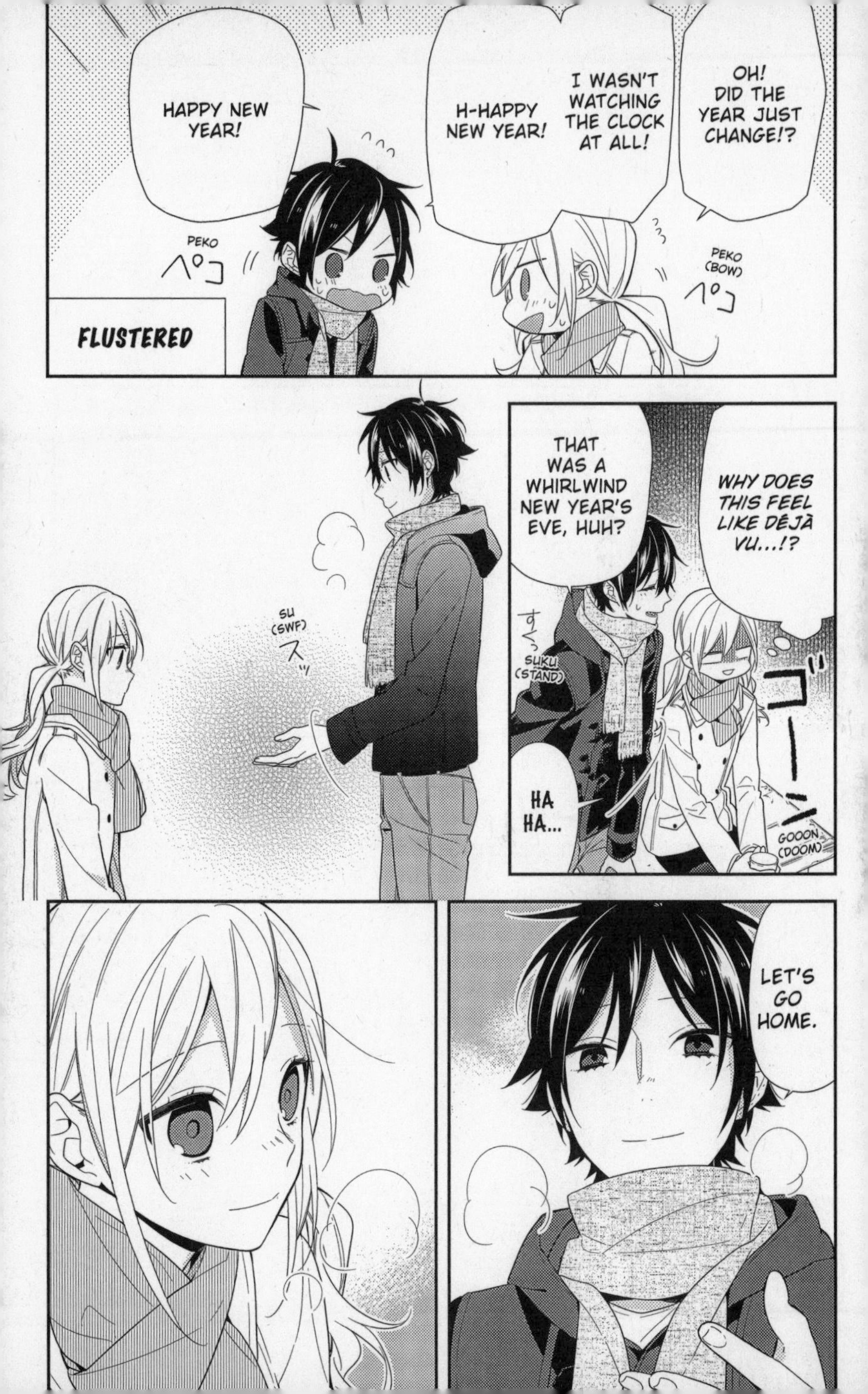
OH! DID THE YEAR JUST CHANGE!?
I WASN'T WATCHING THE CLOCK AT ALL!
H-HAPPY NEW YEAR!
ペコ
PEKO (BOW)
HAPPY NEW YEAR!
ペコ
PEKO
FLUSTERED
WHY DOES THIS FEEL LIKE DÉJÀ VU...!?
THAT WAS A WHIRLWIND NEW YEAR'S EVE, HUH?
すくっ
SUKU (STAND)
ゴーン
GOOON (DOOM)
HA HA...
スッ
SU (SWF)
LET'S GO HOME.

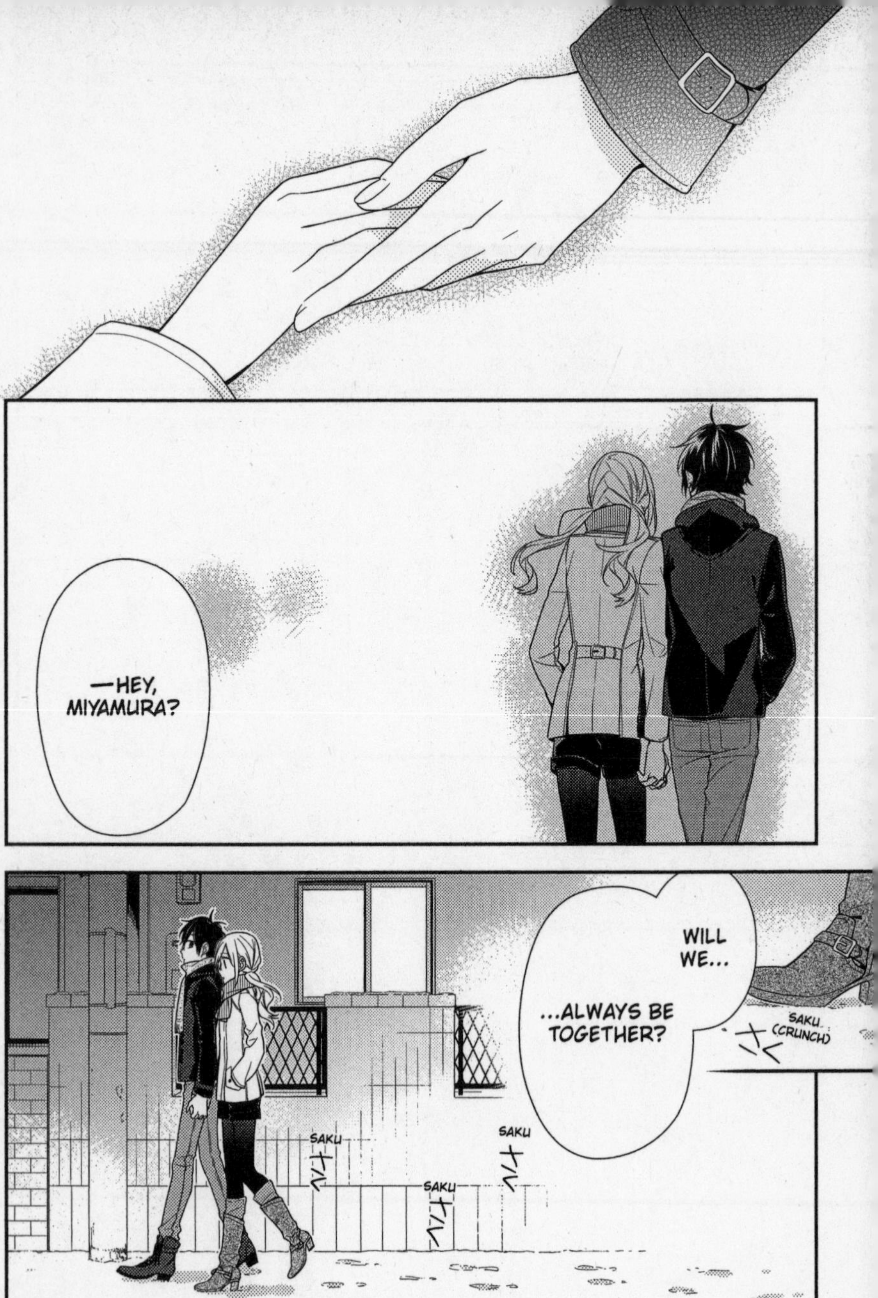
—HEY, MIYAMURA?
WILL WE...
...ALWAYS BE TOGETHER?
SAKU (CRUNCH)
SAKU
SAKU
SAKU

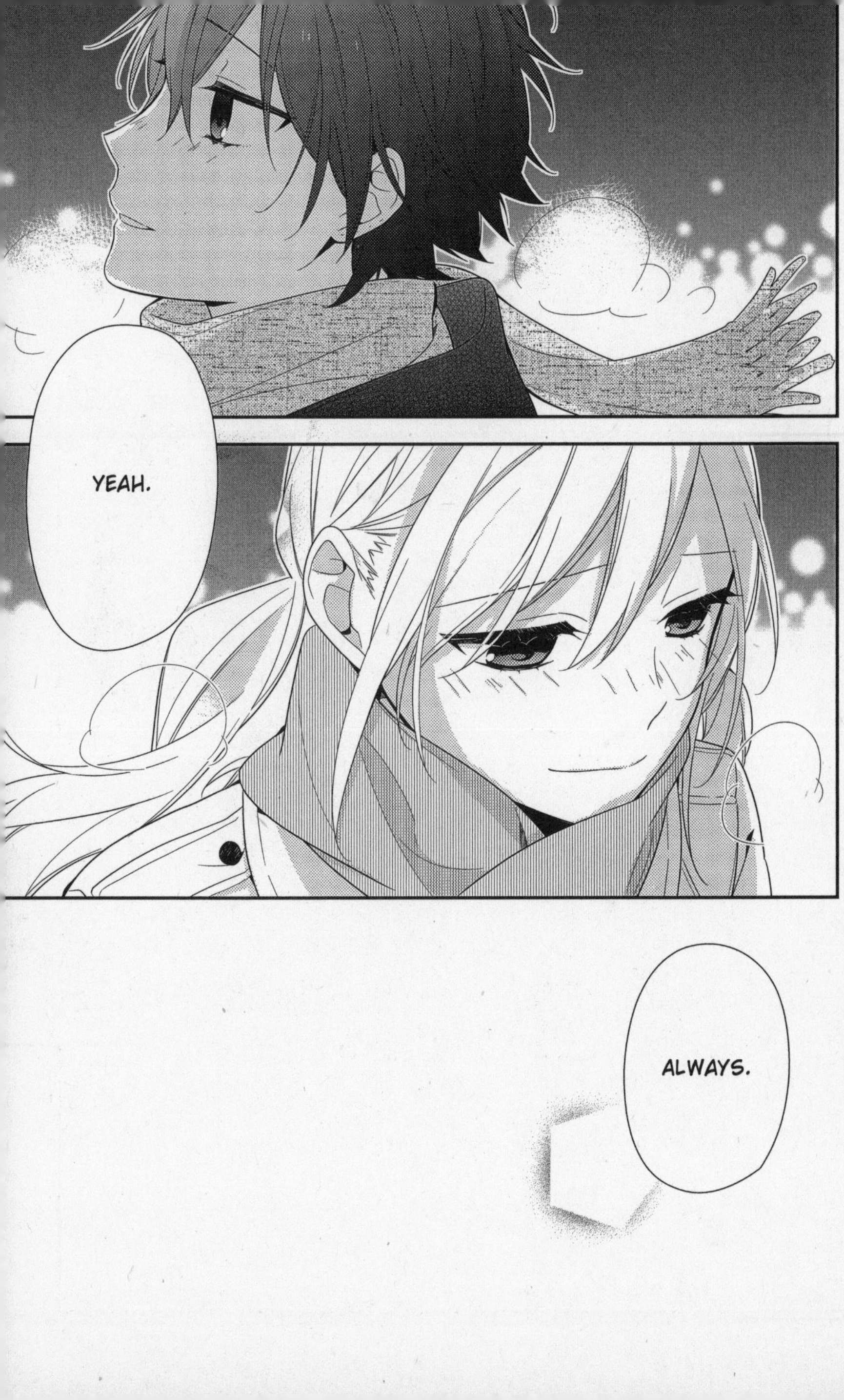
YEAH.
ALWAYS.

HORIMIYA

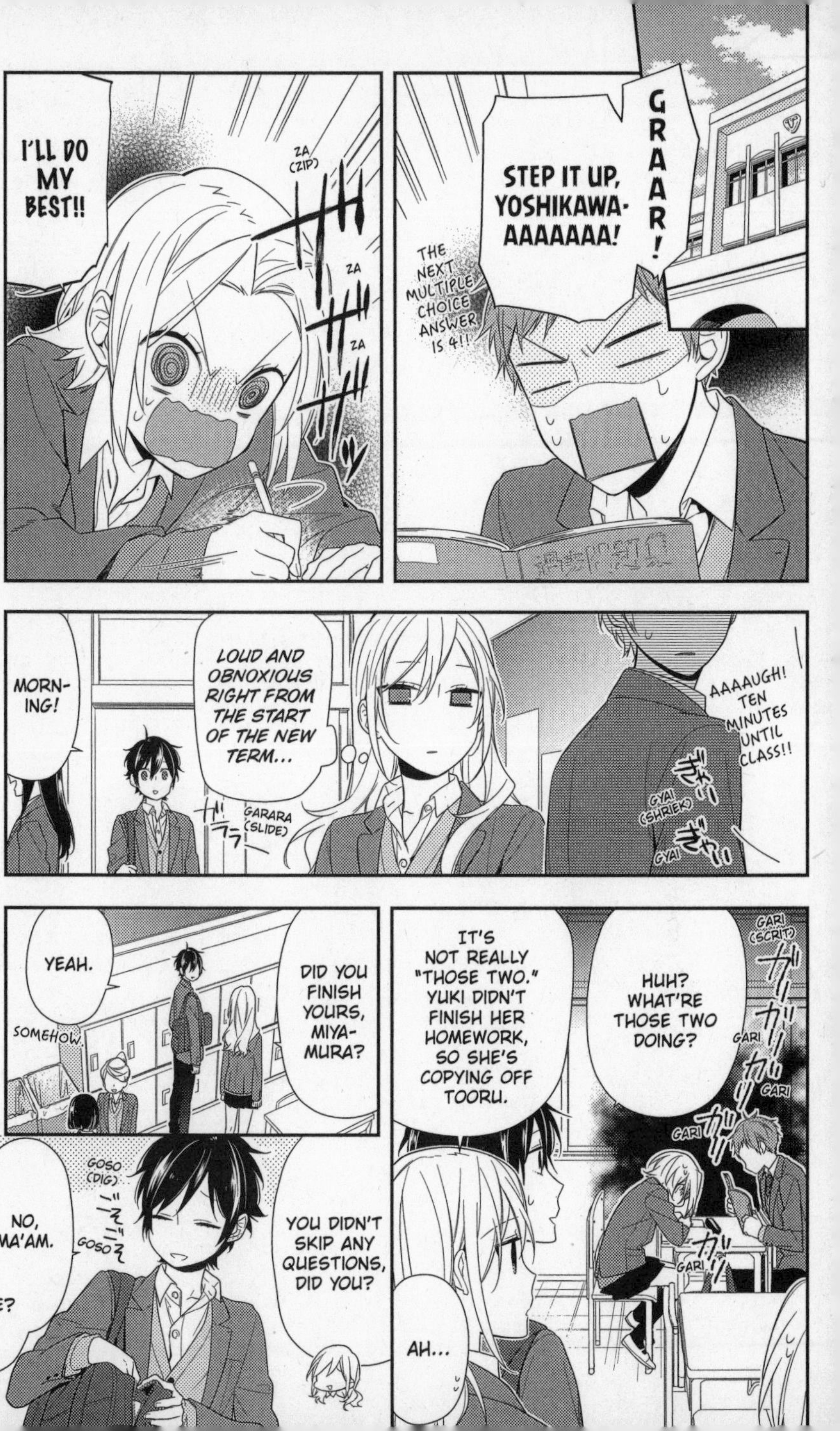
GRAAR!
STEP IT UP, YOSHIKAWA-AAAAAAA!
THE NEXT MULTIPLE CHOICE ANSWER IS 4!!
ZA (ZIP)
ZA
ZA
I'LL DO MY BEST!!
AAAAUGH! TEN MINUTES UNTIL CLASS!!
GYAI (SHRIEK)
GYAI
LOUD AND OBNOXIOUS RIGHT FROM THE START OF THE NEW TERM...
GARARA (SLIDE)
MORN-ING!
GARI (SCRIT)
HUH? WHAT'RE THOSE TWO DOING?
GARI
IT'S NOT REALLY "THOSE TWO." YUKI DIDN'T FINISH HER HOMEWORK, SO SHE'S COPYING OFF TOORU.
GARI
GARI
GARI
AH...
DID YOU FINISH YOURS, MIYA-MURA?
YEAH.
SOMEHOW.
YOU DIDN'T SKIP ANY QUESTIONS, DID YOU?
GOSO (DIG)
GOSO
NO, MA'AM.
SEE?

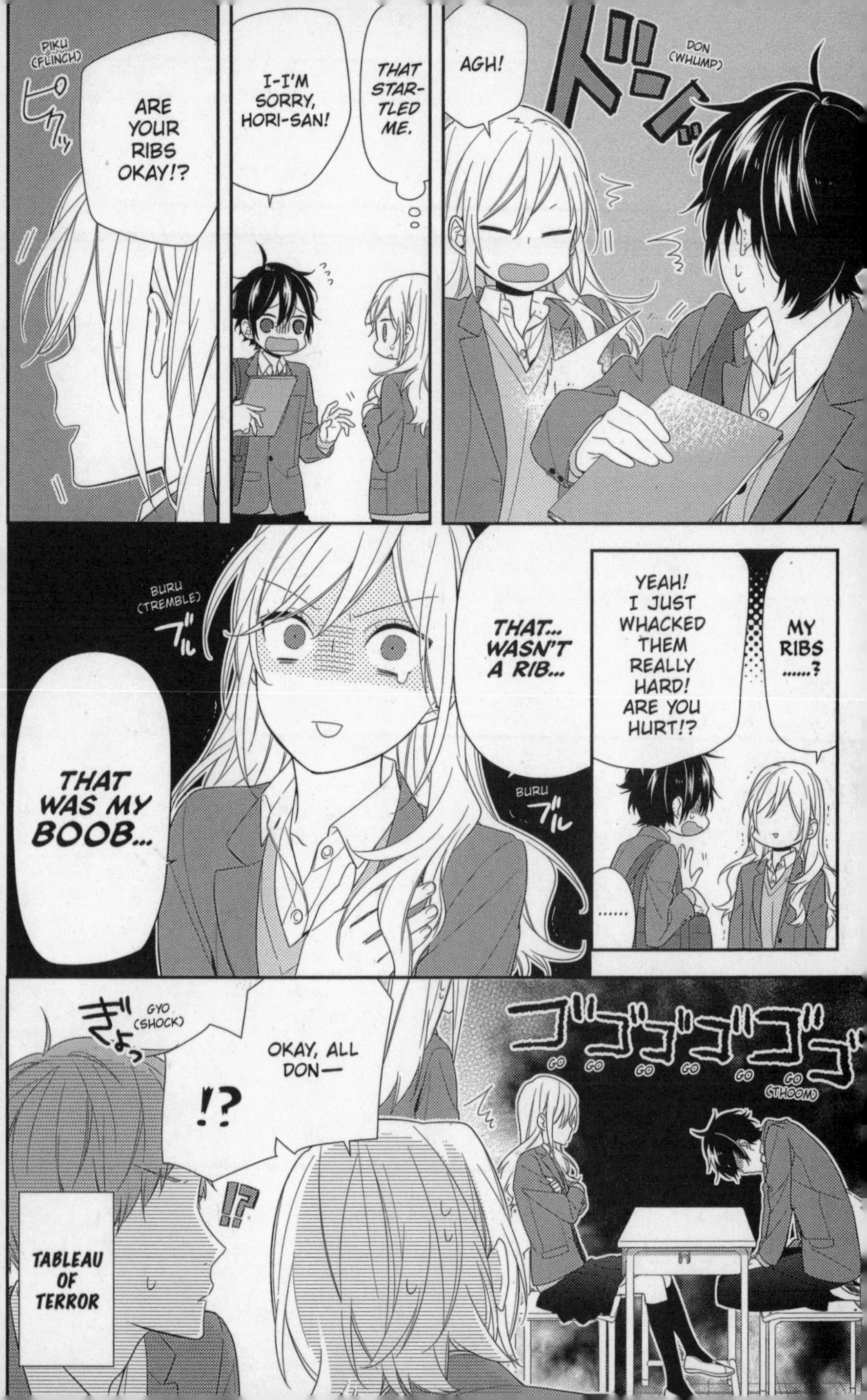
DON (WHUMP)
AGH!
THAT STARTLED ME.
I-I'M SORRY, HORI-SAN!
PIKU (FLINCH)
ARE YOUR RIBS OKAY!?
MY RIBS ......?
YEAH! I JUST WHACKED THEM REALLY HARD! ARE YOU HURT!?
......
THAT... WASN'T A RIB...
BURU (TREMBLE)
BURU
THAT WAS MY BOOB...
GO GO GO GO GO GO (THOOM)
OKAY, ALL DON—
GYO (SHOCK)
!?
!?
TABLEAU OF TERROR

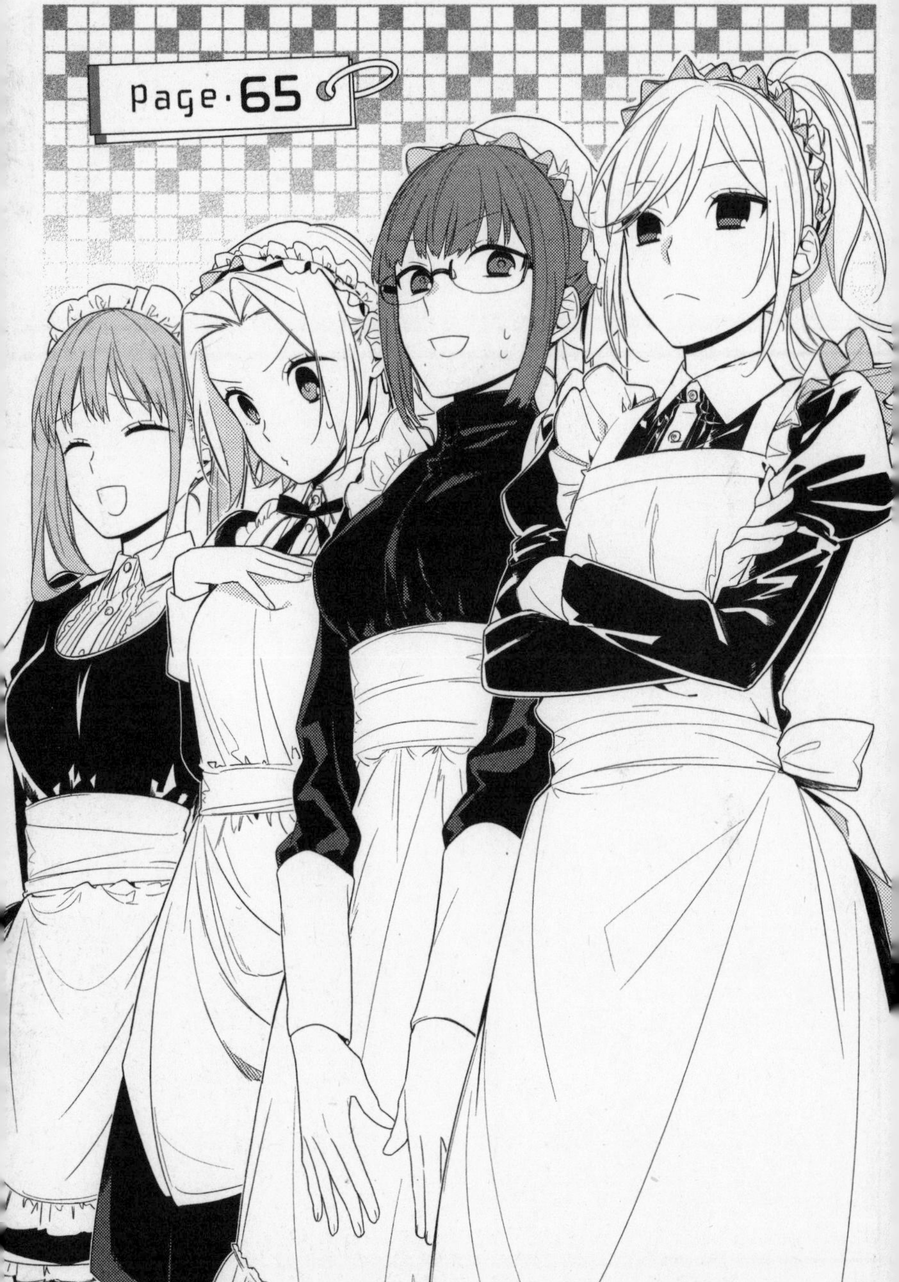
Page·65

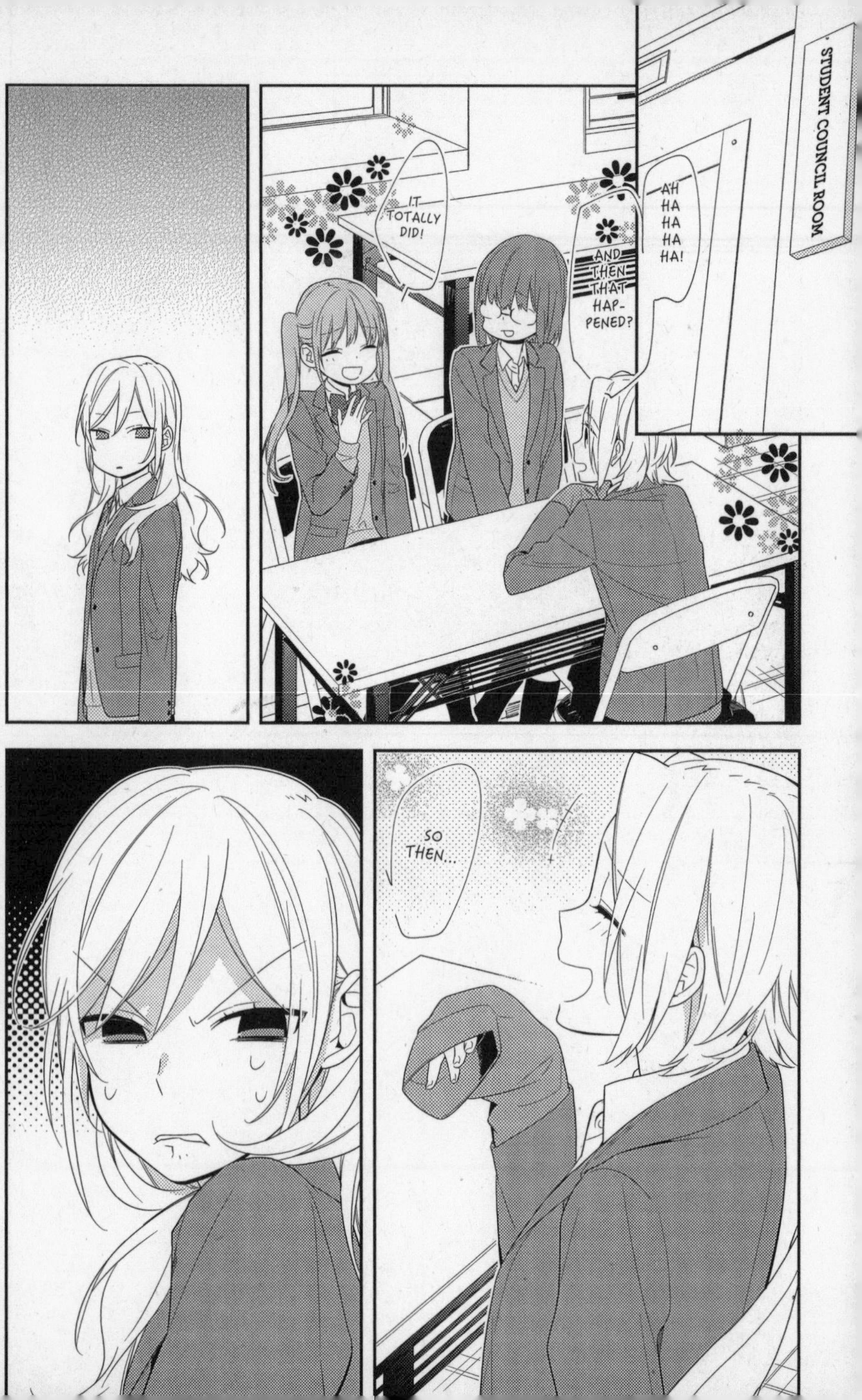
STUDENT COUNCIL ROOM
AH HA HA HA HA!
AND THEN THAT HAP-PENED?
IT TOTALLY DID!
SO THEN...

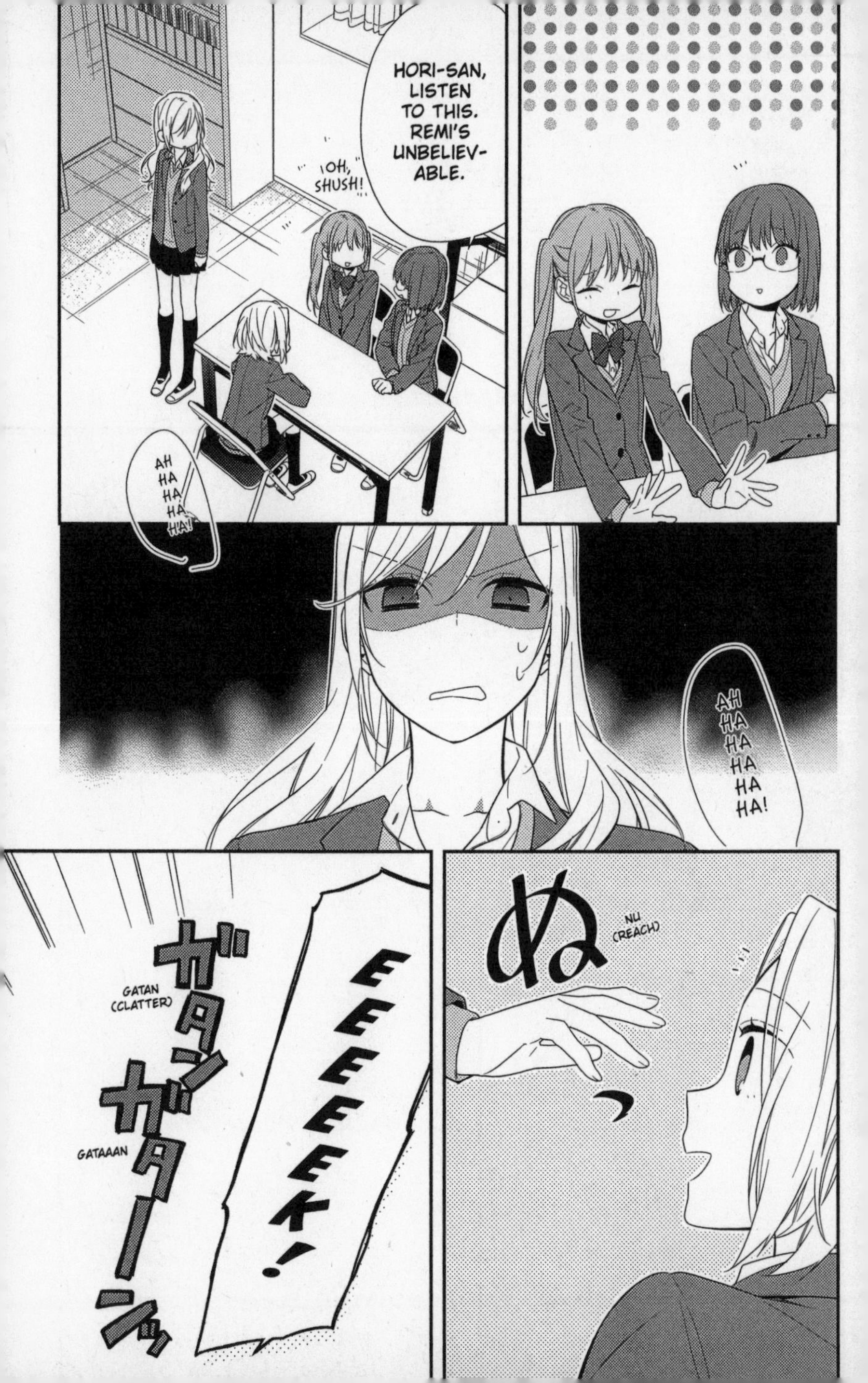
HORI-SAN, LISTEN TO THIS. REMI'S UNBELIEVABLE.
OH, SHUSH!
AH HA HA HA HA!
AH HA HA HA HA HA!
ぬ
NU (REACH)
EEEEEEK!
ガタンガターンッ
GATAN (CLATTER)
GATAAAN

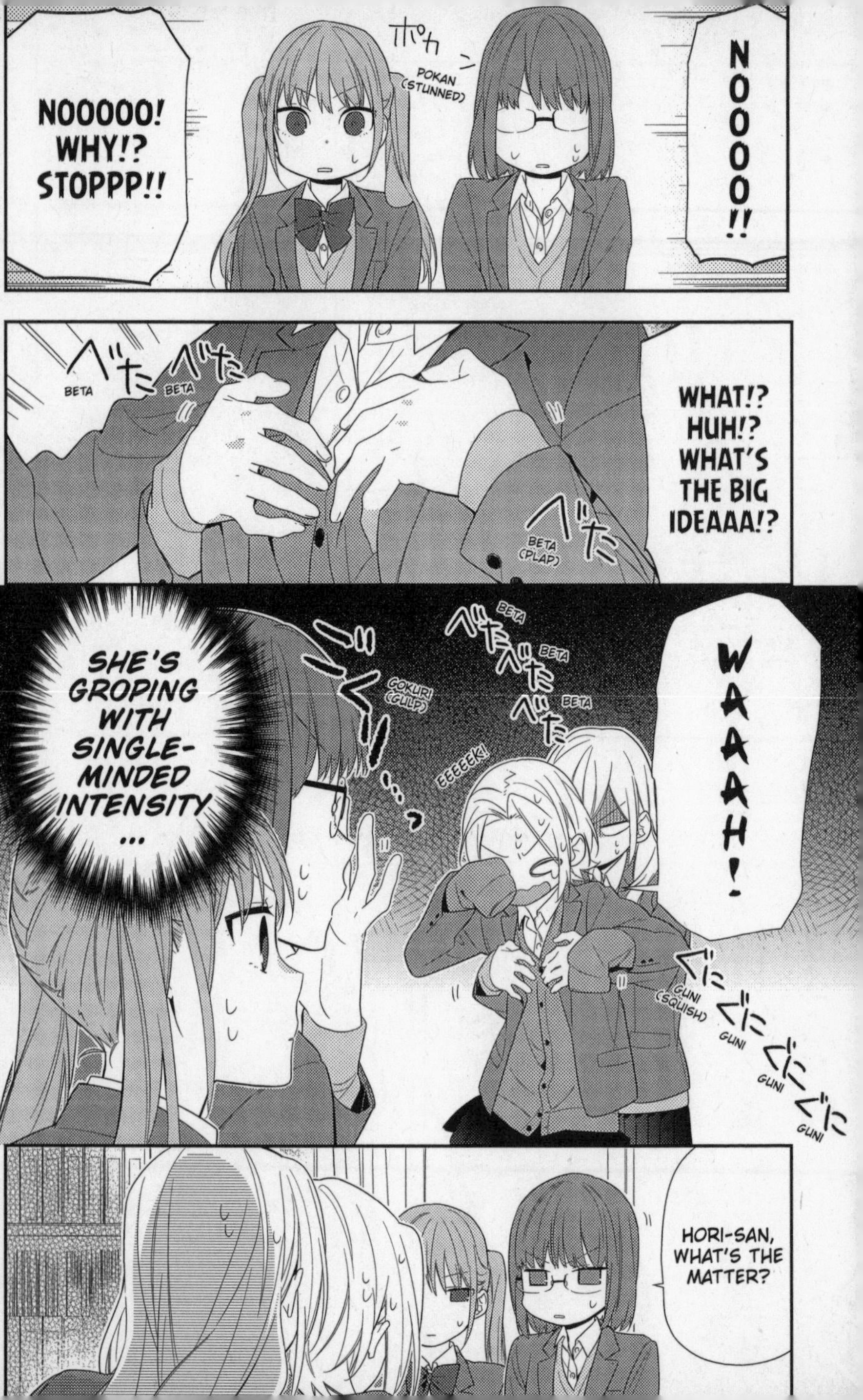
NOOOO!!
ポカン
POKAN (STUNNED)
NOOOOO! WHY!? STOPPP!!
WHAT!? HUH!? WHAT'S THE BIG IDEAAA!?
べたべた
BETA BETA
べた
BETA (PLAP)
WAAAAH!
べたべたべた
BETA BETA BETA
ごくり
GOKURI (GULP)
EEEEEK!
ぐにぐにぐにぐに
GUNI (SQUISH) GUNI GUNI GUNI
SHE'S GROPING WITH SINGLE-MINDED INTENSITY...
HORI-SAN, WHAT'S THE MATTER?

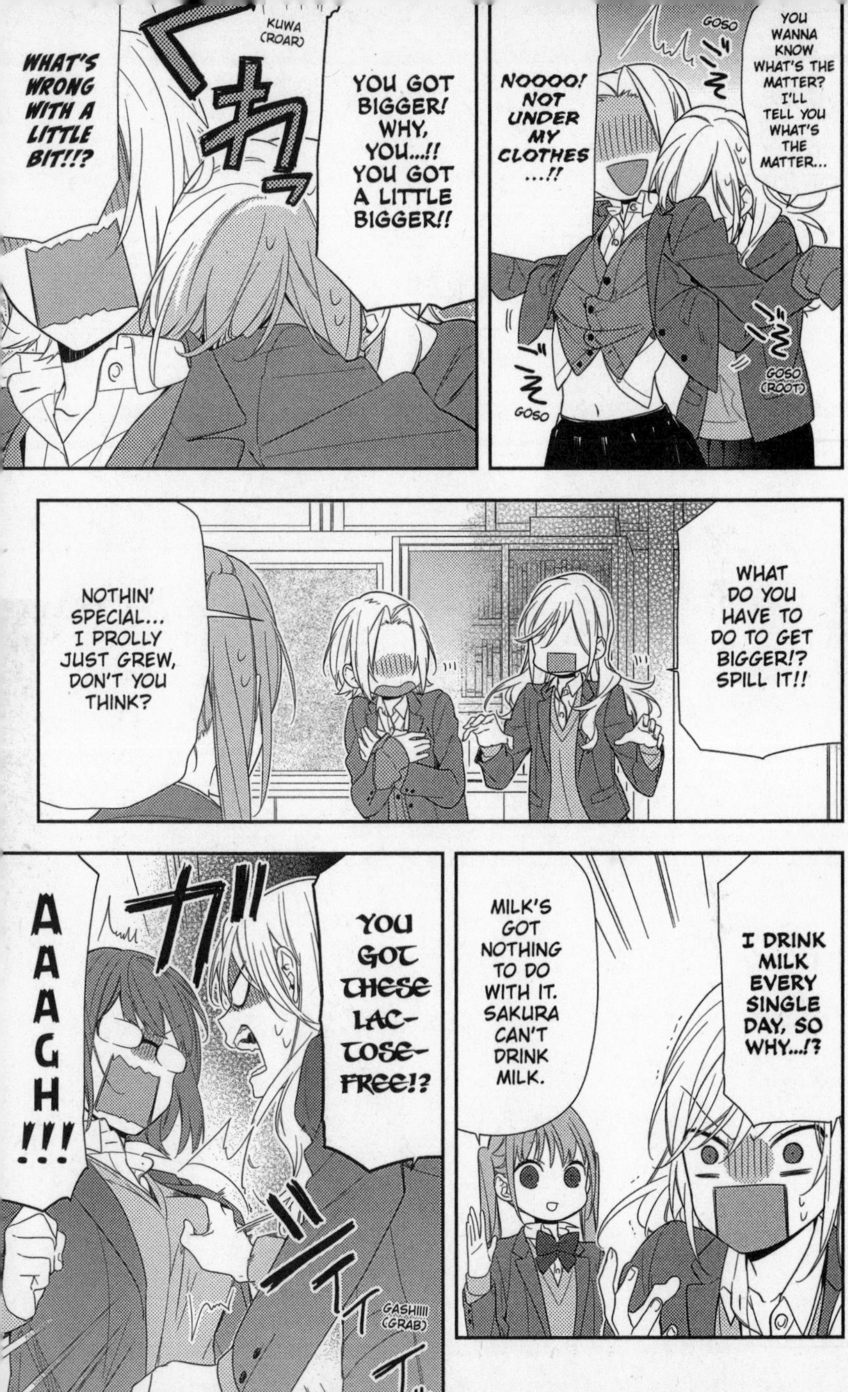
YOU WANNA KNOW WHAT'S THE MATTER? I'LL TELL YOU WHAT'S THE MATTER...
GOSO
NOOOO! NOT UNDER MY CLOTHES...!!
GOSO (ROOT)
GOSO
YOU GOT BIGGER! WHY, YOU...!! YOU GOT A LITTLE BIGGER!!
KUWA (ROAR)
WHAT'S WRONG WITH A LITTLE BIT!!?
WHAT DO YOU HAVE TO DO TO GET BIGGER!? SPILL IT!!
NOTHIN' SPECIAL... I PROLLY JUST GREW, DON'T YOU THINK?
I DRINK MILK EVERY SINGLE DAY, SO WHY...!?
MILK'S GOT NOTHING TO DO WITH IT. SAKURA CAN'T DRINK MILK.
YOU GOT THESE LACTOSE-FREE!?
GASHIIII (GRAB)
AAAAGH!!!

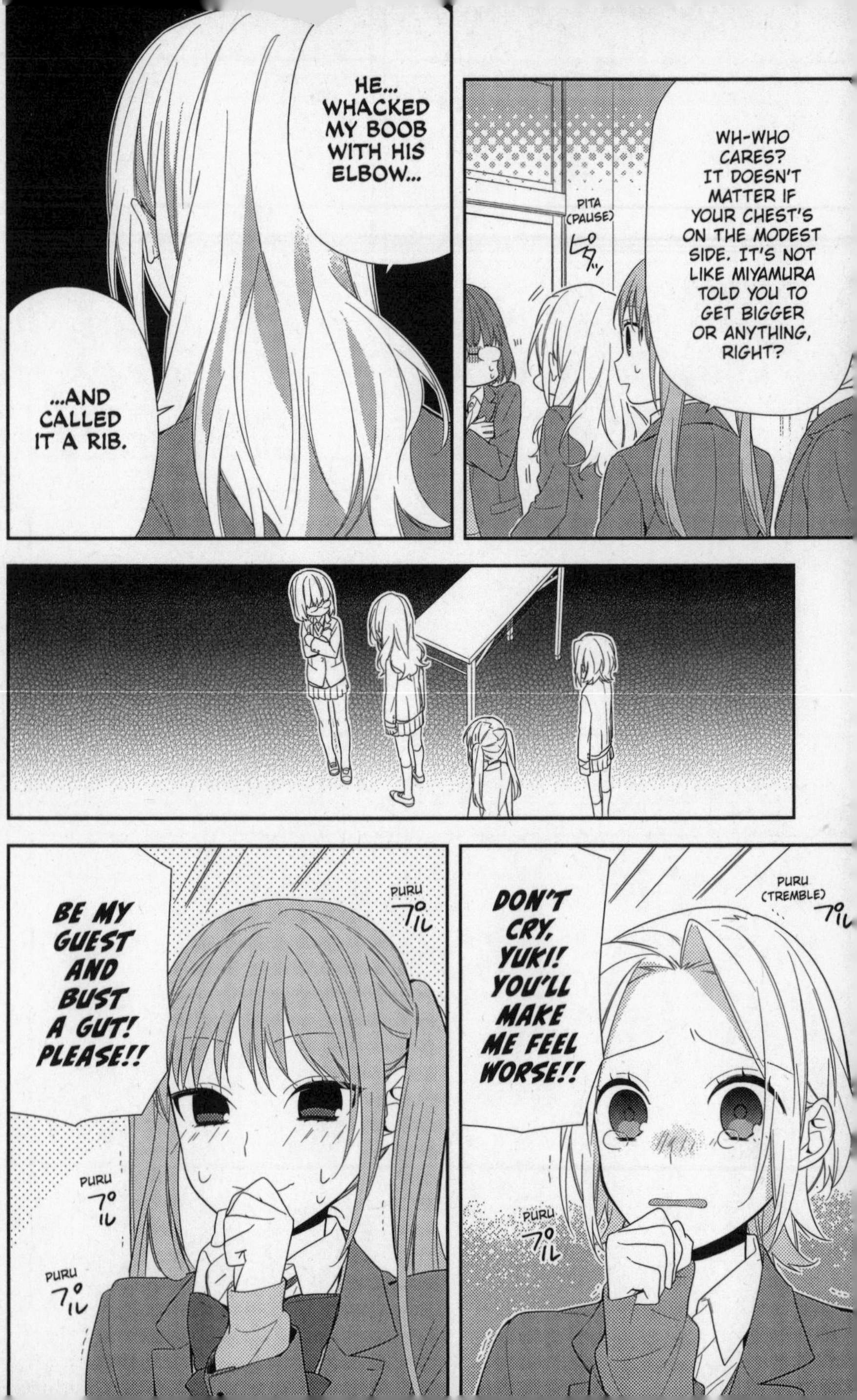
WH-WHO CARES? IT DOESN'T MATTER IF YOUR CHEST'S ON THE MODEST SIDE. IT'S NOT LIKE MIYAMURA TOLD YOU TO GET BIGGER OR ANYTHING, RIGHT?
PITA (PAUSE)
ピタッ
HE... WHACKED MY BOOB WITH HIS ELBOW...
...AND CALLED IT A RIB.
PURU (TREMBLE)
プル
DON'T CRY, YUKI! YOU'LL MAKE ME FEEL WORSE!!
PURU
プル
PURU
プル
BE MY GUEST AND BUST A GUT! PLEASE!!
PURU
プル
PURU
プル

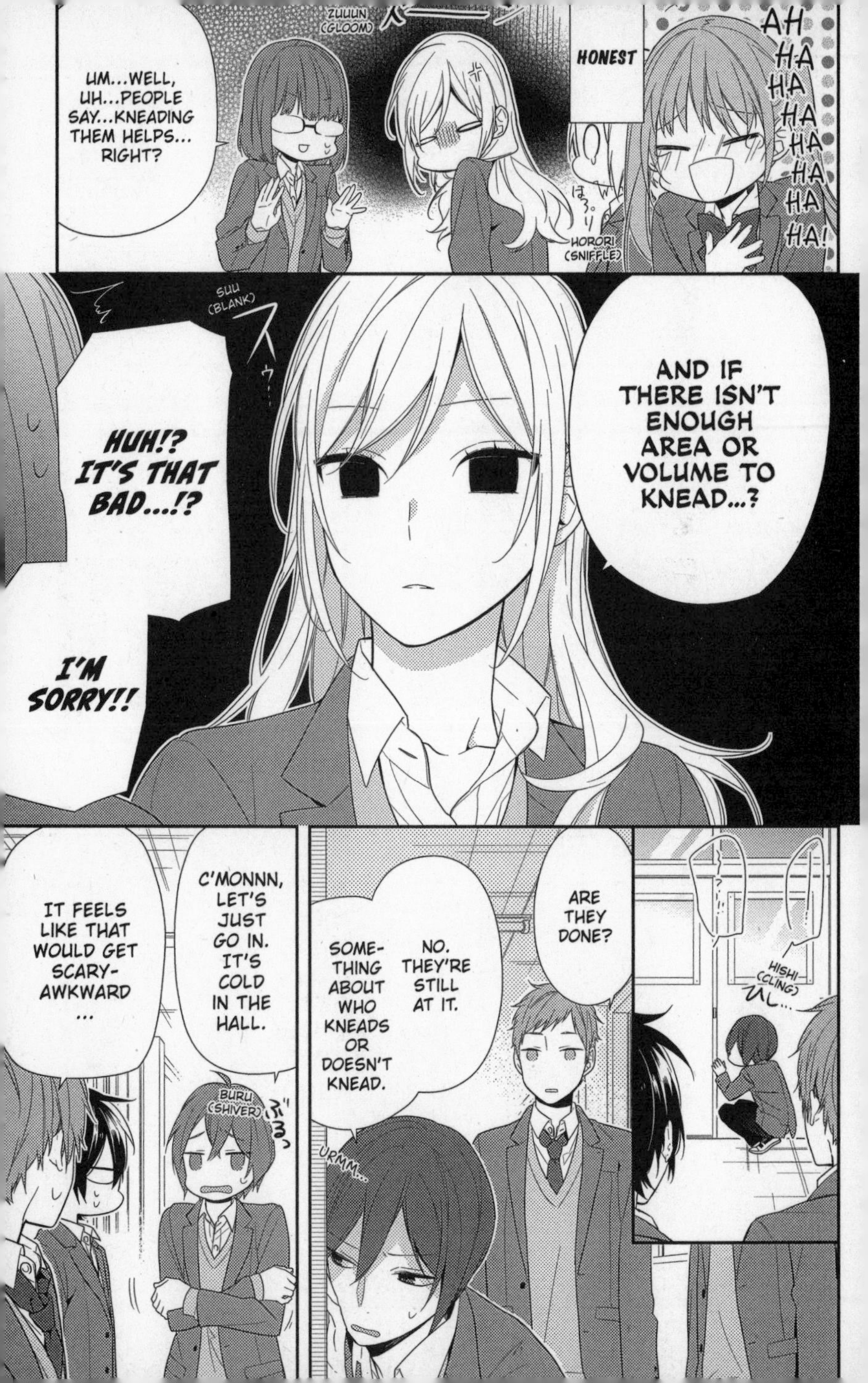
AH HA HA HA HA HA HA HA!
HONEST
HORORI (SNIFFLE)
ZUUUN (GLOOM)
UM...WELL, UH...PEOPLE SAY...KNEADING THEM HELPS... RIGHT?
AND IF THERE ISN'T ENOUGH AREA OR VOLUME TO KNEAD...?
SUU (BLANK)
HUH!? IT'S THAT BAD...!?
I'M SORRY!!
HISHI (CLING)
ARE THEY DONE?
NO. THEY'RE STILL AT IT.
SOME-THING ABOUT WHO KNEADS OR DOESN'T KNEAD.
URMM...
C'MONNN, LET'S JUST GO IN. IT'S COLD IN THE HALL.
BURU (SHIVER)
IT FEELS LIKE THAT WOULD GET SCARY-AWKWARD...

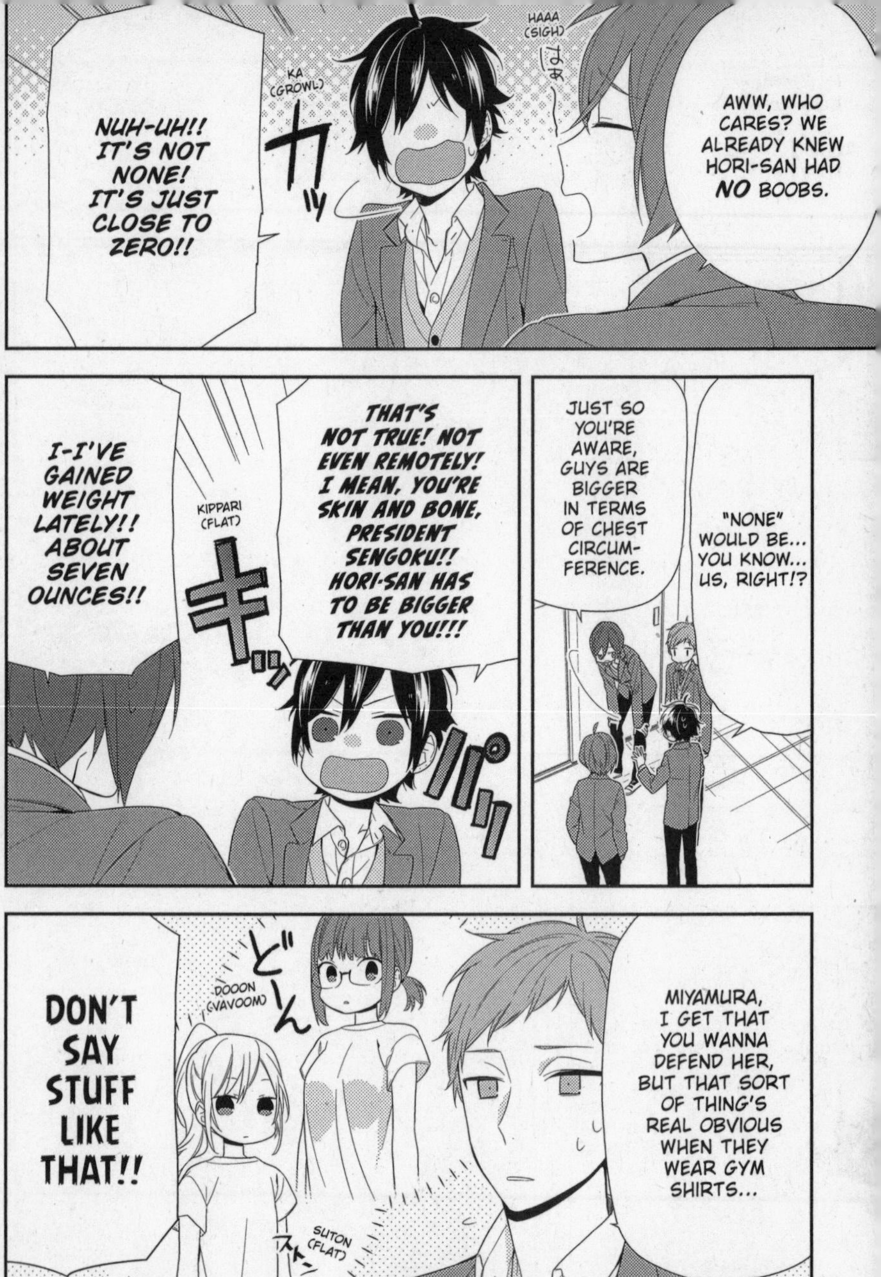
AWW, WHO CARES? WE ALREADY KNEW HORI-SAN HAD NO BOOBS.
HAAA (SIGH)
KA (GROWL)
NUH-UH!! IT'S NOT NONE! IT'S JUST CLOSE TO ZERO!!
"NONE" WOULD BE... YOU KNOW... US, RIGHT!?
JUST SO YOU'RE AWARE, GUYS ARE BIGGER IN TERMS OF CHEST CIRCUM-FERENCE.
THAT'S NOT TRUE! NOT EVEN REMOTELY! I MEAN, YOU'RE SKIN AND BONE, PRESIDENT SENGOKU!! HORI-SAN HAS TO BE BIGGER THAN YOU!!!
KIPPARI (FLAT)
I-I'VE GAINED WEIGHT LATELY!! ABOUT SEVEN OUNCES!!
MIYAMURA, I GET THAT YOU WANNA DEFEND HER, BUT THAT SORT OF THING'S REAL OBVIOUS WHEN THEY WEAR GYM SHIRTS...
DOOON (VAVOOM)
SUTON (FLAT)
DON'T SAY STUFF LIKE THAT!!

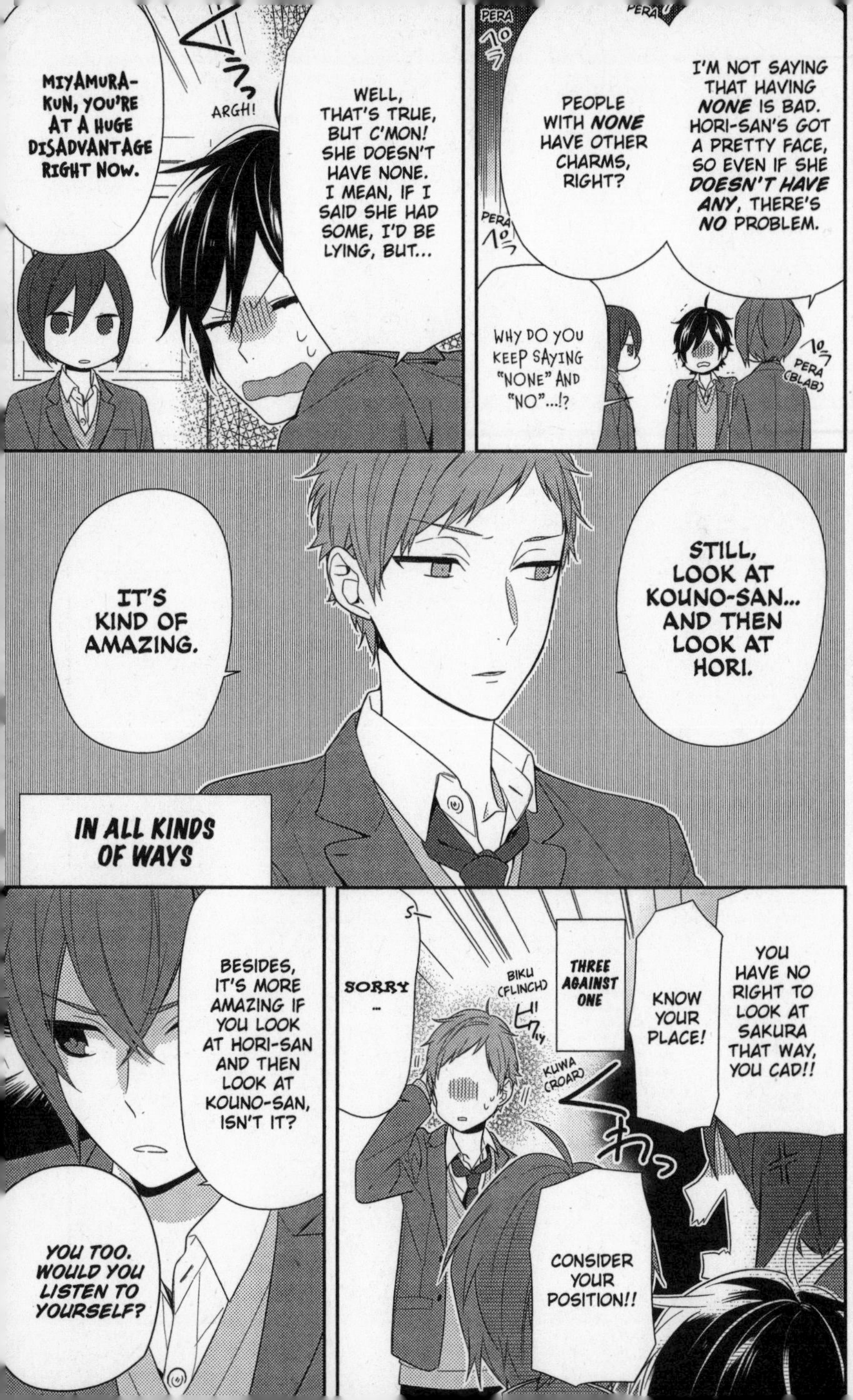
PERA
PERA
I'M NOT SAYING THAT HAVING ***NONE*** IS BAD. HORI-SAN'S GOT A PRETTY FACE, SO EVEN IF SHE ***DOESN'T HAVE ANY***, THERE'S ***NO*** PROBLEM.
PEOPLE WITH ***NONE*** HAVE OTHER CHARMS, RIGHT?
PERA
PERA (BLAB)
WHY DO YOU KEEP SAYING "NONE" AND "NO"...!?
WELL, THAT'S TRUE, BUT C'MON! SHE DOESN'T HAVE NONE. I MEAN, IF I SAID SHE HAD SOME, I'D BE LYING, BUT...
ARGH!
MIYAMURA-KUN, YOU'RE AT A HUGE DISADVANTAGE RIGHT NOW.
STILL, LOOK AT KOUNO-SAN... AND THEN LOOK AT HORI.
IT'S KIND OF AMAZING.
IN ALL KINDS OF WAYS
YOU HAVE NO RIGHT TO LOOK AT SAKURA THAT WAY, YOU CAD!!
KNOW YOUR PLACE!
THREE AGAINST ONE
KUWA (ROAR)
BIKU (FLINCH)
SORRY...
CONSIDER YOUR POSITION!!
BESIDES, IT'S MORE AMAZING IF YOU LOOK AT HORI-SAN AND THEN LOOK AT KOUNO-SAN, ISN'T IT?
YOU TOO. WOULD YOU LISTEN TO YOURSELF?

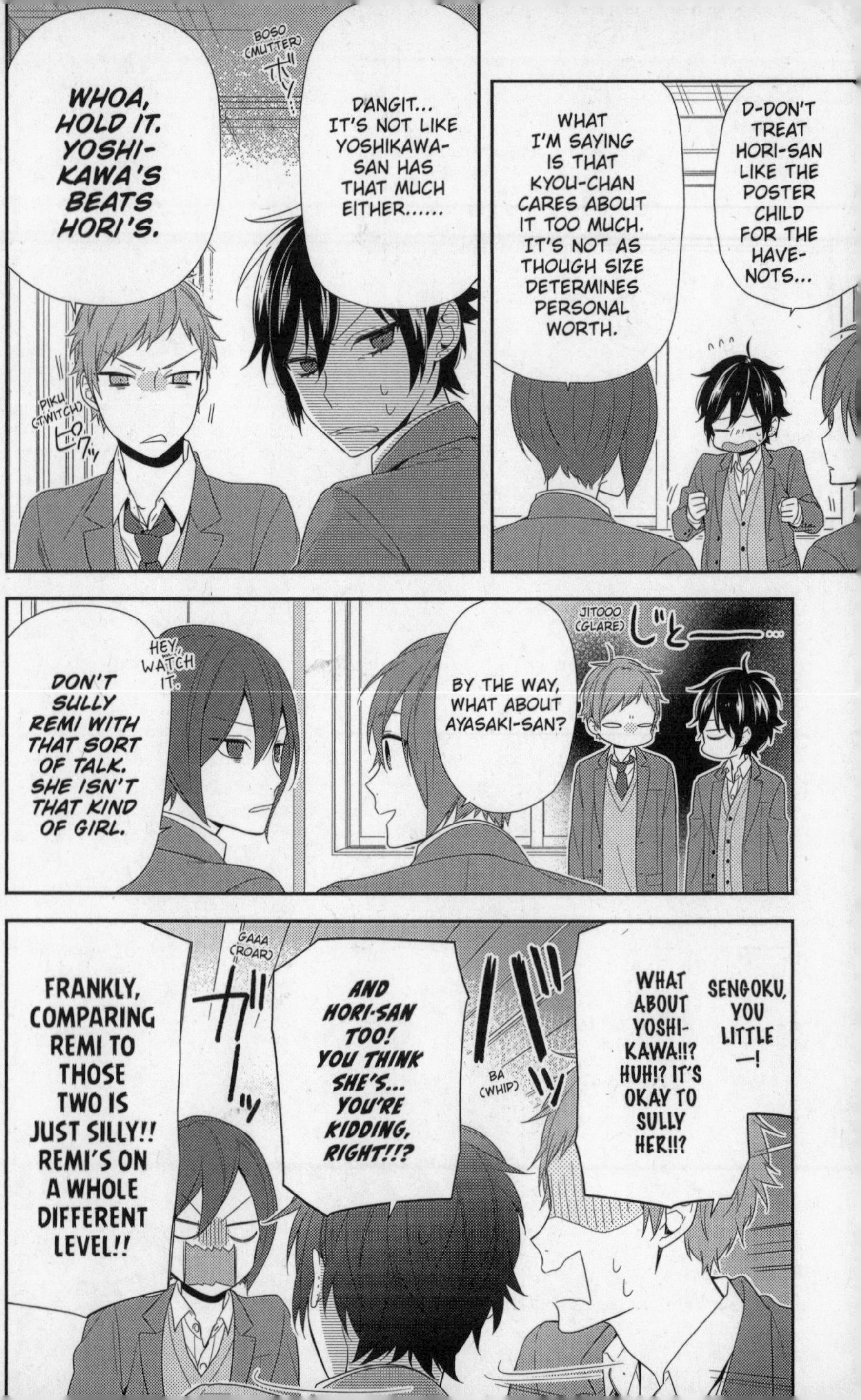
D-DON'T TREAT HORI-SAN LIKE THE POSTER CHILD FOR THE HAVE-NOTS...
WHAT I'M SAYING IS THAT KYOU-CHAN CARES ABOUT IT TOO MUCH. IT'S NOT AS THOUGH SIZE DETERMINES PERSONAL WORTH.
DANGIT... IT'S NOT LIKE YOSHIKAWA-SAN HAS THAT MUCH EITHER......
BOSO (MUTTER)
WHOA, HOLD IT. YOSHIKAWA'S BEATS HORI'S.
PIKU (TWITCH)
JITOOO (GLARE)
BY THE WAY, WHAT ABOUT AYASAKI-SAN?
HEY, WATCH IT.
DON'T SULLY REMI WITH THAT SORT OF TALK. SHE ISN'T THAT KIND OF GIRL.
SENGOKU, YOU LITTLE—!
WHAT ABOUT YOSHIKAWA!!? HUH!? IT'S OKAY TO SULLY HER!!?
BA (WHIP)
AND HORI-SAN TOO! YOU THINK SHE'S... YOU'RE KIDDING, RIGHT!!?
GAAA (ROAR)
FRANKLY, COMPARING REMI TO THOSE TWO IS JUST SILLY!! REMI'S ON A WHOLE DIFFERENT LEVEL!!

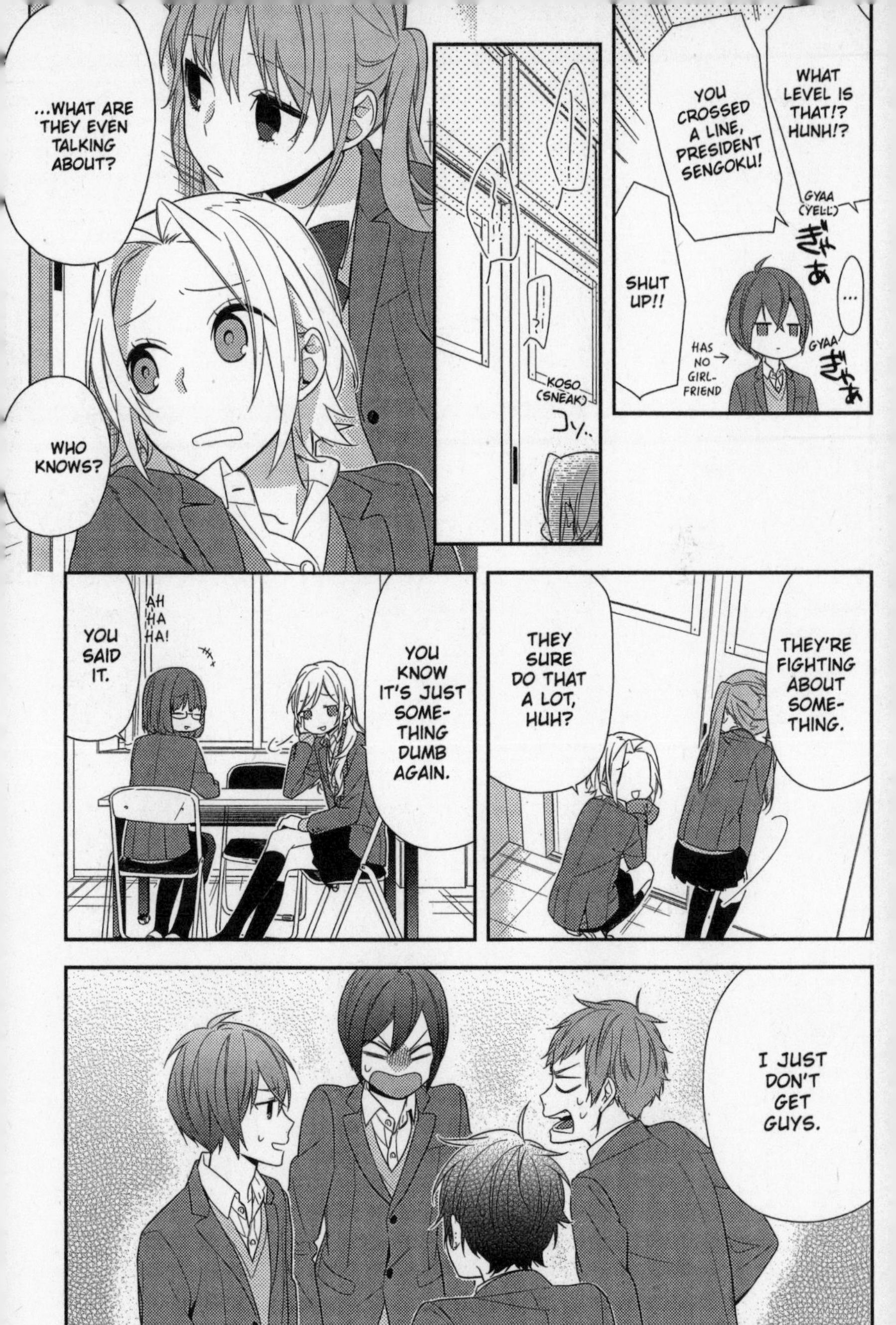
WHAT LEVEL IS THAT!? HUNH!?
YOU CROSSED A LINE, PRESIDENT SENGOKU!
GYAA (YELL)
ぎゃあ
...
SHUT UP!!
GYAA
ぎゃあ
HAS NO GIRLFRIEND
KOSO (SNEAK)
...WHAT ARE THEY EVEN TALKING ABOUT?
WHO KNOWS?
THEY'RE FIGHTING ABOUT SOMETHING.
THEY SURE DO THAT A LOT, HUH?
YOU KNOW IT'S JUST SOMETHING DUMB AGAIN.
AH HA HA!
YOU SAID IT.
I JUST DON'T GET GUYS.

HORIMIYA

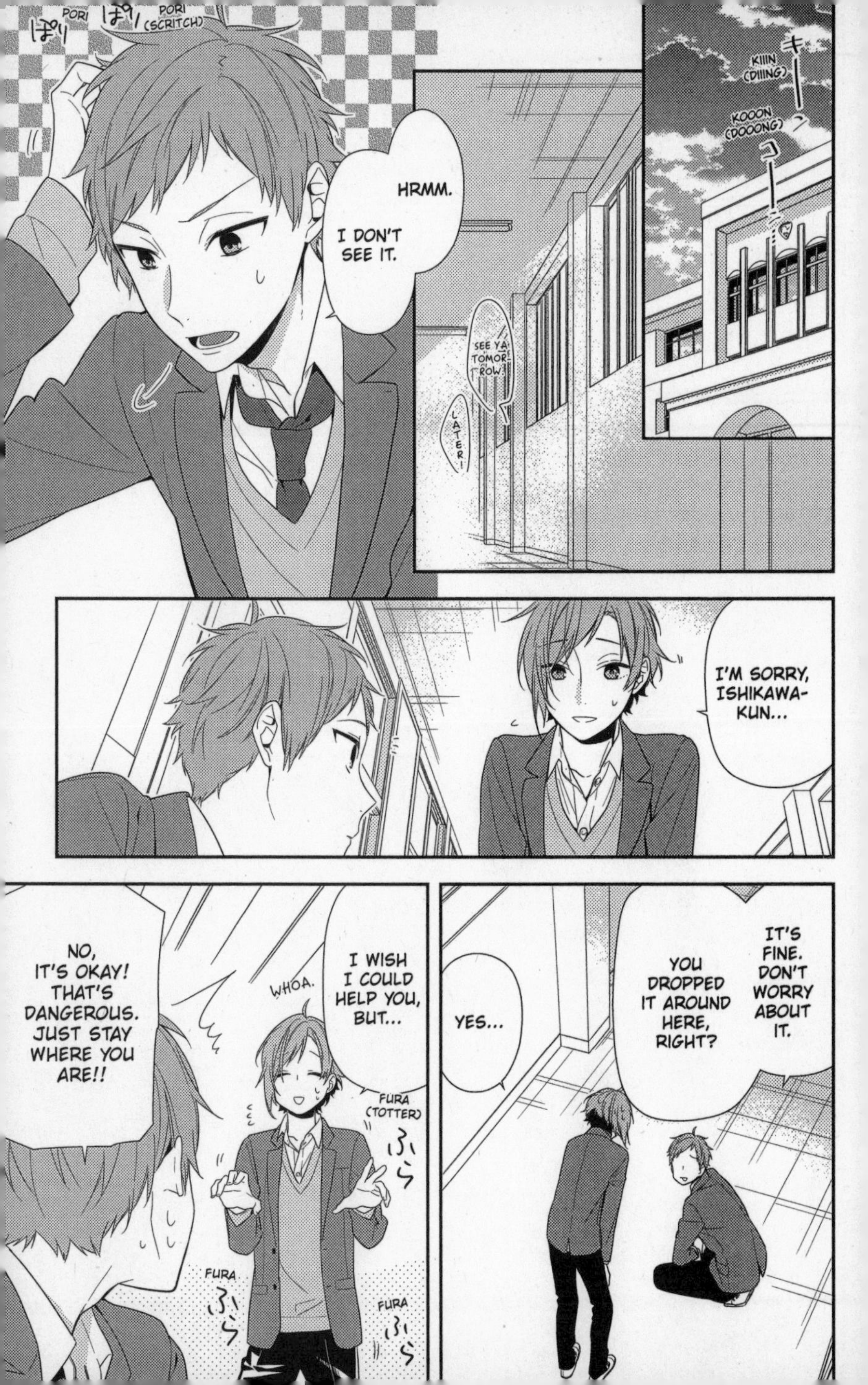
KIIIN (DIIING)
キーン
KOOON (DOOONG)
コーン
SEE YA TOMORROW.
LATER!
PORI ぽり
PORI (SCRITCH) ぽり
HRMM.
I DON'T SEE IT.
I'M SORRY, ISHIKAWA-KUN...
IT'S FINE. DON'T WORRY ABOUT IT.
YOU DROPPED IT AROUND HERE, RIGHT?
YES...
I WISH I COULD HELP YOU, BUT...
WHOA.
FURA (TOTTER) ふら
NO, IT'S OKAY! THAT'S DANGEROUS. JUST STAY WHERE YOU ARE!!
FURA ふら
FURA ふら

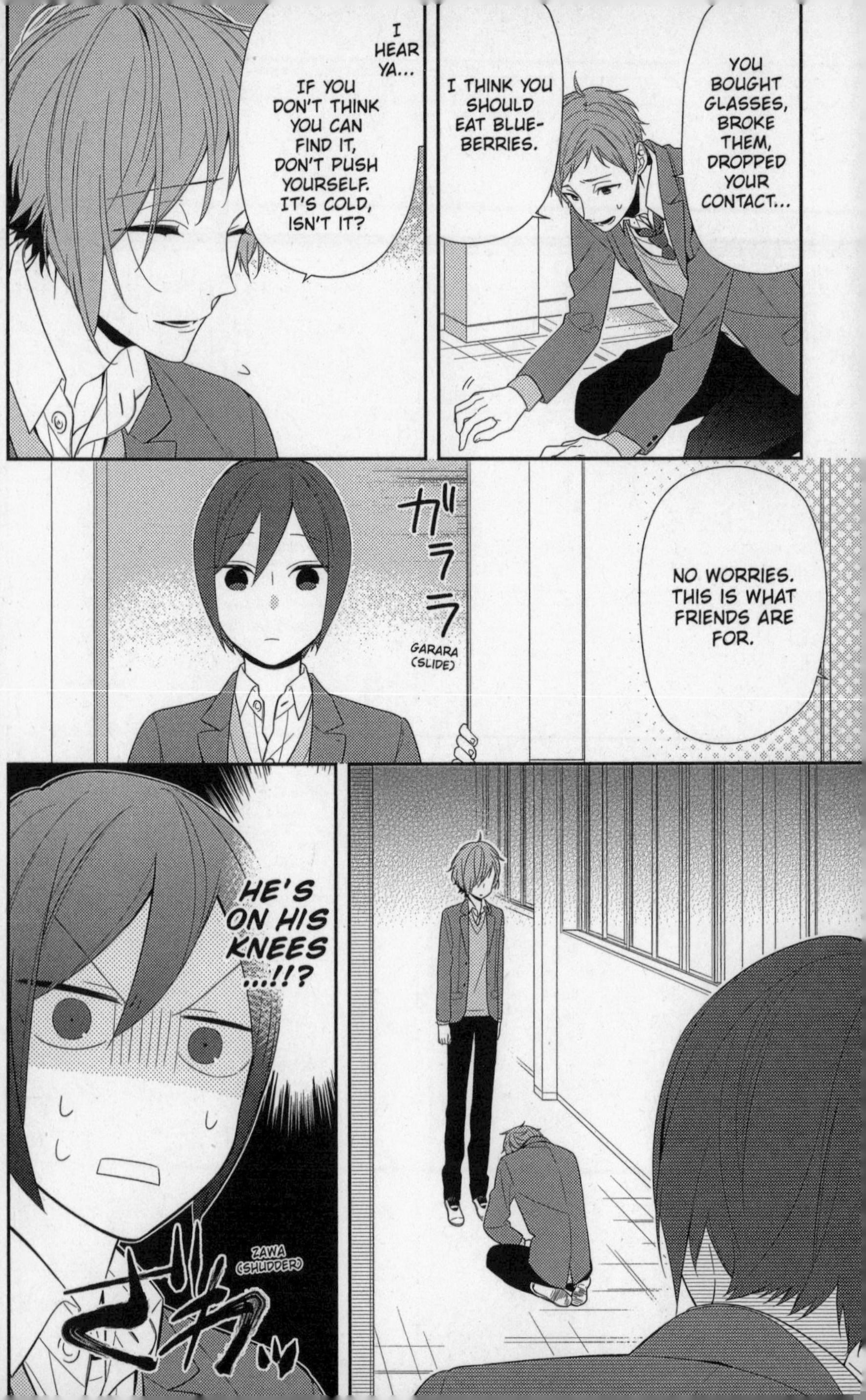

YOU BOUGHT GLASSES, BROKE THEM, DROPPED YOUR CONTACT...
I THINK YOU SHOULD EAT BLUE-BERRIES.
I HEAR YA...
IF YOU DON'T THINK YOU CAN FIND IT, DON'T PUSH YOURSELF. IT'S COLD, ISN'T IT?
NO WORRIES. THIS IS WHAT FRIENDS ARE FOR.
ガララ
GARARA (SLIDE)
HE'S ON HIS KNEES...!!?
ZAWA (SHUDDER)

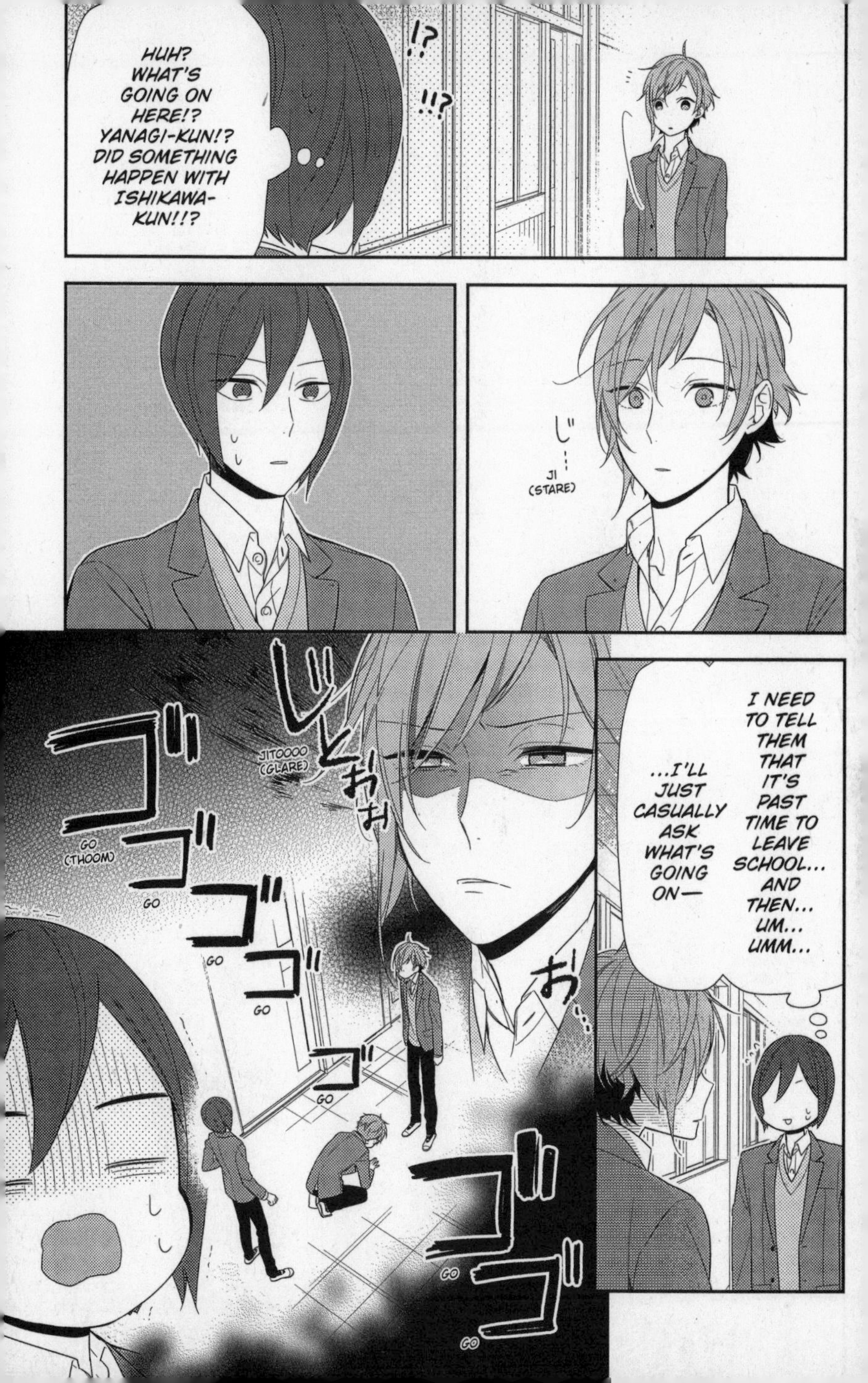
!?
!!?
HUH? WHAT'S GOING ON HERE!? YANAGI-KUN!? DID SOMETHING HAPPEN WITH ISHIKAWA-KUN!!?
じ…
JI (STARE)
I NEED TO TELL THEM THAT IT'S PAST TIME TO LEAVE SCHOOL... AND THEN... UM... UMM...
...I'LL JUST CASUALLY ASK WHAT'S GOING ON—
じとぉぉ…
JITOOOO (GLARE)
ゴゴゴゴゴゴ
GO (THOOM)
GO
GO
GO
GO
GO
GO

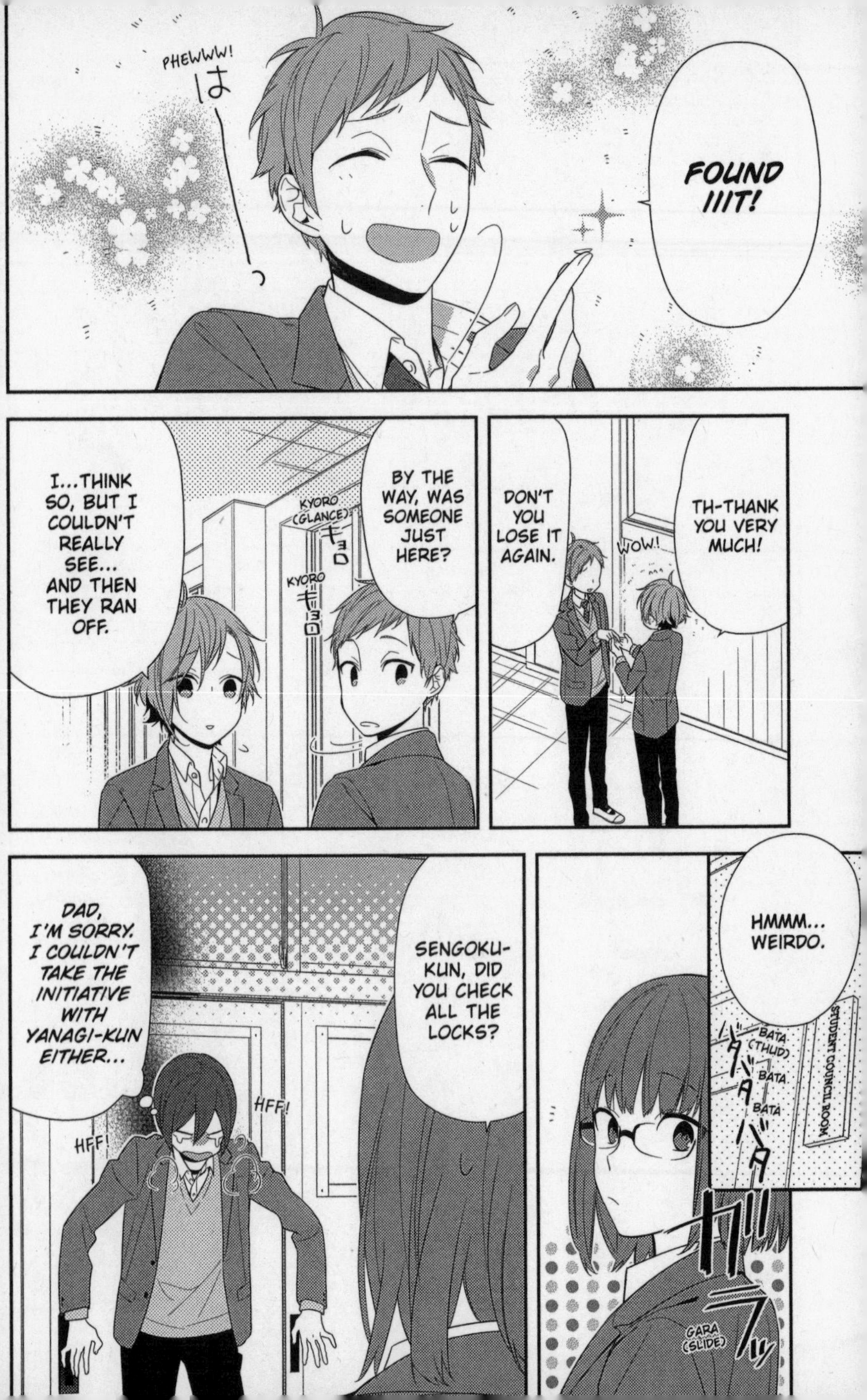
FOUND IIIT!
PHEWWW!
は
TH-THANK YOU VERY MUCH!
WOW!
DON'T YOU LOSE IT AGAIN.
BY THE WAY, WAS SOMEONE JUST HERE?
KYORO (GLANCE)
KYORO
I...THINK SO, BUT I COULDN'T REALLY SEE... AND THEN THEY RAN OFF.
HMMM... WEIRDO.
STUDENT COUNCIL ROOM
BATA (THUD)
BATA
BATA
GARA (SLIDE)
SENGOKU-KUN, DID YOU CHECK ALL THE LOCKS?
DAD, I'M SORRY. I COULDN'T TAKE THE INITIATIVE WITH YANAGI-KUN EITHER...
HFF!
HFF!

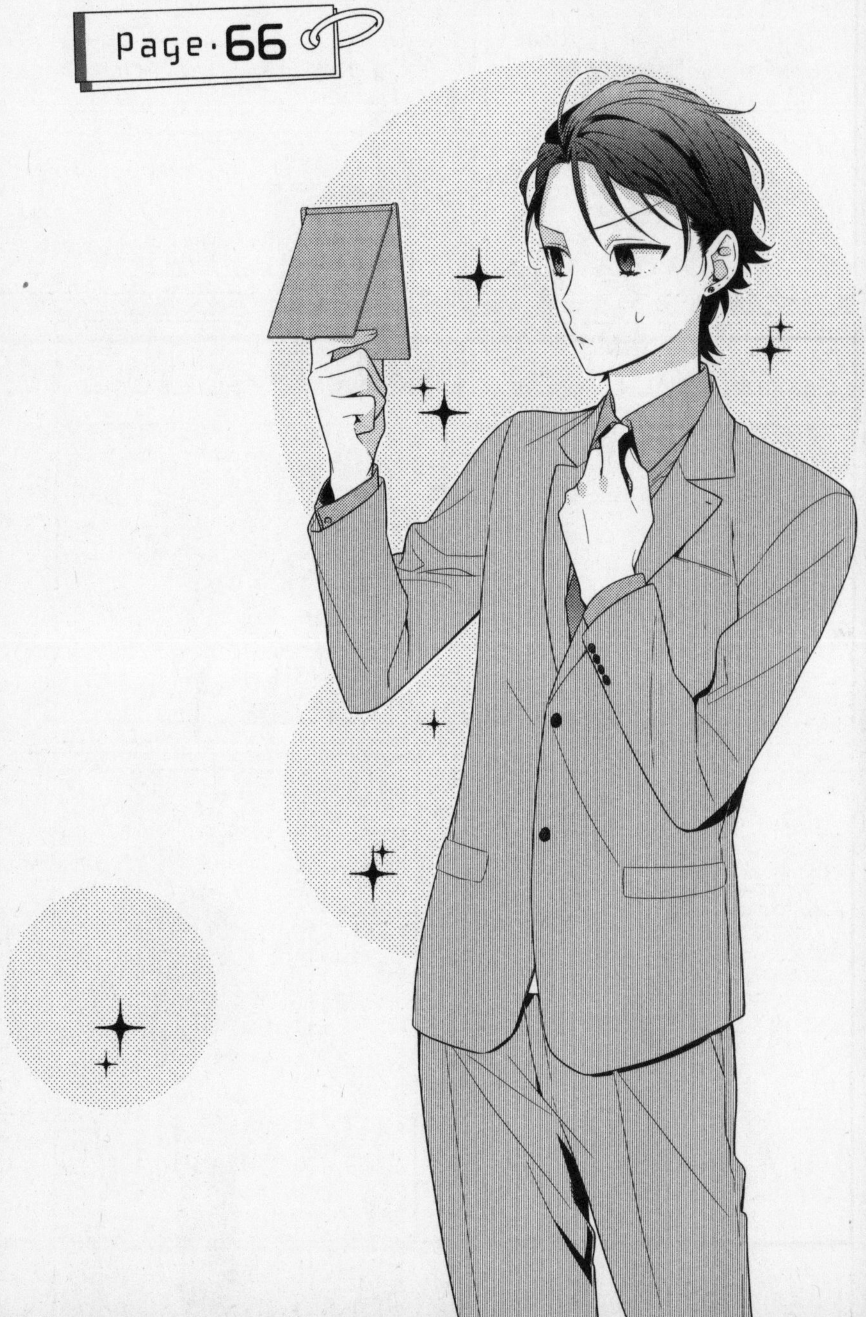
Page·66

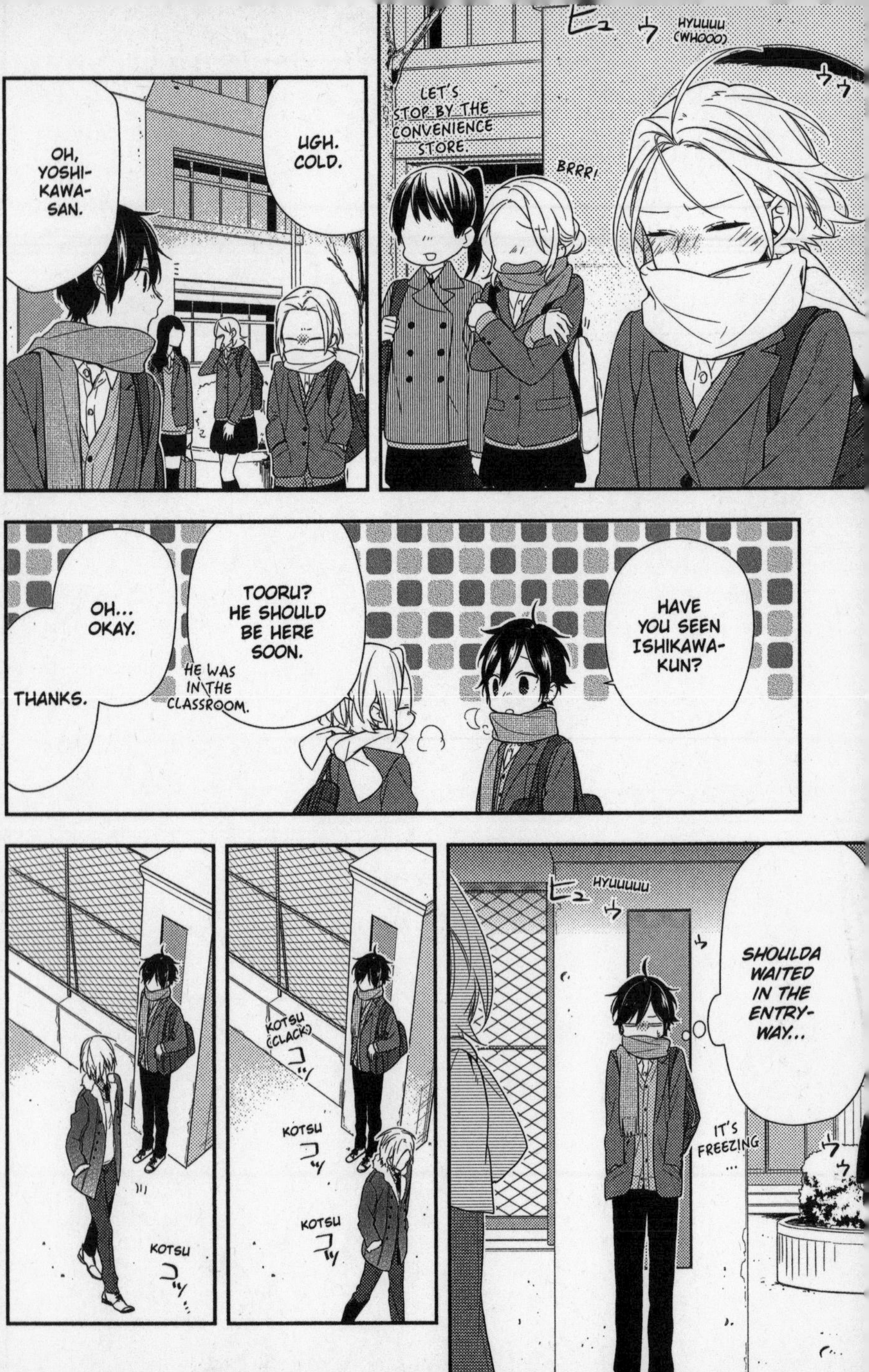
HYUUUU (WHOOO)
LET'S STOP BY THE CONVENIENCE STORE.
BRRR!
UGH. COLD.
OH, YOSHI-KAWA-SAN.
HAVE YOU SEEN ISHIKAWA-KUN?
TOORU? HE SHOULD BE HERE SOON.
HE WAS IN THE CLASSROOM.
OH... OKAY.
THANKS.
HYUUUUU
SHOULDA WAITED IN THE ENTRY-WAY...
IT'S FREEZING...
KOTSU (CLACK)
KOTSU
KOTSU
KOTSU

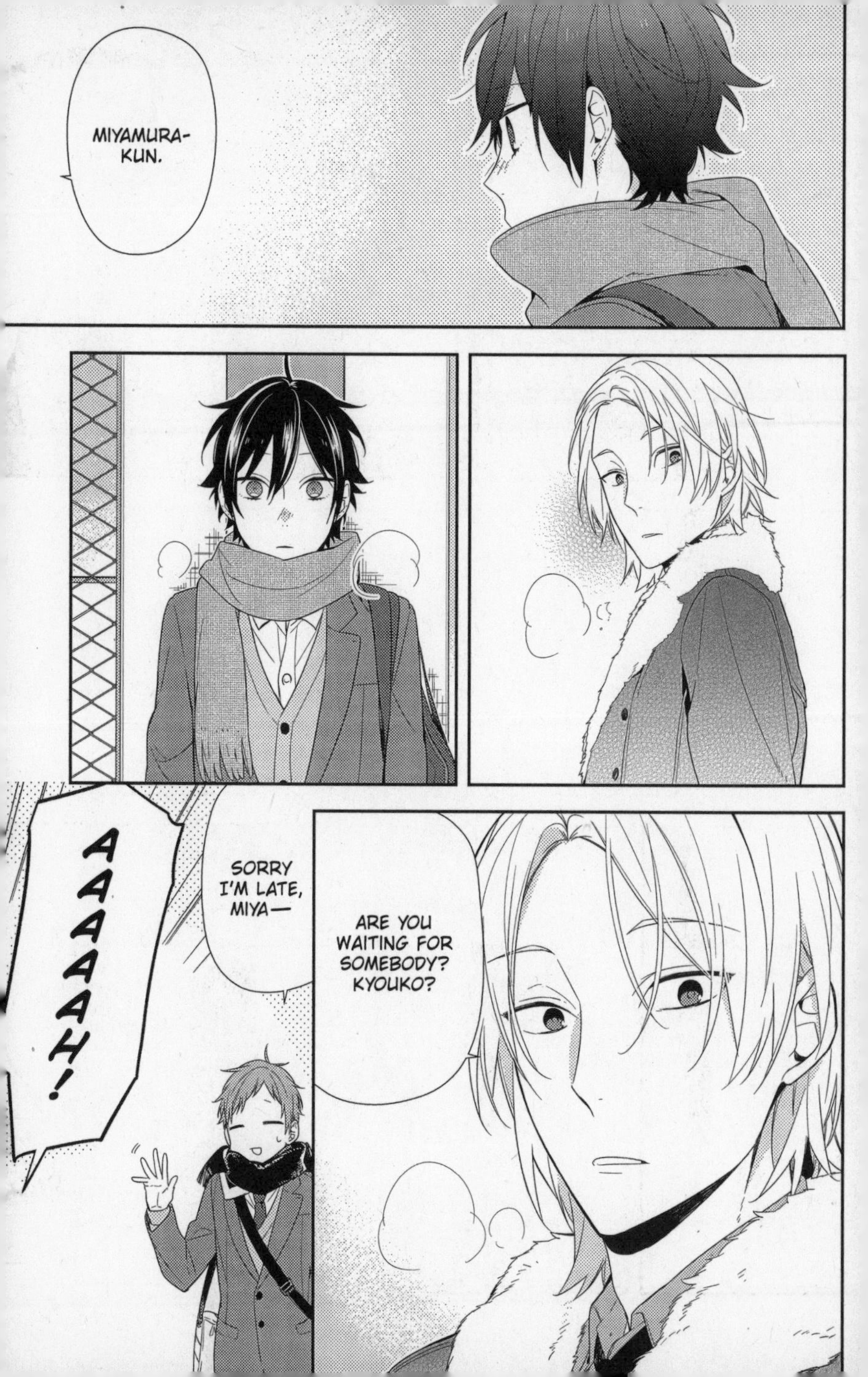
MIYAMURA-KUN.
ARE YOU WAITING FOR SOMEBODY? KYOUKO?
SORRY I'M LATE, MIYA—
AAAAAAH!

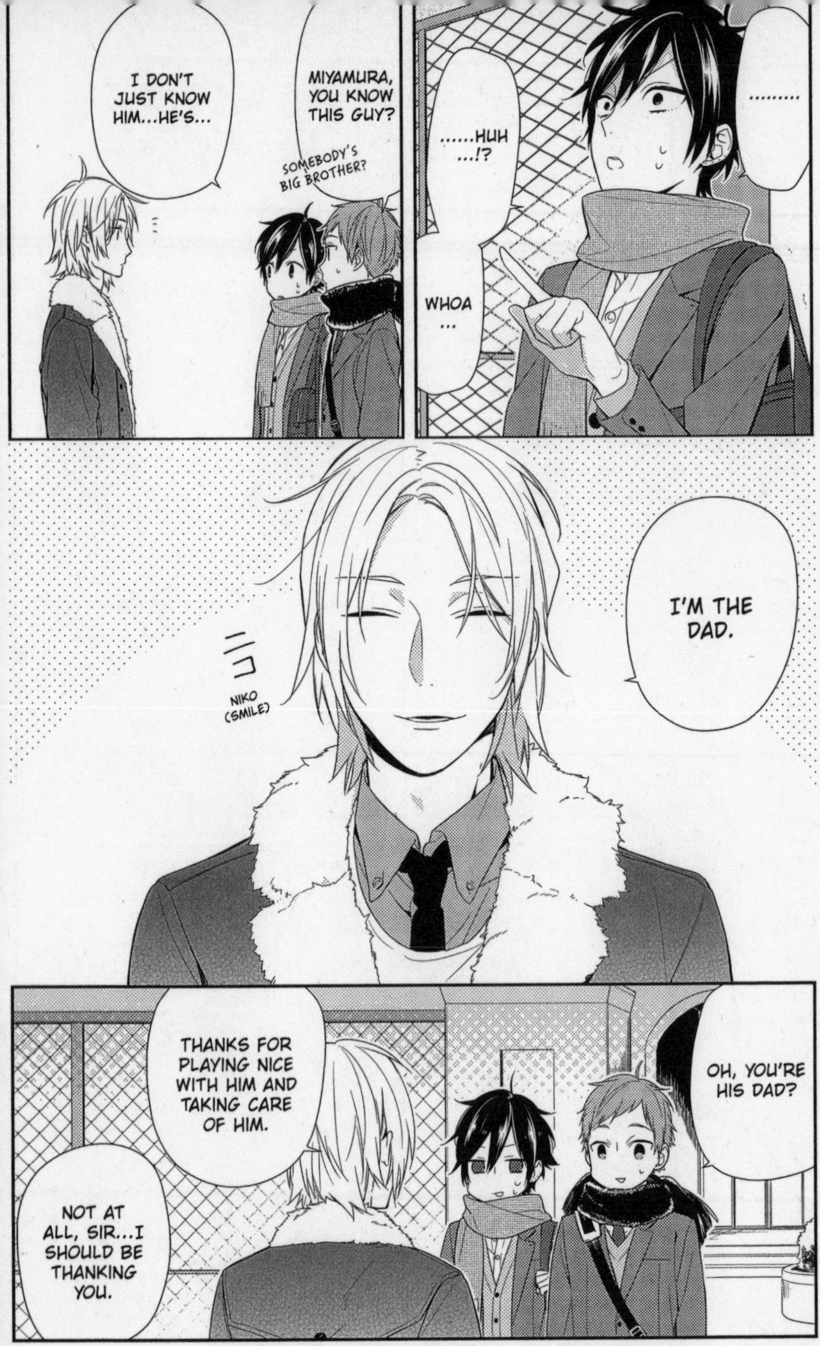
....
......HUH ...!?
WHOA ...
MIYAMURA, YOU KNOW THIS GUY?
SOMEBODY'S BIG BROTHER?
I DON'T JUST KNOW HIM...HE'S...
I'M THE DAD.
ニコ
NIKO (SMILE)
OH, YOU'RE HIS DAD?
THANKS FOR PLAYING NICE WITH HIM AND TAKING CARE OF HIM.
NOT AT ALL, SIR...I SHOULD BE THANKING YOU.

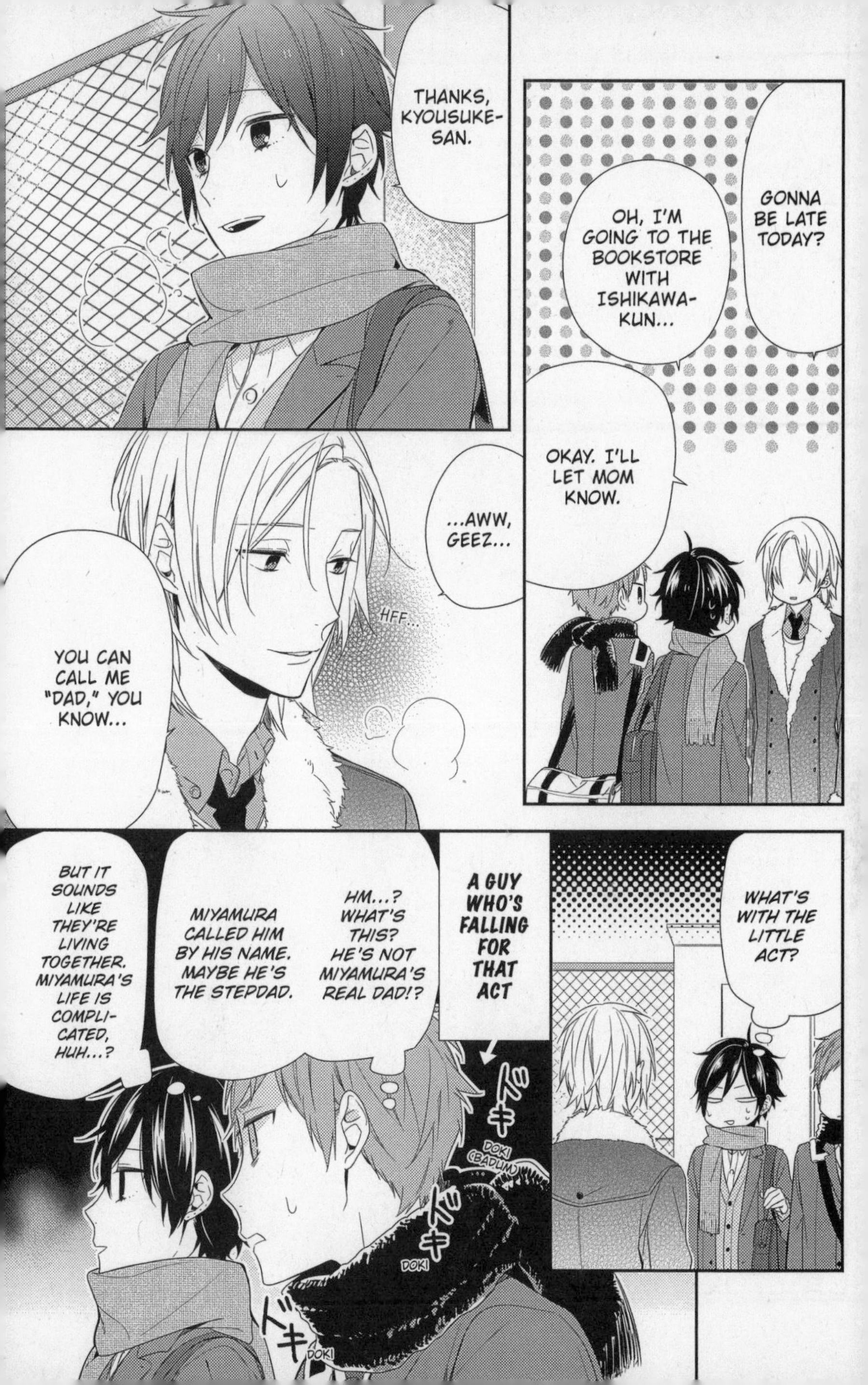
GONNA BE LATE TODAY?
OH, I'M GOING TO THE BOOKSTORE WITH ISHIKAWA-KUN...
OKAY. I'LL LET MOM KNOW.
THANKS, KYOUSUKE-SAN.
...AWW, GEEZ...
HFF...
YOU CAN CALL ME "DAD," YOU KNOW...
WHAT'S WITH THE LITTLE ACT?
A GUY WHO'S FALLING FOR THAT ACT
HM...? WHAT'S THIS? HE'S NOT MIYAMURA'S REAL DAD!?
MIYAMURA CALLED HIM BY HIS NAME. MAYBE HE'S THE STEPDAD.
BUT IT SOUNDS LIKE THEY'RE LIVING TOGETHER. MIYAMURA'S LIFE IS COMPLI-CATED, HUH...?
DOKI (BADUM)
DOKI
DOKI

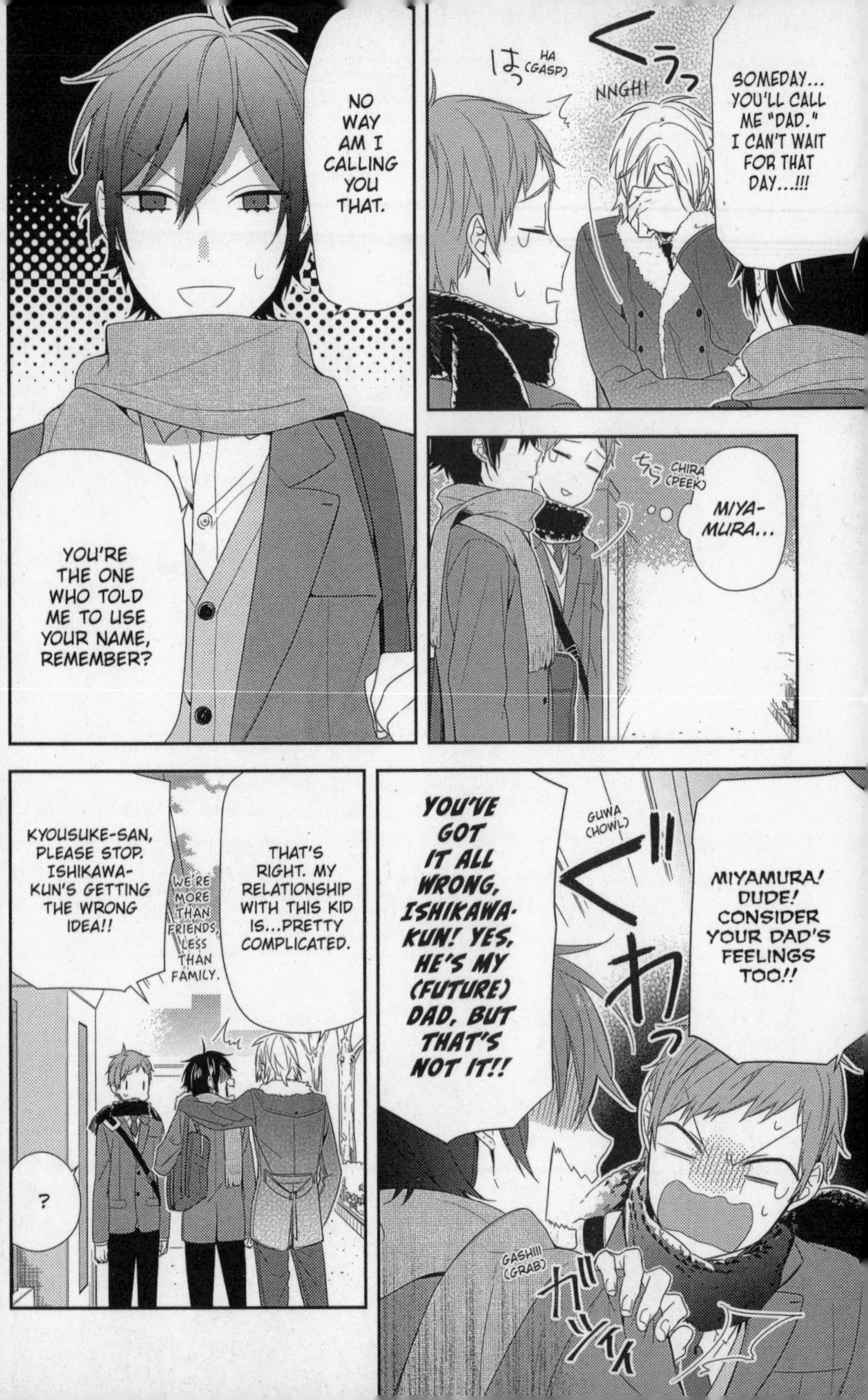
はっ HA (GASP)
くうっ NNGH!
SOMEDAY... YOU'LL CALL ME "DAD." I CAN'T WAIT FOR THAT DAY...!!!
ちら CHIRA (PEEK)
MIYA-MURA...
NO WAY AM I CALLING YOU THAT.
YOU'RE THE ONE WHO TOLD ME TO USE YOUR NAME, REMEMBER?
MIYAMURA! DUDE! CONSIDER YOUR DAD'S FEELINGS TOO!!
GUWA (HOWL)
YOU'VE GOT IT ALL WRONG, ISHIKAWA-KUN! YES, HE'S MY (FUTURE) DAD, BUT THAT'S NOT IT!!
GASHIII (GRAB)
THAT'S RIGHT. MY RELATIONSHIP WITH THIS KID IS...PRETTY COMPLICATED.
WE'RE MORE THAN FRIENDS, LESS THAN FAMILY.
KYOUSUKE-SAN, PLEASE STOP. ISHIKAWA-KUN'S GETTING THE WRONG IDEA!!
?

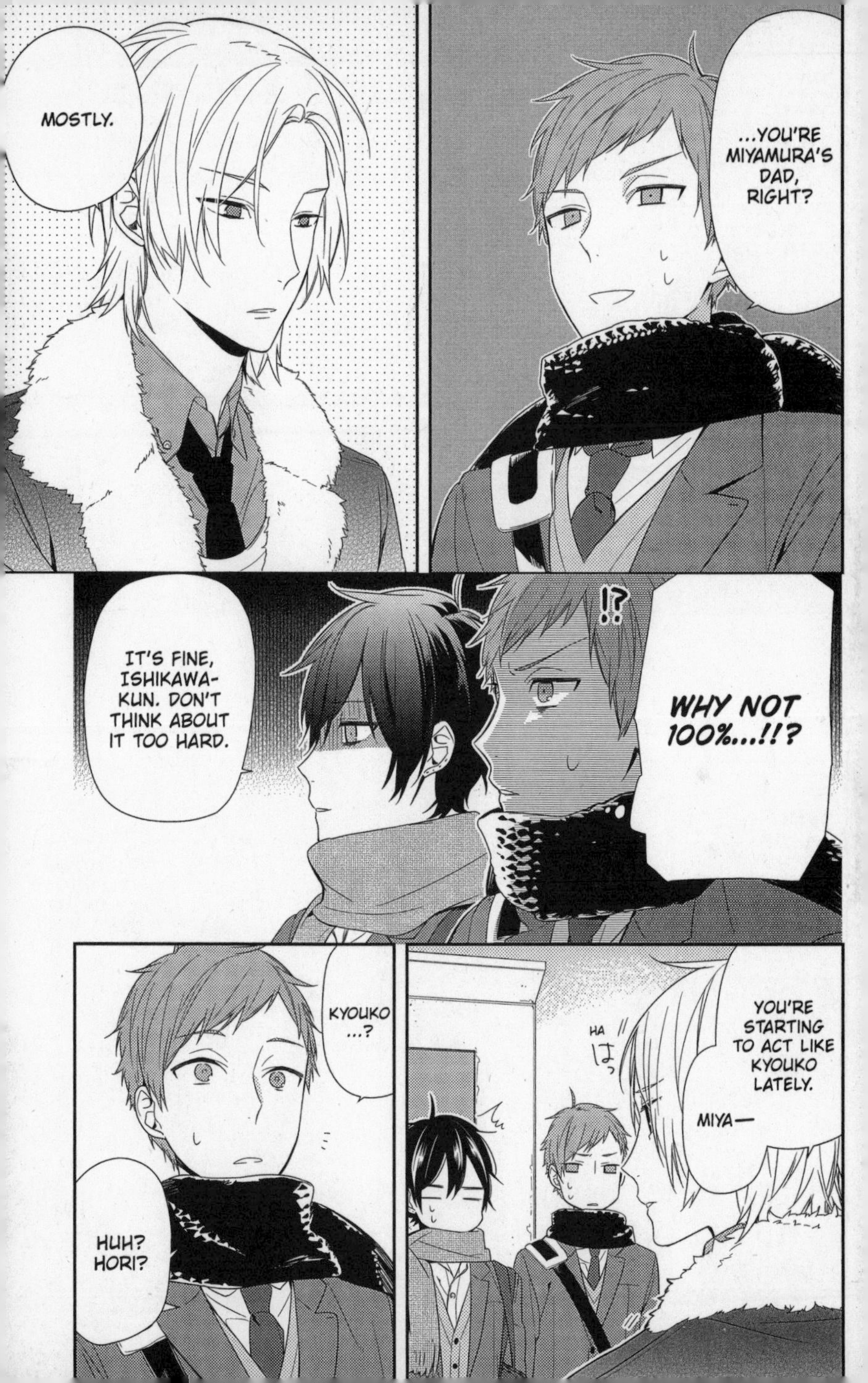
...YOU'RE MIYAMURA'S DAD, RIGHT?
MOSTLY.
!?
WHY NOT 100%...!!?
IT'S FINE, ISHIKAWA-KUN. DON'T THINK ABOUT IT TOO HARD.
YOU'RE STARTING TO ACT LIKE KYOUKO LATELY.
HA
MIYA—
KYOUKO ...?
HUH? HORI?

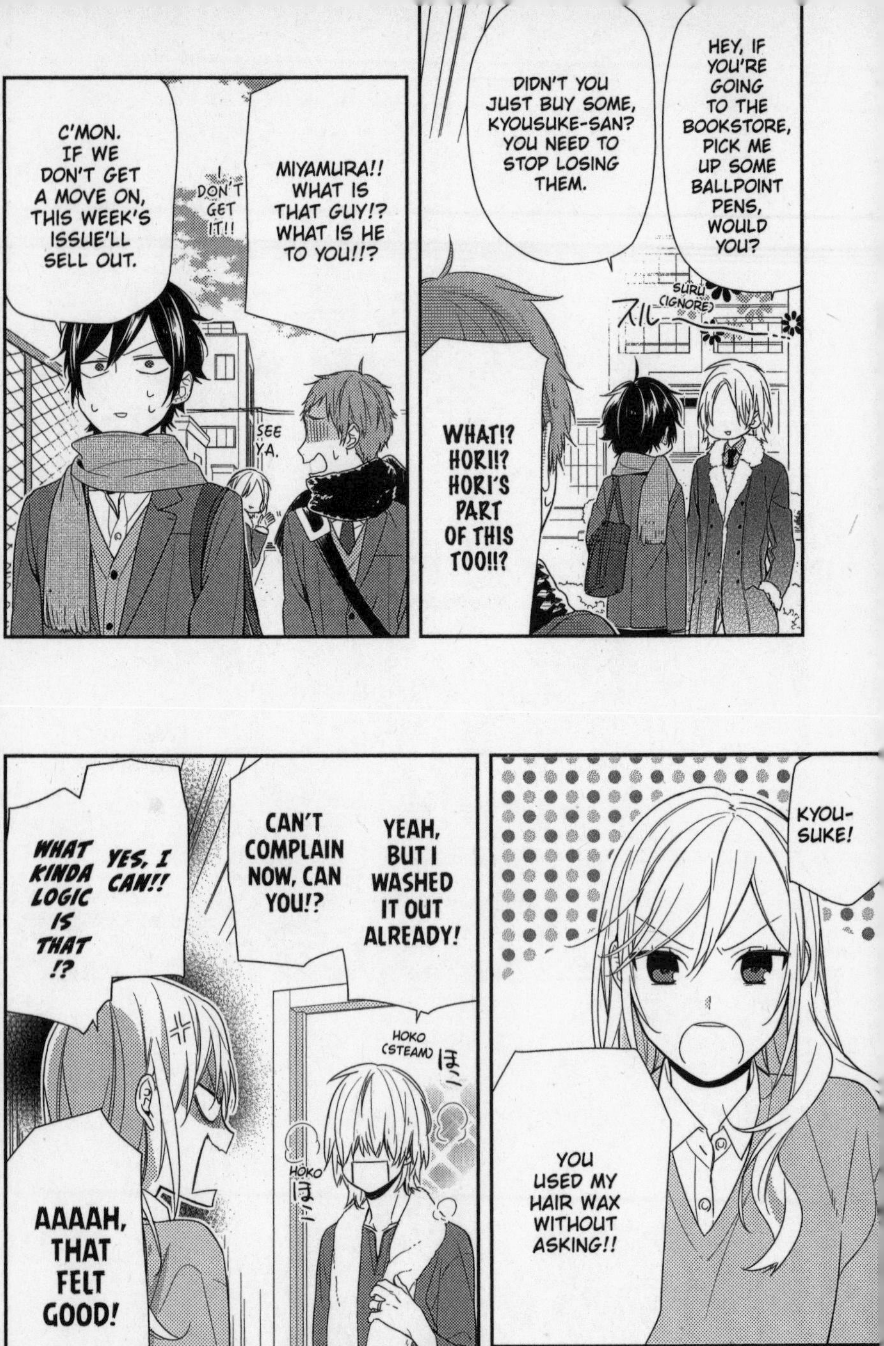
HEY, IF YOU'RE GOING TO THE BOOKSTORE, PICK ME UP SOME BALLPOINT PENS, WOULD YOU?
DIDN'T YOU JUST BUY SOME, KYOUSUKE-SAN? YOU NEED TO STOP LOSING THEM.
スルー
SURU (IGNORE)
WHAT!? HORI!? HORI'S PART OF THIS TOO!!?
MIYAMURA!! WHAT IS THAT GUY!? WHAT IS HE TO YOU!!?
I DON'T GET IT!!
C'MON. IF WE DON'T GET A MOVE ON, THIS WEEK'S ISSUE'LL SELL OUT.
SEE YA.
KYOU-SUKE!
YOU USED MY HAIR WAX WITHOUT ASKING!!
YEAH, BUT I WASHED IT OUT ALREADY!
CAN'T COMPLAIN NOW, CAN YOU!?
YES, I CAN!!
WHAT KINDA LOGIC IS THAT!?
ほこ
HOKO (STEAM)
ほこ
HOKO
AAAAH, THAT FELT GOOD!

HORIMIYA

HORIMIYA

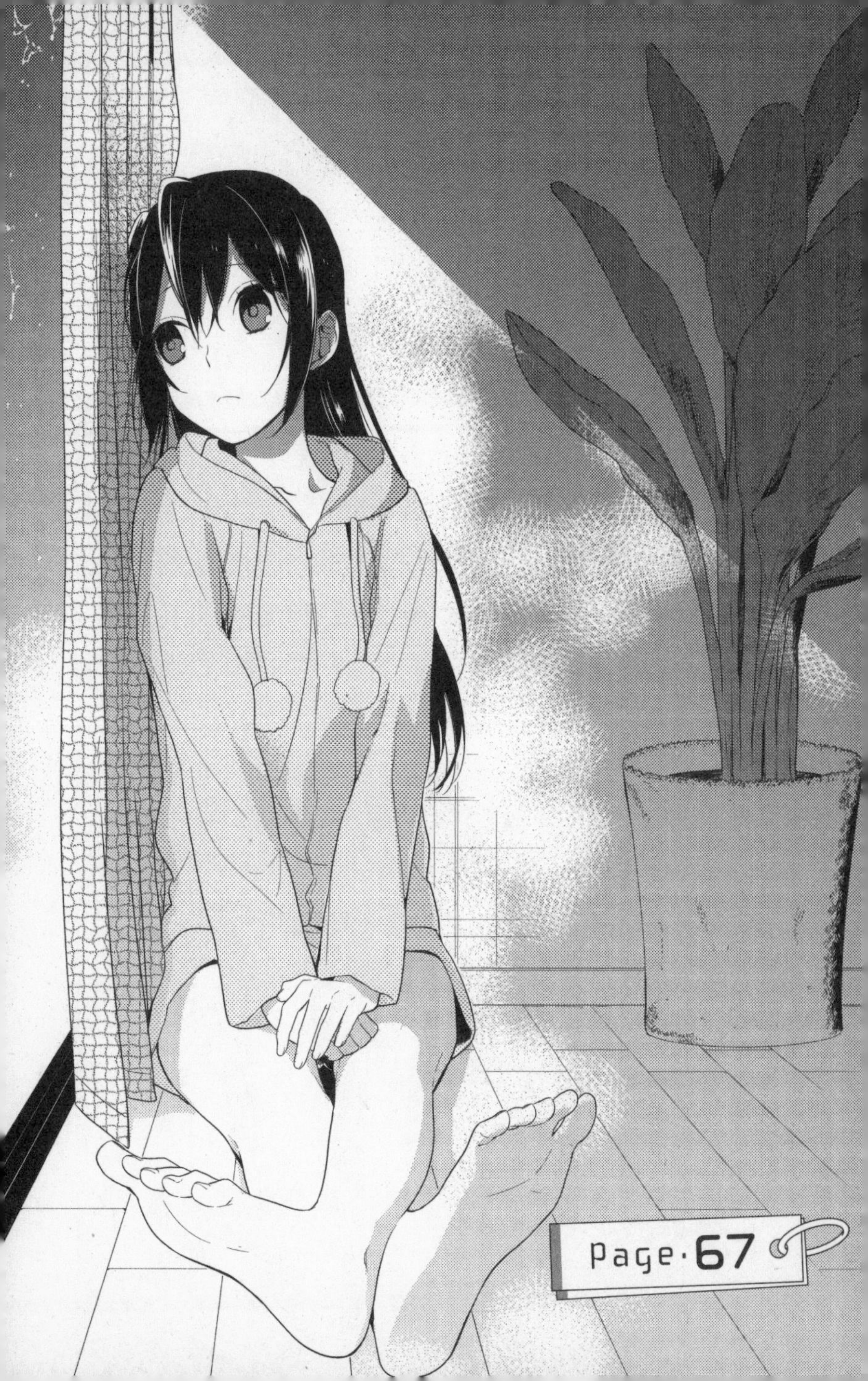
Page·67

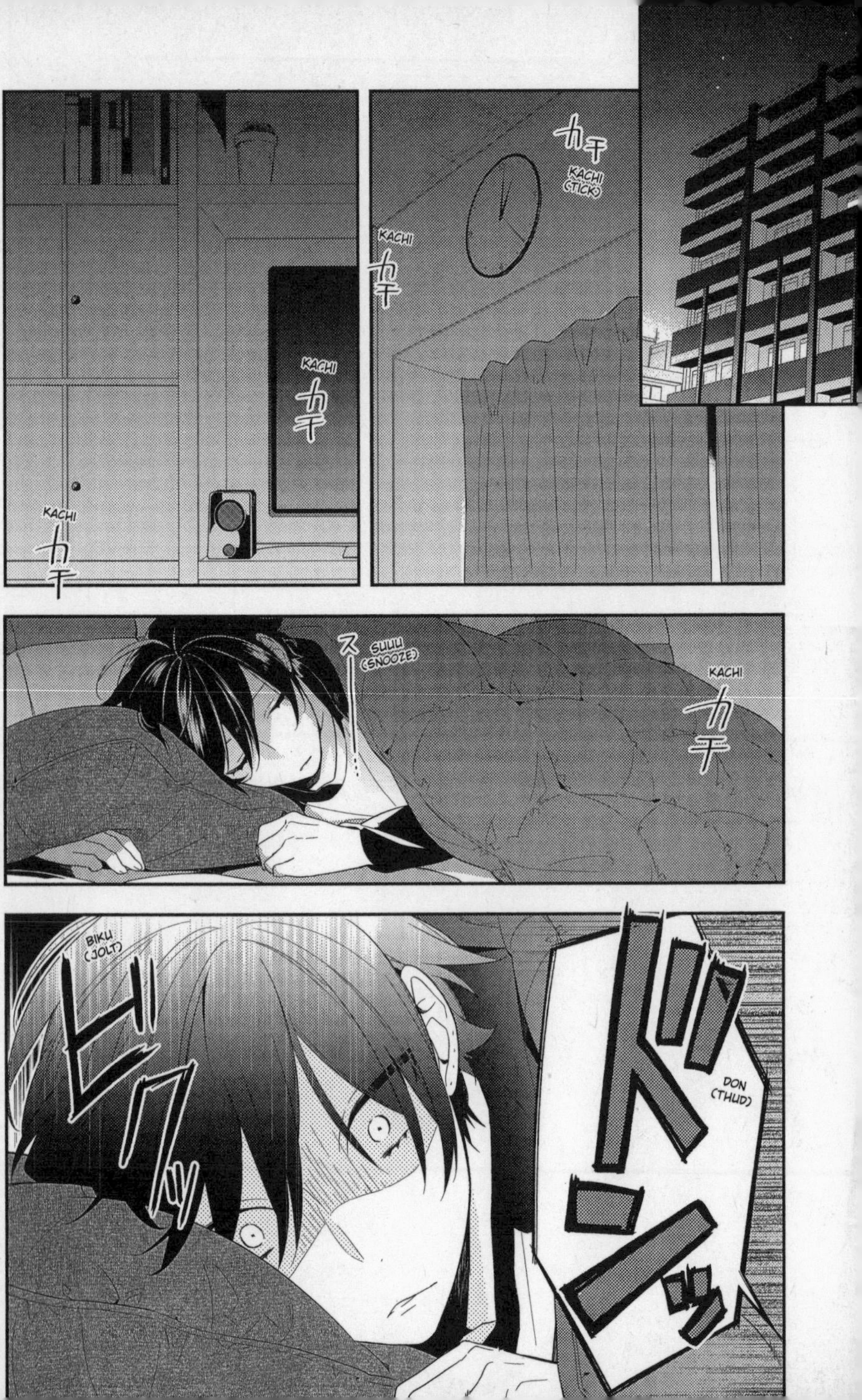

カチ
KACHI (TICK)
KACHI
カチ
KACHI
カチ
KACHI
カチ
KACHI
カチ
SUUU (SNOOZE)
スー
ドン
DON (THUD)
BIKU (JOLT)
ビクッ

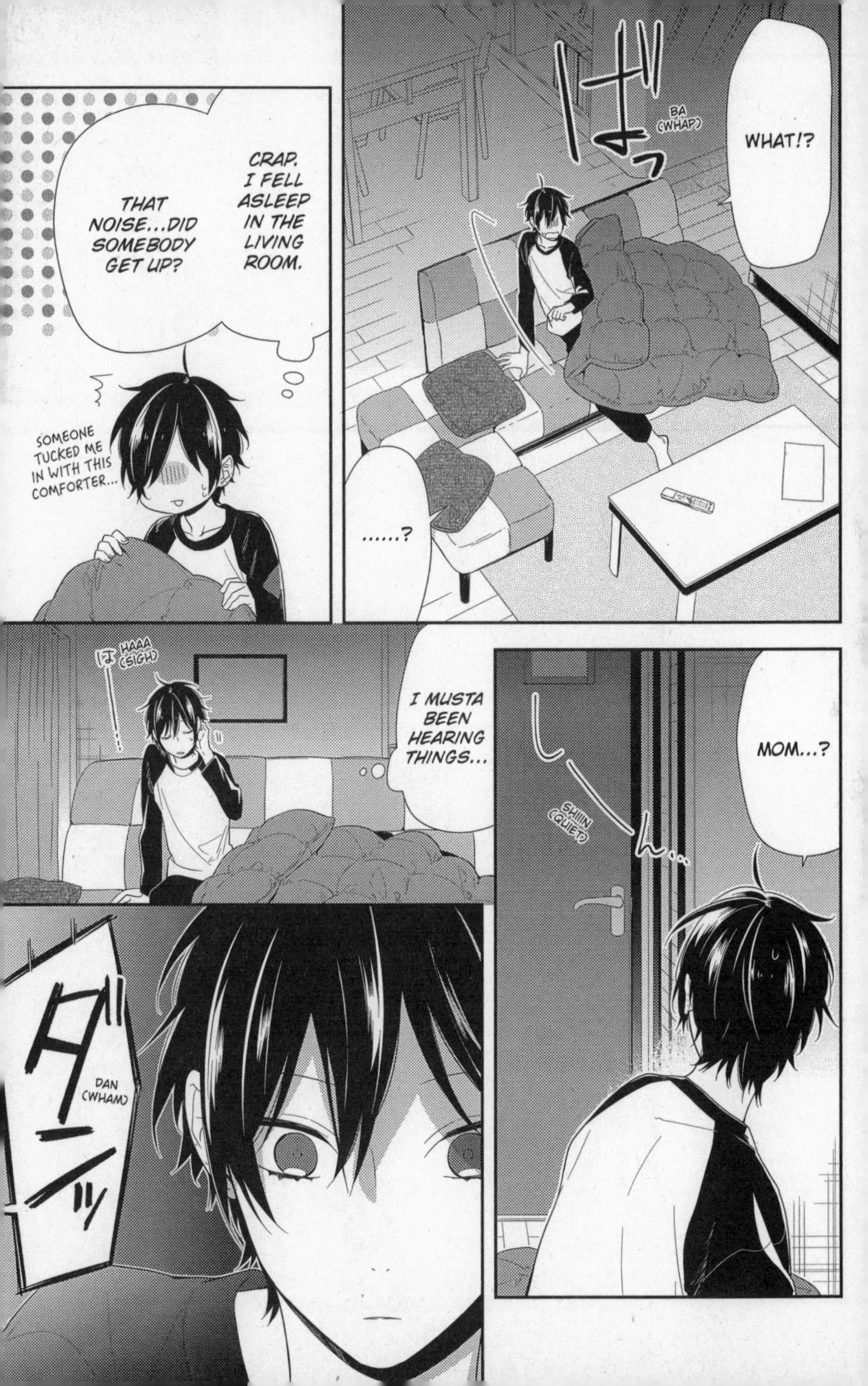
WHAT!?
BA (WHAP)
......?
CRAP. I FELL ASLEEP IN THE LIVING ROOM.
THAT NOISE...DID SOMEBODY GET UP?
SOMEONE TUCKED ME IN WITH THIS COMFORTER...
MOM...?
SHIIN (QUIET)
HAAA (SIGH)
I MUSTA BEEN HEARING THINGS...
DAN (WHAM)

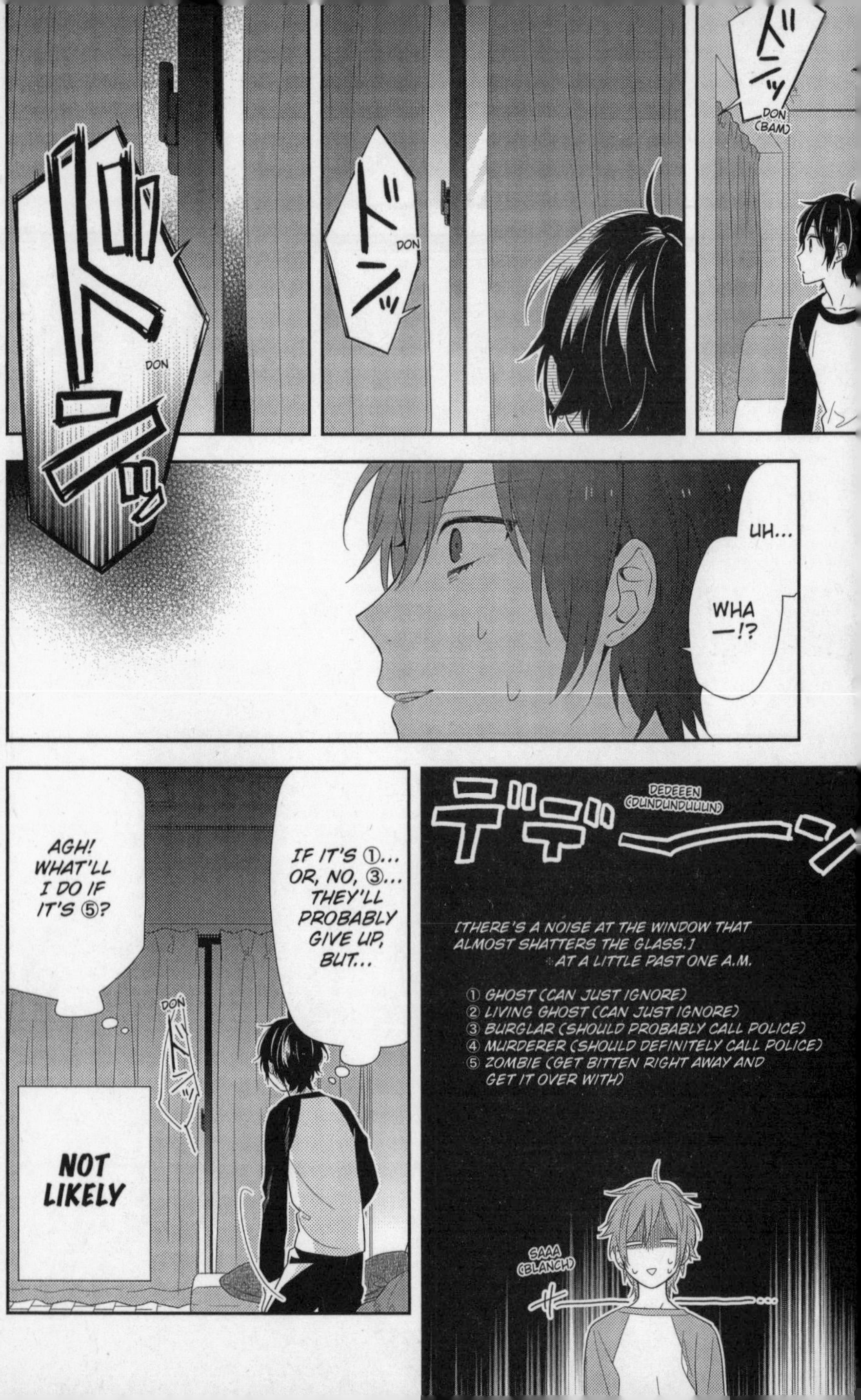
DON (BAM)
DON
DON
UH...
WHA—!?
DEDEEEN (DUNDUNDUUUN)
[THERE'S A NOISE AT THE WINDOW THAT ALMOST SHATTERS THE GLASS.]
*AT A LITTLE PAST ONE A.M.
① GHOST (CAN JUST IGNORE)
② LIVING GHOST (CAN JUST IGNORE)
③ BURGLAR (SHOULD PROBABLY CALL POLICE)
④ MURDERER (SHOULD DEFINITELY CALL POLICE)
⑤ ZOMBIE (GET BITTEN RIGHT AWAY AND GET IT OVER WITH)
SAAA (BLANCH)
IF IT'S ①... OR, NO, ③... THEY'LL PROBABLY GIVE UP, BUT...
AGH! WHAT'LL I DO IF IT'S ⑤?
DON
NOT LIKELY

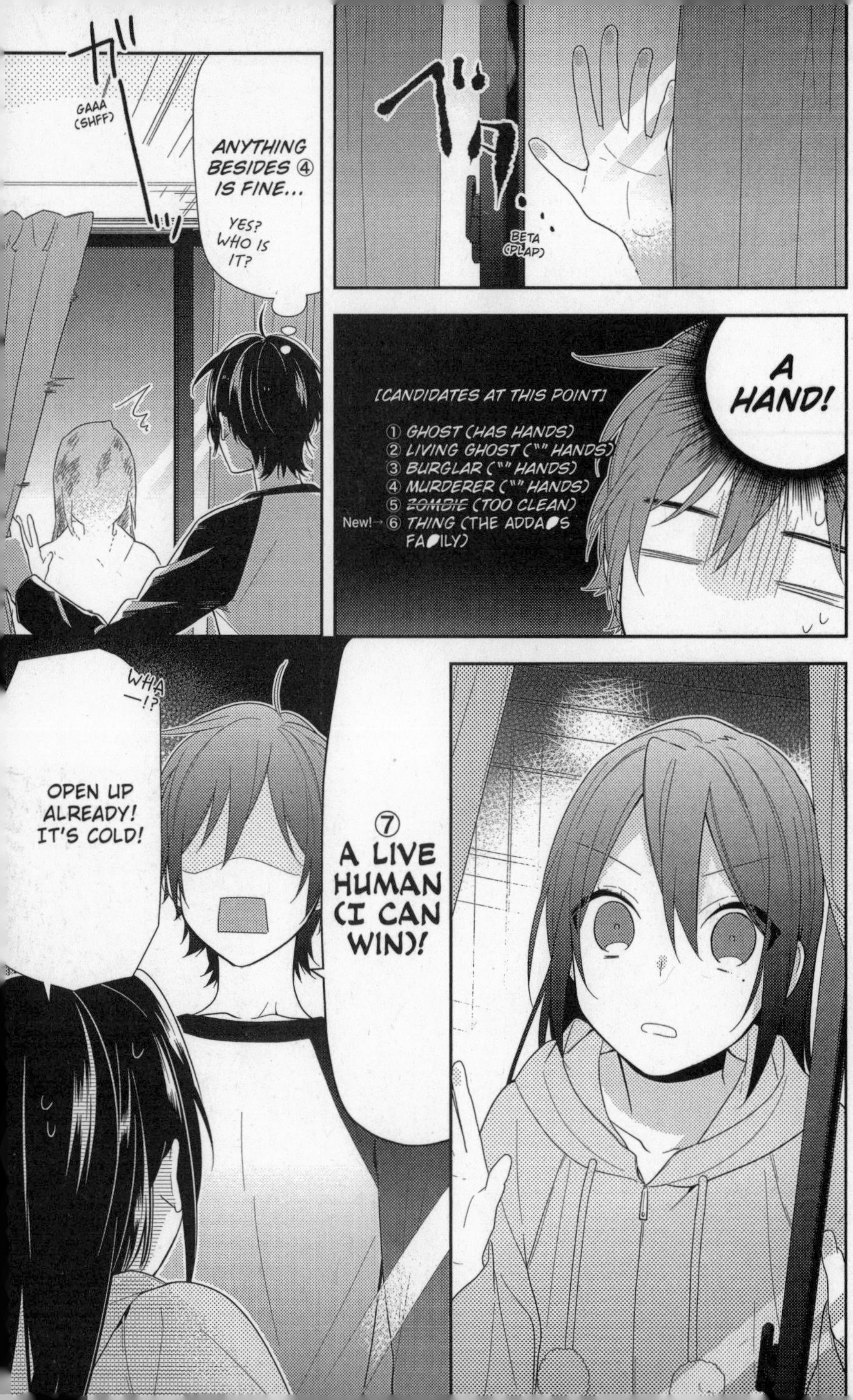

BETA (PLAP)
A HAND!
[CANDIDATES AT THIS POINT]
① GHOST (HAS HANDS)
② LIVING GHOST ("" HANDS)
③ BURGLAR ("" HANDS)
④ MURDERER ("" HANDS)
⑤ ~~ZOMBIE~~ (TOO CLEAN)
New!→ ⑥ THING (THE ADDA[redacted]S FA[redacted]ILY)
GAAA (SHFF)
ANYTHING BESIDES ④ IS FINE...
YES? WHO IS IT?
⑦ A LIVE HUMAN (I CAN WIN)!
WHA—!?
OPEN UP ALREADY! IT'S COLD!

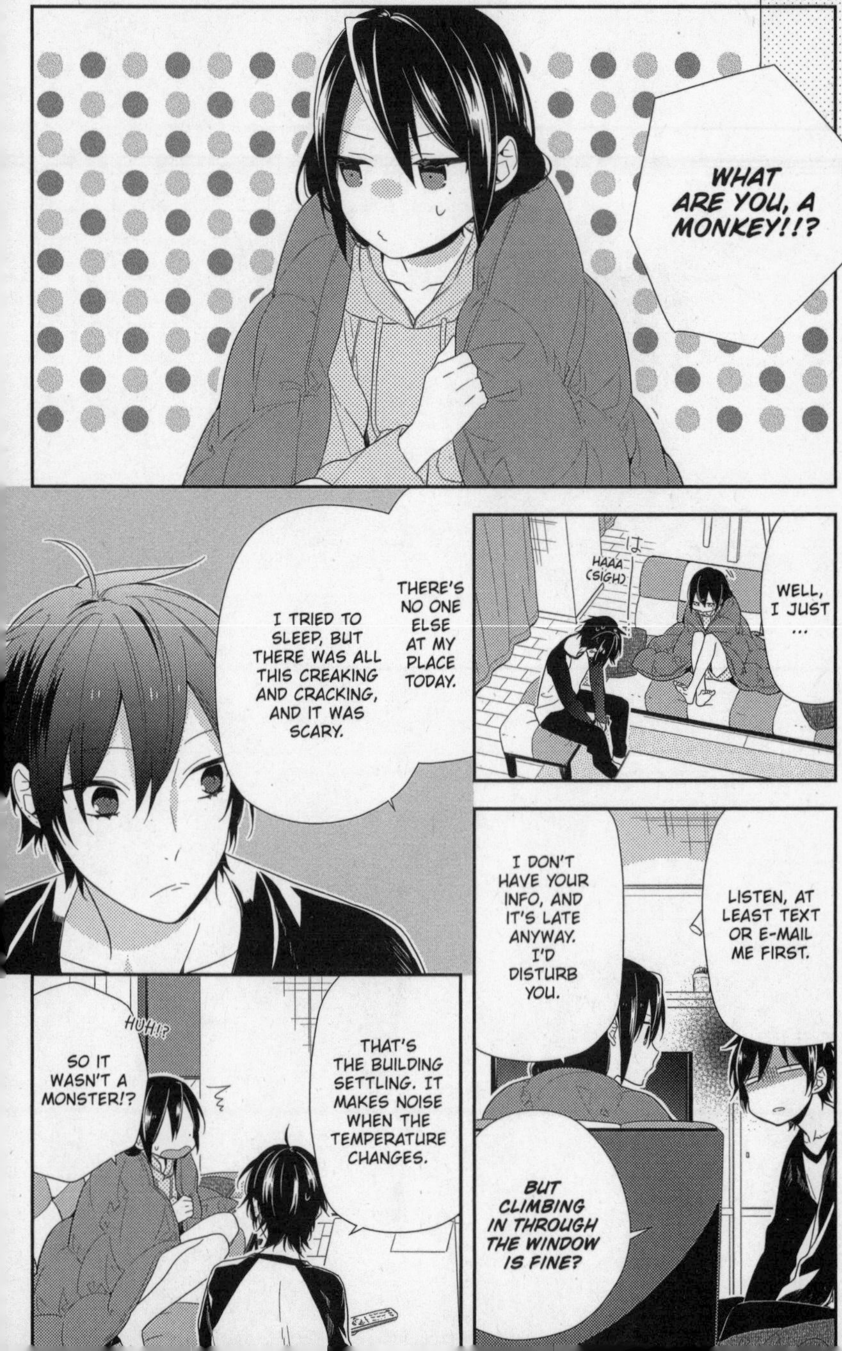

WHAT ARE YOU, A MONKEY!!?
は
HAAA (SIGH)
WELL, I JUST ...
THERE'S NO ONE ELSE AT MY PLACE TODAY.
I TRIED TO SLEEP, BUT THERE WAS ALL THIS CREAKING AND CRACKING, AND IT WAS SCARY.
LISTEN, AT LEAST TEXT OR E-MAIL ME FIRST.
I DON'T HAVE YOUR INFO, AND IT'S LATE ANYWAY. I'D DISTURB YOU.
BUT CLIMBING IN THROUGH THE WINDOW IS FINE?
THAT'S THE BUILDING SETTLING. IT MAKES NOISE WHEN THE TEMPERATURE CHANGES.
HUH!?
SO IT WASN'T A MONSTER!?

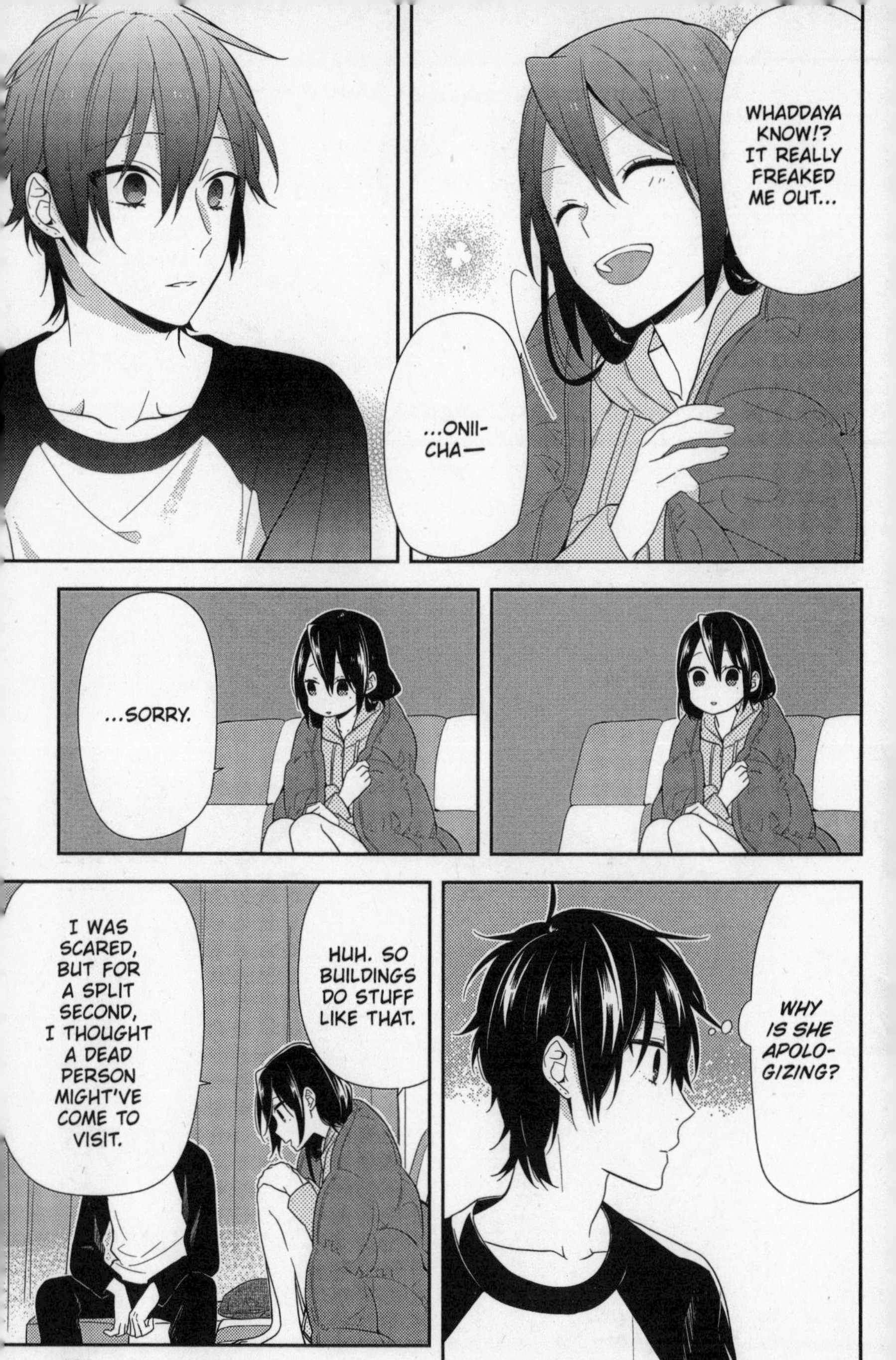
WHADDAYA KNOW!? IT REALLY FREAKED ME OUT...
...ONII-CHA—
...SORRY.
WHY IS SHE APOLO-GIZING?
HUH. SO BUILDINGS DO STUFF LIKE THAT.
I WAS SCARED, BUT FOR A SPLIT SECOND, I THOUGHT A DEAD PERSON MIGHT'VE COME TO VISIT.

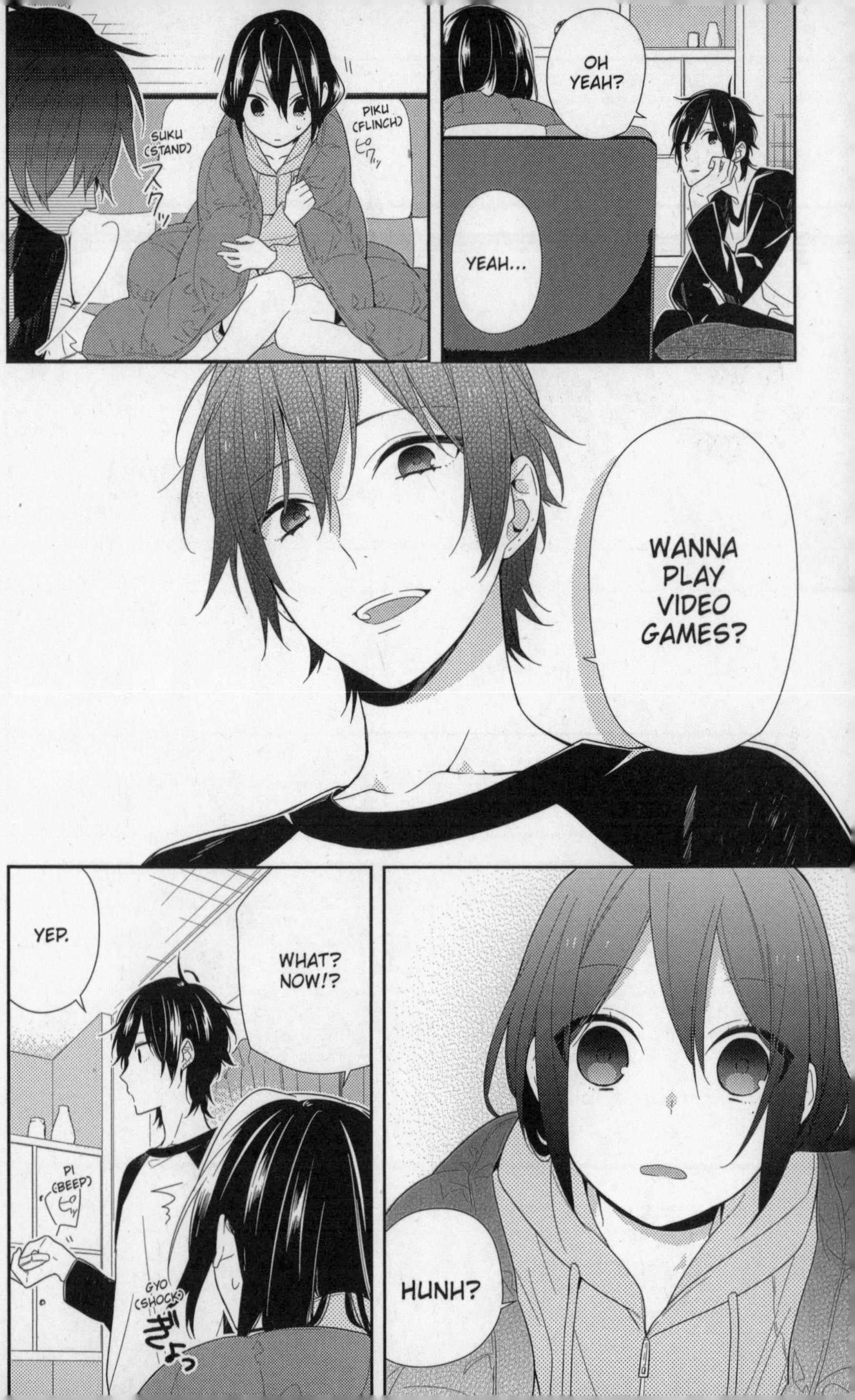
OH YEAH?
YEAH...
PIKU (FLINCH)
SUKU (STAND)
WANNA PLAY VIDEO GAMES?
HUNH?
WHAT? NOW!?
YEP.
PI (BEEP)
GYO (SHOCK)

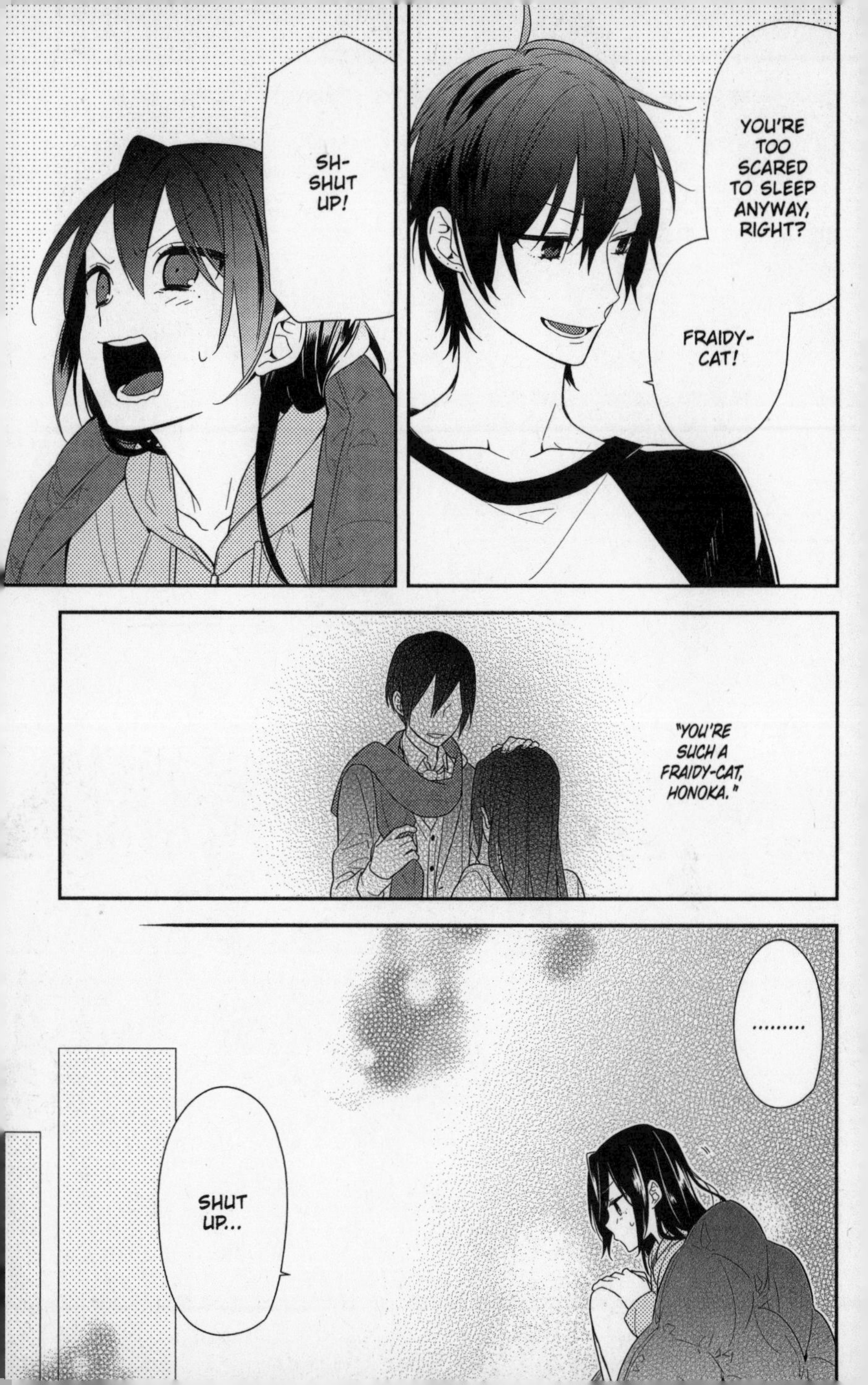
YOU'RE TOO SCARED TO SLEEP ANYWAY, RIGHT?
FRAIDY-CAT!
SH-SHUT UP!
"YOU'RE SUCH A FRAIDY-CAT, HONOKA."
....
SHUT UP...

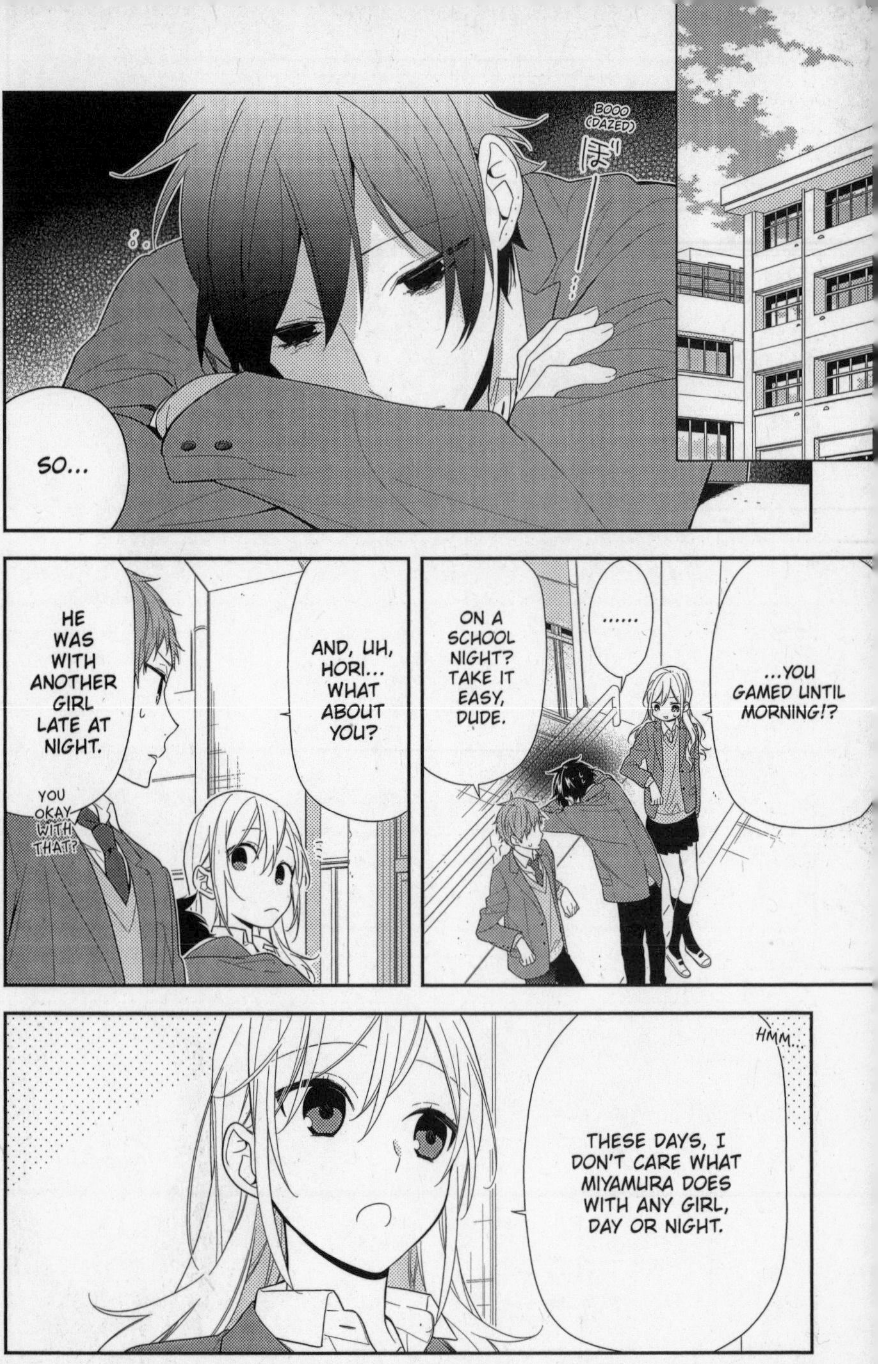
BOOO (DAZED)
ぼー
SO...
...YOU GAMED UNTIL MORNING!?
......
ON A SCHOOL NIGHT? TAKE IT EASY, DUDE.
AND, UH, HORI... WHAT ABOUT YOU?
HE WAS WITH ANOTHER GIRL LATE AT NIGHT.
YOU OKAY WITH THAT?
HMM...
THESE DAYS, I DON'T CARE WHAT MIYAMURA DOES WITH ANY GIRL, DAY OR NIGHT.

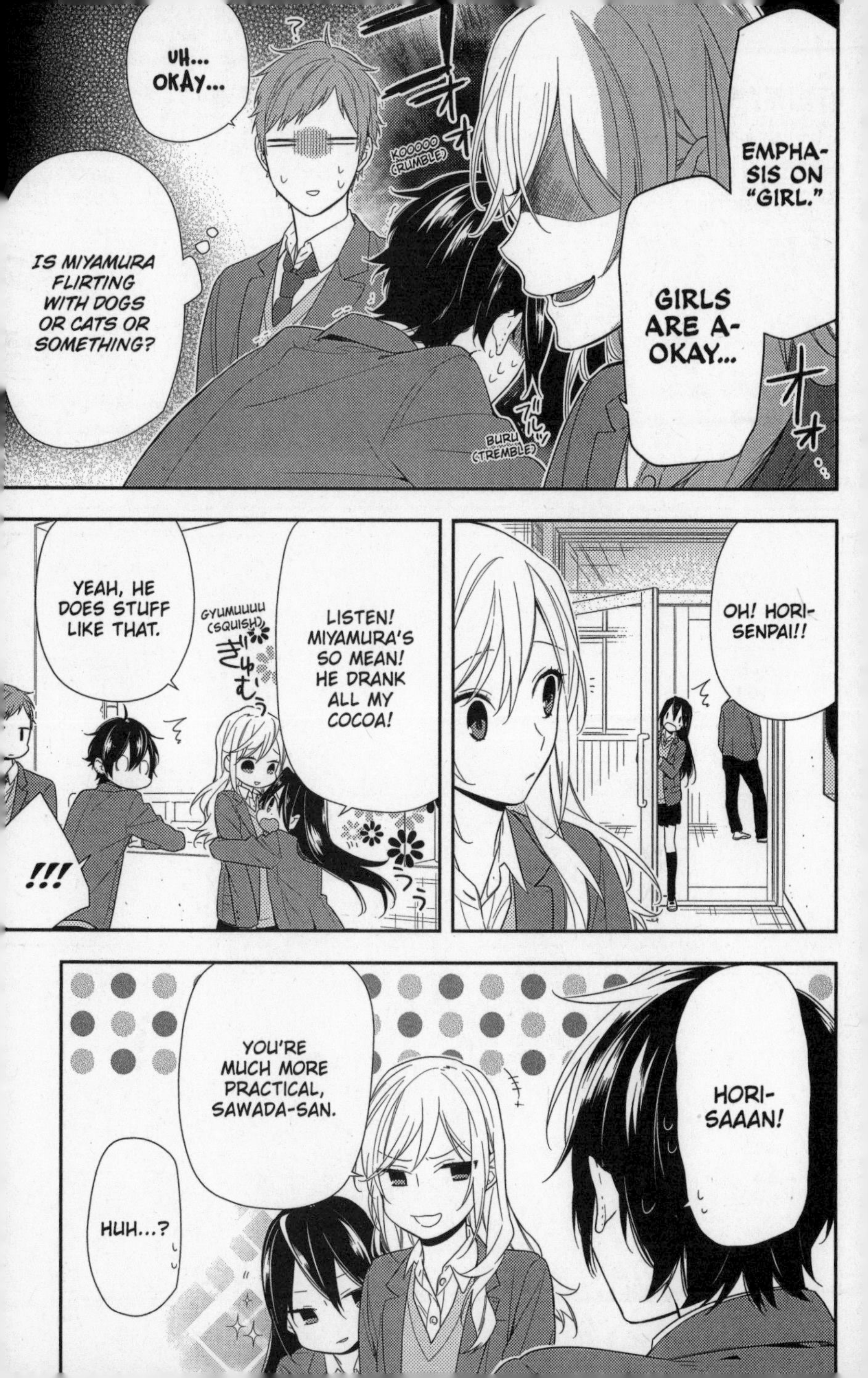
EMPHASIS ON "GIRL."
GIRLS ARE A-OKAY...
KOOOOO (RUMBLE)
BURU (TREMBLE)
UH... OKAY...
IS MIYAMURA FLIRTING WITH DOGS OR CATS OR SOMETHING?
OH! HORI-SENPAI!!
LISTEN! MIYAMURA'S SO MEAN! HE DRANK ALL MY COCOA!
GYUMUUUU (SQUISH)
YEAH, HE DOES STUFF LIKE THAT.
!!!
HORI-SAAAN!
YOU'RE MUCH MORE PRACTICAL, SAWADA-SAN.
HUH...?

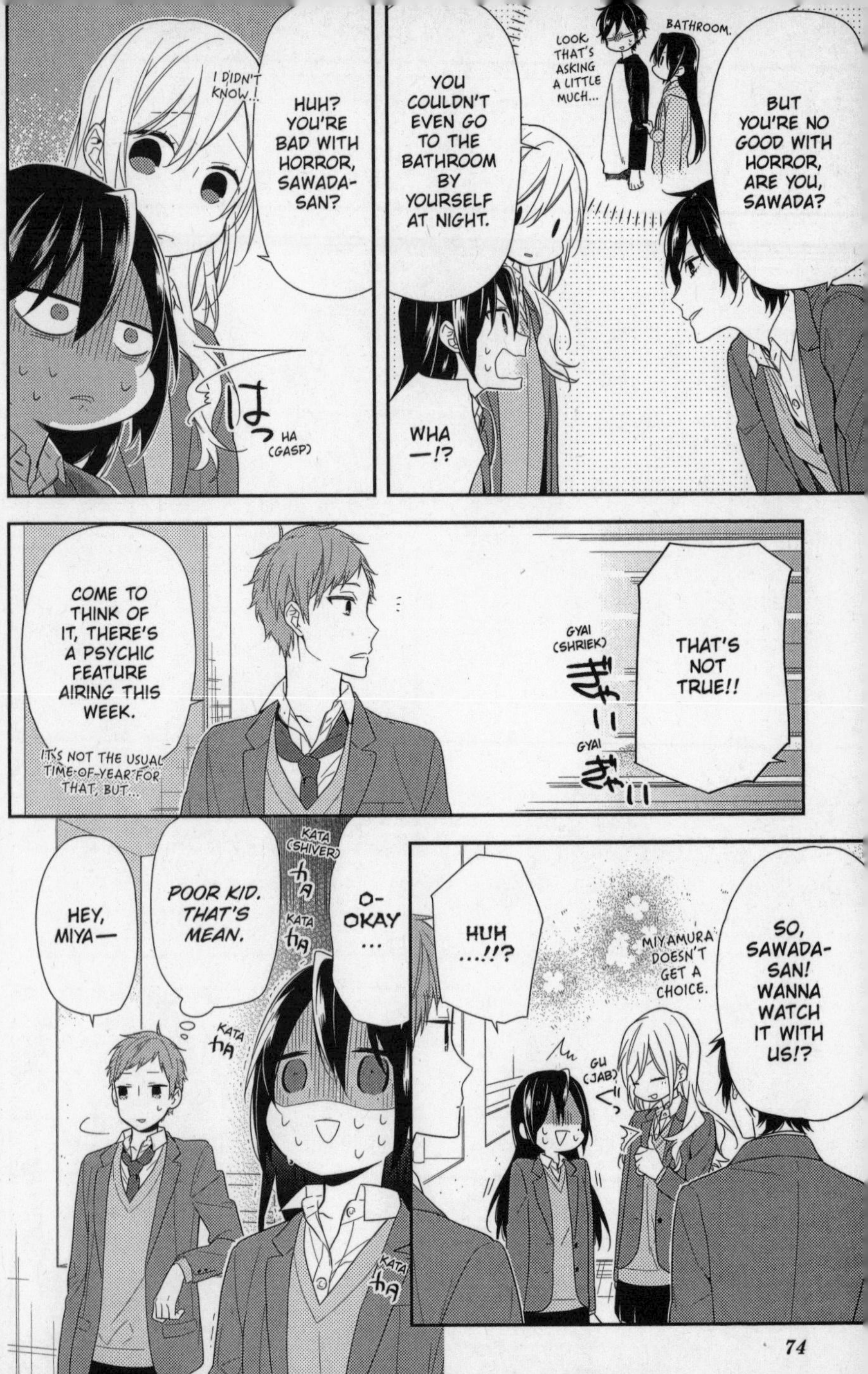
BATHROOM.
LOOK THAT'S ASKING A LITTLE MUCH...
BUT YOU'RE NO GOOD WITH HORROR, ARE YOU, SAWADA?
YOU COULDN'T EVEN GO TO THE BATHROOM BY YOURSELF AT NIGHT.
WHA—!?
HUH? YOU'RE BAD WITH HORROR, SAWADA-SAN?
I DIDN'T KNOW...
HA (GASP)
THAT'S NOT TRUE!!
GYAI (SHRIEK)
GYAI
COME TO THINK OF IT, THERE'S A PSYCHIC FEATURE AIRING THIS WEEK.
IT'S NOT THE USUAL TIME-OF-YEAR FOR THAT, BUT...
SO, SAWADA-SAN! WANNA WATCH IT WITH US!?
MIYAMURA DOESN'T GET A CHOICE.
GU (JAB)
HUH ...!!?
O-OKAY ...
KATA (SHIVER)
KATA
KATA
KATA
POOR KID. THAT'S MEAN.
HEY, MIYA—

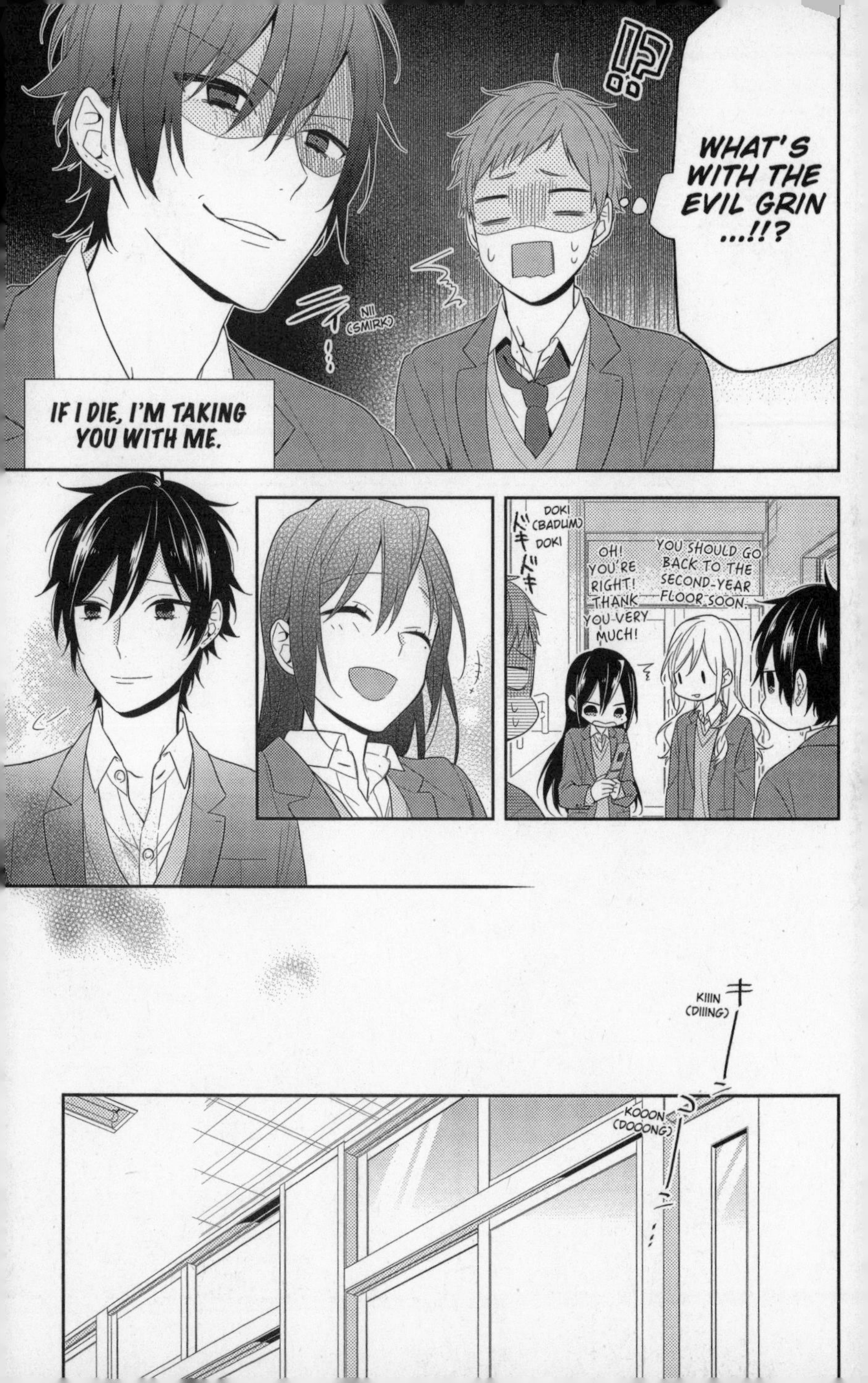
!?
WHAT'S WITH THE EVIL GRIN ...!!?
NII (SMIRK)
IF I DIE, I'M TAKING YOU WITH ME.
DOKI (BADUM) DOKI
YOU SHOULD GO BACK TO THE SECOND-YEAR FLOOR SOON.
OH! YOU'RE RIGHT! THANK YOU VERY MUCH!
KIIIN (DIIING)
KOOON (DOOONG)

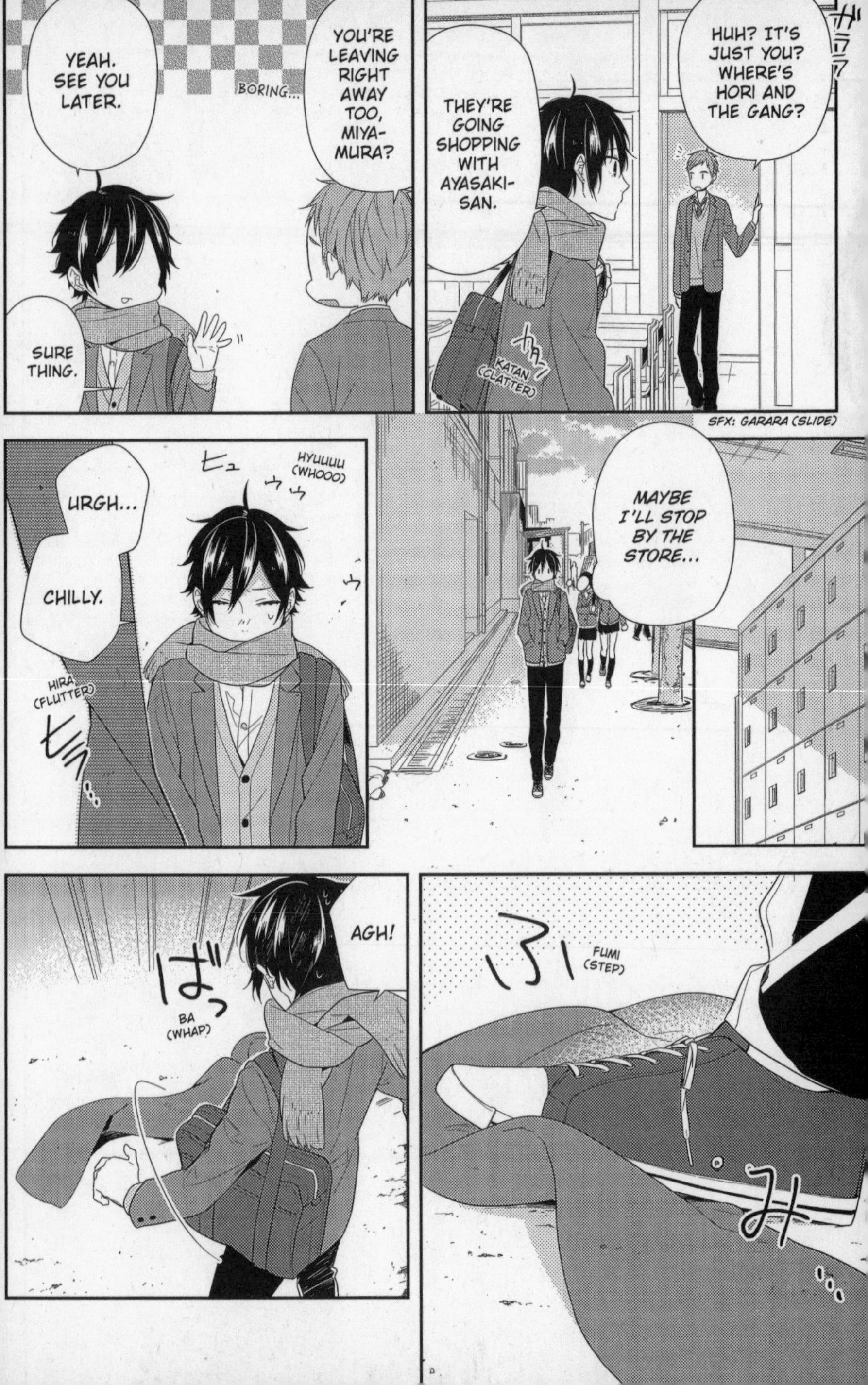
HUH? IT'S JUST YOU? WHERE'S HORI AND THE GANG?
THEY'RE GOING SHOPPING WITH AYASAKI-SAN.
KATAN (CLATTER)
SFX: GARARA (SLIDE)
YOU'RE LEAVING RIGHT AWAY TOO, MIYAMURA?
YEAH. SEE YOU LATER.
BORING...
SURE THING.
MAYBE I'LL STOP BY THE STORE...
HYUUUU (WHOOO)
URGH...
CHILLY.
HIRA (FLUTTER)
FUMI (STEP)
AGH!
BA (WHAP)

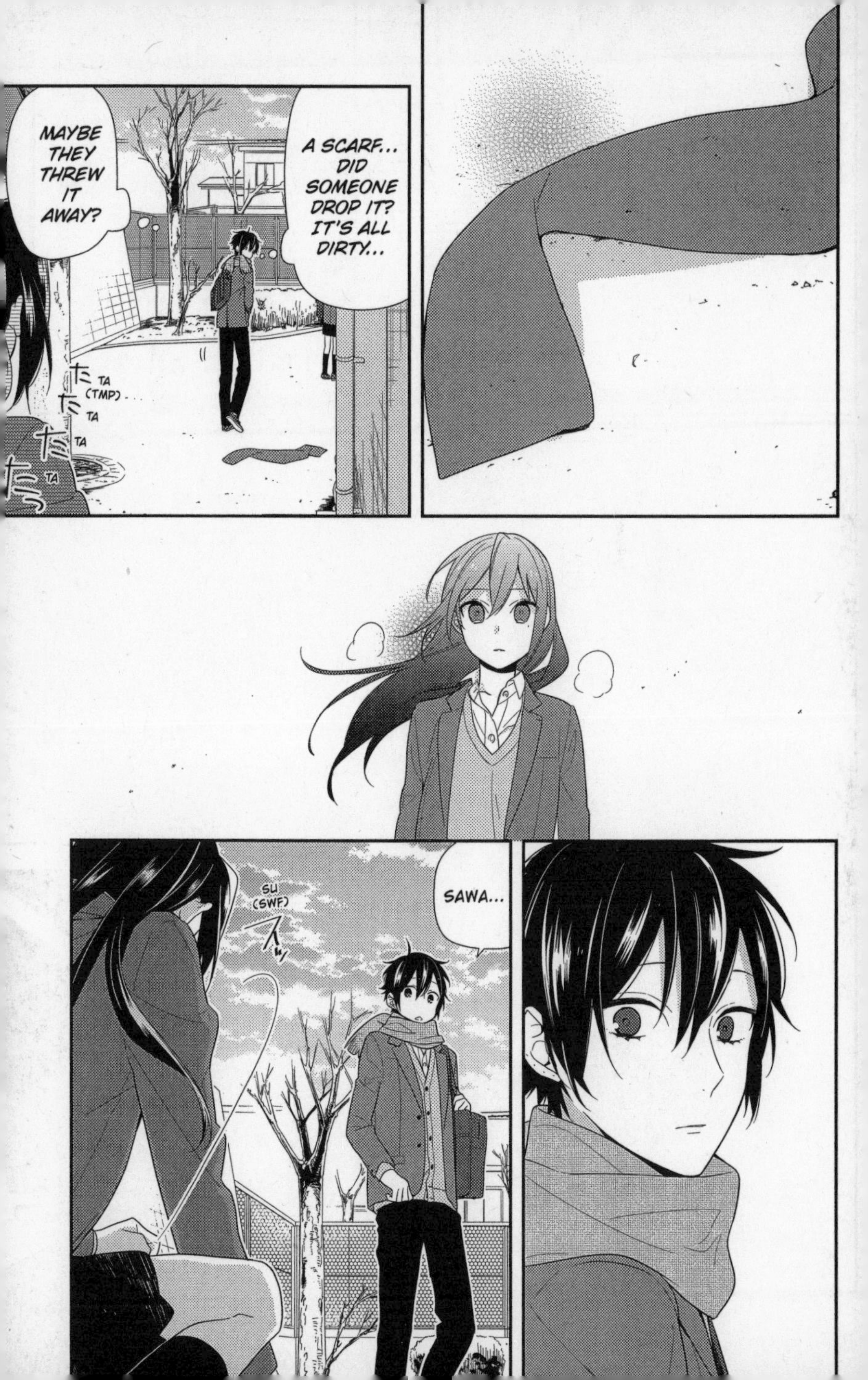
A SCARF... DID SOMEONE DROP IT? IT'S ALL DIRTY...
MAYBE THEY THREW IT AWAY?
た TA (TMP)
た TA
た TA
たっ TA
SAWA...
SU (SWF)

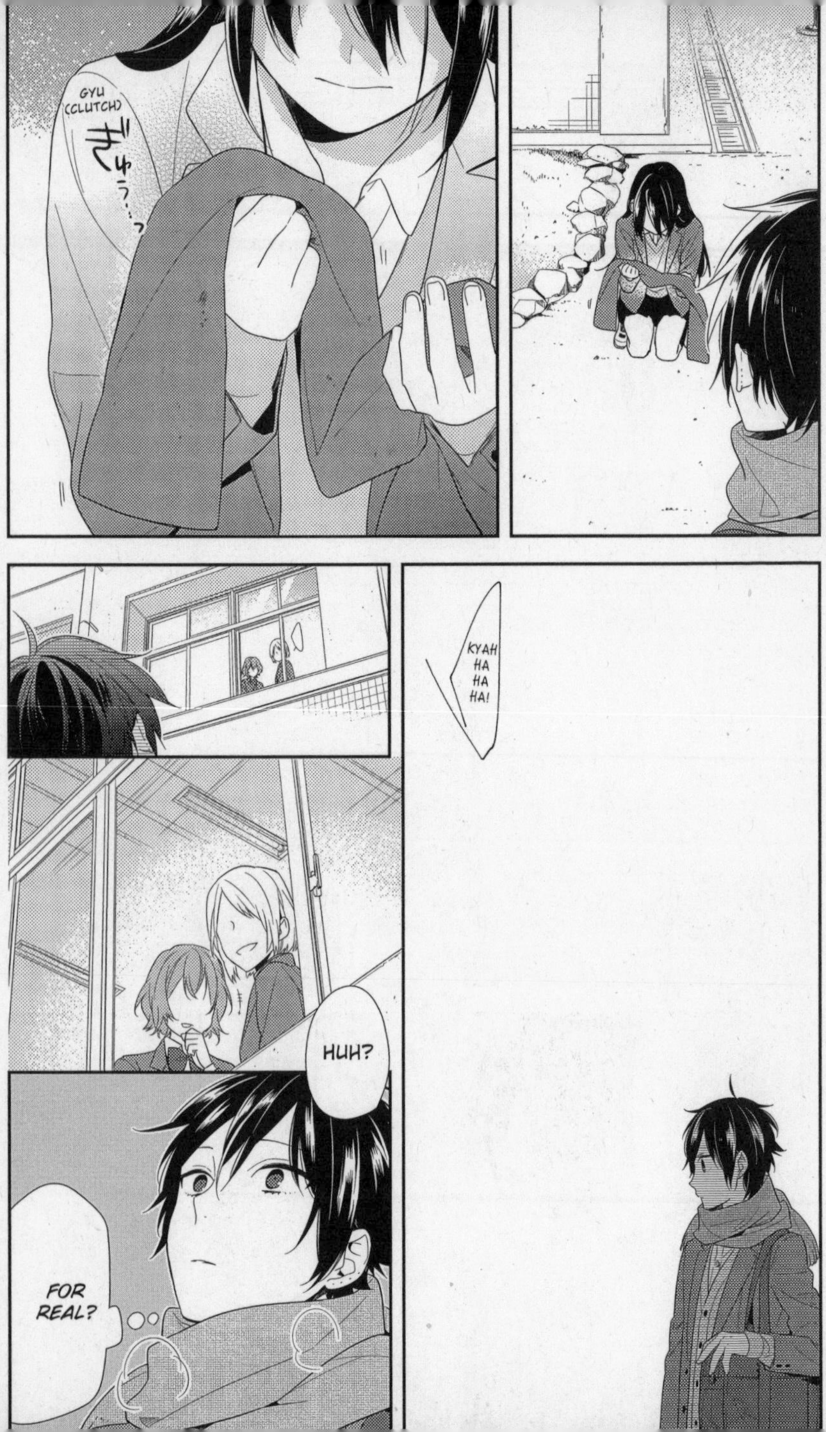
GYU (CLUTCH)
ぎゅう…っ
KYAH HA HA HA!
HUH?
FOR REAL?

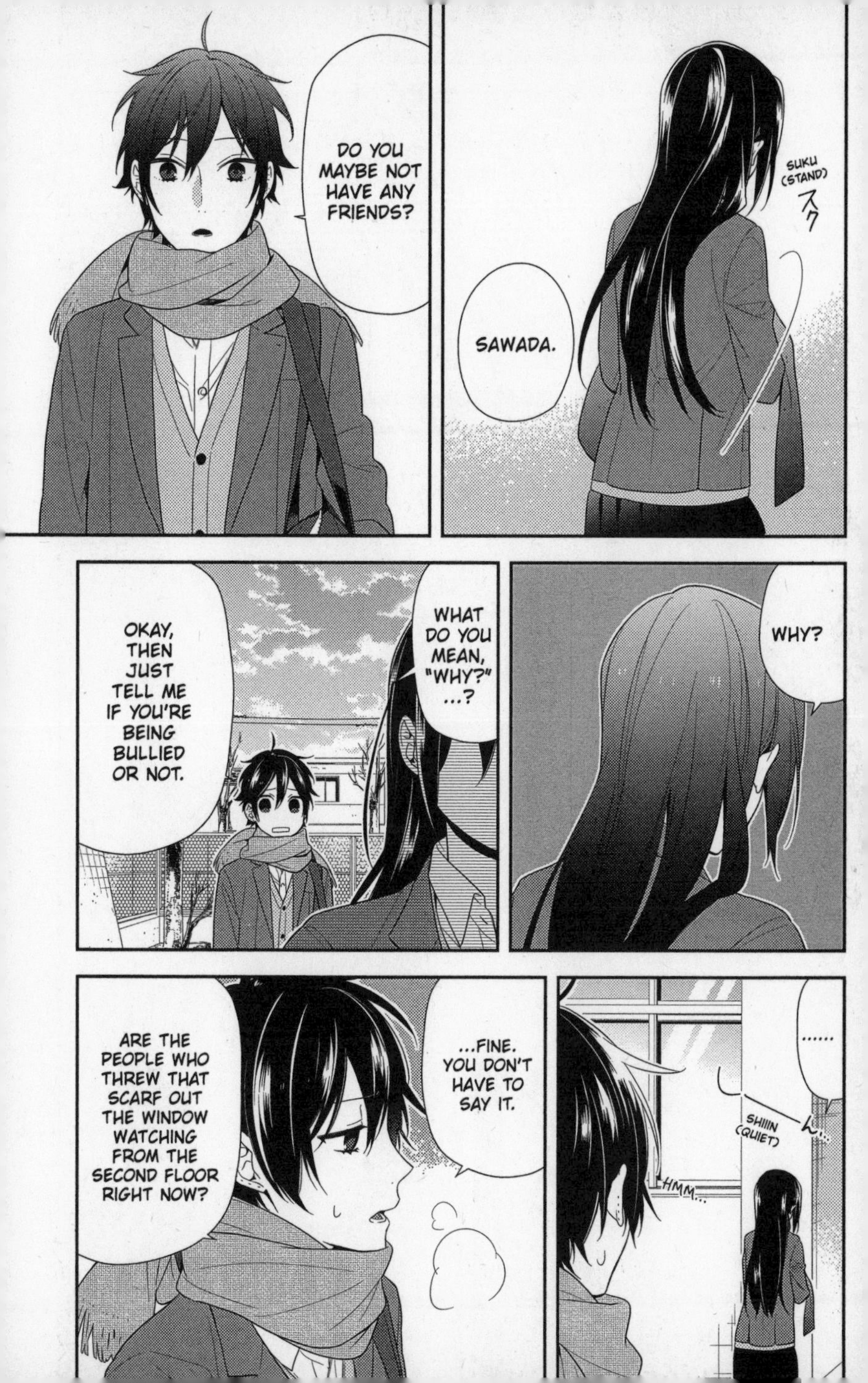
SUKU (STAND)
スク
SAWADA.
DO YOU MAYBE NOT HAVE ANY FRIENDS?
WHY?
WHAT DO YOU MEAN, "WHY?" ...?
OKAY, THEN JUST TELL ME IF YOU'RE BEING BULLIED OR NOT.
......
SHIIIN (QUIET)
HMM...
...FINE. YOU DON'T HAVE TO SAY IT.
ARE THE PEOPLE WHO THREW THAT SCARF OUT THE WINDOW WATCHING FROM THE SECOND FLOOR RIGHT NOW?

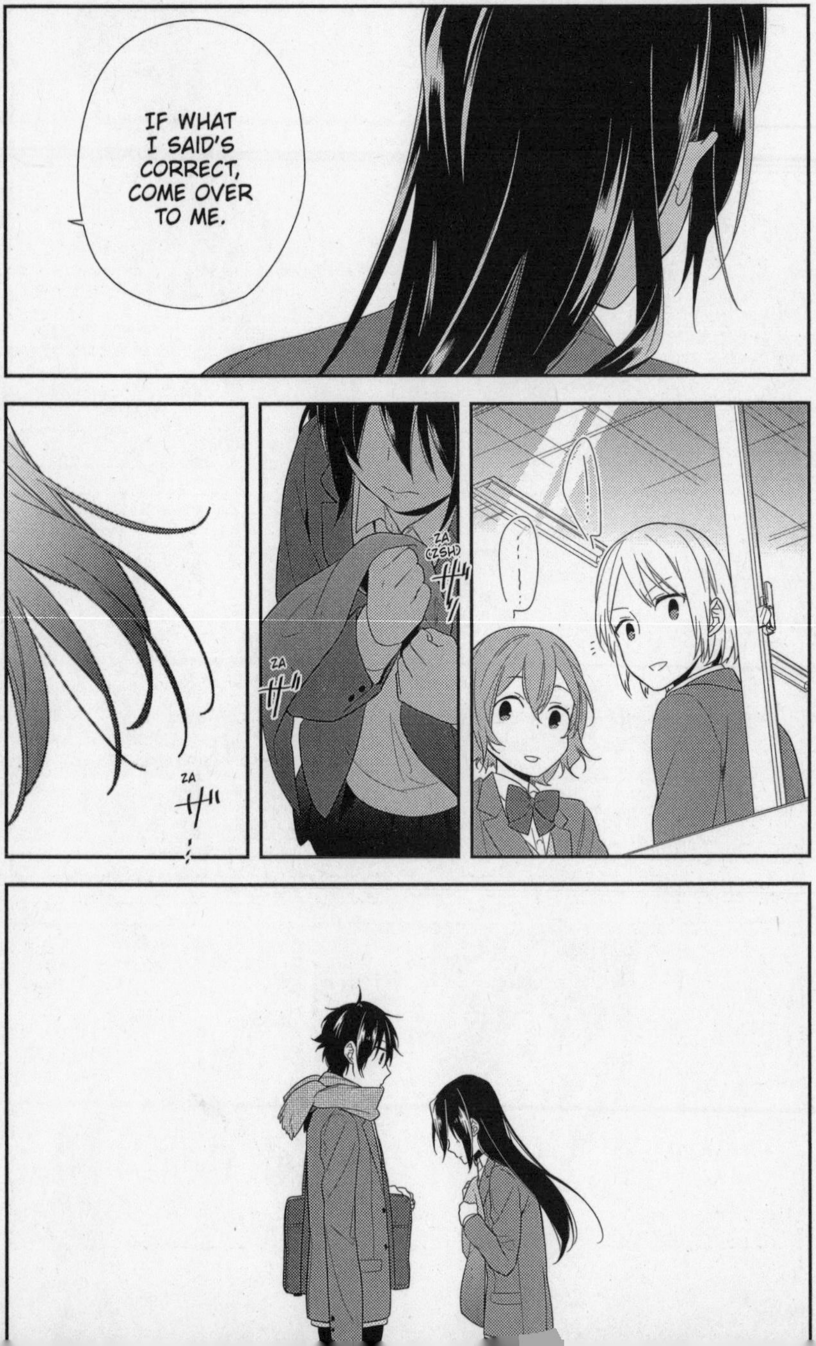
IF WHAT I SAID'S CORRECT, COME OVER TO ME.
ZA (ZSH)
ZA
ZA

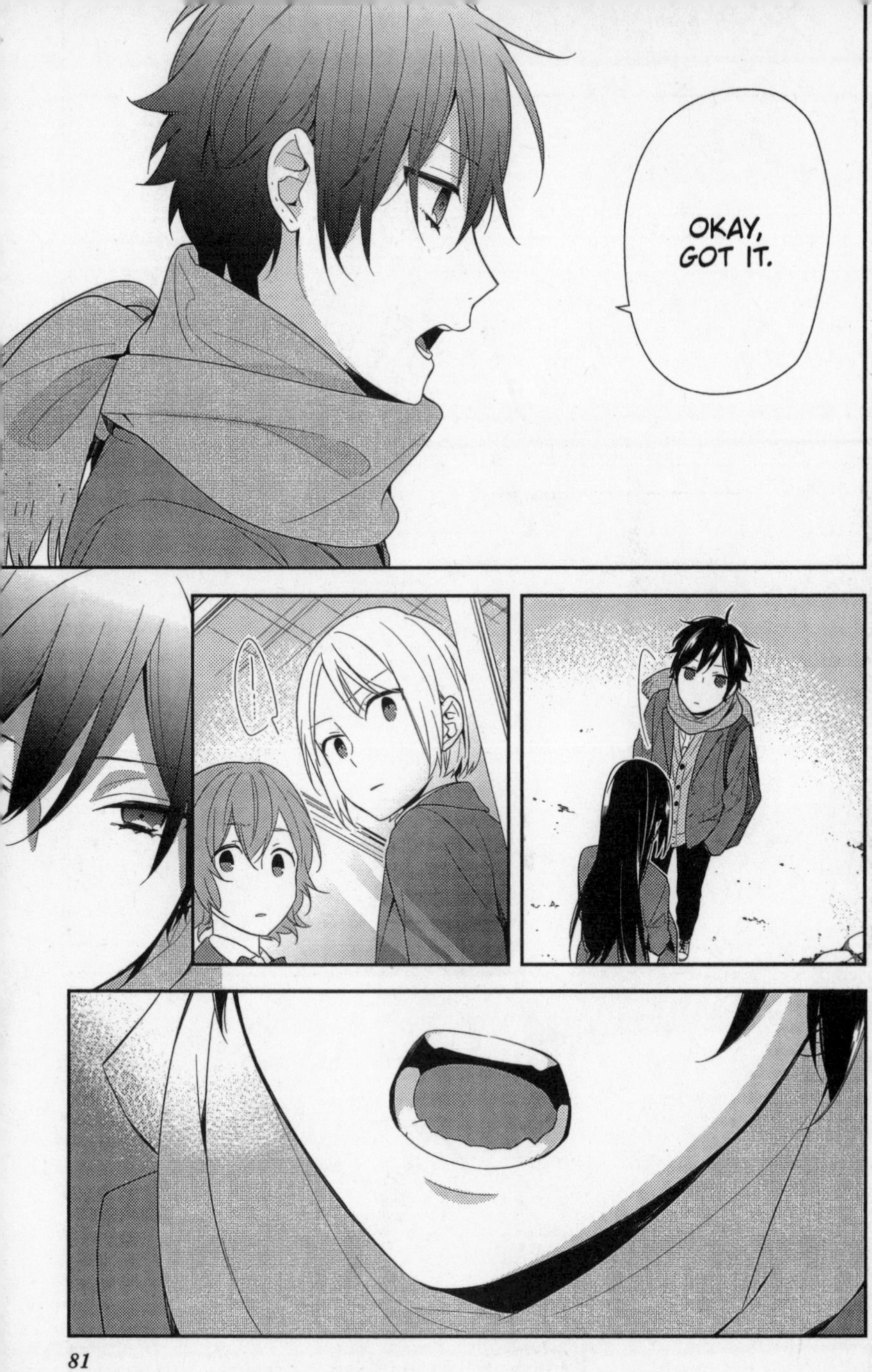
OKAY, GOT IT.

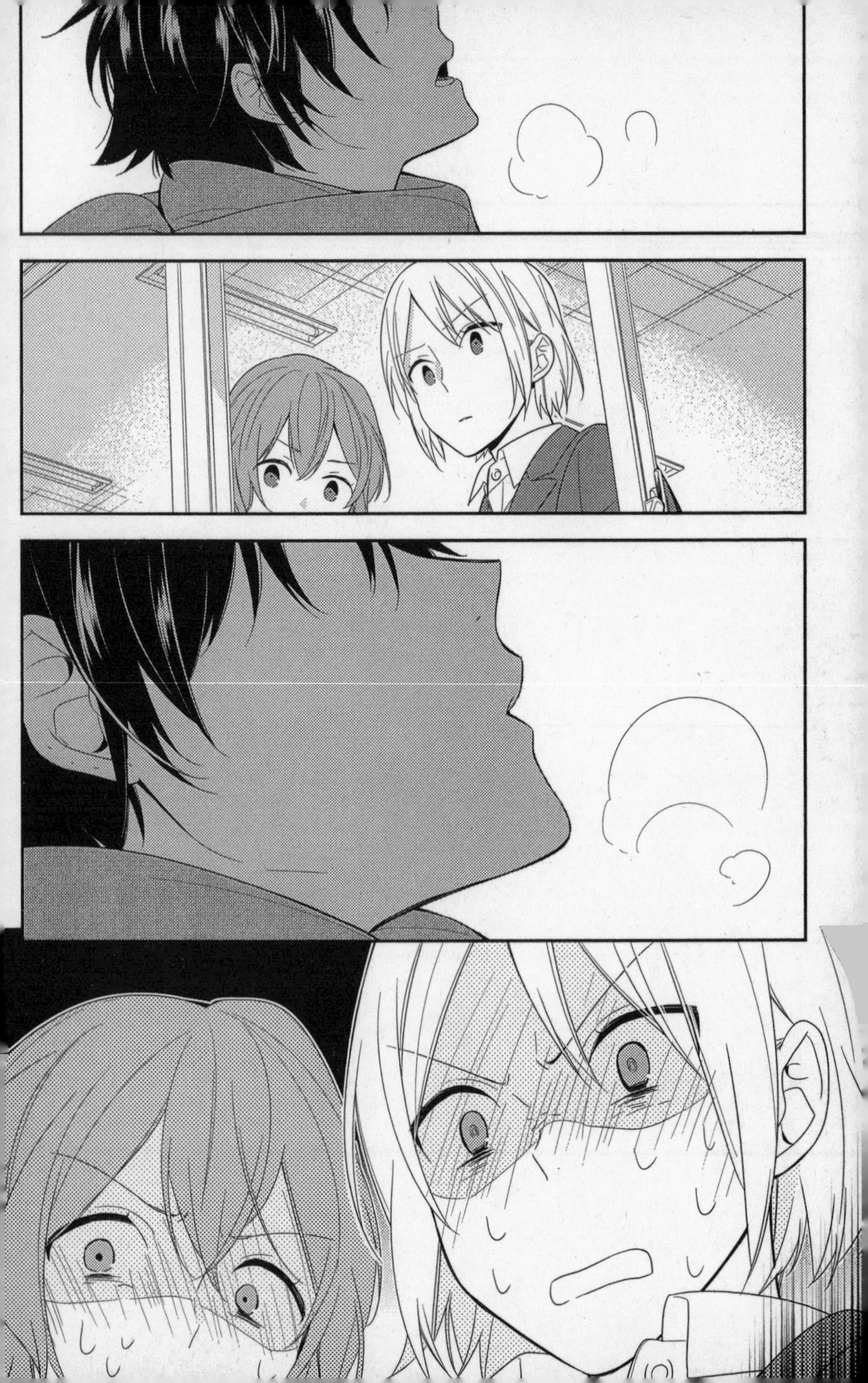

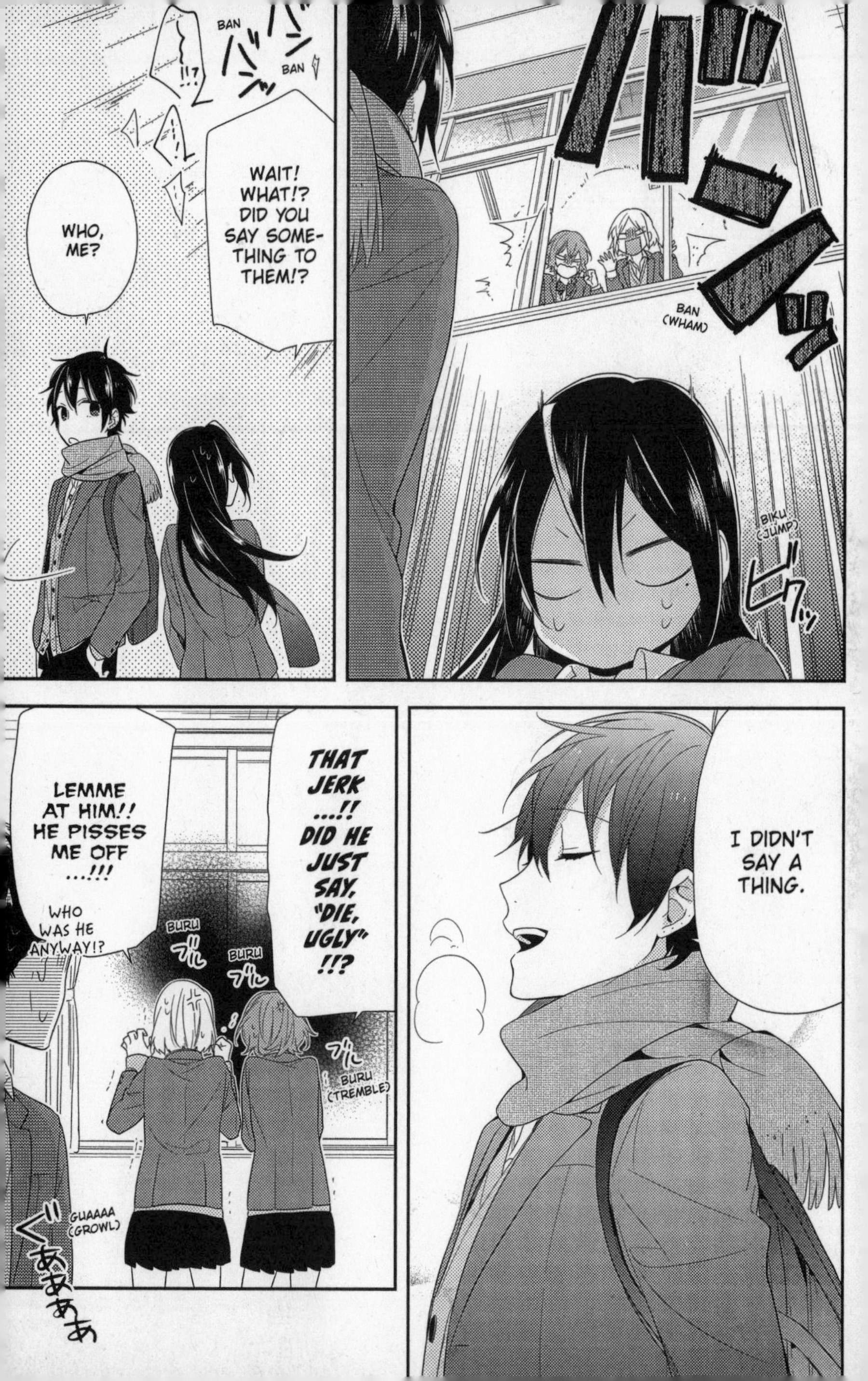
BAN (WHAM)
BIKU (JUMP)
BAN
BAN
!!?
WAIT! WHAT!? DID YOU SAY SOME-THING TO THEM!?
WHO, ME?
I DIDN'T SAY A THING.
THAT JERK ....!! DID HE JUST SAY, "DIE, UGLY" !!?
LEMME AT HIM!! HE PISSES ME OFF ....!!!
WHO WAS HE ANYWAY!?
BURU
BURU
BURU (TREMBLE)
GUAAAA (GROWL)

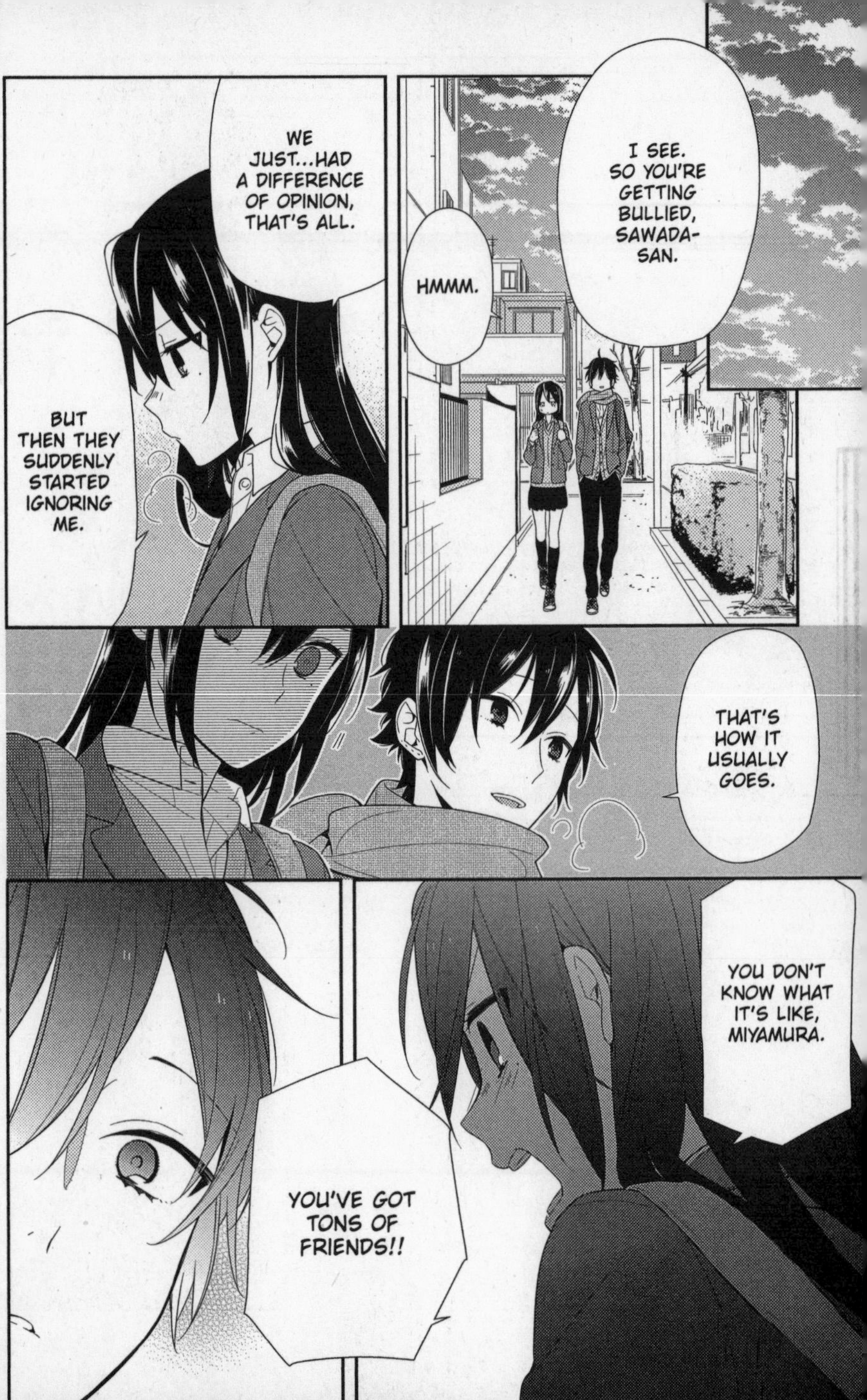
I SEE. SO YOU'RE GETTING BULLIED, SAWADA-SAN.
HMMM.
WE JUST...HAD A DIFFERENCE OF OPINION, THAT'S ALL.
BUT THEN THEY SUDDENLY STARTED IGNORING ME.
THAT'S HOW IT USUALLY GOES.
YOU DON'T KNOW WHAT IT'S LIKE, MIYAMURA.
YOU'VE GOT TONS OF FRIENDS!!

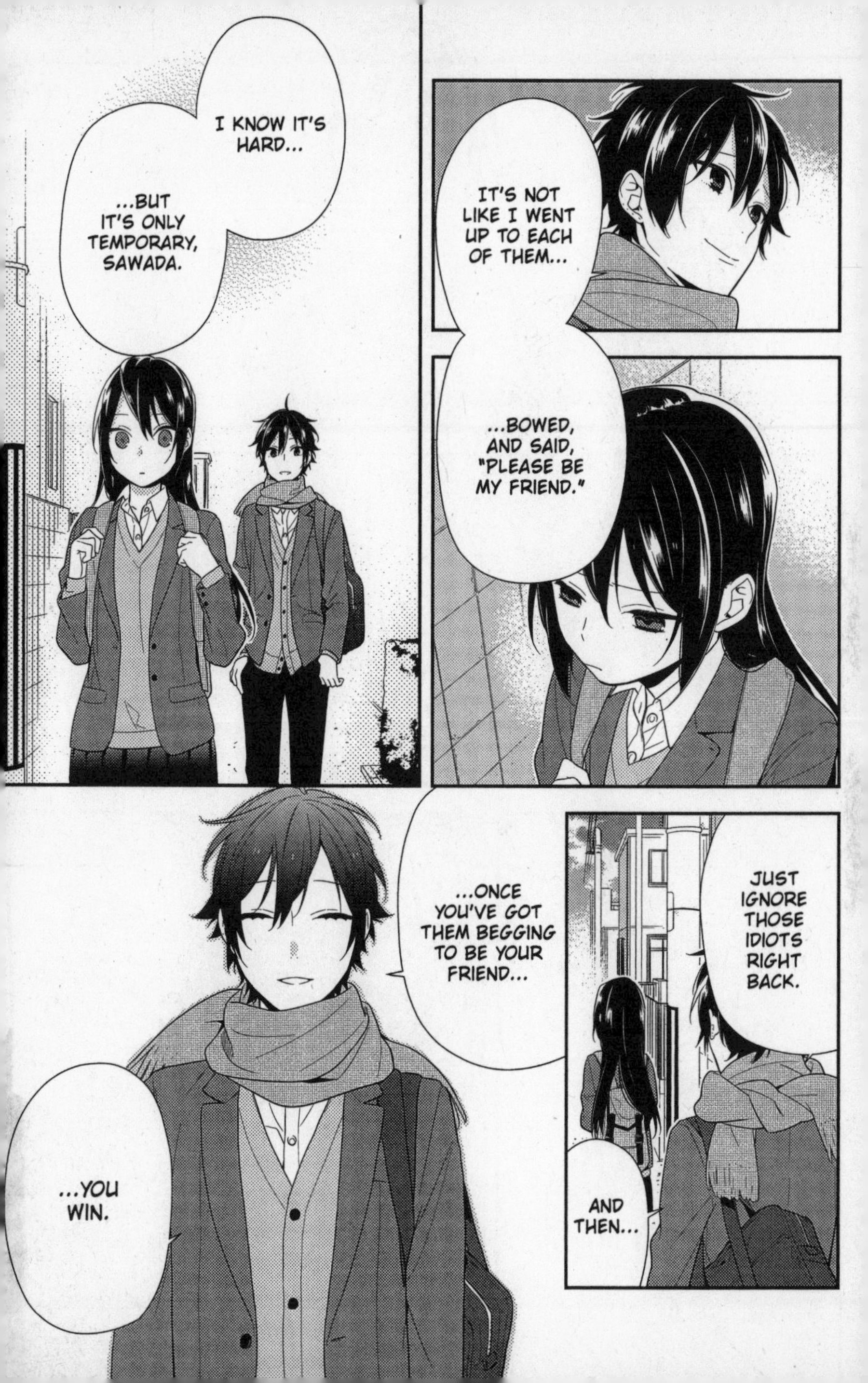
IT'S NOT LIKE I WENT UP TO EACH OF THEM...
...BOWED, AND SAID, "PLEASE BE MY FRIEND."
I KNOW IT'S HARD...
...BUT IT'S ONLY TEMPORARY, SAWADA.
JUST IGNORE THOSE IDIOTS RIGHT BACK.
AND THEN...
...ONCE YOU'VE GOT THEM BEGGING TO BE YOUR FRIEND...
...YOU WIN.

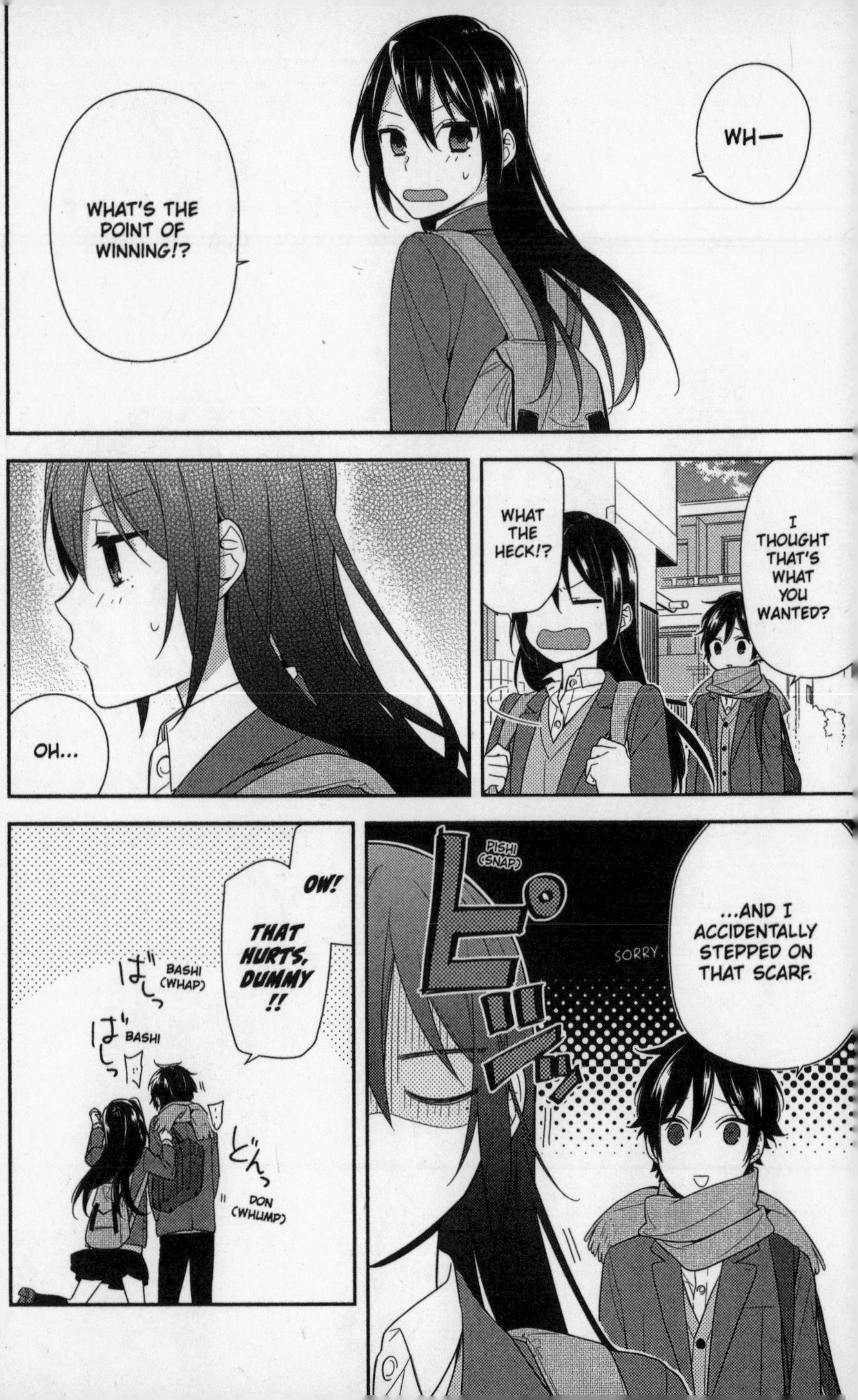
WH—
WHAT'S THE POINT OF WINNING!?
I THOUGHT THAT'S WHAT YOU WANTED?
WHAT THE HECK!?
OH...
PISHI (SNAP)
SORRY.
...AND I ACCIDENTALLY STEPPED ON THAT SCARF.
OW! THAT HURTS, DUMMY!!
ばしっ BASHI (WHAP)
ばしっ BASHI
どんっ DON (WHUMP)

HORIMIYA

HORIMIYA

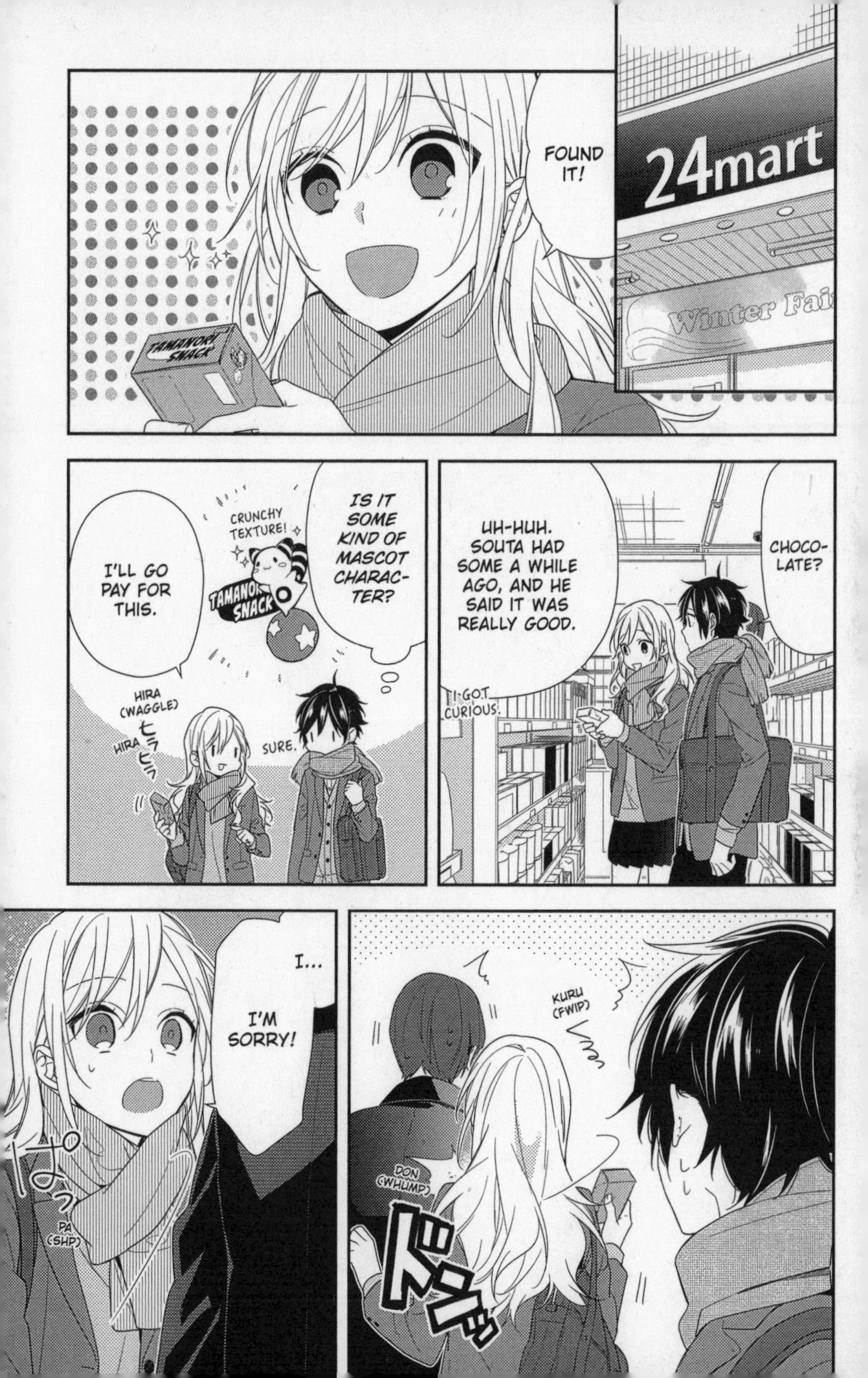
24mart
Winter Fai
FOUND IT!
TAMANORI SNACK
CHOCO-LATE?
UH-HUH. SOUTA HAD SOME A WHILE AGO, AND HE SAID IT WAS REALLY GOOD.
I GOT CURIOUS.
IS IT SOME KIND OF MASCOT CHARAC-TER?
CRUNCHY TEXTURE!
TAMANORI SNACK
I'LL GO PAY FOR THIS.
SURE.
HIRA (WAGGLE)
HIRA
KURU (FWIP)
DON (WHUMP)
I...
I'M SORRY!
PA (SHP)

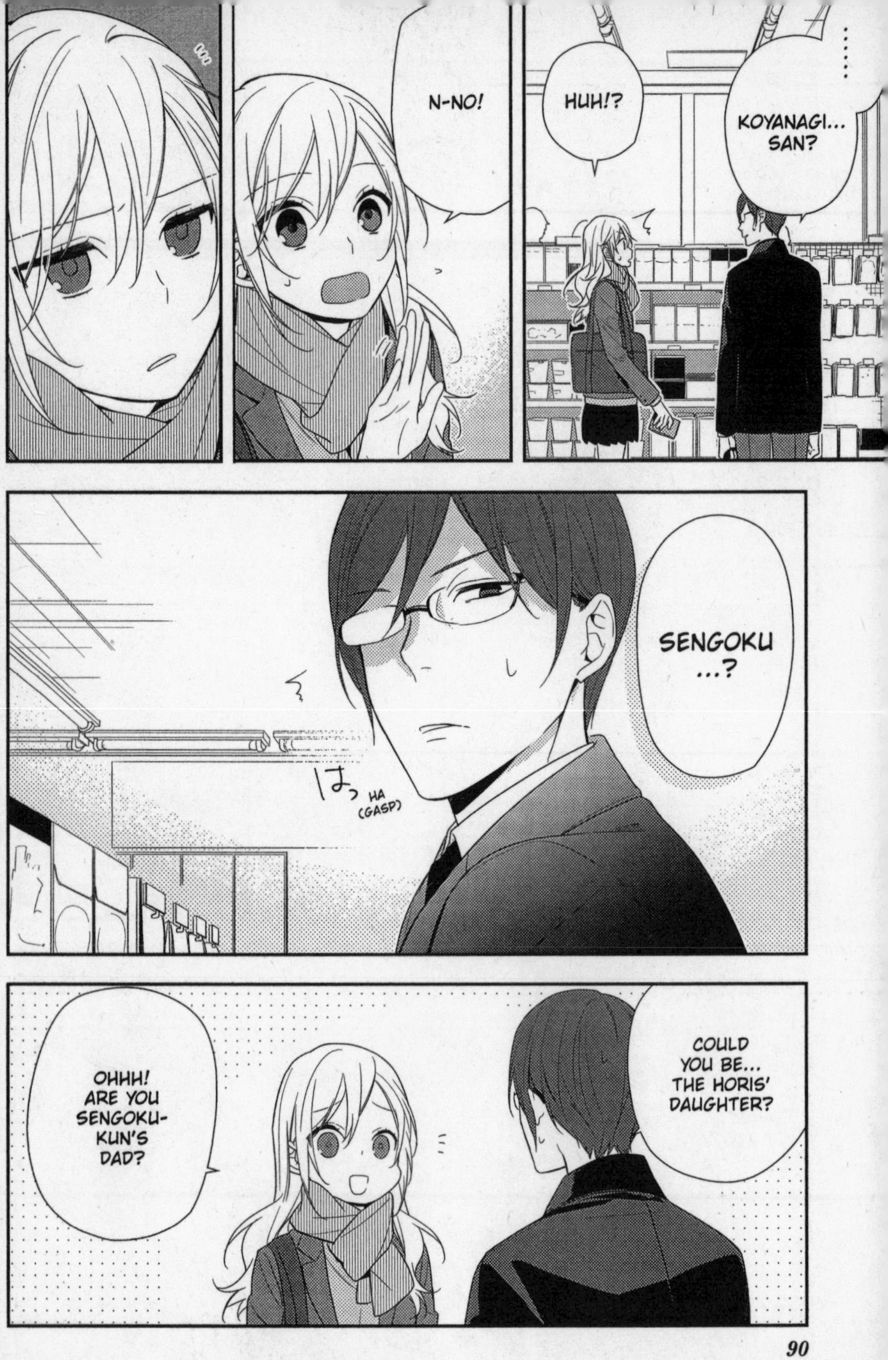
......
KOYANAGI... SAN?
HUH!?
N-NO!
SENGOKU ...?
はっ
HA (GASP)
COULD YOU BE... THE HORIS' DAUGHTER?
OHHH! ARE YOU SENGOKU-KUN'S DAD?

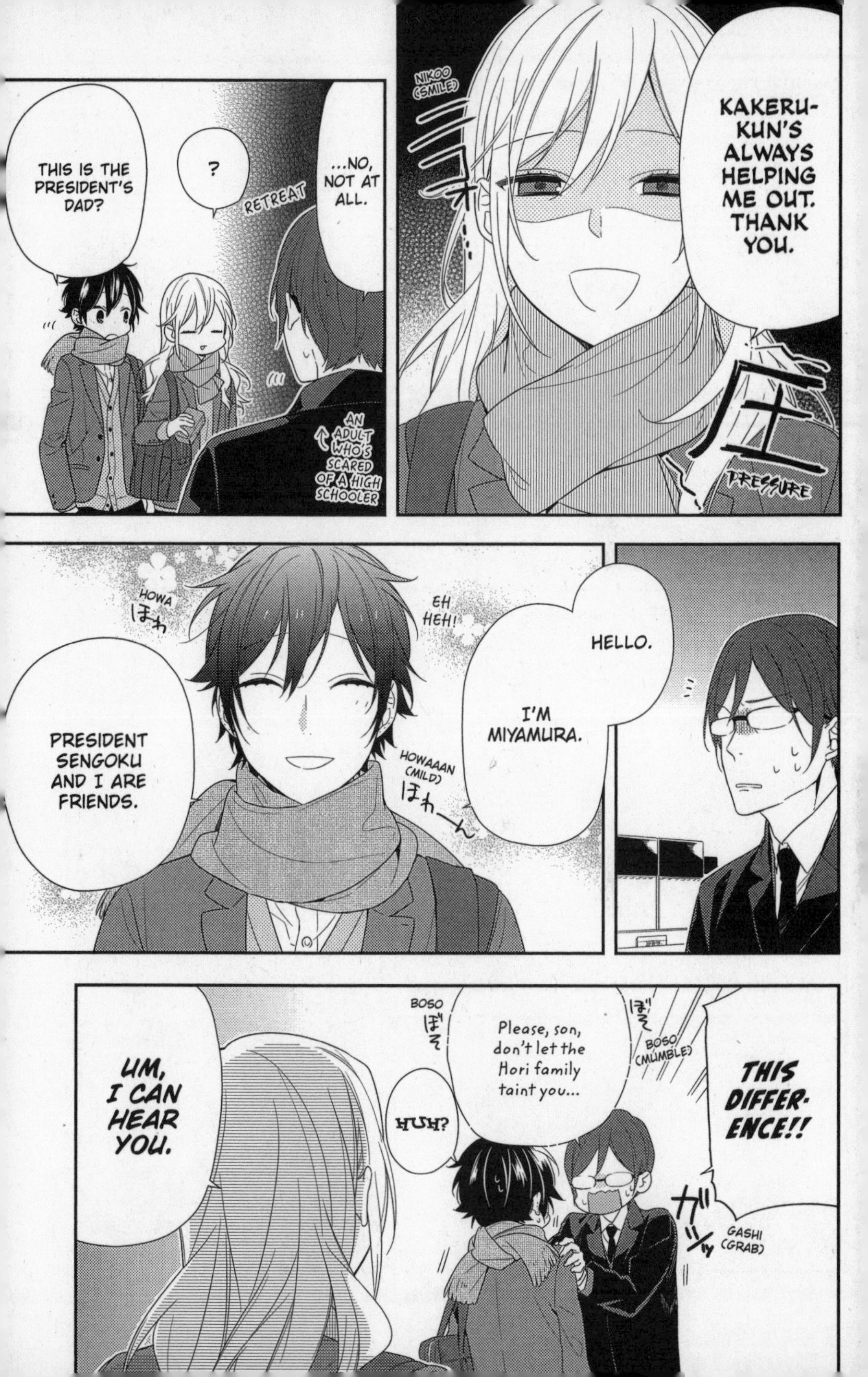
NIKOO (SMILE)
KAKERU-KUN'S ALWAYS HELPING ME OUT. THANK YOU.
圧
PRESSURE
...NO, NOT AT ALL.
RETREAT
?
THIS IS THE PRESIDENT'S DAD?
AN ADULT WHO'S SCARED OF A HIGH SCHOOLER
HELLO.
I'M MIYAMURA.
EH HEH!
HOWAAAN (MILD)
ほわ～ん
HOWA
ほわ
PRESIDENT SENGOKU AND I ARE FRIENDS.
THIS DIFFERENCE!!
GASHI (GRAB)
ぼそ
BOSO (MUMBLE)
Please, son, don't let the Hori family taint you...
BOSO
ぼそ
HUH?
UM, I CAN HEAR YOU.

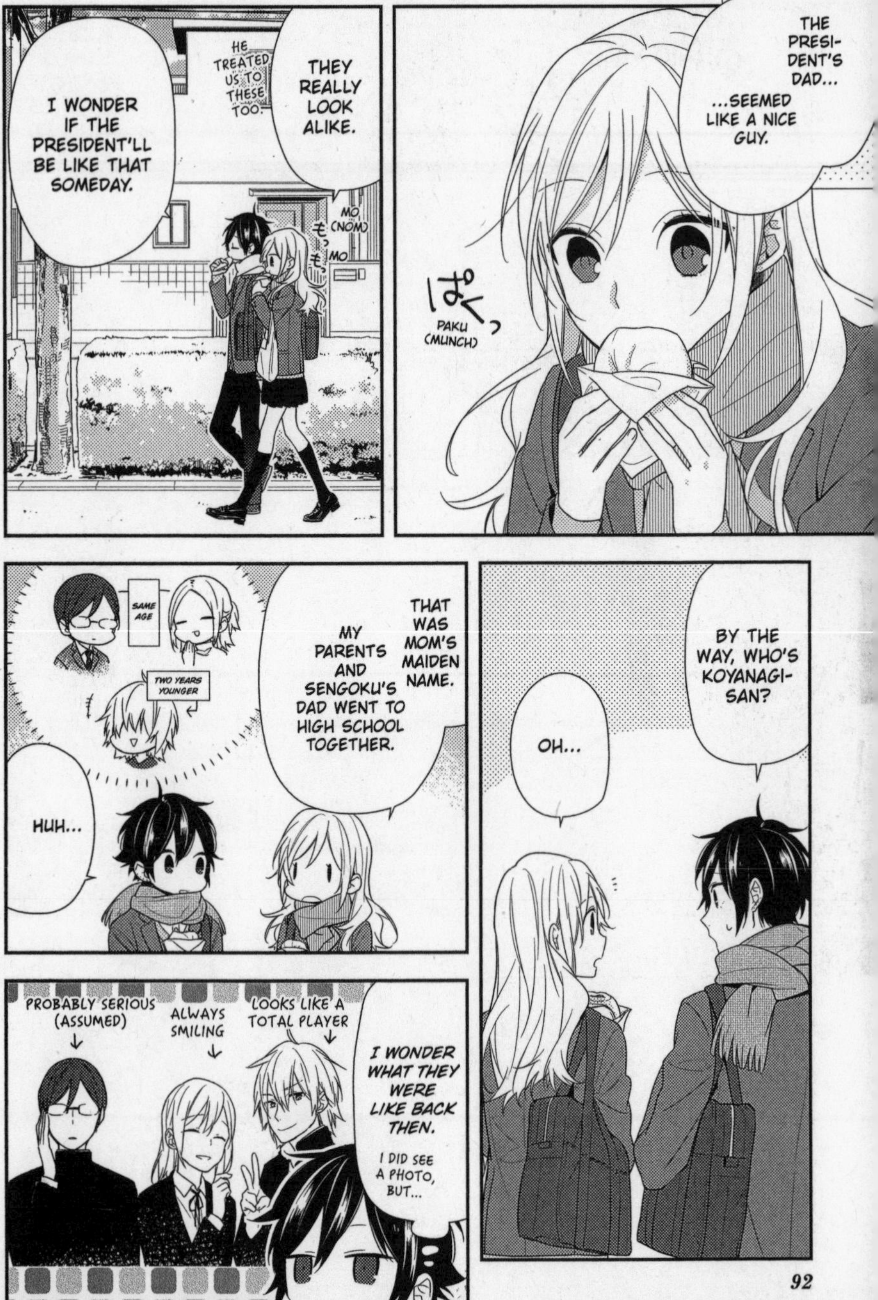
THE PRESIDENT'S DAD...
...SEEMED LIKE A NICE GUY.
ぱくっ
PAKU (MUNCH)
THEY REALLY LOOK ALIKE.
HE TREATED US TO THESE TOO.
MO (NOM) MO
もっもっ
I WONDER IF THE PRESIDENT'LL BE LIKE THAT SOMEDAY.
BY THE WAY, WHO'S KOYANAGI-SAN?
OH...
THAT WAS MOM'S MAIDEN NAME.
MY PARENTS AND SENGOKU'S DAD WENT TO HIGH SCHOOL TOGETHER.
SAME AGE
TWO YEARS YOUNGER
HUH...
I WONDER WHAT THEY WERE LIKE BACK THEN.
I DID SEE A PHOTO, BUT...
LOOKS LIKE A TOTAL PLAYER
ALWAYS SMILING
PROBABLY SERIOUS (ASSUMED)

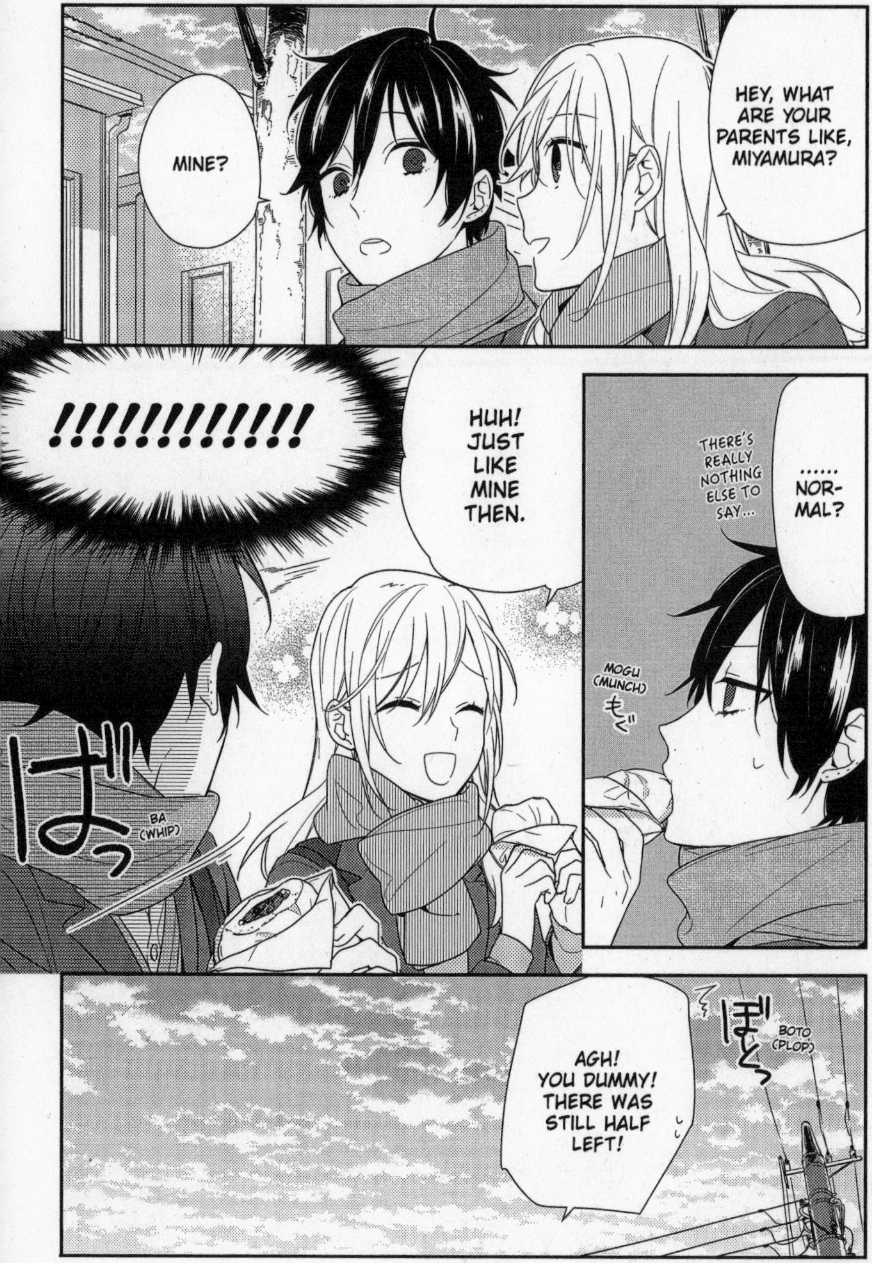
HEY, WHAT ARE YOUR PARENTS LIKE, MIYAMURA?
MINE?
......NOR-MAL?
THERE'S REALLY NOTHING ELSE TO SAY...
MOGU (MUNCH)
もぐ
HUH! JUST LIKE MINE THEN.
!!!!!!!!!!!!!
ばっ
BA (WHIP)
ぼとっ
BOTO (PLOP)
AGH! YOU DUMMY! THERE WAS STILL HALF LEFT!

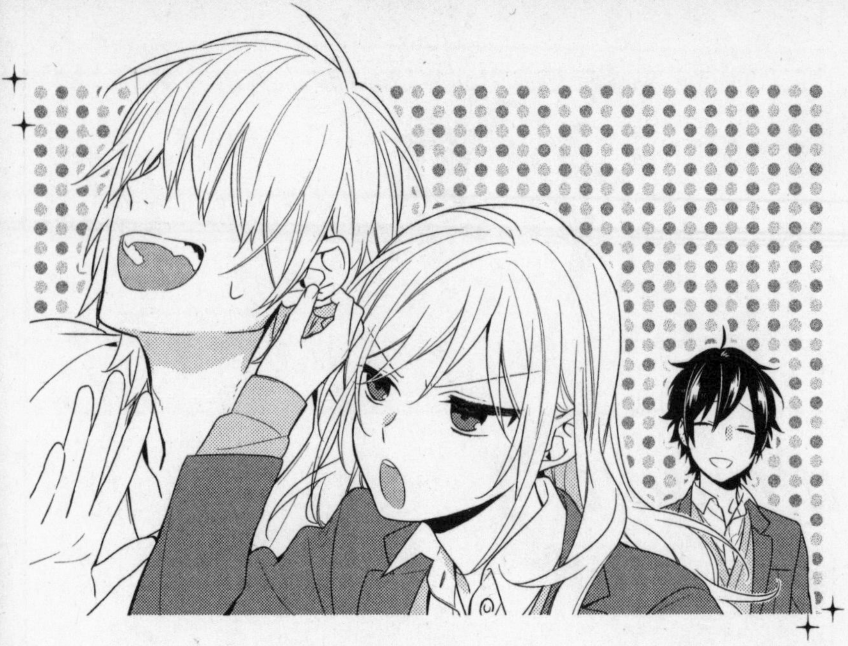

page·68

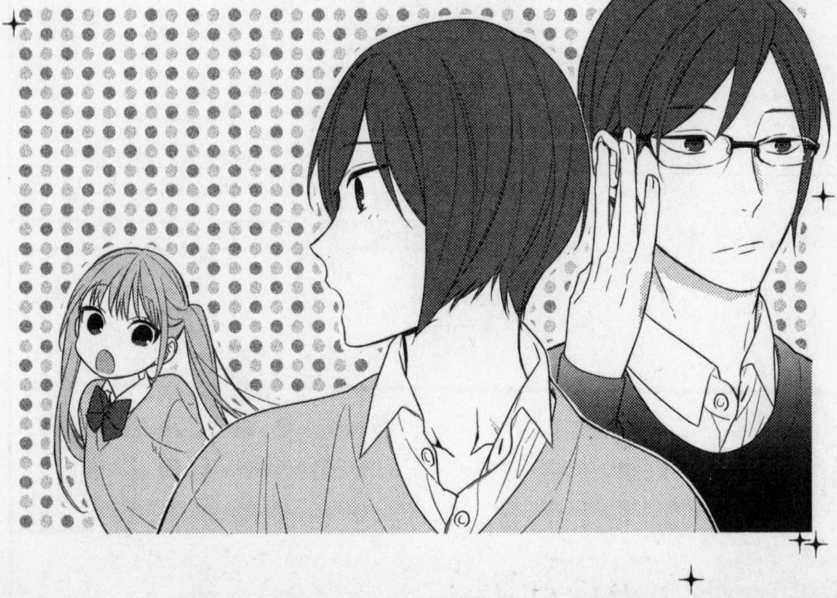

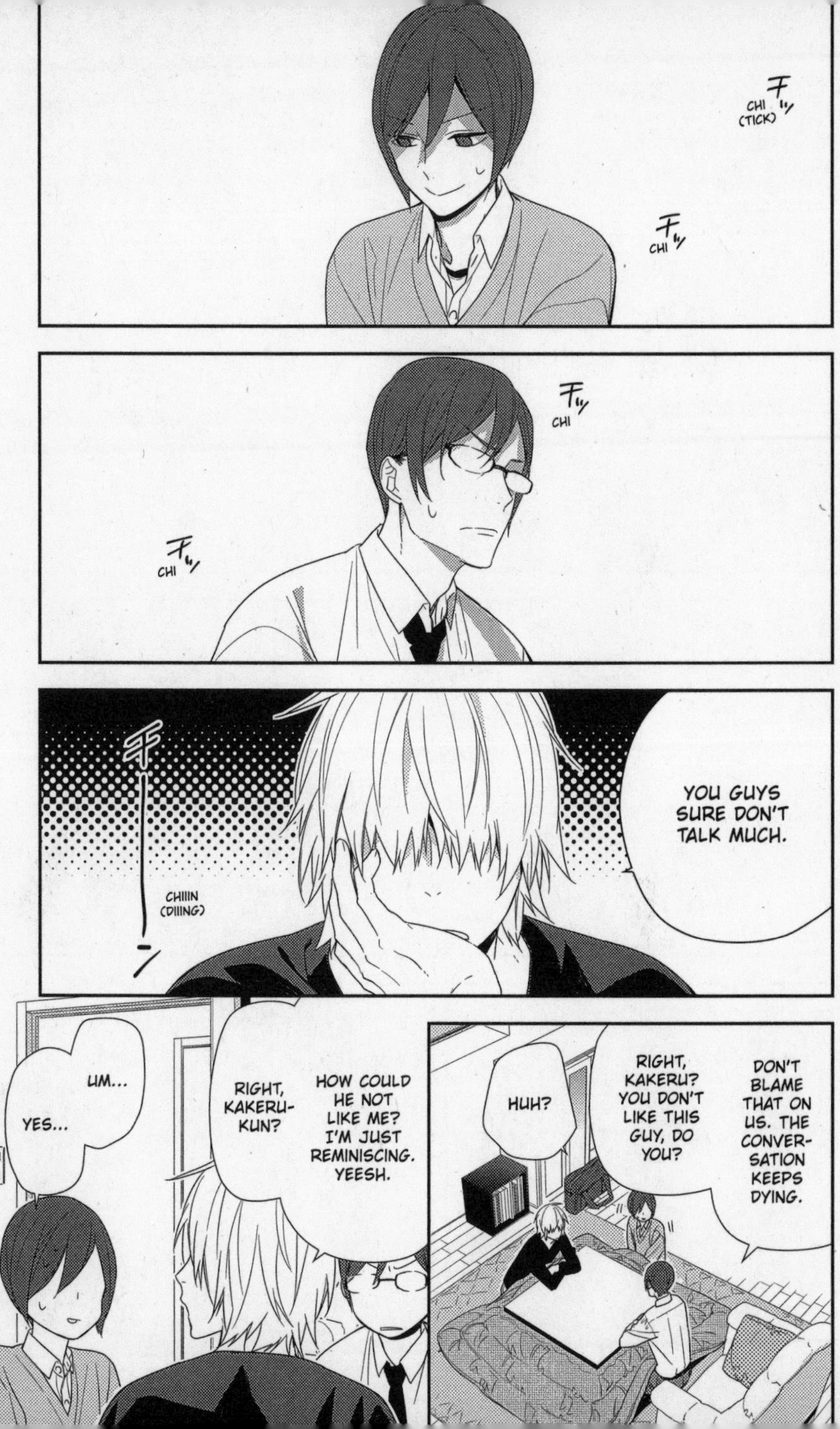
CHI (TICK)
CHI
CHI
CHI
YOU GUYS SURE DON'T TALK MUCH.
CHIIIN (DIIING)
DON'T BLAME THAT ON US. THE CONVER-SATION KEEPS DYING.
RIGHT, KAKERU? YOU DON'T LIKE THIS GUY, DO YOU?
HUH?
HOW COULD HE NOT LIKE ME? I'M JUST REMINISCING. YEESH.
RIGHT, KAKERU-KUN?
UM... YES...

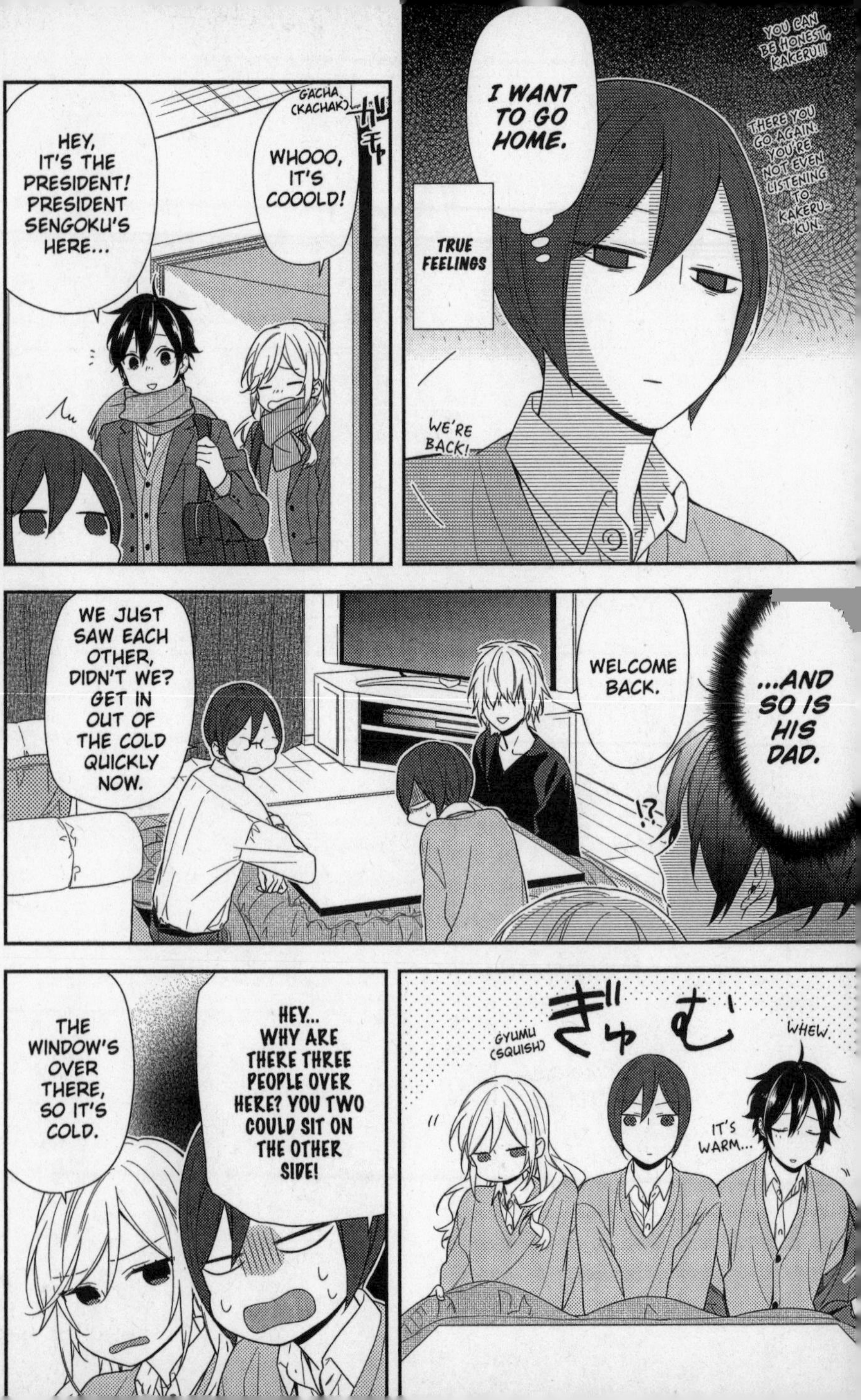
YOU CAN BE HONEST, KAKERU!!
THERE YOU GO AGAIN. YOU'RE NOT EVEN LISTENING TO KAKERU-KUN.
I WANT TO GO HOME.
TRUE FEELINGS
WE'RE BACK!
ガチャ
GACHA (KACHAK)
WHOOO, IT'S COOOLD!
HEY, IT'S THE PRESIDENT! PRESIDENT SENGOKU'S HERE...
...AND SO IS HIS DAD.
!?
WELCOME BACK.
WE JUST SAW EACH OTHER, DIDN'T WE? GET IN OUT OF THE COLD QUICKLY NOW.
WHEW.
ぎゅむ
GYUMU (SQUISH)
IT'S WARM...
HEY... WHY ARE THERE THREE PEOPLE OVER HERE? YOU TWO COULD SIT ON THE OTHER SIDE!
THE WINDOW'S OVER THERE, SO IT'S COLD.

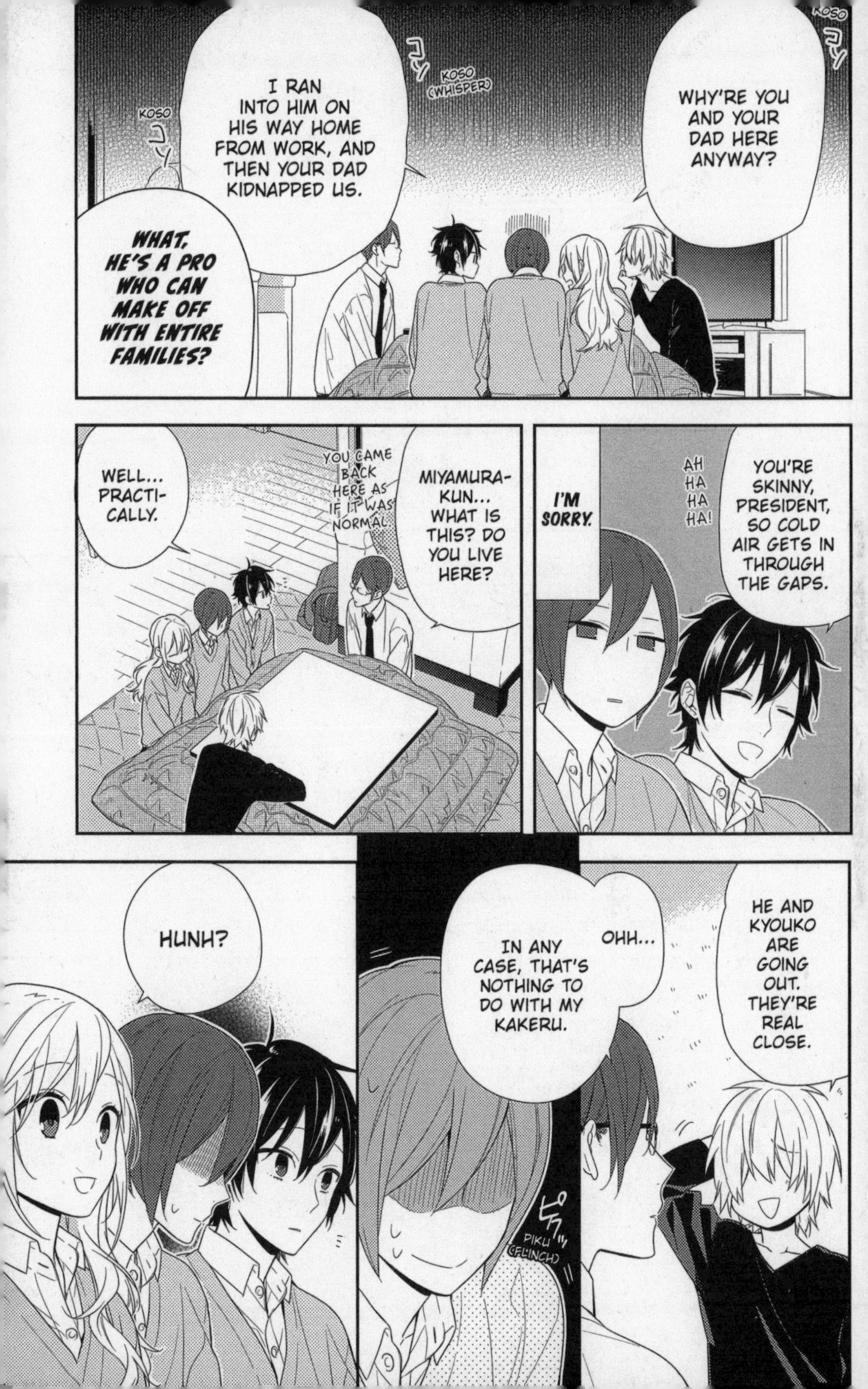
KOSO
WHY'RE YOU AND YOUR DAD HERE ANYWAY?
KOSO (WHISPER)
I RAN INTO HIM ON HIS WAY HOME FROM WORK, AND THEN YOUR DAD KIDNAPPED US.
KOSO
WHAT, HE'S A PRO WHO CAN MAKE OFF WITH ENTIRE FAMILIES?
YOU'RE SKINNY, PRESIDENT, SO COLD AIR GETS IN THROUGH THE GAPS.
AH HA HA HA!
I'M SORRY.
MIYAMURA-KUN... WHAT IS THIS? DO YOU LIVE HERE?
YOU CAME BACK HERE AS IF IT WAS NORMAL
WELL... PRACTI-CALLY.
HE AND KYOUKO ARE GOING OUT. THEY'RE REAL CLOSE.
OHH...
IN ANY CASE, THAT'S NOTHING TO DO WITH MY KAKERU.
PIKU (FLINCH)
HUNH?

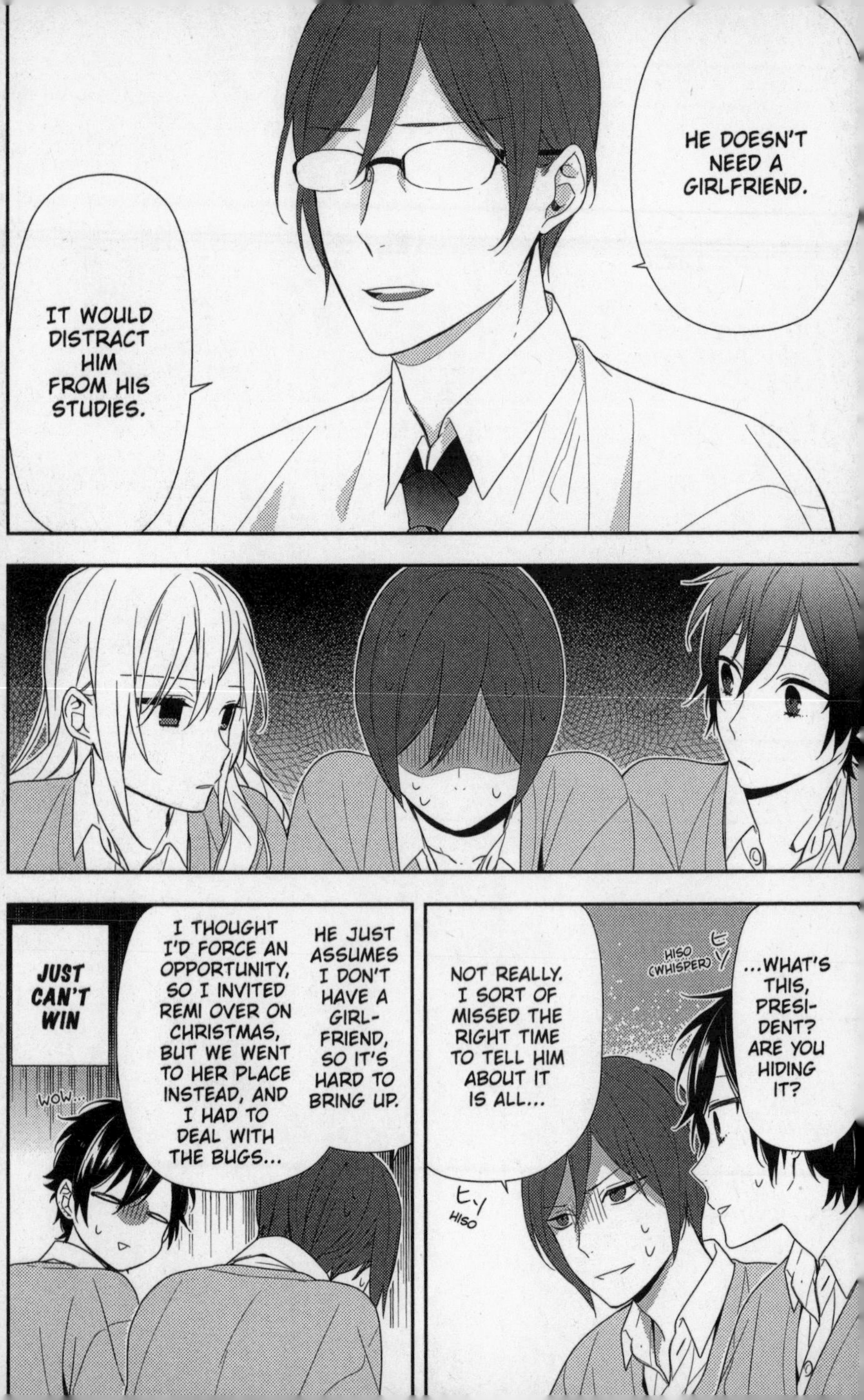

HE DOESN'T NEED A GIRLFRIEND.
IT WOULD DISTRACT HIM FROM HIS STUDIES.
ヒソ HISO (WHISPER)
...WHAT'S THIS, PRESIDENT? ARE YOU HIDING IT?
NOT REALLY. I SORT OF MISSED THE RIGHT TIME TO TELL HIM ABOUT IT IS ALL...
ヒソ HISO
HE JUST ASSUMES I DON'T HAVE A GIRLFRIEND, SO IT'S HARD TO BRING UP.
I THOUGHT I'D FORCE AN OPPORTUNITY, SO I INVITED REMI OVER ON CHRISTMAS, BUT WE WENT TO HER PLACE INSTEAD, AND I HAD TO DEAL WITH THE BUGS...
JUST CAN'T WIN
WOW...

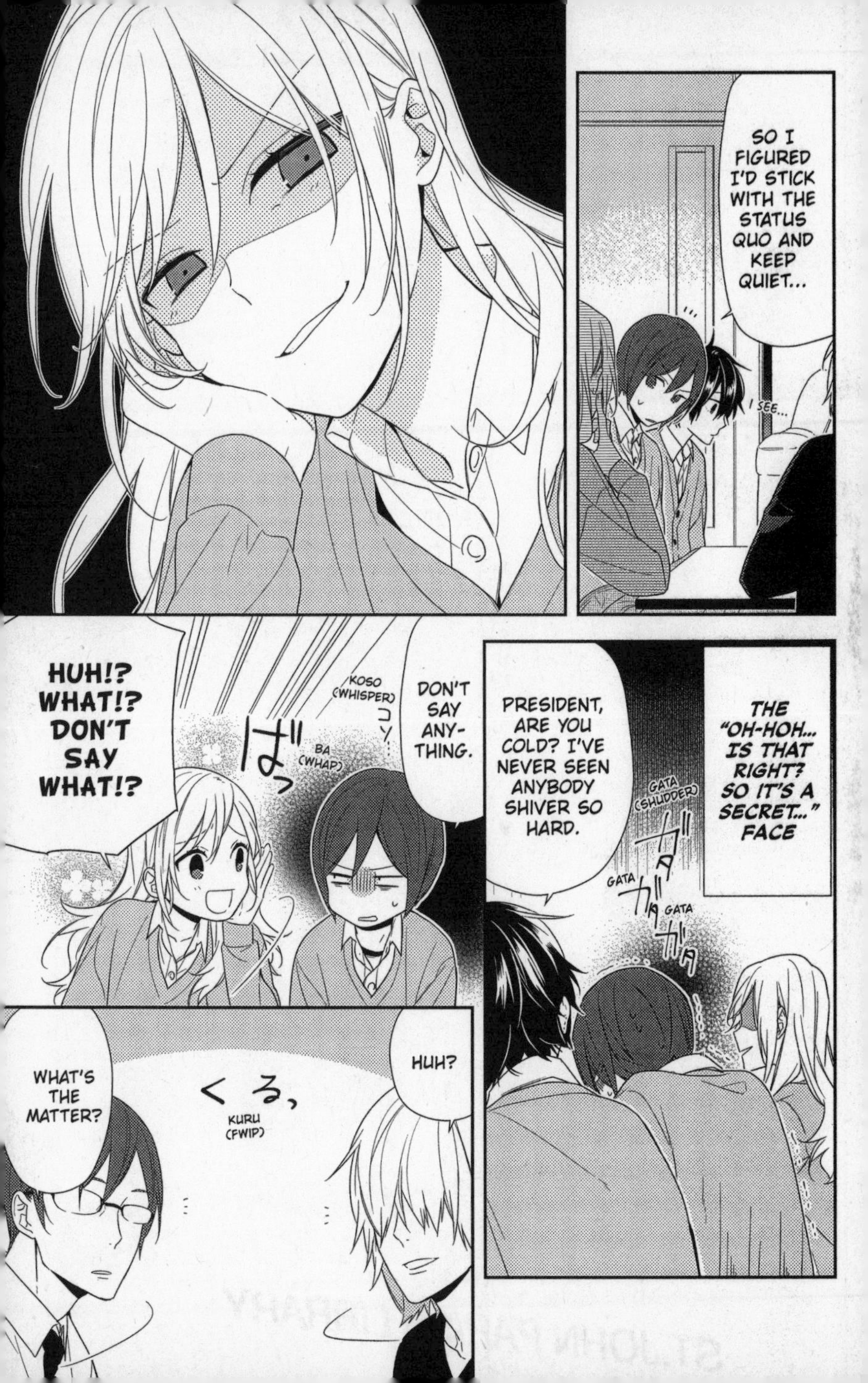
SO I FIGURED I'D STICK WITH THE STATUS QUO AND KEEP QUIET...
I SEE...
THE "OH-HOH... IS THAT RIGHT? SO IT'S A SECRET..." FACE
PRESIDENT, ARE YOU COLD? I'VE NEVER SEEN ANYBODY SHIVER SO HARD.
GATA (SHUDDER)
GATA
GATA
DON'T SAY ANYTHING.
KOSO (WHISPER)
コソ
BA (WHAP)
ばっ
HUH!? WHAT!? DON'T SAY WHAT!?
HUH?
くるっ
KURU (FWIP)
WHAT'S THE MATTER?

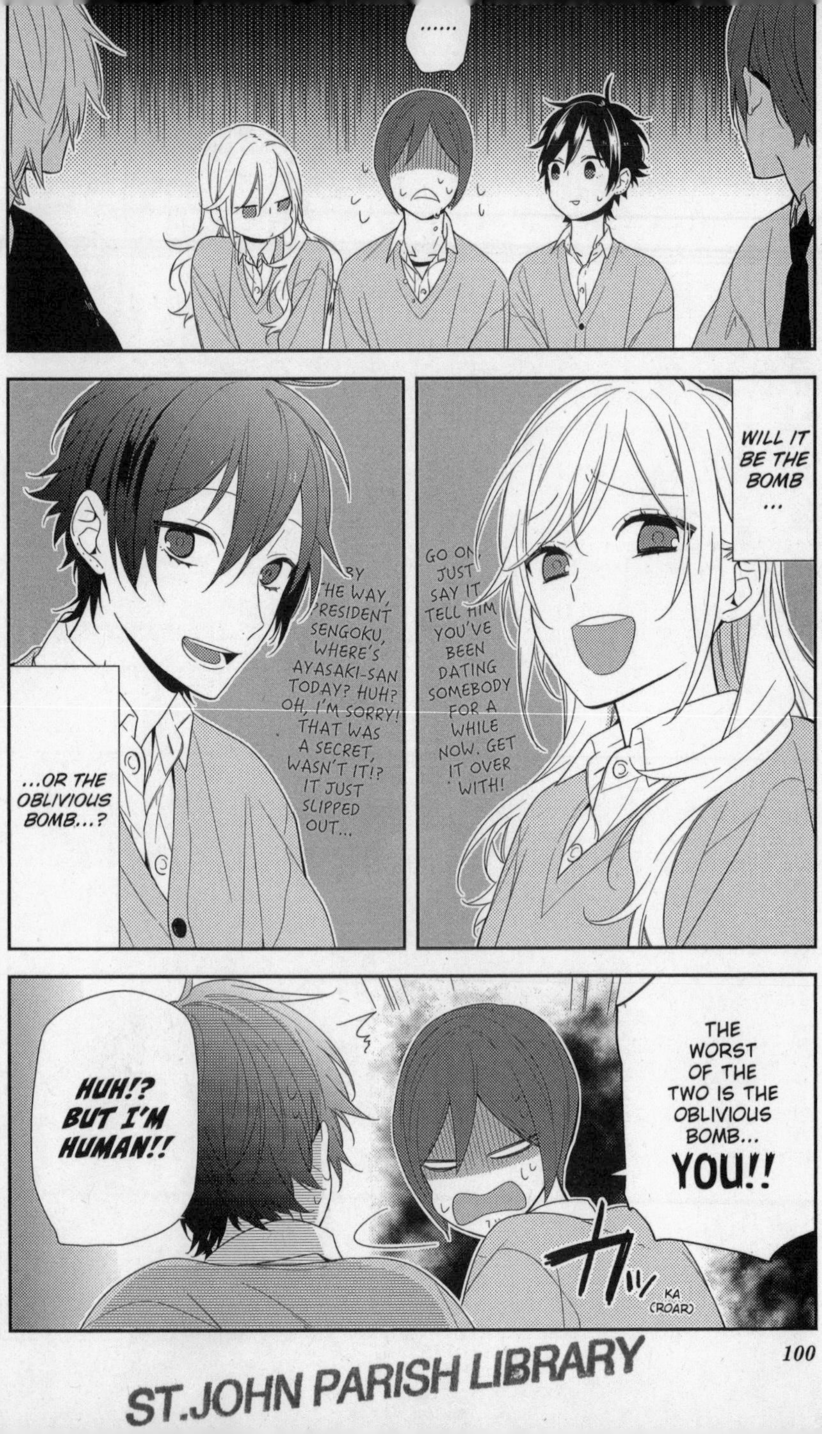
......
WILL IT BE THE BOMB ...
GO ON. JUST SAY IT. TELL HIM YOU'VE BEEN DATING SOMEBODY FOR A WHILE NOW. GET IT OVER WITH!
BY THE WAY, PRESIDENT SENGOKU, WHERE'S AYASAKI-SAN TODAY? HUH? OH, I'M SORRY! THAT WAS A SECRET, WASN'T IT!? IT JUST SLIPPED OUT...
...OR THE OBLIVIOUS BOMB...?
THE WORST OF THE TWO IS THE OBLIVIOUS BOMB... YOU!!
HUH!? BUT I'M HUMAN!!
KA (ROAR)

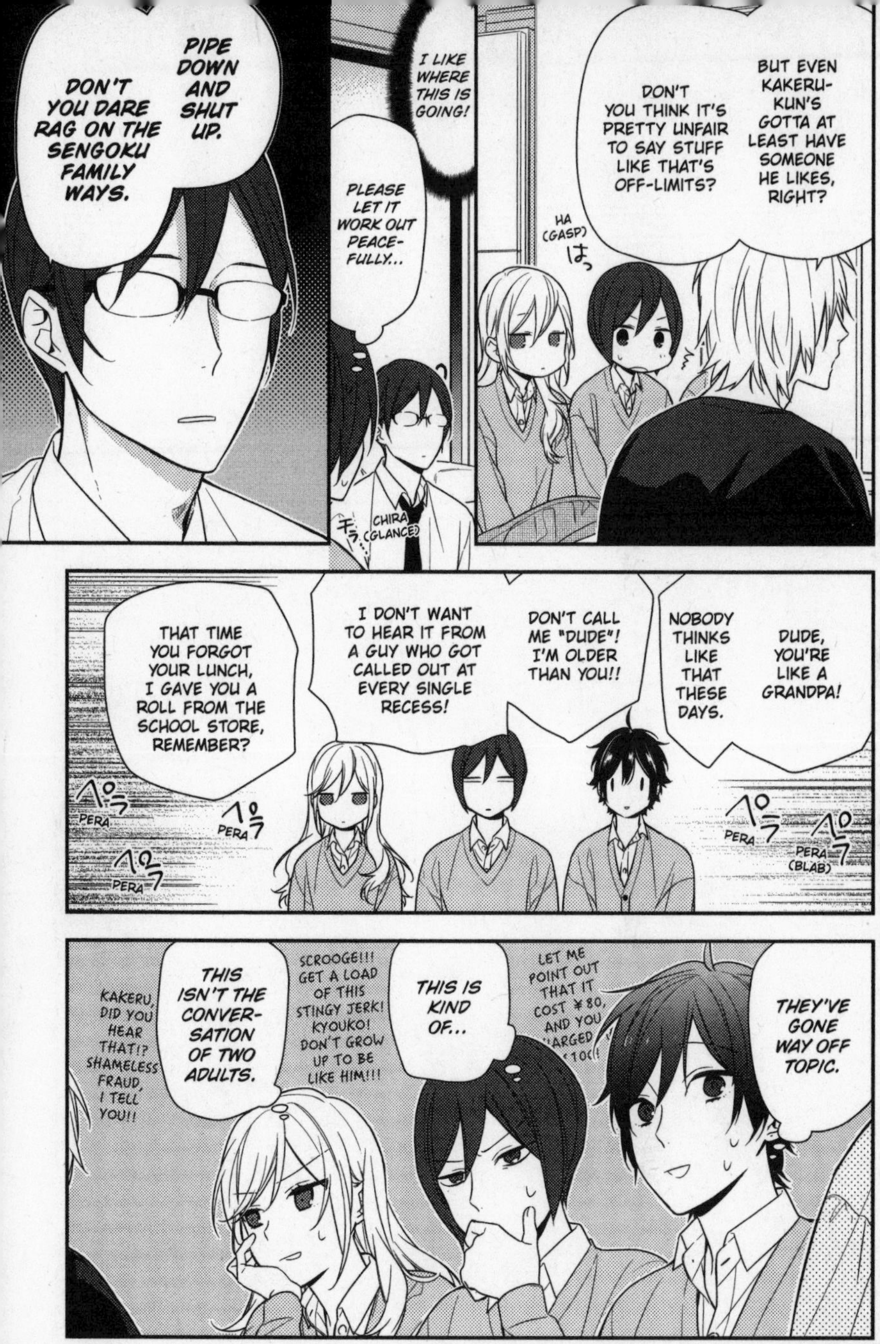
BUT EVEN KAKERU-KUN'S GOTTA AT LEAST HAVE SOMEONE HE LIKES, RIGHT?
DON'T YOU THINK IT'S PRETTY UNFAIR TO SAY STUFF LIKE THAT'S OFF-LIMITS?
はっ
HA (GASP)
I LIKE WHERE THIS IS GOING!
PLEASE LET IT WORK OUT PEACEFULLY...
チラ
CHIRA (GLANCED)
PIPE DOWN AND SHUT UP.
DON'T YOU DARE RAG ON THE SENGOKU FAMILY WAYS.
DUDE, YOU'RE LIKE A GRANDPA!
NOBODY THINKS LIKE THAT THESE DAYS.
DON'T CALL ME "DUDE"! I'M OLDER THAN YOU!!
I DON'T WANT TO HEAR IT FROM A GUY WHO GOT CALLED OUT AT EVERY SINGLE RECESS!
THAT TIME YOU FORGOT YOUR LUNCH, I GAVE YOU A ROLL FROM THE SCHOOL STORE, REMEMBER?
PERA (BLAB)
PERA
PERA
PERA
PERA
THEY'VE GONE WAY OFF TOPIC.
LET ME POINT OUT THAT IT COST ¥80, AND YOU
THIS IS KIND OF...
SCROOGE!!! GET A LOAD OF THIS STINGY JERK! KYOUKO! DON'T GROW UP TO BE LIKE HIM!!!
THIS ISN'T THE CONVERSATION OF TWO ADULTS.
KAKERU, DID YOU HEAR THAT!? SHAMELESS FRAUD, I TELL YOU!!

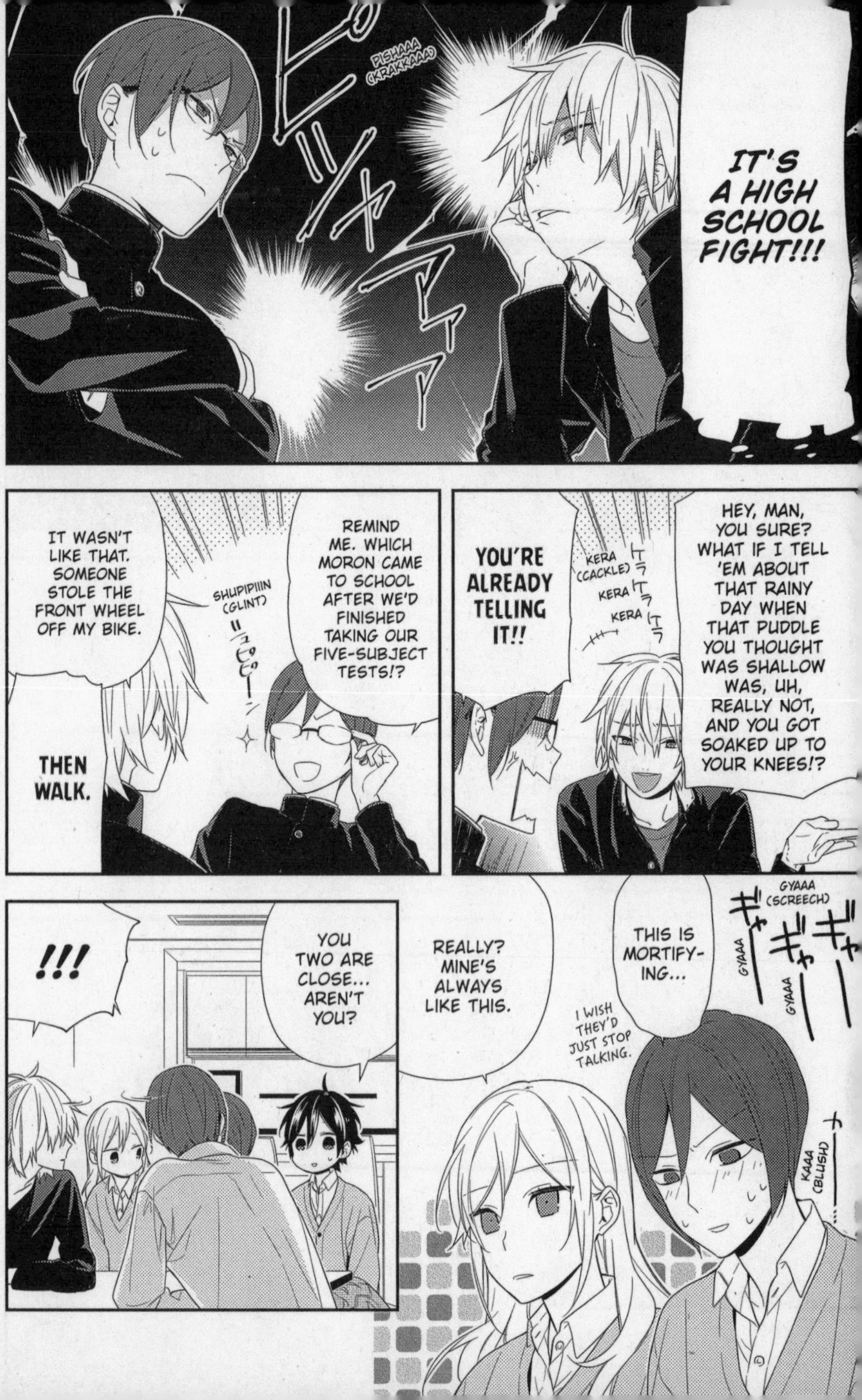
IT'S A HIGH SCHOOL FIGHT!!!
PISHAAA (KRAKKAAA)
HEY, MAN, YOU SURE? WHAT IF I TELL 'EM ABOUT THAT RAINY DAY WHEN THAT PUDDLE YOU THOUGHT WAS SHALLOW WAS, UH, REALLY NOT, AND YOU GOT SOAKED UP TO YOUR KNEES!?
KERA (CACKLE) KERA KERA
YOU'RE ALREADY TELLING IT!!
REMIND ME. WHICH MORON CAME TO SCHOOL AFTER WE'D FINISHED TAKING OUR FIVE-SUBJECT TESTS!?
SHUPIPIIIN (GLINT)
IT WASN'T LIKE THAT. SOMEONE STOLE THE FRONT WHEEL OFF MY BIKE.
THEN WALK.
GYAAA (SCREECH)
GYAAA
GYAAA
THIS IS MORTIFYING...
I WISH THEY'D JUST STOP TALKING.
KAAA (BLUSH)
REALLY? MINE'S ALWAYS LIKE THIS.
YOU TWO ARE CLOSE... AREN'T YOU?
!!!

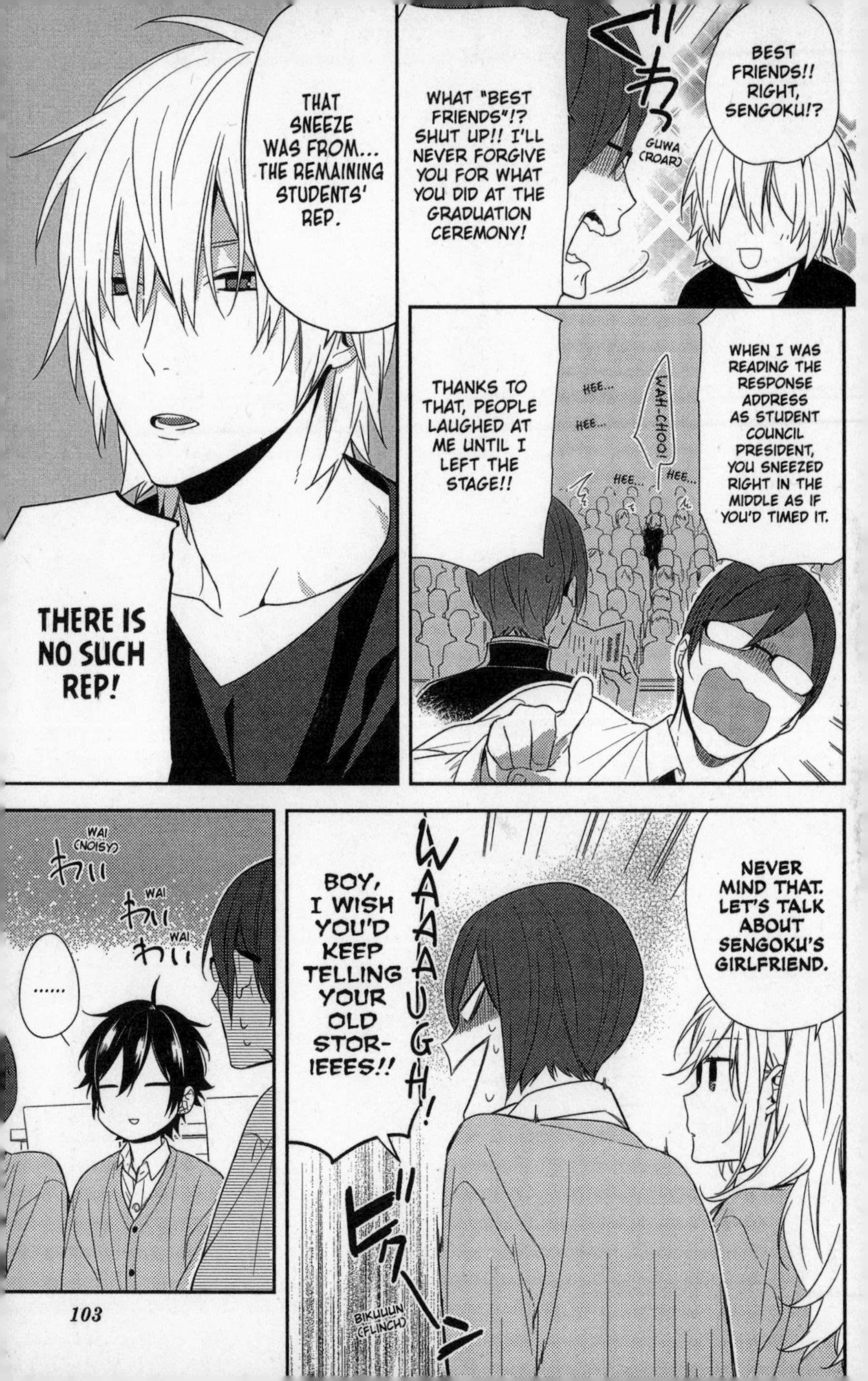
BEST FRIENDS!! RIGHT, SENGOKU!?
GUWA (ROAR)
WHAT "BEST FRIENDS"!? SHUT UP!! I'LL NEVER FORGIVE YOU FOR WHAT YOU DID AT THE GRADUATION CEREMONY!
WHEN I WAS READING THE RESPONSE ADDRESS AS STUDENT COUNCIL PRESIDENT, YOU SNEEZED RIGHT IN THE MIDDLE AS IF YOU'D TIMED IT.
HEE... HEE...
WAH-CHOO!
HEE... HEE...
THANKS TO THAT, PEOPLE LAUGHED AT ME UNTIL I LEFT THE STAGE!!
THAT SNEEZE WAS FROM... THE REMAINING STUDENTS' REP.
THERE IS NO SUCH REP!
NEVER MIND THAT. LET'S TALK ABOUT SENGOKU'S GIRLFRIEND.
WAAAAUGH!
BOY, I WISH YOU'D KEEP TELLING YOUR OLD STOR-IEEES!!
BIKUUUN (FLINCH)
WAI (NOISY)
WAI
WAI
......

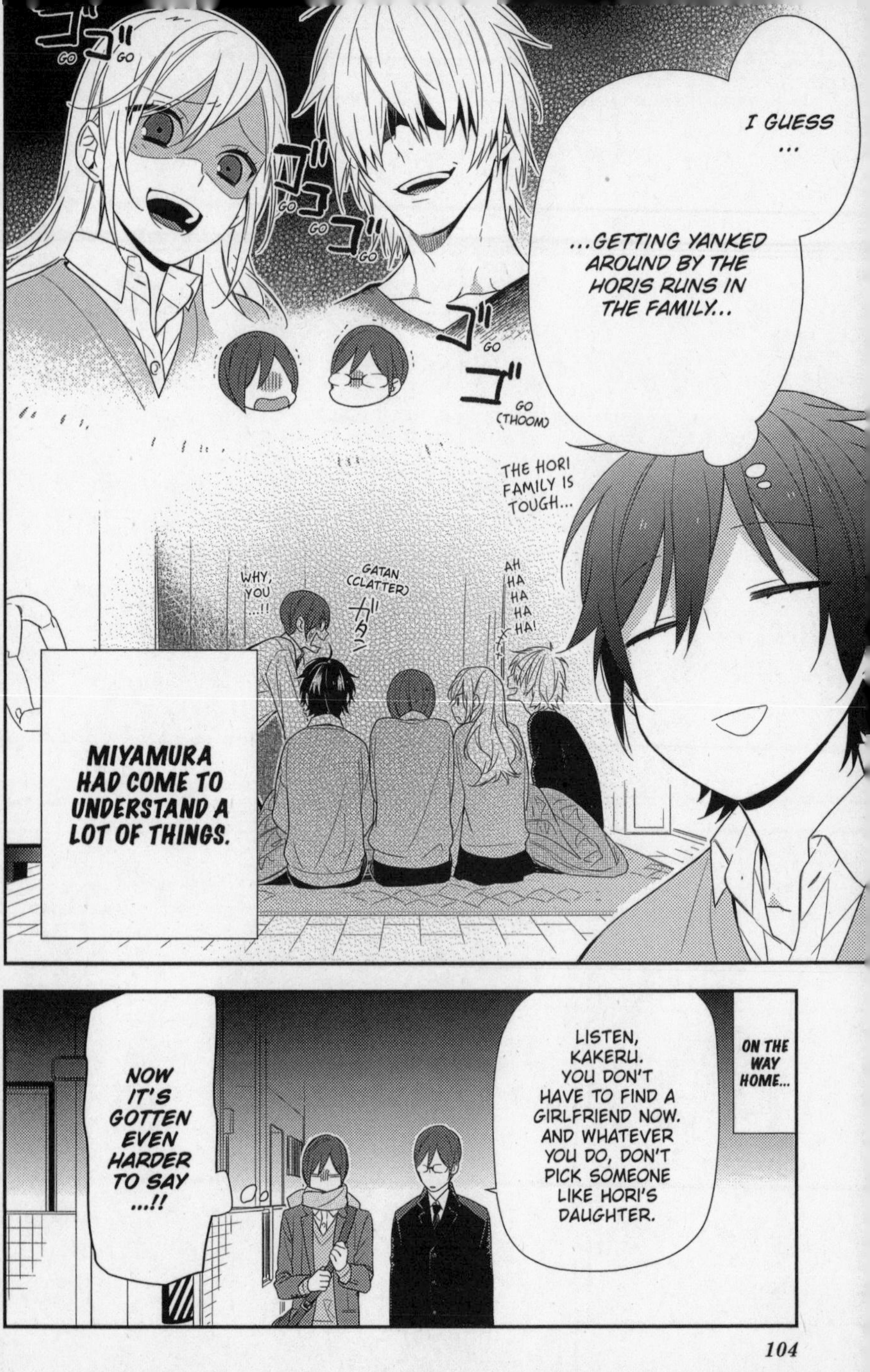
I GUESS ...
...GETTING YANKED AROUND BY THE HORIS RUNS IN THE FAMILY...
GO GO
GO GO GO
GO
GO (THOOM)
THE HORI FAMILY IS TOUGH...
AH HA HA HA HA!
GATAN (CLATTER)
WHY, YOU ...!!
MIYAMURA HAD COME TO UNDERSTAND A LOT OF THINGS.
ON THE WAY HOME...
LISTEN, KAKERU. YOU DON'T HAVE TO FIND A GIRLFRIEND NOW. AND WHATEVER YOU DO, DON'T PICK SOMEONE LIKE HORI'S DAUGHTER.
NOW IT'S GOTTEN EVEN HARDER TO SAY ...!!

HORIMIYA

HORIMIYA

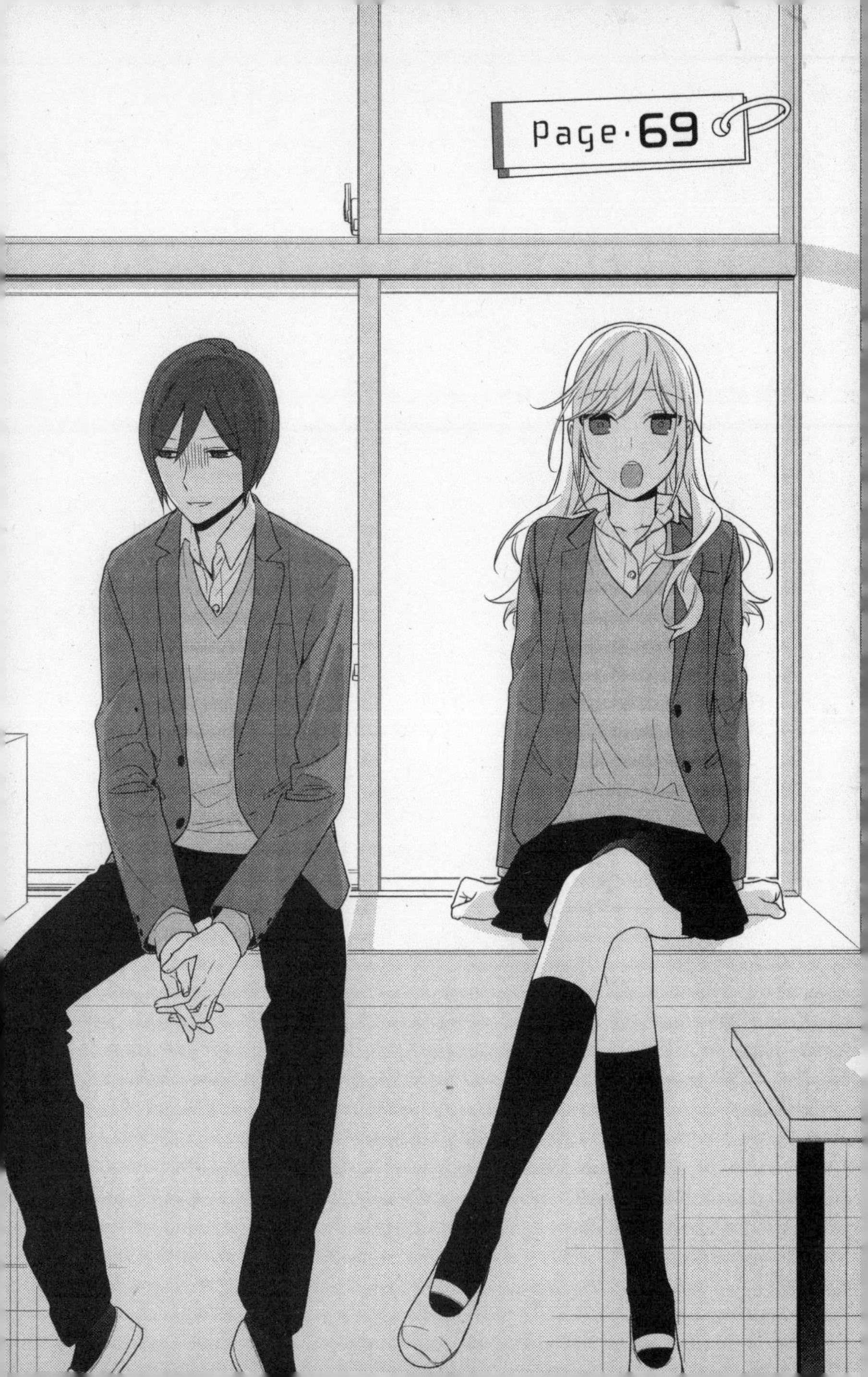
Page·69

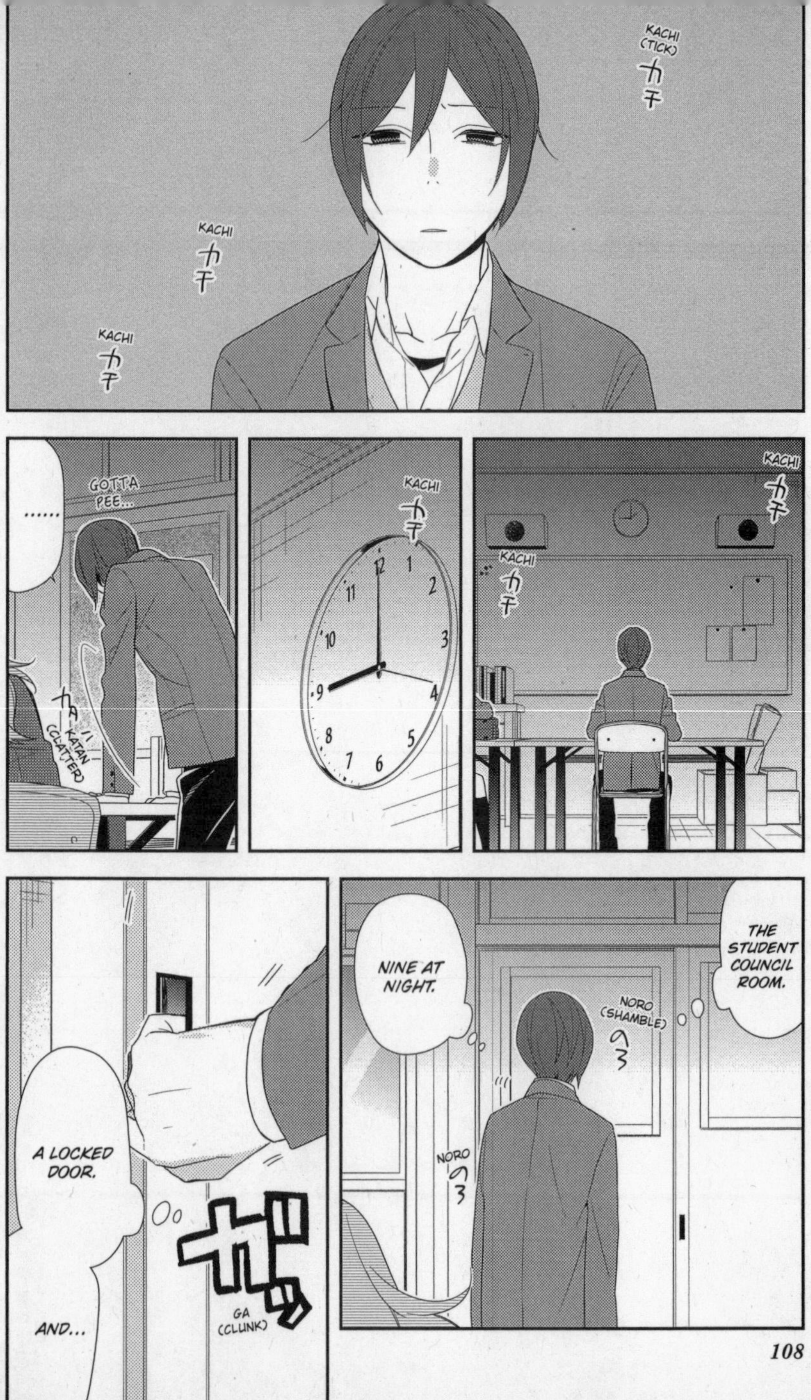
KACHI (TICK)
カチ
KACHI
カチ
KACHI
カチ
KACHI
カチ
KACHI
カチ
KACHI
カチ
GOTTA PEE...
....
KATAN (CLATTER)
カタン
THE STUDENT COUNCIL ROOM.
NINE AT NIGHT.
NORO (SHAMBLE)
のろ
NORO
のろ
A LOCKED DOOR.
GA (CLUNK)
ガッ
AND...

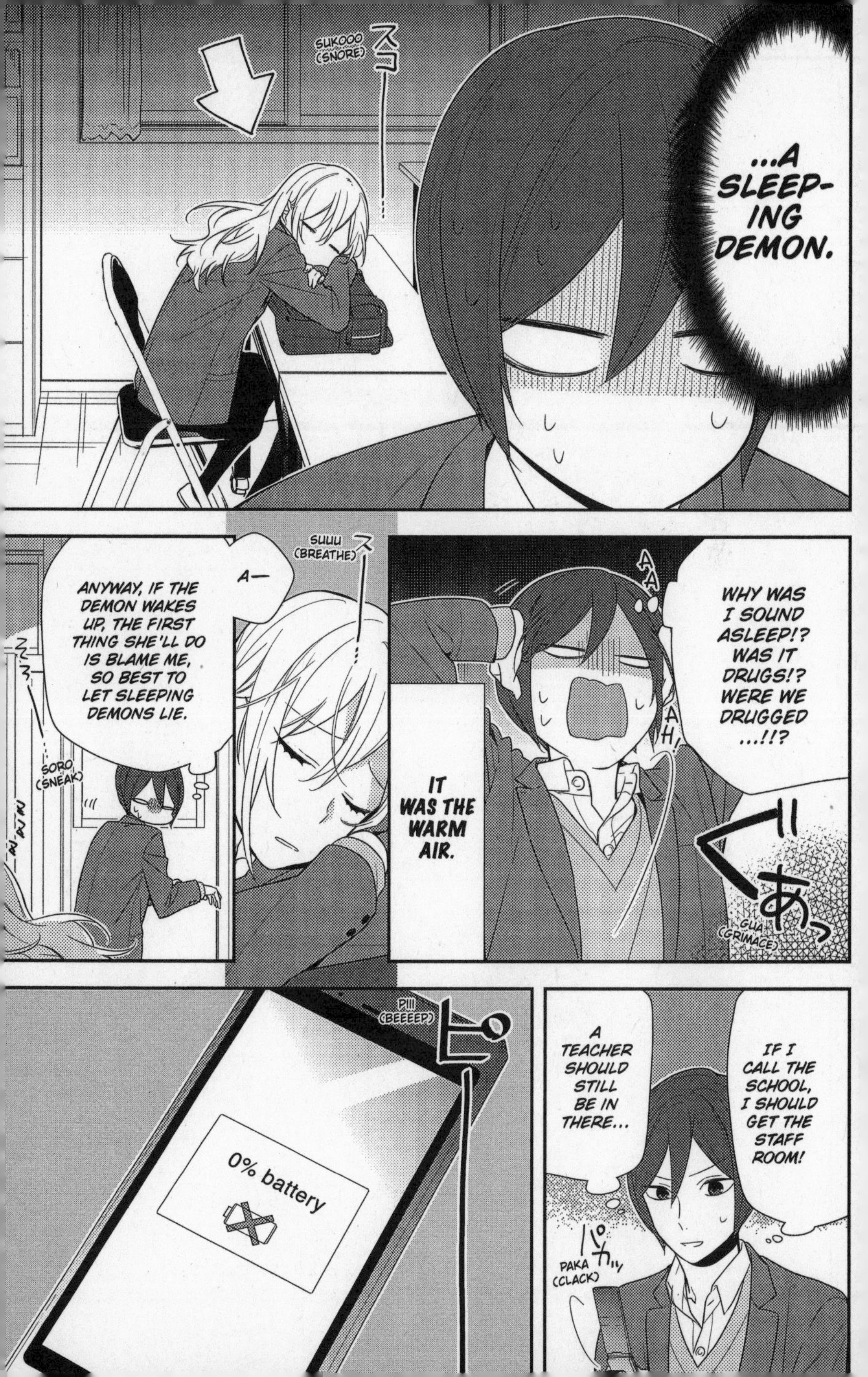
...A SLEEP-ING DEMON.
SUKOOO (SNORE)
AA
WHY WAS I SOUND ASLEEP!? WAS IT DRUGS!? WERE WE DRUGGED ...!!?
AH!
IT WAS THE WARM AIR.
GUA (GRIMACE)
SUUU (BREATHE)
A—
ANYWAY, IF THE DEMON WAKES UP, THE FIRST THING SHE'LL DO IS BLAME ME, SO BEST TO LET SLEEPING DEMONS LIE.
SORO (SNEAK)
IF I CALL THE SCHOOL, I SHOULD GET THE STAFF ROOM!
A TEACHER SHOULD STILL BE IN THERE...
PAKA (CLACK)
PIII (BEEEEP)
0% battery

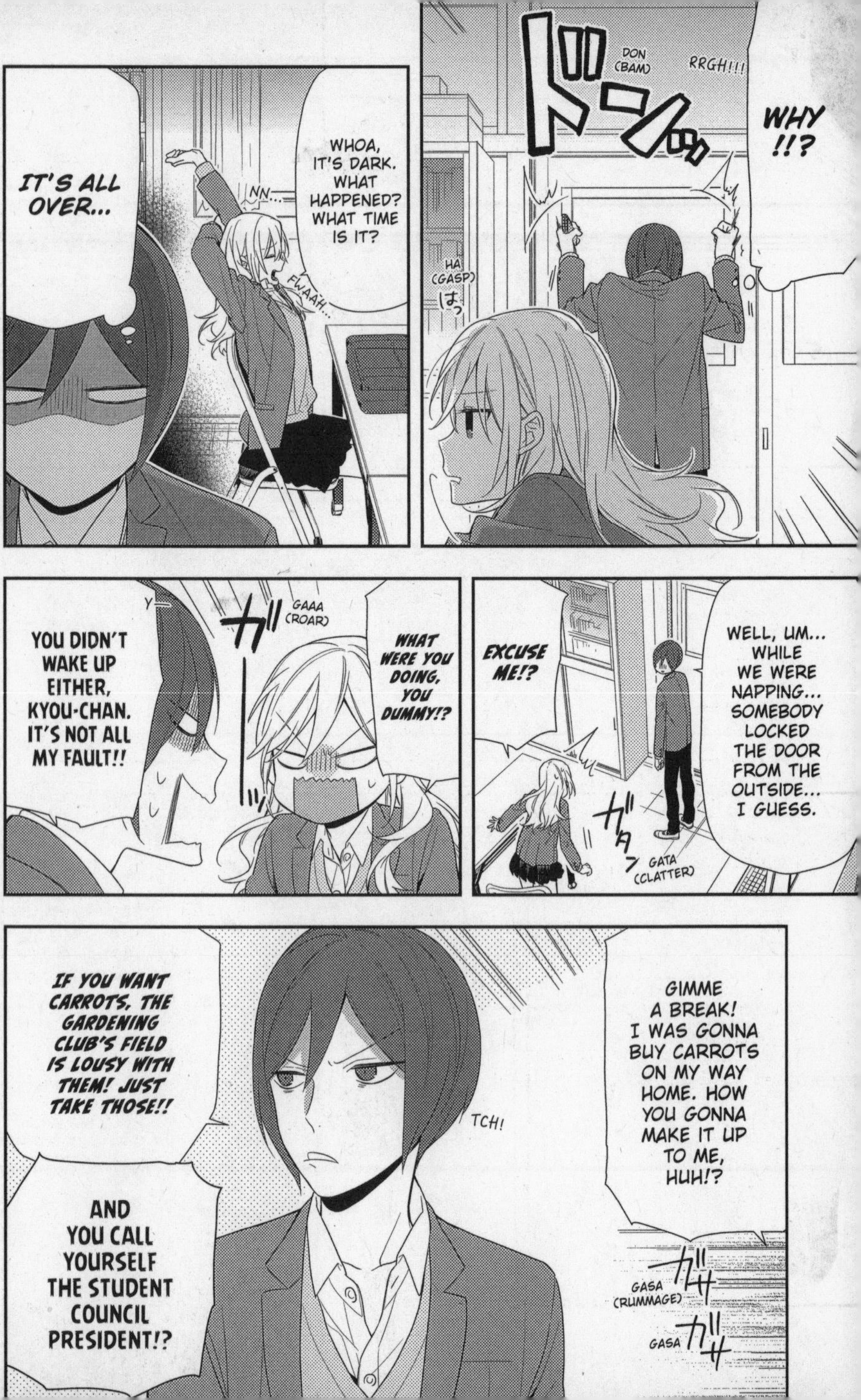
DON (BAM)
RRGH!!!
WHY!!?
HA (GASP)
WHOA, IT'S DARK. WHAT HAPPENED? WHAT TIME IS IT?
NN...
FWAAAH...
IT'S ALL OVER...
WELL, UM... WHILE WE WERE NAPPING... SOMEBODY LOCKED THE DOOR FROM THE OUTSIDE... I GUESS.
EXCUSE ME!?
GATA (CLATTER)
WHAT WERE YOU DOING, YOU DUMMY!?
GAAA (ROAR)
Y—
YOU DIDN'T WAKE UP EITHER, KYOU-CHAN. IT'S NOT ALL MY FAULT!!
GIMME A BREAK! I WAS GONNA BUY CARROTS ON MY WAY HOME. HOW YOU GONNA MAKE IT UP TO ME, HUH!?
TCH!
IF YOU WANT CARROTS, THE GARDENING CLUB'S FIELD IS LOUSY WITH THEM! JUST TAKE THOSE!!
AND YOU CALL YOURSELF THE STUDENT COUNCIL PRESIDENT!?
GASA (RUMMAGE)
GASA

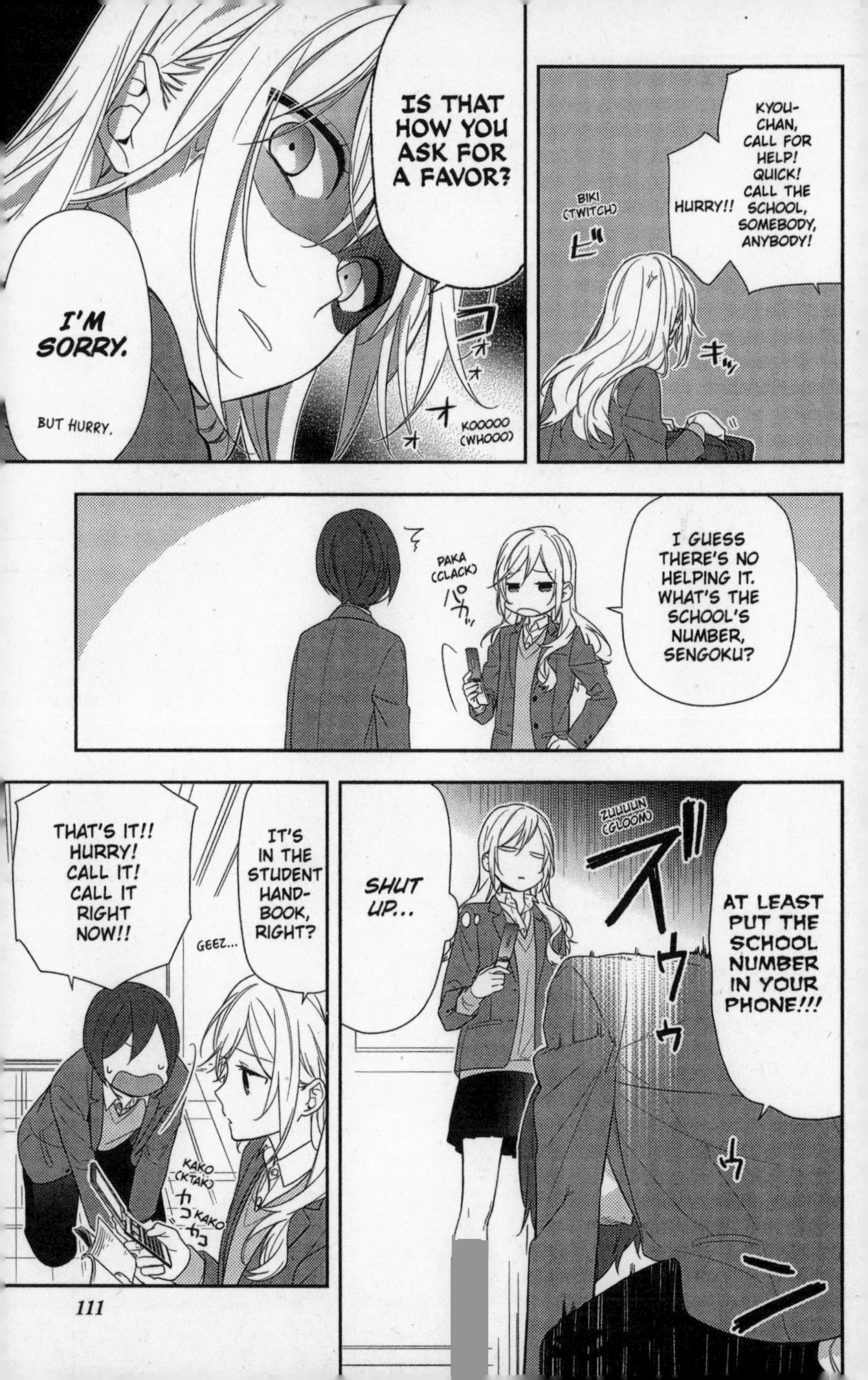

KYOU-CHAN, CALL FOR HELP! QUICK! CALL THE SCHOOL, SOMEBODY, ANYBODY!
HURRY!!
BIKI (TWITCH)
IS THAT HOW YOU ASK FOR A FAVOR?
KOOOOO (WHOOO)
I'M SORRY.
BUT HURRY.
I GUESS THERE'S NO HELPING IT. WHAT'S THE SCHOOL'S NUMBER, SENGOKU?
PAKA (CLACK)
AT LEAST PUT THE SCHOOL NUMBER IN YOUR PHONE!!!
ZUUUUUN (GLOOM)
SHUT UP...
IT'S IN THE STUDENT HAND-BOOK, RIGHT?
THAT'S IT!! HURRY! CALL IT! CALL IT RIGHT NOW!!
GEEZ...
KAKO (KTAK)
KAKO

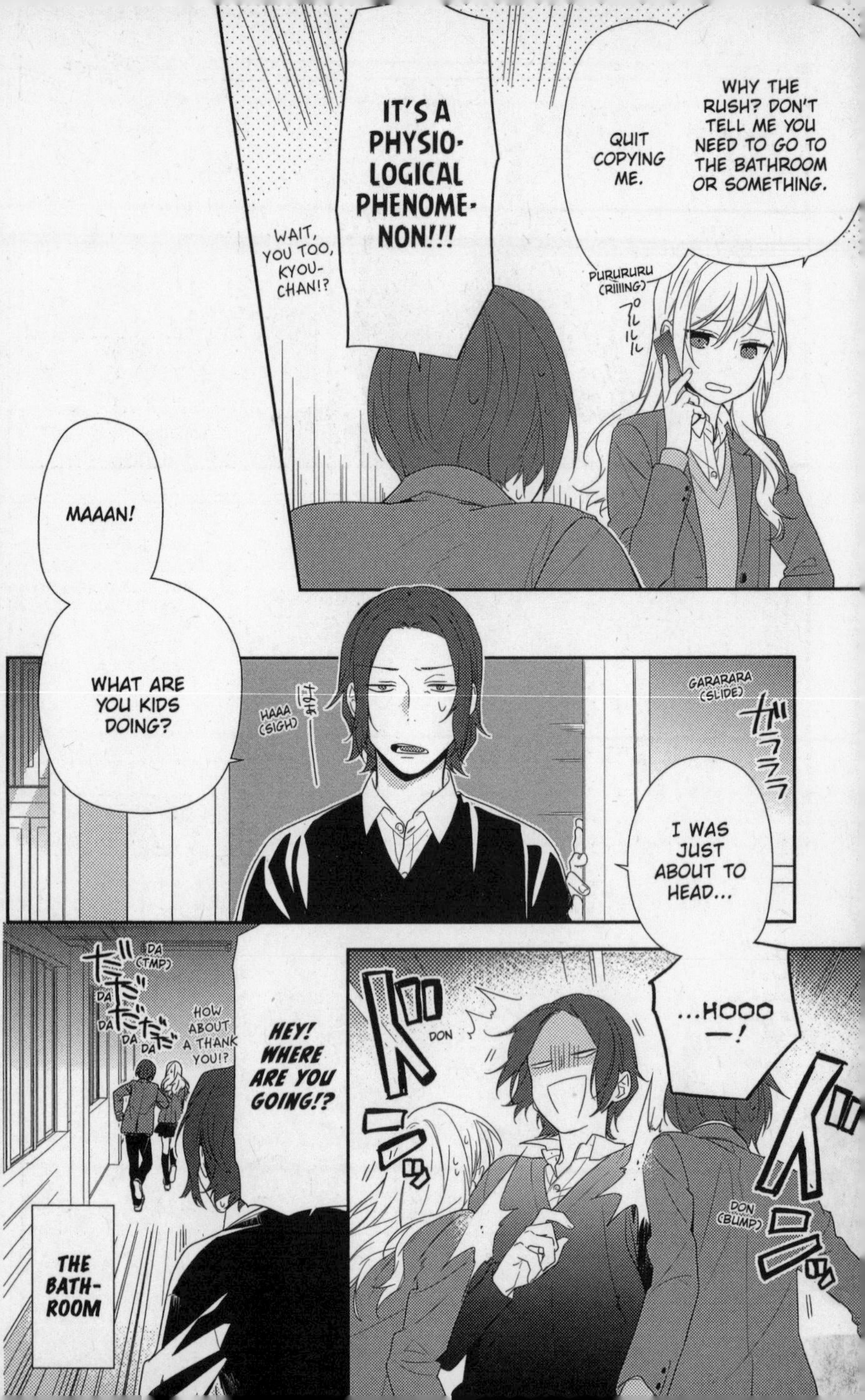
WHY THE RUSH? DON'T TELL ME YOU NEED TO GO TO THE BATHROOM OR SOMETHING.
QUIT COPYING ME.
PURURURU (RIIIING)
プルルル
IT'S A PHYSIO-LOGICAL PHENOME-NON!!!
WAIT, YOU TOO, KYOU-CHAN!?
GARARARA (SLIDE)
ガラララ
I WAS JUST ABOUT TO HEAD...
HAAA (SIGH)
はぁー
MAAAN!
WHAT ARE YOU KIDS DOING?
...HOOO—!
DON (BUMP)
DON
HEY! WHERE ARE YOU GOING!?
HOW ABOUT A THANK YOU!?
DA (TMP) DA DA DA DA
だだだだだ
THE BATH-ROOM

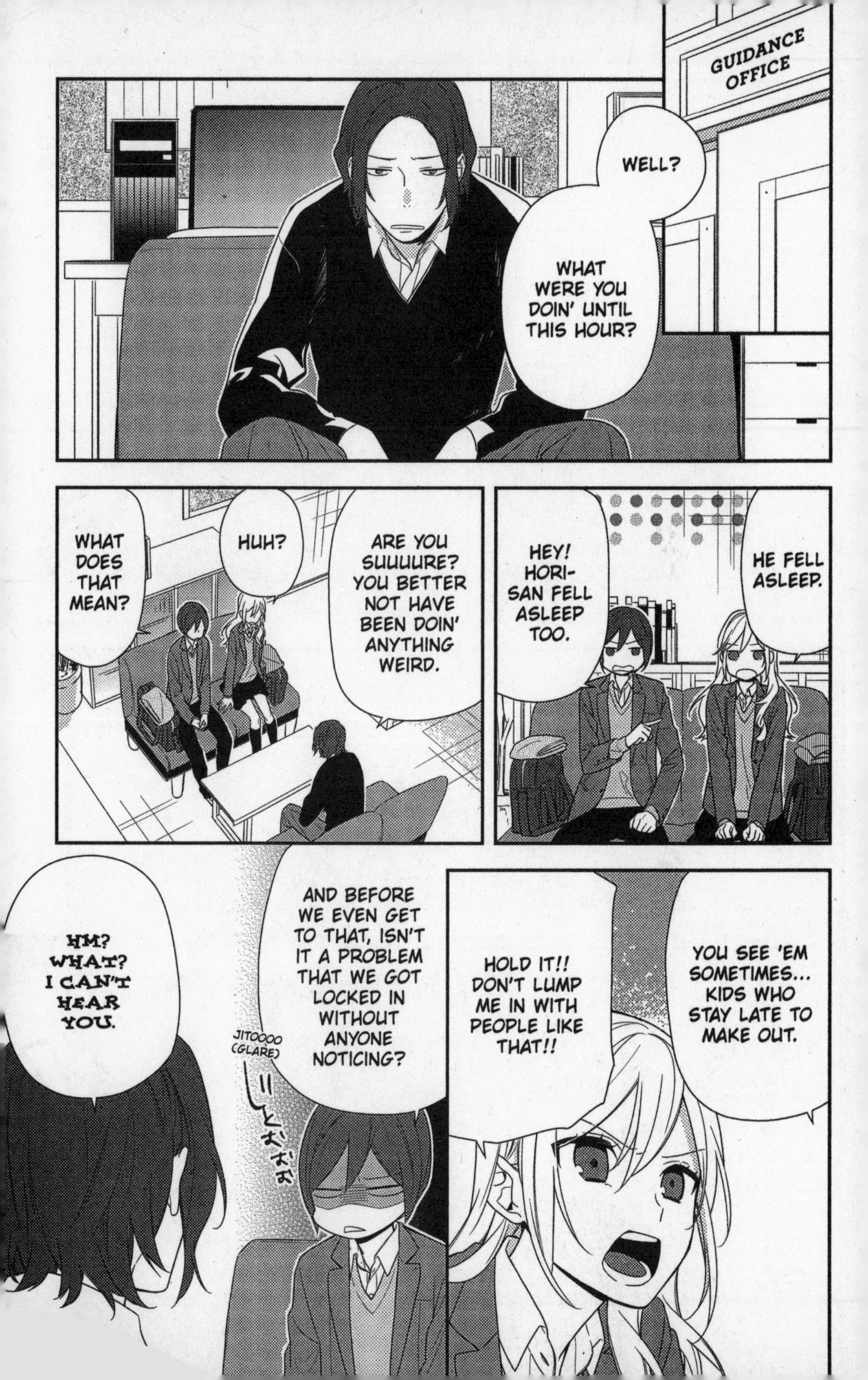
GUIDANCE OFFICE
WELL?
WHAT WERE YOU DOIN' UNTIL THIS HOUR?
HE FELL ASLEEP.
HEY! HORI-SAN FELL ASLEEP TOO.
ARE YOU SUUUURE? YOU BETTER NOT HAVE BEEN DOIN' ANYTHING WEIRD.
HUH?
WHAT DOES THAT MEAN?
YOU SEE 'EM SOMETIMES... KIDS WHO STAY LATE TO MAKE OUT.
HOLD IT!! DON'T LUMP ME IN WITH PEOPLE LIKE THAT!!
AND BEFORE WE EVEN GET TO THAT, ISN'T IT A PROBLEM THAT WE GOT LOCKED IN WITHOUT ANYONE NOTICING?
JITOOOO (GLARE)
HM? WHAT? I CAN'T HEAR YOU.

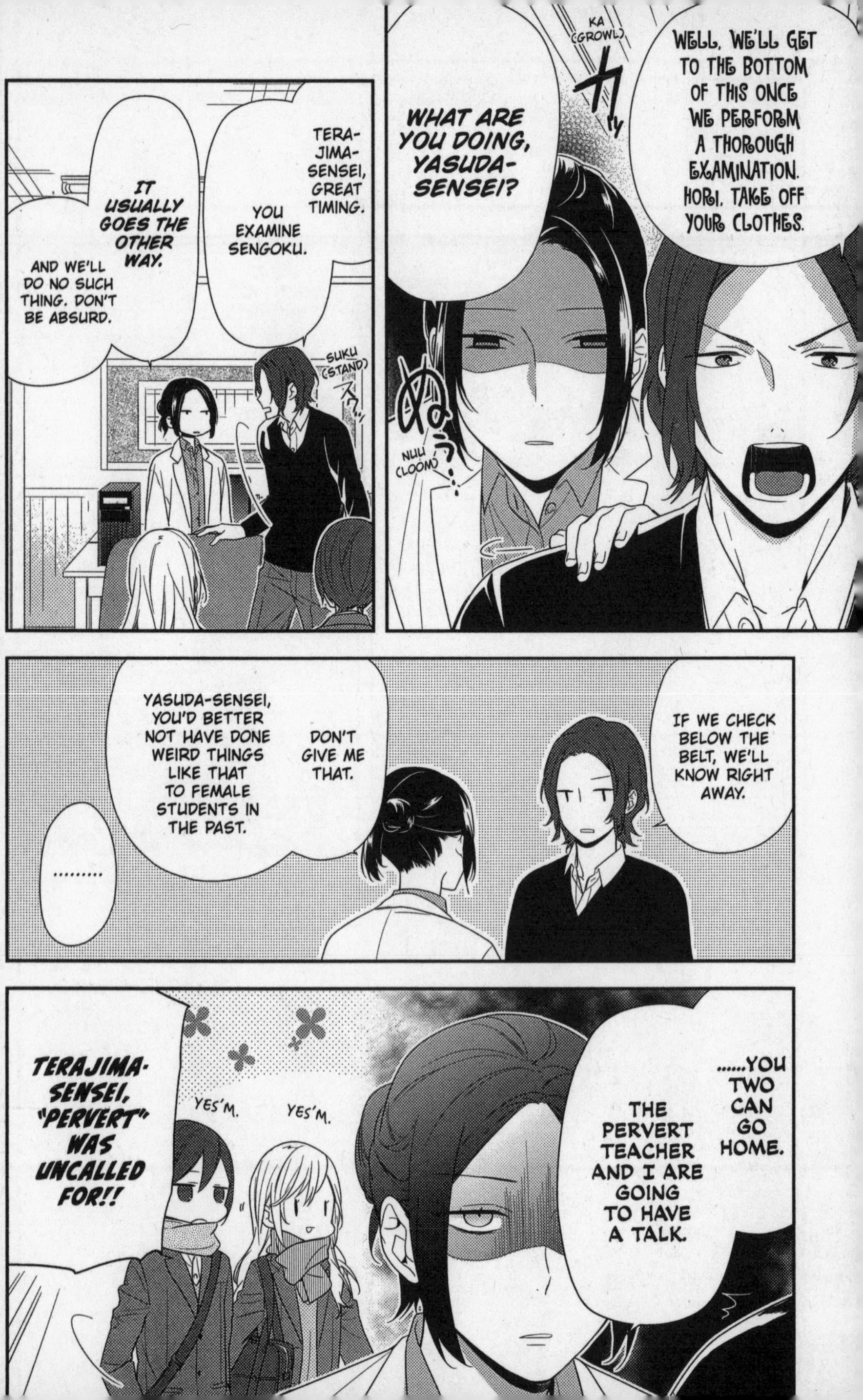
WELL, WE'LL GET TO THE BOTTOM OF THIS ONCE WE PERFORM A THOROUGH EXAMINATION. HORI, TAKE OFF YOUR CLOTHES.
KA (GROWL)
WHAT ARE YOU DOING, YASUDA-SENSEI?
NUU (LOOM)
TERAJIMA-SENSEI, GREAT TIMING.
YOU EXAMINE SENGOKU.
SUKU (STAND)
IT USUALLY GOES THE OTHER WAY.
AND WE'LL DO NO SUCH THING. DON'T BE ABSURD.
IF WE CHECK BELOW THE BELT, WE'LL KNOW RIGHT AWAY.
DON'T GIVE ME THAT.
YASUDA-SENSEI, YOU'D BETTER NOT HAVE DONE WEIRD THINGS LIKE THAT TO FEMALE STUDENTS IN THE PAST.
....
......YOU TWO CAN GO HOME.
THE PERVERT TEACHER AND I ARE GOING TO HAVE A TALK.
YES'M.
YES'M.
TERAJIMA-SENSEI, "PERVERT" WAS UNCALLED FOR!!

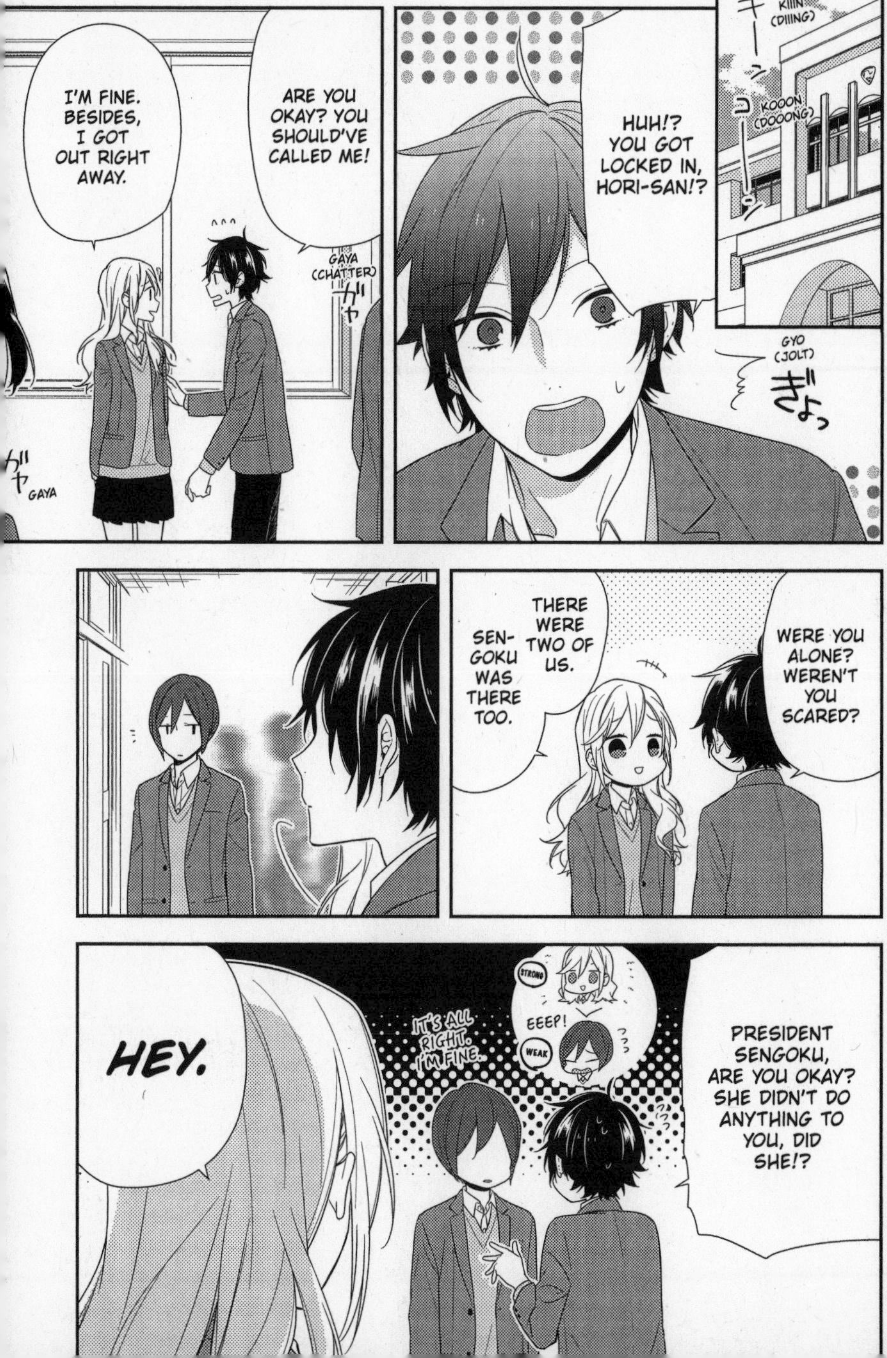
KIIIN (DIIING)
KOOON (DOOONG)
GYO (JOLT)
HUH!? YOU GOT LOCKED IN, HORI-SAN!?
ARE YOU OKAY? YOU SHOULD'VE CALLED ME!
I'M FINE. BESIDES, I GOT OUT RIGHT AWAY.
GAYA (CHATTER)
GAYA
WERE YOU ALONE? WEREN'T YOU SCARED?
THERE WERE TWO OF US.
SEN-GOKU WAS THERE TOO.
PRESIDENT SENGOKU, ARE YOU OKAY? SHE DIDN'T DO ANYTHING TO YOU, DID SHE!?
STRONG
EEEP!
WEAK
IT'S ALL RIGHT. I'M FINE.
HEY.

HORIMIYA

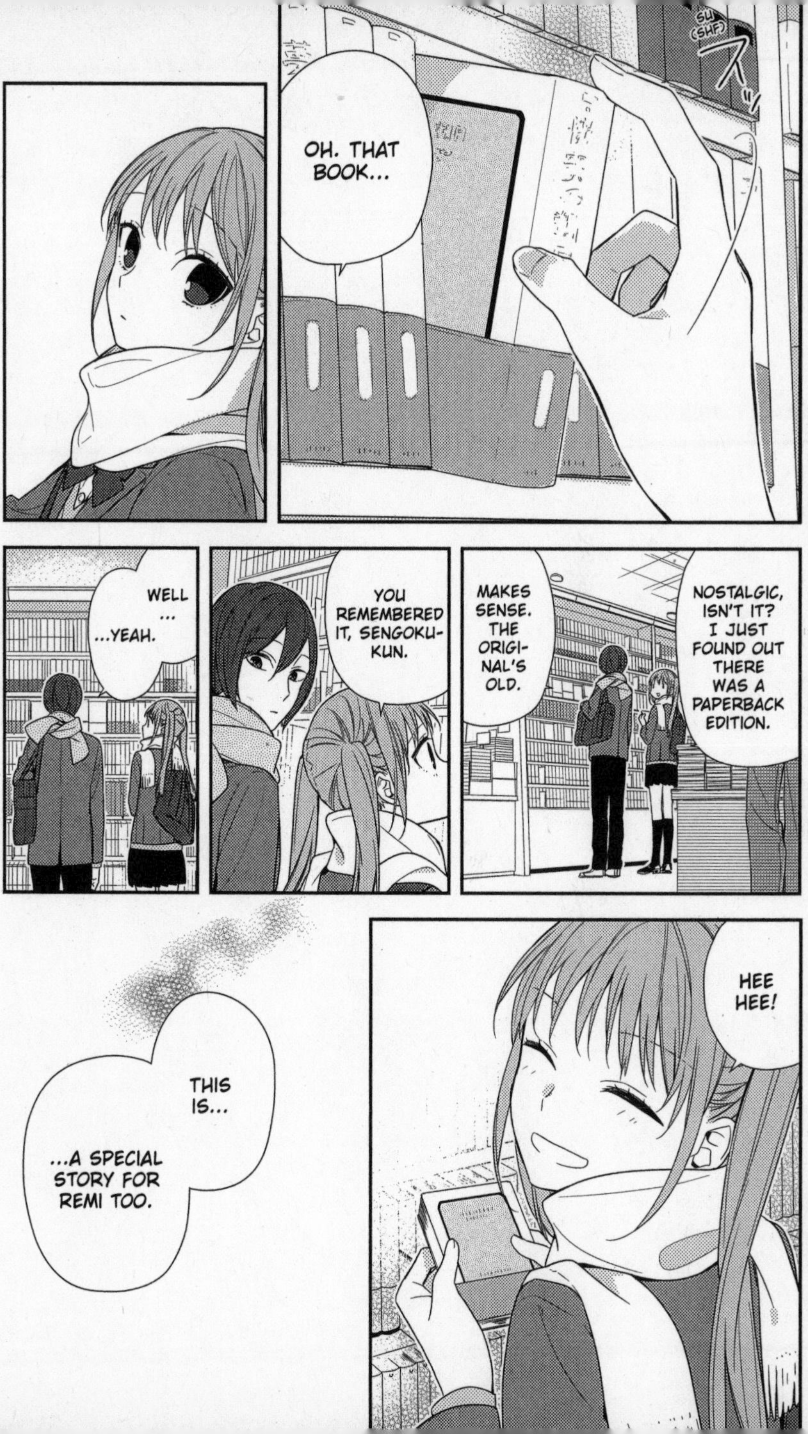
SU (SHF)
スッ
OH. THAT BOOK...
NOSTALGIC, ISN'T IT? I JUST FOUND OUT THERE WAS A PAPERBACK EDITION.
MAKES SENSE. THE ORIGINAL'S OLD.
YOU REMEMBERED IT, SENGOKU-KUN.
WELL ...
...YEAH.
HEE HEE!
THIS IS...
...A SPECIAL STORY FOR REMI TOO.

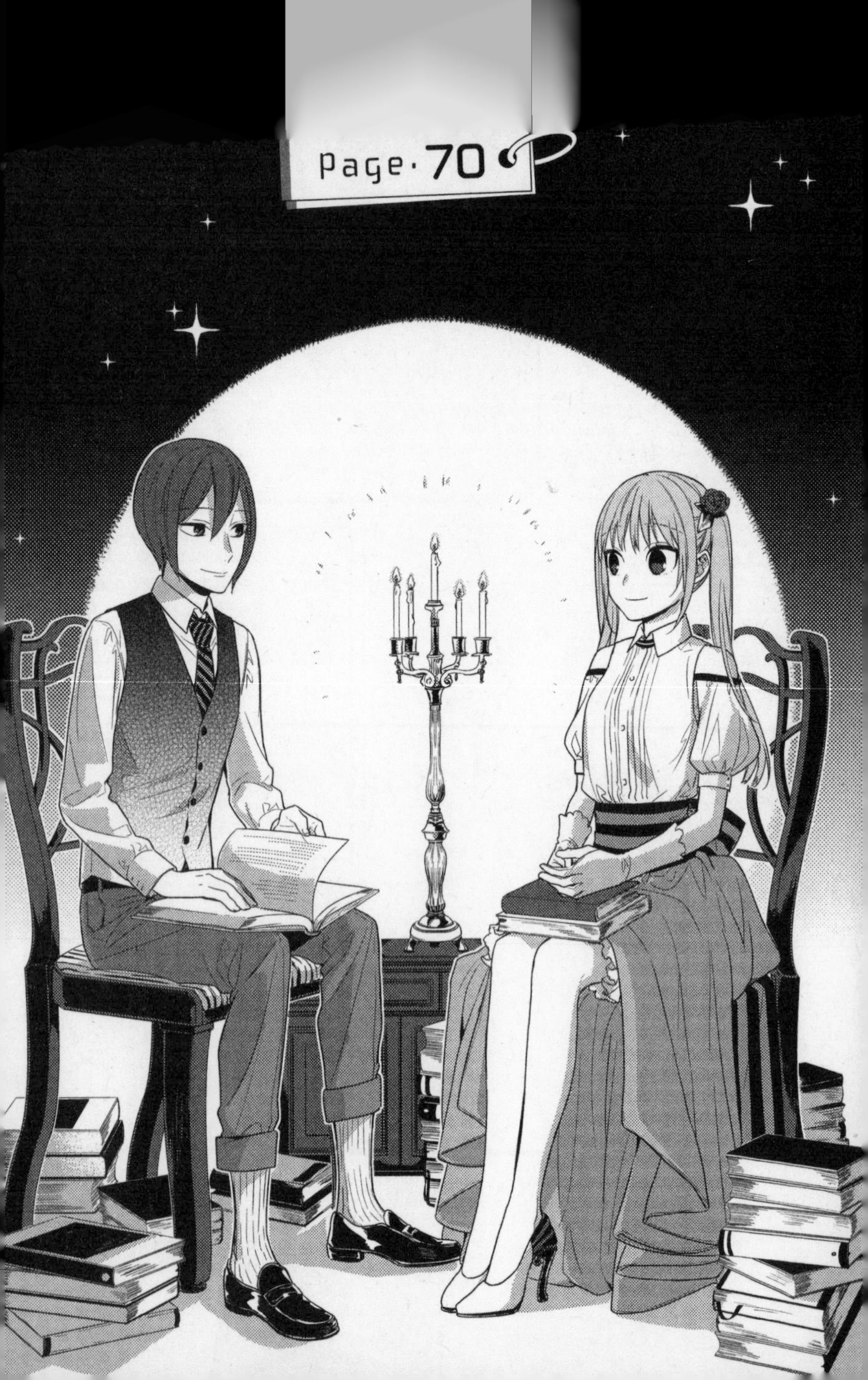
Page·70

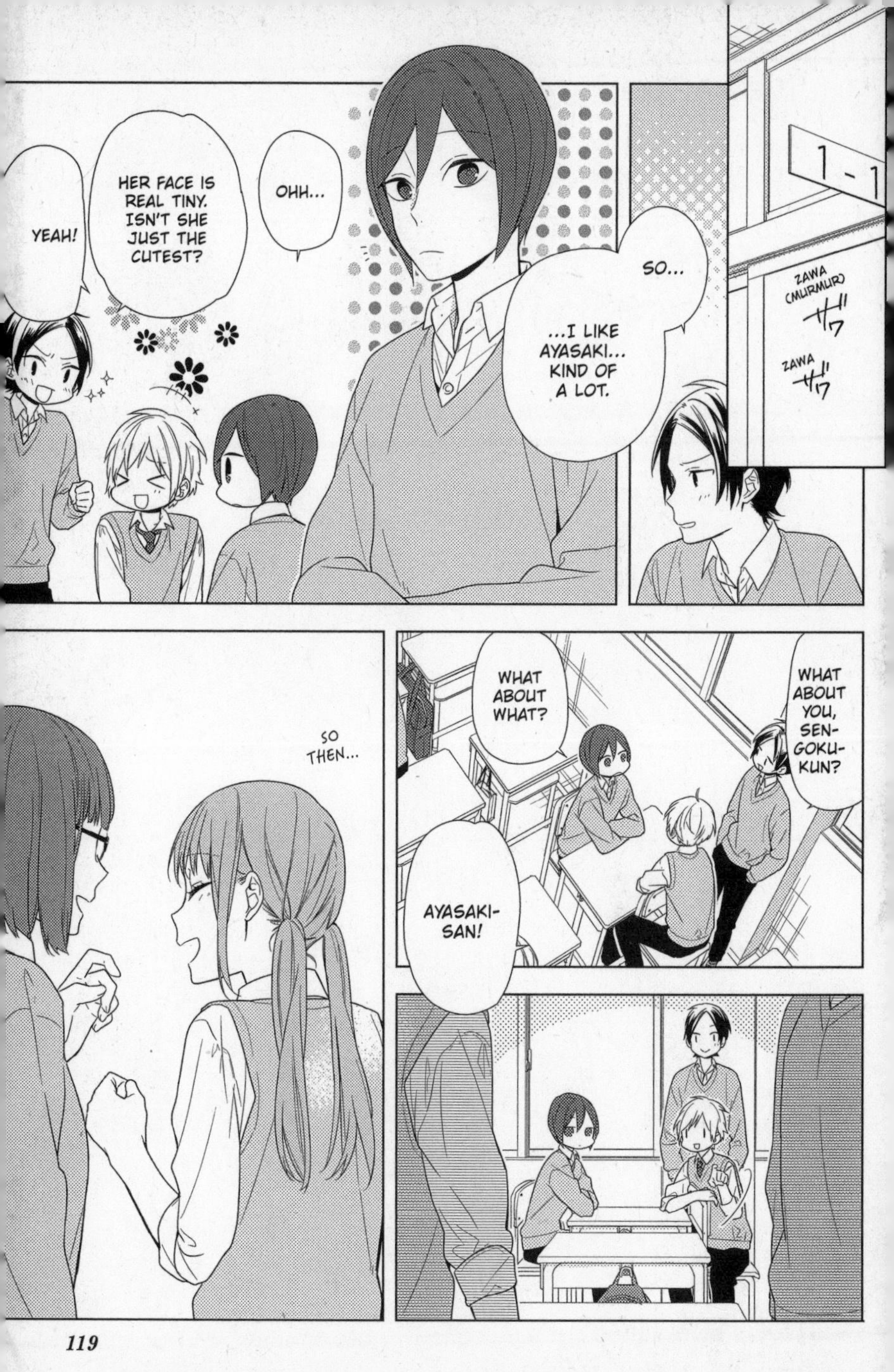
ZAWA (MURMUR)
ZAWA
SO...
...I LIKE AYASAKI... KIND OF A LOT.
OHH...
HER FACE IS REAL TINY. ISN'T SHE JUST THE CUTEST?
YEAH!
WHAT ABOUT YOU, SEN-GOKU-KUN?
WHAT ABOUT WHAT?
AYASAKI-SAN!
SO THEN...

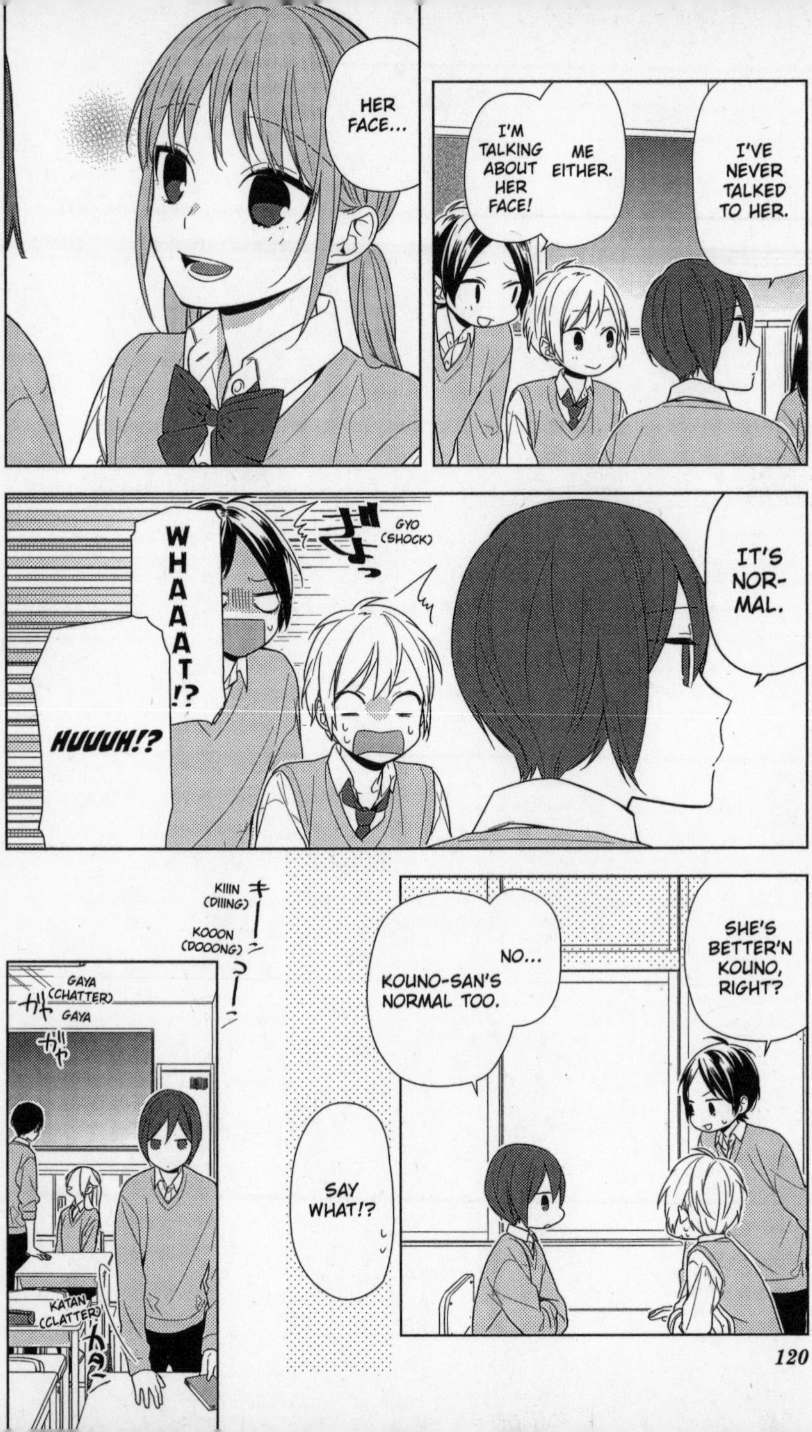
I'VE NEVER TALKED TO HER.
ME EITHER.
I'M TALKING ABOUT HER FACE!
HER FACE...
IT'S NOR-MAL.
GYO (SHOCK)
WHAAAAT!?
HUUUH!?
SHE'S BETTER'N KOUNO, RIGHT?
NO... KOUNO-SAN'S NORMAL TOO.
SAY WHAT!?
KIIIN (DIIING)
KOOON (DOOONG)
GAYA (CHATTER) GAYA
KATAN (CLATTER)

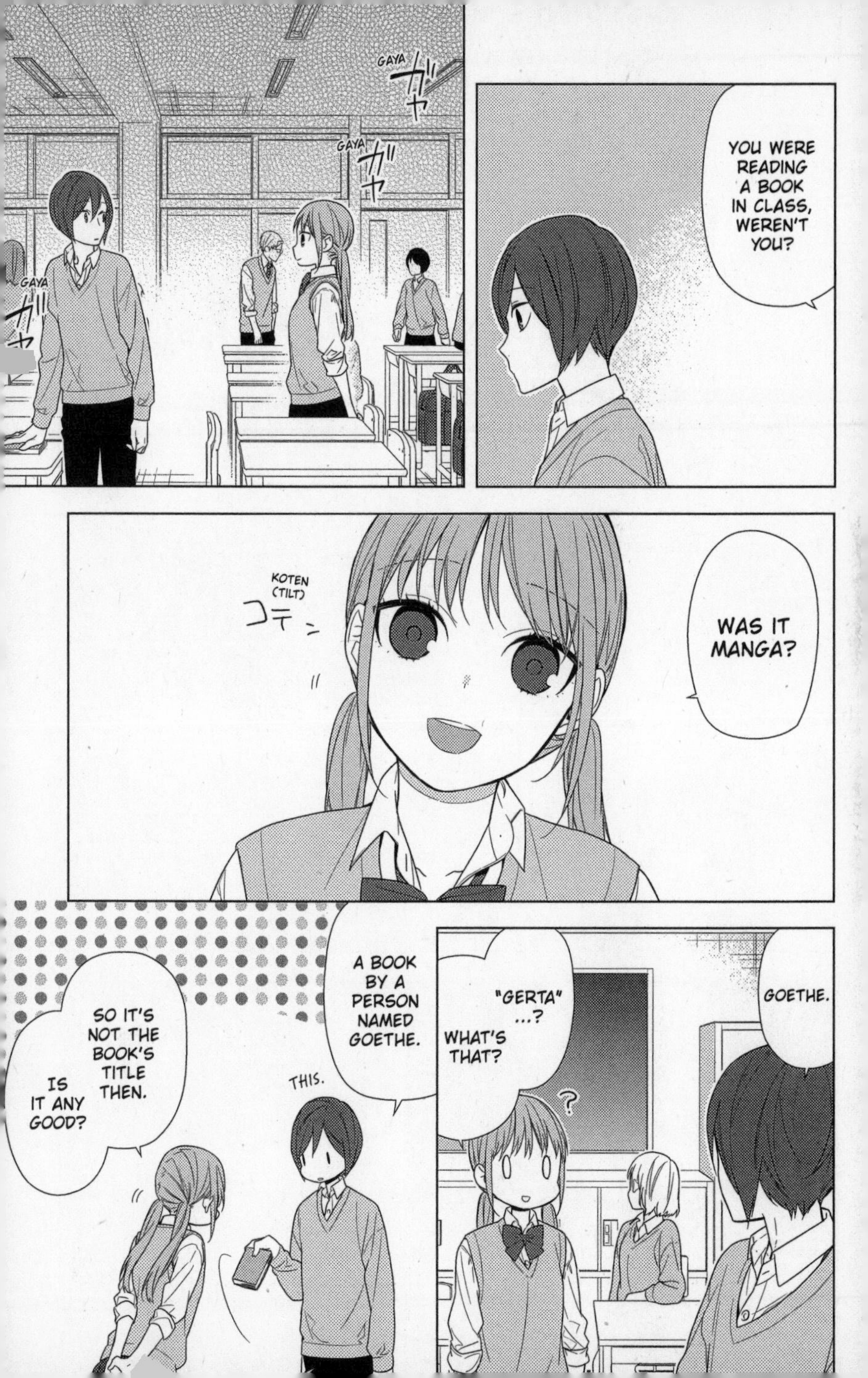
YOU WERE READING A BOOK IN CLASS, WEREN'T YOU?
GAYA
ガヤ
GAYA
ガヤ
GAYA
WAS IT MANGA?
KOTEN (TILT)
コテ
GOETHE.
"GERTA" ...?
WHAT'S THAT?
A BOOK BY A PERSON NAMED GOETHE.
THIS.
SO IT'S NOT THE BOOK'S TITLE THEN.
IS IT ANY GOOD?

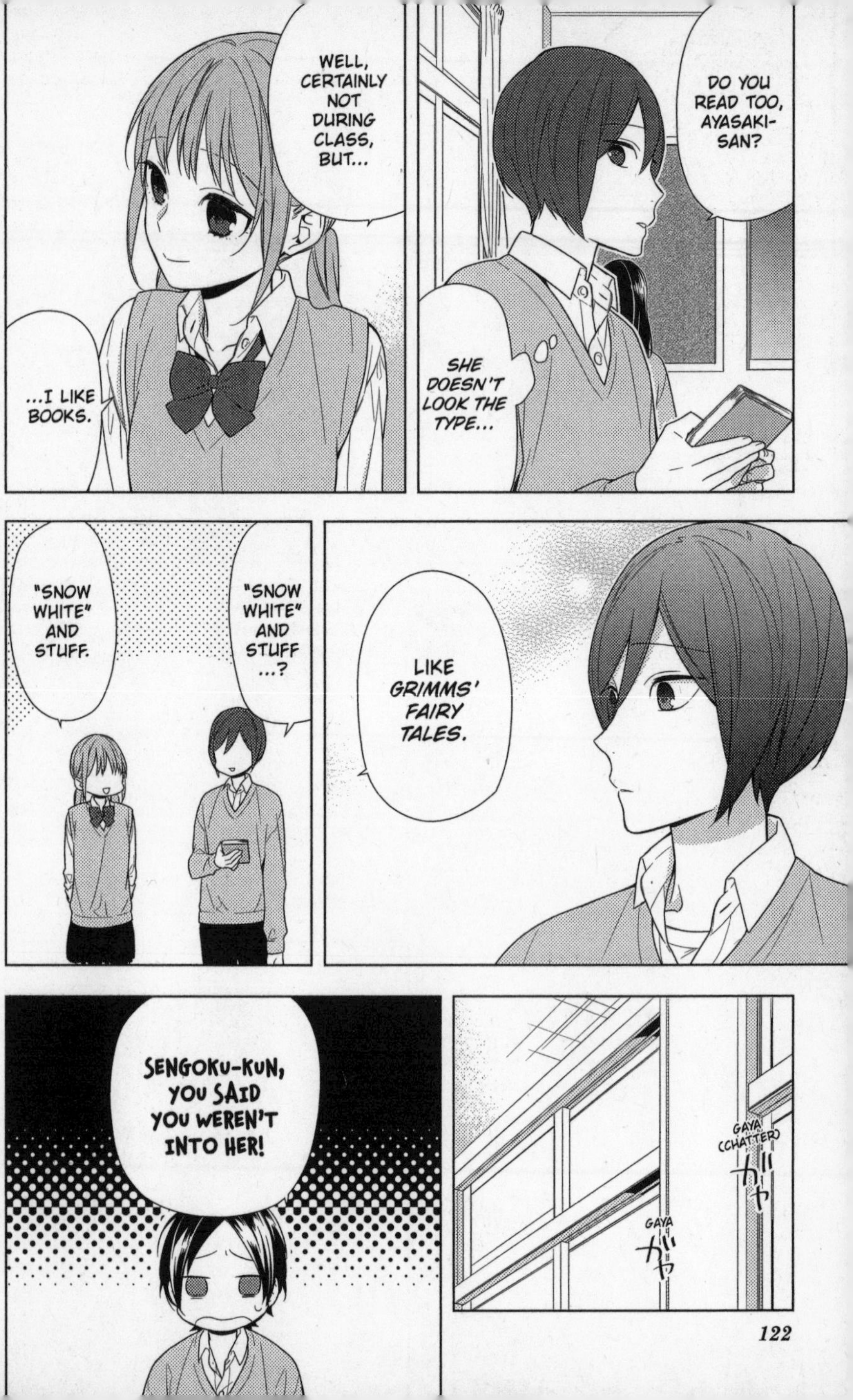
DO YOU READ TOO, AYASAKI-SAN?
SHE DOESN'T LOOK THE TYPE...
WELL, CERTAINLY NOT DURING CLASS, BUT...
...I LIKE BOOKS.
LIKE GRIMMS' FAIRY TALES.
"SNOW WHITE" AND STUFF ...?
"SNOW WHITE" AND STUFF.
GAYA (CHATTER)
ガヤ
GAYA
ガヤ
SENGOKU-KUN, YOU SAID YOU WEREN'T INTO HER!

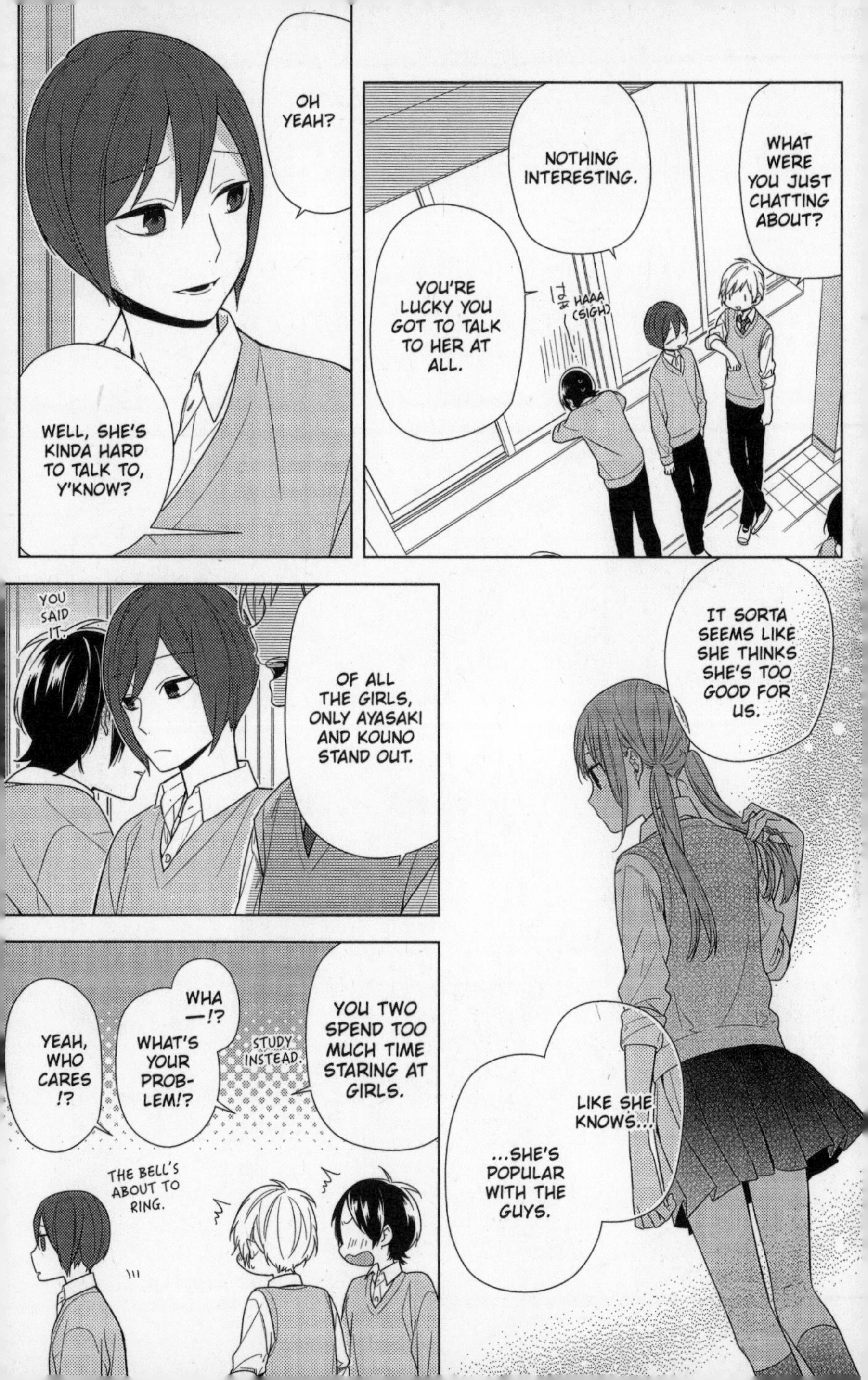
WHAT WERE YOU JUST CHATTING ABOUT?
NOTHING INTERESTING.
はぁ HAAA (SIGH)
YOU'RE LUCKY YOU GOT TO TALK TO HER AT ALL.
OH YEAH?
WELL, SHE'S KINDA HARD TO TALK TO, Y'KNOW?
IT SORTA SEEMS LIKE SHE THINKS SHE'S TOO GOOD FOR US.
LIKE SHE KNOWS...!
...SHE'S POPULAR WITH THE GUYS.
OF ALL THE GIRLS, ONLY AYASAKI AND KOUNO STAND OUT.
YOU SAID IT.
YOU TWO SPEND TOO MUCH TIME STARING AT GIRLS.
STUDY INSTEAD.
WHA—!?
WHAT'S YOUR PROBLEM!?
YEAH, WHO CARES!?
THE BELL'S ABOUT TO RING.

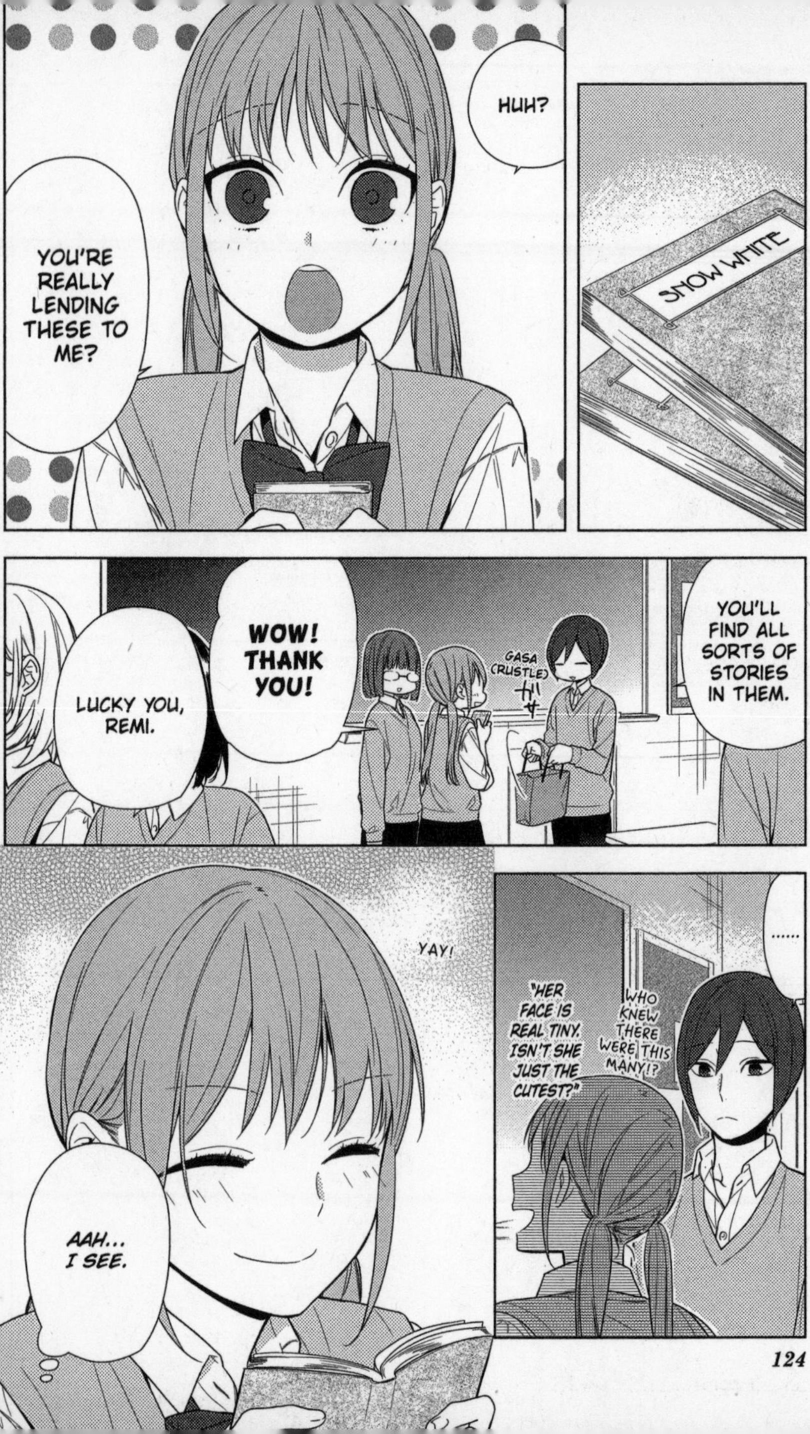
SNOW WHITE
HUH?
YOU'RE REALLY LENDING THESE TO ME?
YOU'LL FIND ALL SORTS OF STORIES IN THEM.
GASA (RUSTLE)
WOW! THANK YOU!
LUCKY YOU, REMI.
......
WHO KNEW THERE WERE THIS MANY!?
"HER FACE IS REAL TINY. ISN'T SHE JUST THE CUTEST?"
YAY!
AAH... I SEE.

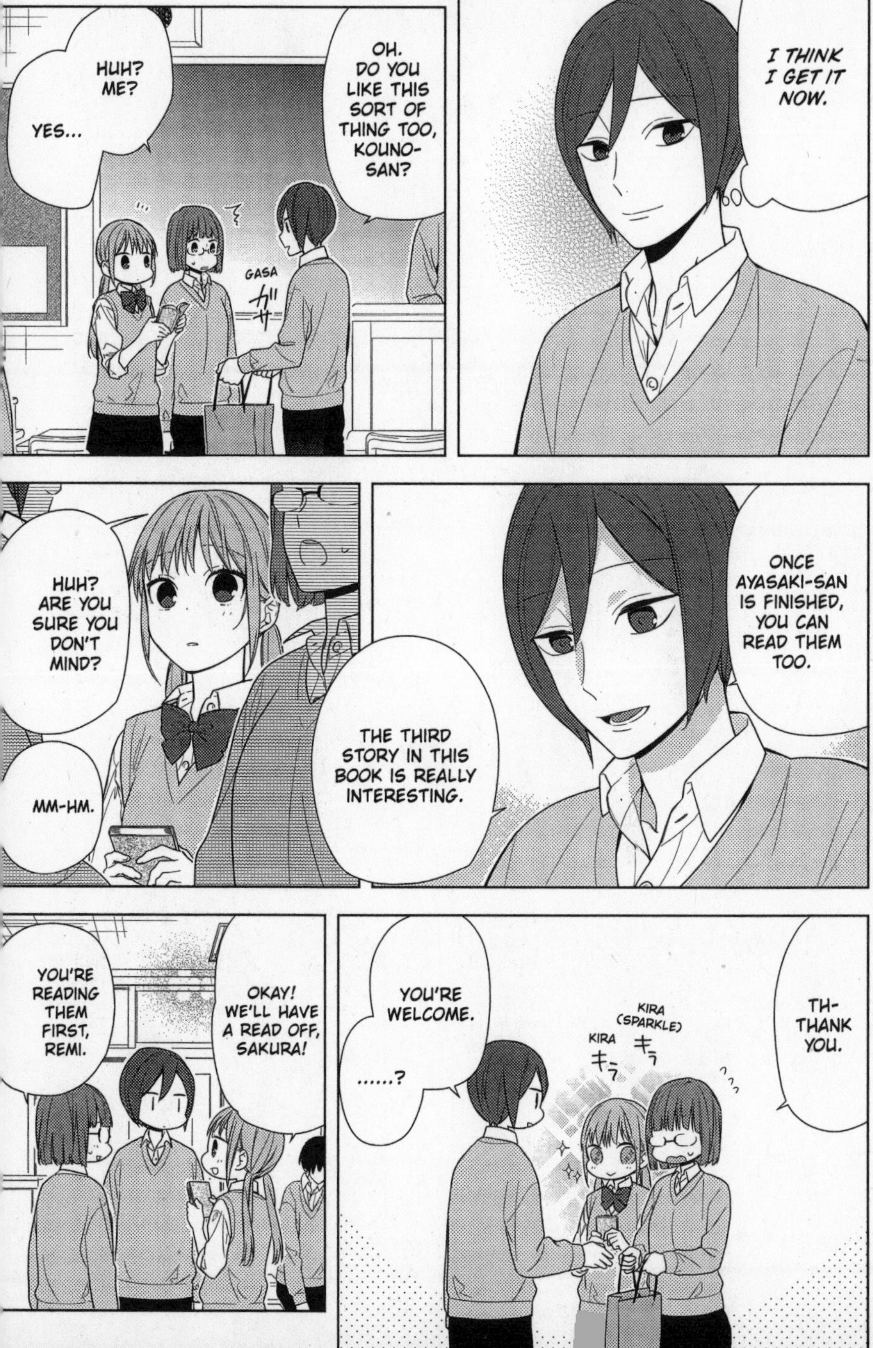
I THINK I GET IT NOW.
OH. DO YOU LIKE THIS SORT OF THING TOO, KOUNO-SAN?
GASA
HUH? ME?
YES...
ONCE AYASAKI-SAN IS FINISHED, YOU CAN READ THEM TOO.
THE THIRD STORY IN THIS BOOK IS REALLY INTERESTING.
HUH? ARE YOU SURE YOU DON'T MIND?
MM-HM.
TH-THANK YOU.
KIRA (SPARKLE)
KIRA
YOU'RE WELCOME.
......?
OKAY! WE'LL HAVE A READ OFF, SAKURA!
YOU'RE READING THEM FIRST, REMI.

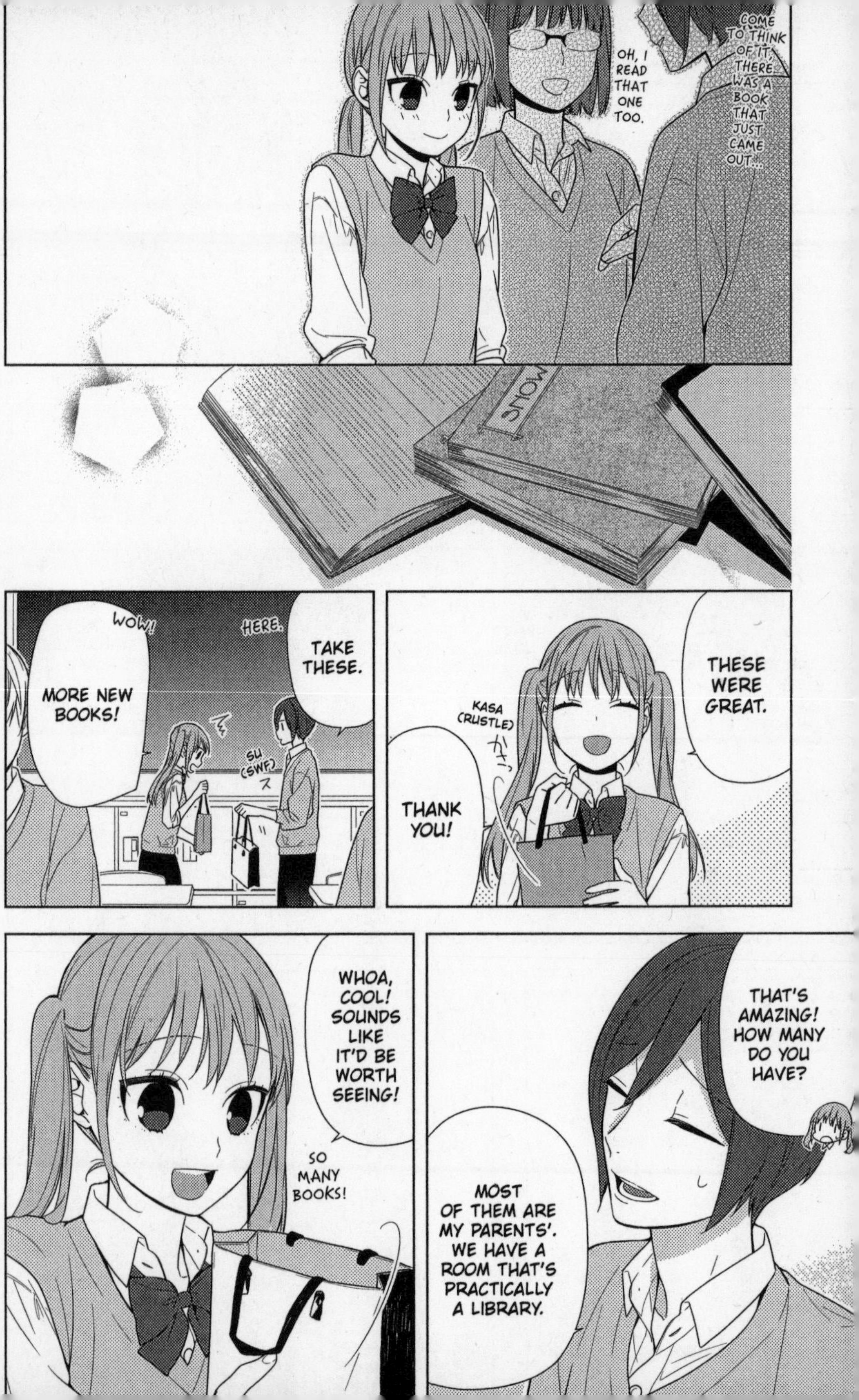
COME TO THINK OF IT, THERE WAS A BOOK THAT JUST CAME OUT...
OH, I READ THAT ONE TOO.
THESE WERE GREAT.
KASA (RUSTLE)
THANK YOU!
TAKE THESE.
HERE.
SU (SWF)
WOW!
MORE NEW BOOKS!
THAT'S AMAZING! HOW MANY DO YOU HAVE?
MOST OF THEM ARE MY PARENTS'. WE HAVE A ROOM THAT'S PRACTICALLY A LIBRARY.
WHOA, COOL! SOUNDS LIKE IT'D BE WORTH SEEING!
SO MANY BOOKS!

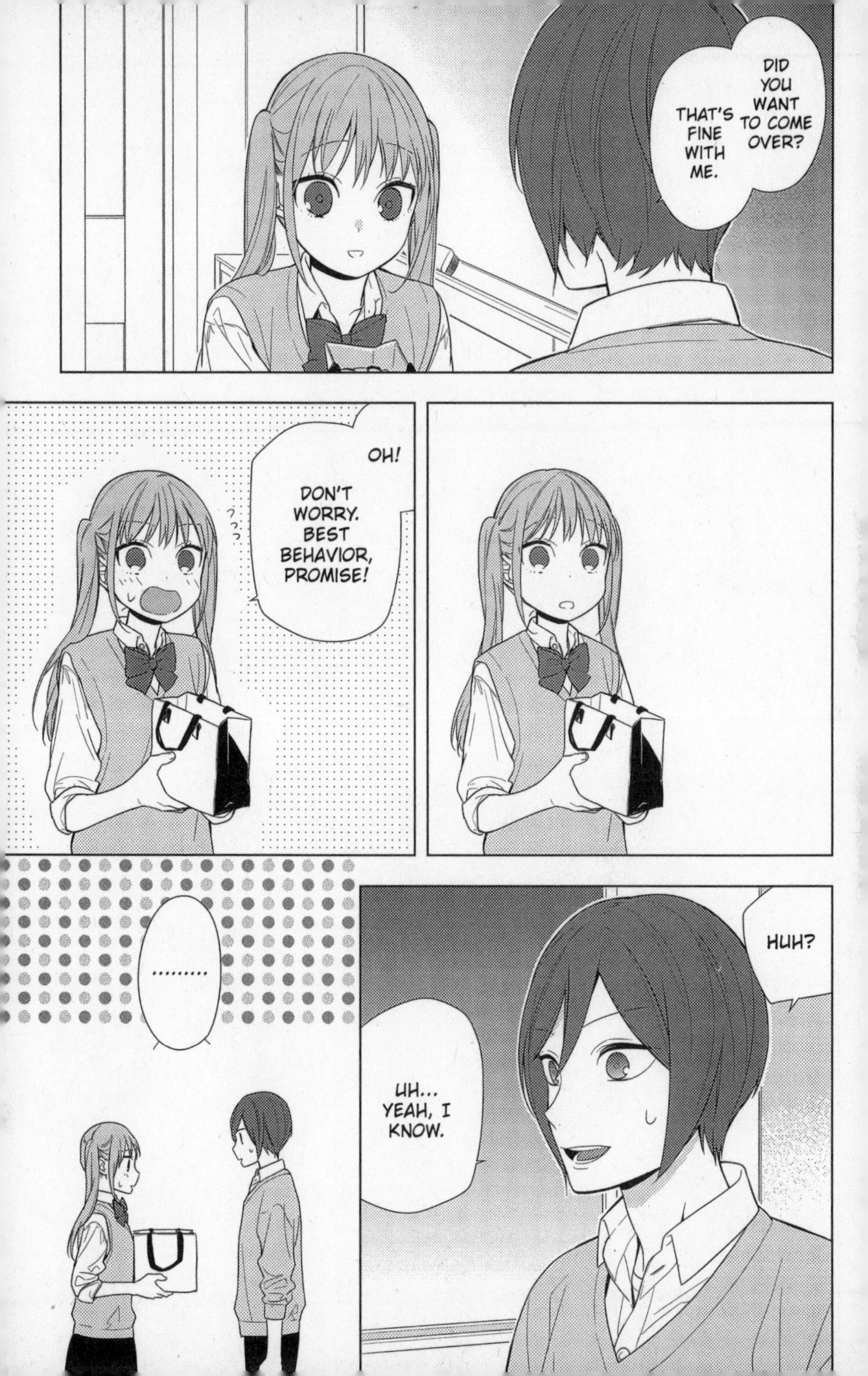
DID YOU WANT TO COME OVER?
THAT'S FINE WITH ME.
OH!
DON'T WORRY. BEST BEHAVIOR, PROMISE!
HUH?
UH... YEAH, I KNOW.
....

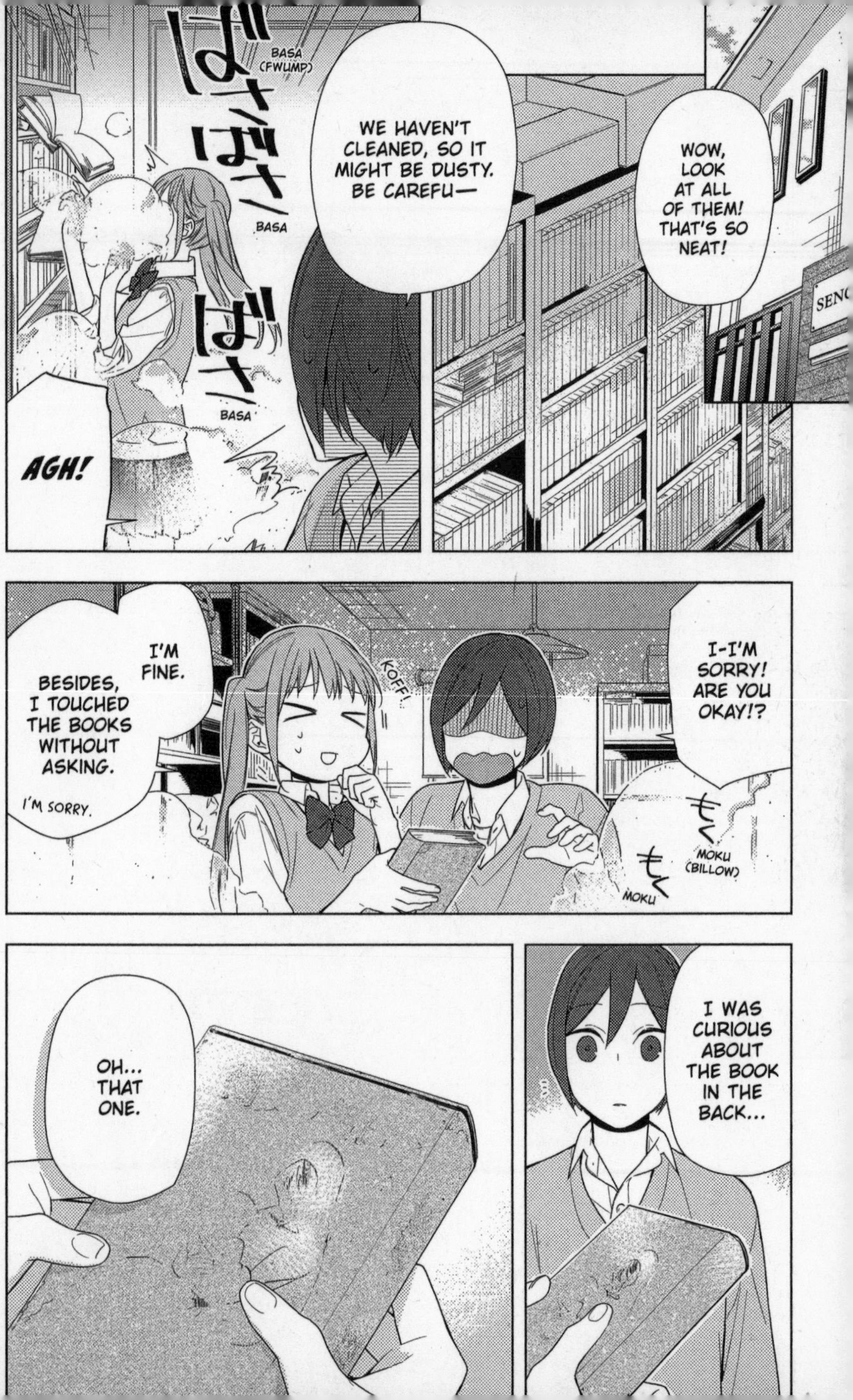

WOW, LOOK AT ALL OF THEM! THAT'S SO NEAT!
SENO
WE HAVEN'T CLEANED, SO IT MIGHT BE DUSTY. BE CAREFU—
ばさ BASA (FWUMP)
ばさ BASA
ばさ BASA
AGH!
I-I'M SORRY! ARE YOU OKAY!?
もく MOKU (BILLOW)
もく MOKU
KOFF!
I'M FINE.
BESIDES, I TOUCHED THE BOOKS WITHOUT ASKING.
I'M SORRY.
I WAS CURIOUS ABOUT THE BOOK IN THE BACK...
OH... THAT ONE.

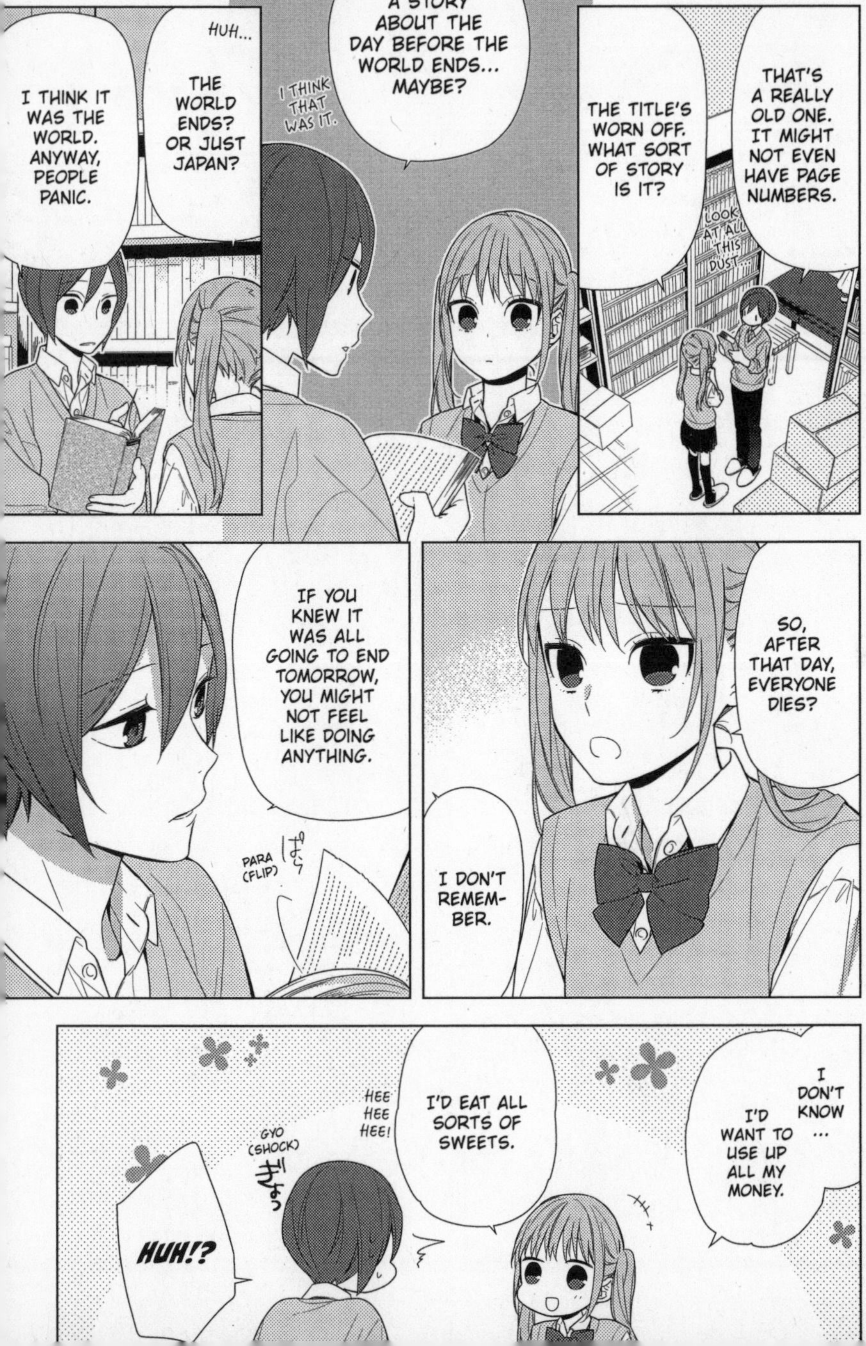
THAT'S A REALLY OLD ONE. IT MIGHT NOT EVEN HAVE PAGE NUMBERS.
LOOK AT ALL THIS DUST...
THE TITLE'S WORN OFF. WHAT SORT OF STORY IS IT?
A STORY ABOUT THE DAY BEFORE THE WORLD ENDS... MAYBE?
I THINK THAT WAS IT.
HUH...
THE WORLD ENDS? OR JUST JAPAN?
I THINK IT WAS THE WORLD. ANYWAY, PEOPLE PANIC.
SO, AFTER THAT DAY, EVERYONE DIES?
I DON'T REMEMBER.
IF YOU KNEW IT WAS ALL GOING TO END TOMORROW, YOU MIGHT NOT FEEL LIKE DOING ANYTHING.
PARA (FLIP)
I DON'T KNOW ...
I'D WANT TO USE UP ALL MY MONEY.
I'D EAT ALL SORTS OF SWEETS.
HEE HEE HEE!
GYO (SHOCK)
HUH!?

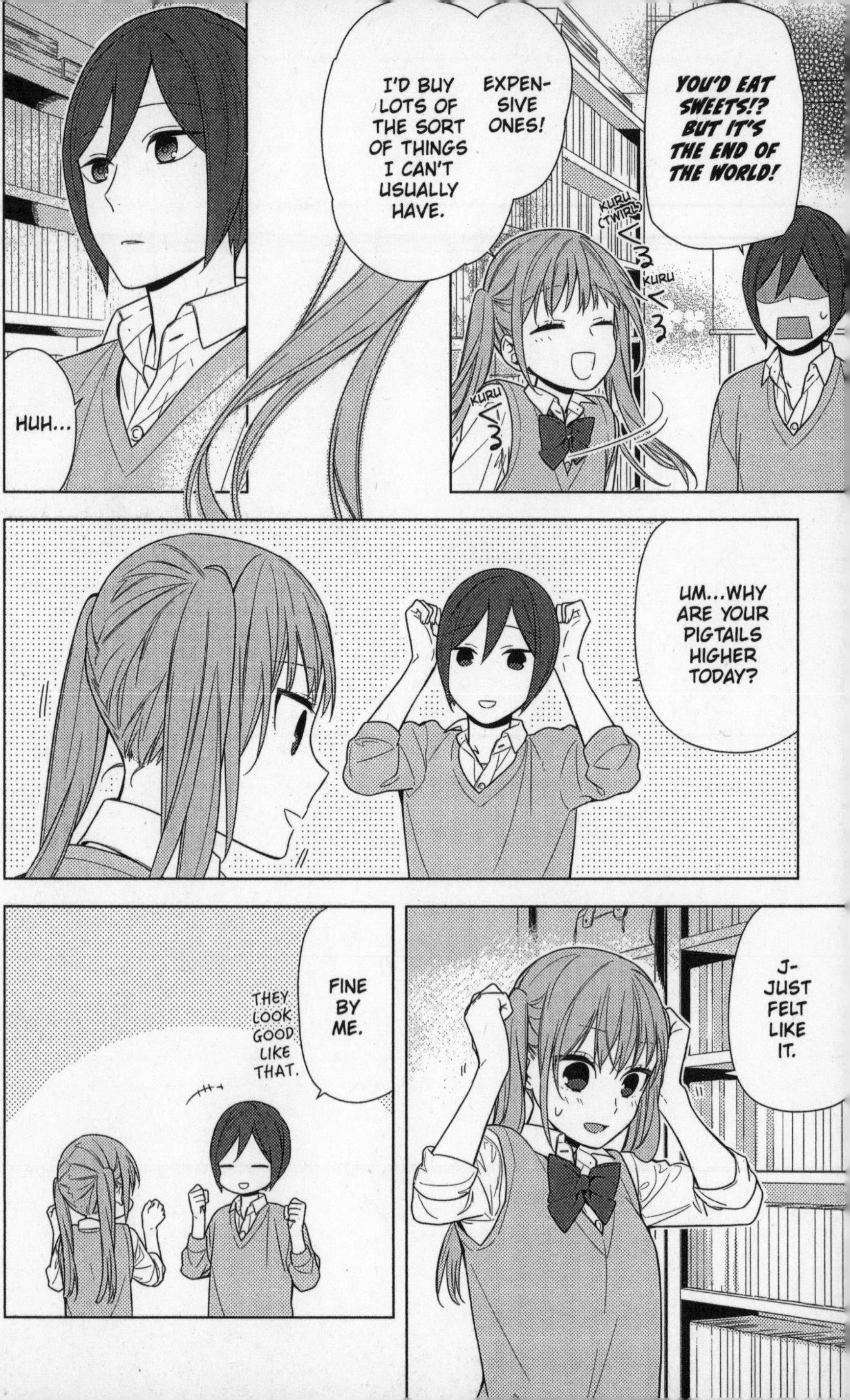
YOU'D EAT SWEETS!? BUT IT'S THE END OF THE WORLD!
KURU (TWIRL)
KURU
KURU
I'D BUY LOTS OF THE SORT OF THINGS I CAN'T USUALLY HAVE. EXPENSIVE ONES!
HUH...
UM...WHY ARE YOUR PIGTAILS HIGHER TODAY?
J-JUST FELT LIKE IT.
FINE BY ME.
THEY LOOK GOOD LIKE THAT.

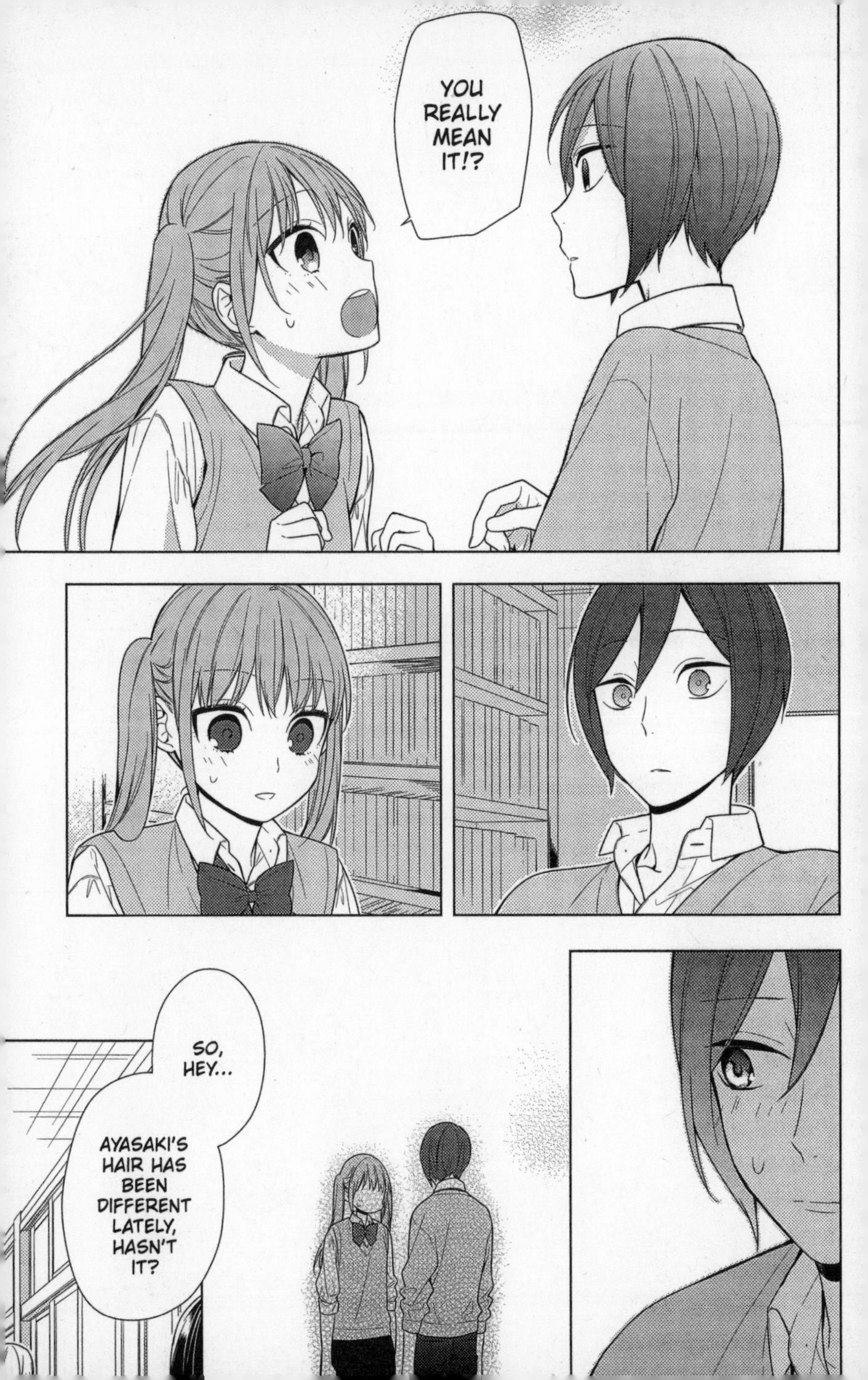
YOU REALLY MEAN IT!?
SO, HEY...
AYASAKI'S HAIR HAS BEEN DIFFERENT LATELY, HASN'T IT?

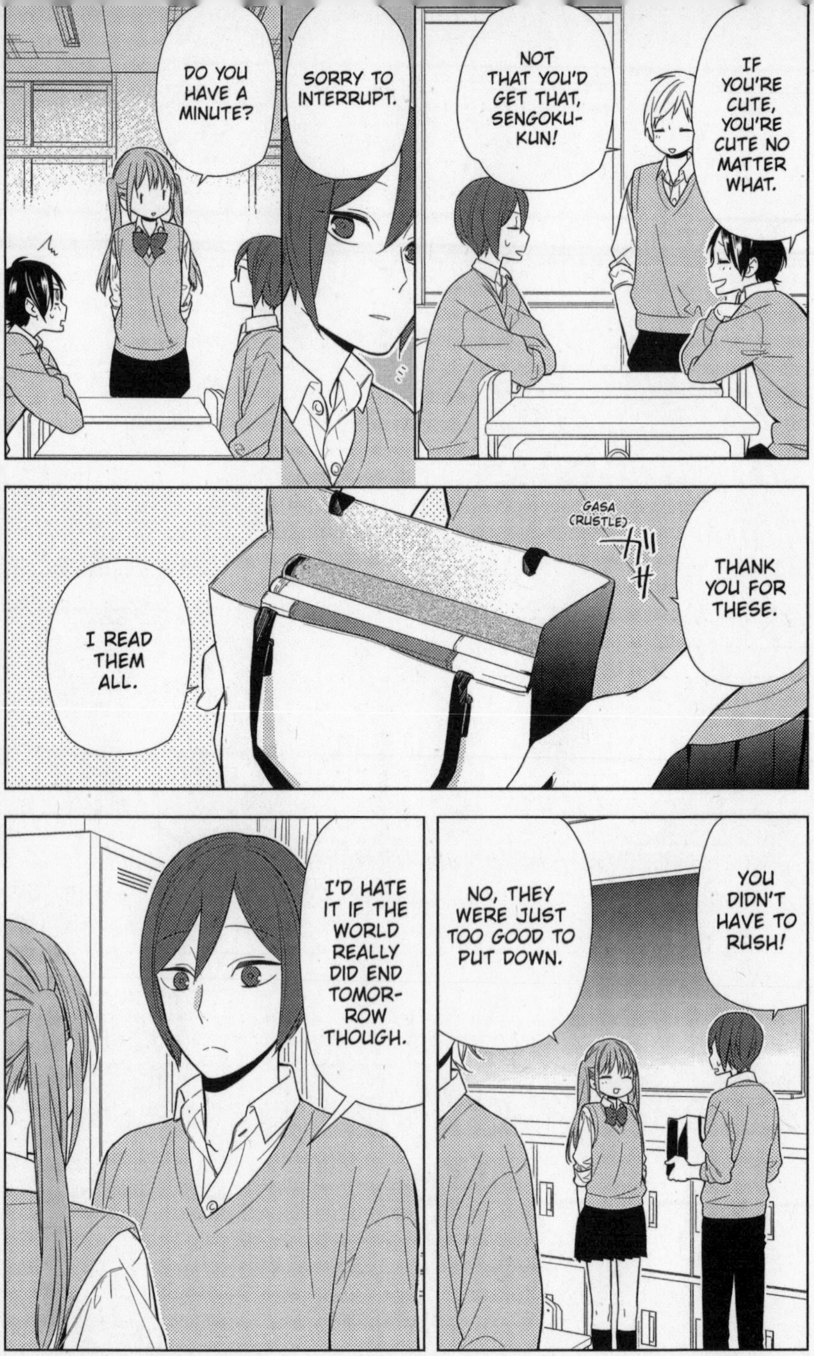

IF YOU'RE CUTE, YOU'RE CUTE NO MATTER WHAT.
NOT THAT YOU'D GET THAT, SENGOKU-KUN!
SORRY TO INTERRUPT.
DO YOU HAVE A MINUTE?
GASA (RUSTLE)
THANK YOU FOR THESE.
I READ THEM ALL.
YOU DIDN'T HAVE TO RUSH!
NO, THEY WERE JUST TOO GOOD TO PUT DOWN.
I'D HATE IT IF THE WORLD REALLY DID END TOMORROW THOUGH.

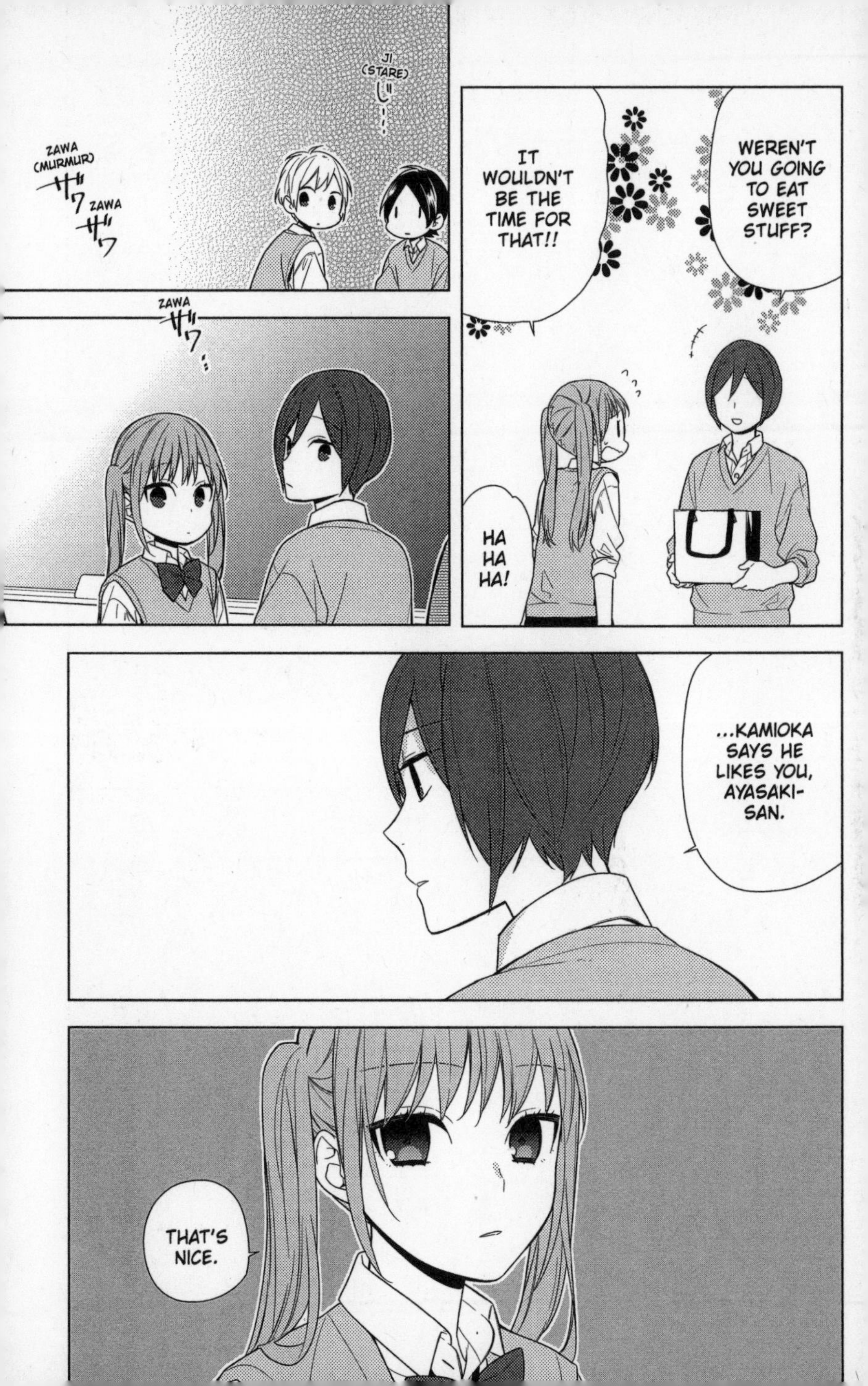
WEREN'T YOU GOING TO EAT SWEET STUFF?
IT WOULDN'T BE THE TIME FOR THAT!!
HA HA HA!
JI (STARE)
じ
ZAWA (MURMUR)
ザワ
ZAWA
ザワ
ZAWA
ザワ
...KAMIOKA SAYS HE LIKES YOU, AYASAKI-SAN.
THAT'S NICE.

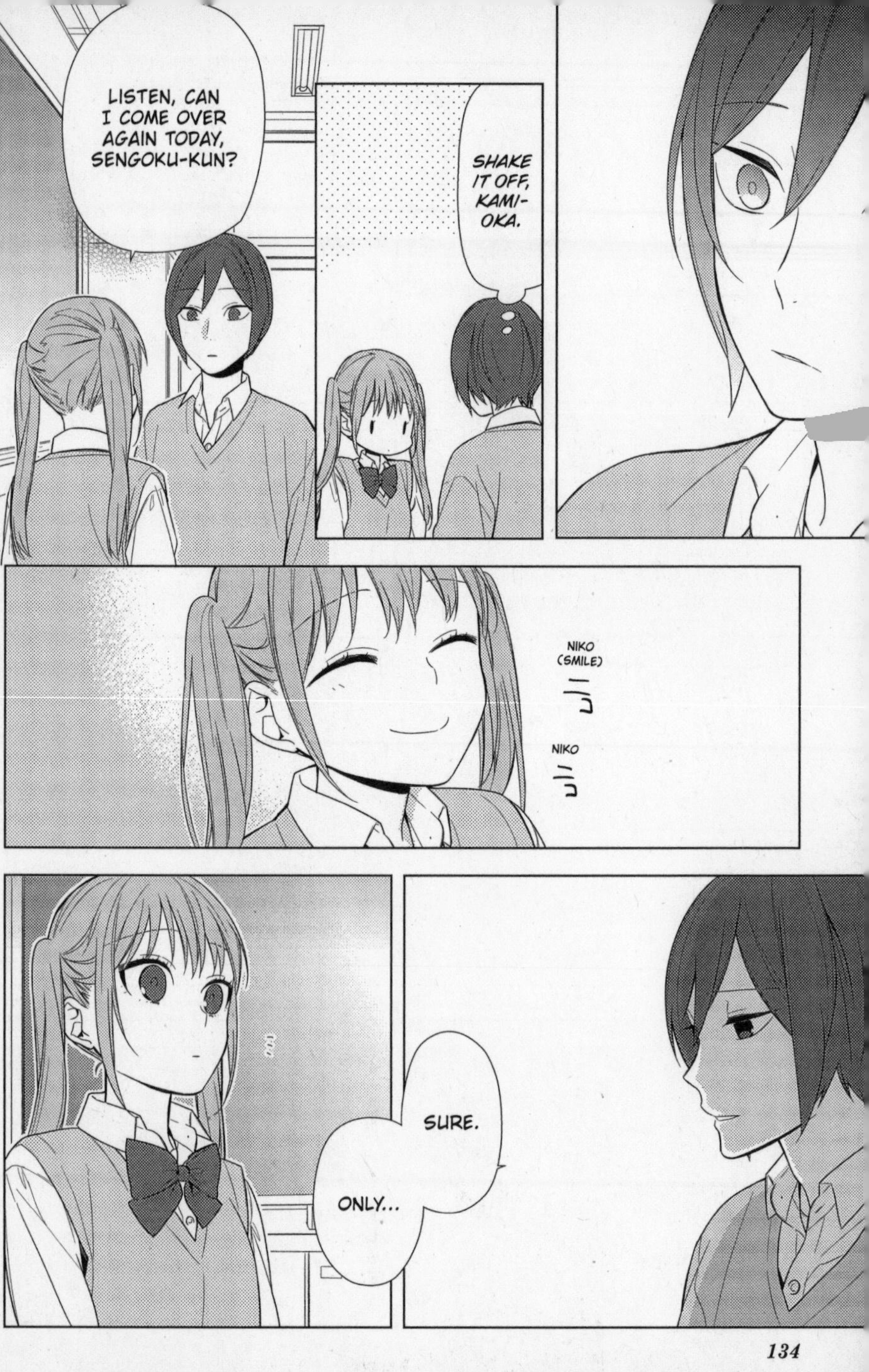
SHAKE IT OFF, KAMI-OKA.
LISTEN, CAN I COME OVER AGAIN TODAY, SENGOKU-KUN?
NIKO (SMILE)
NIKO
SURE.
ONLY...

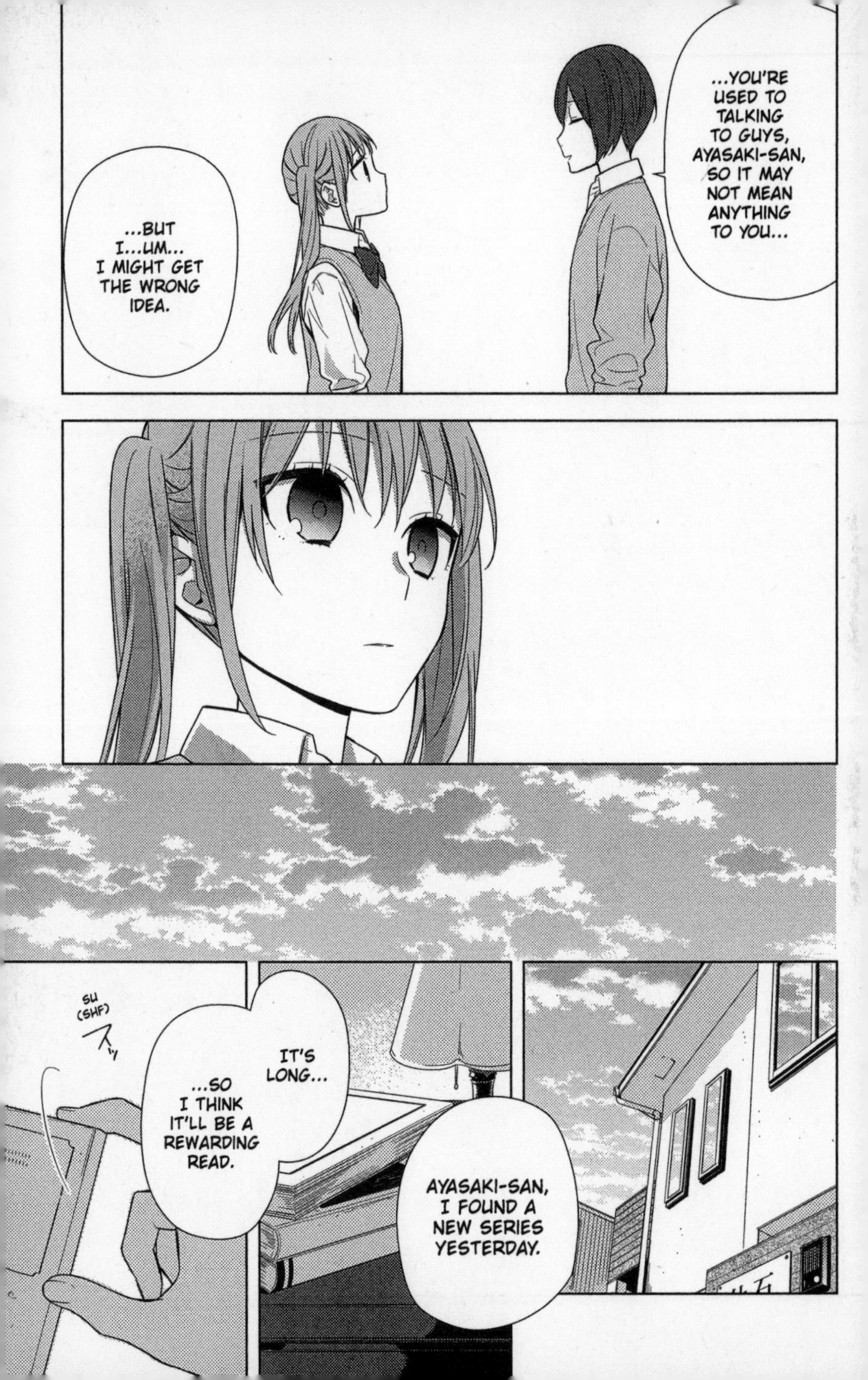
...YOU'RE USED TO TALKING TO GUYS, AYASAKI-SAN, SO IT MAY NOT MEAN ANYTHING TO YOU...
...BUT I...UM... I MIGHT GET THE WRONG IDEA.
AYASAKI-SAN, I FOUND A NEW SERIES YESTERDAY.
IT'S LONG...
...SO I THINK IT'LL BE A REWARDING READ.
SU (SHF)
スッ

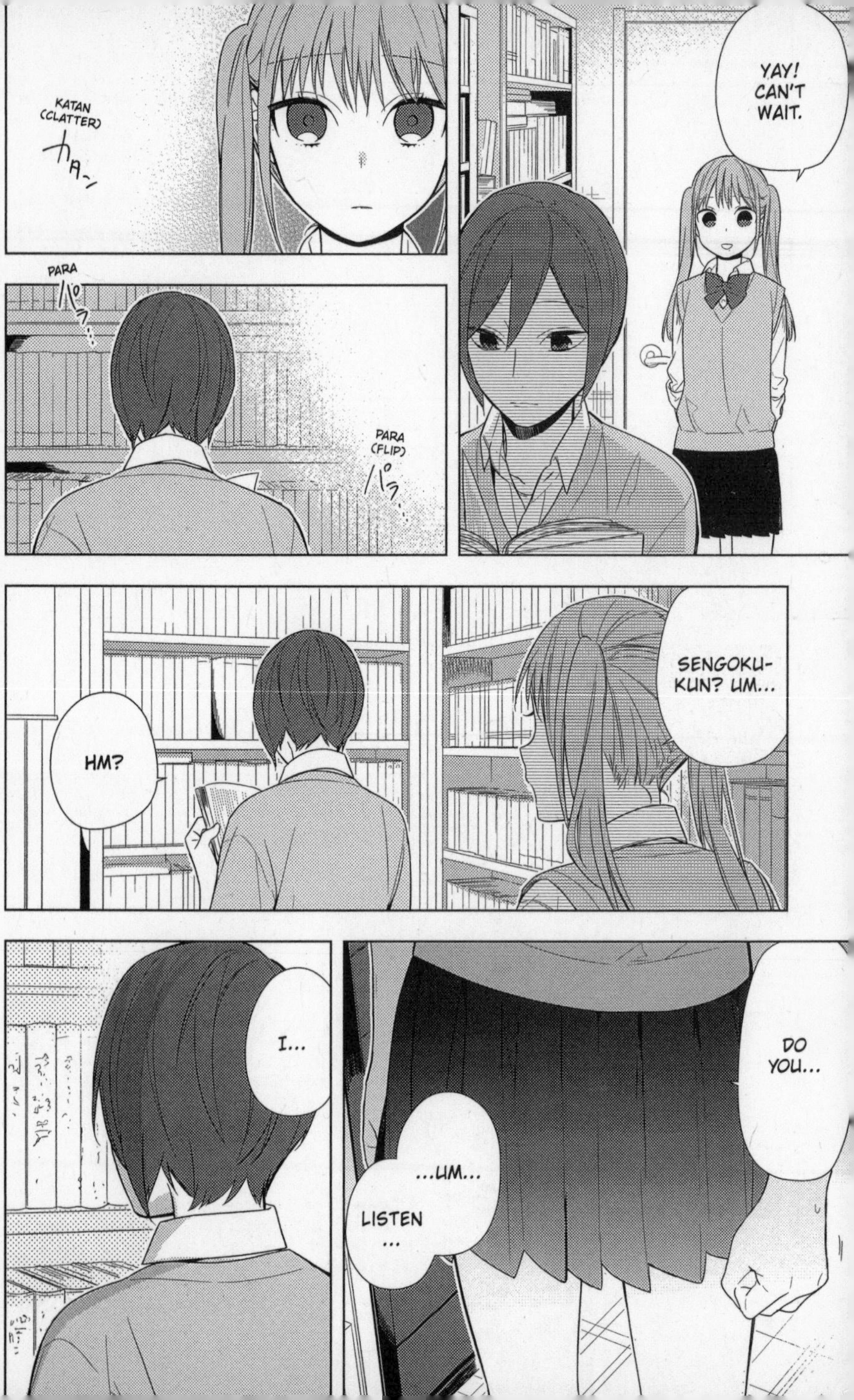
YAY! CAN'T WAIT.
KATAN (CLATTER)
PARA
PARA (FLIP)
SENGOKU-KUN? UM...
HM?
DO YOU...
...UM...
LISTEN ...
I...

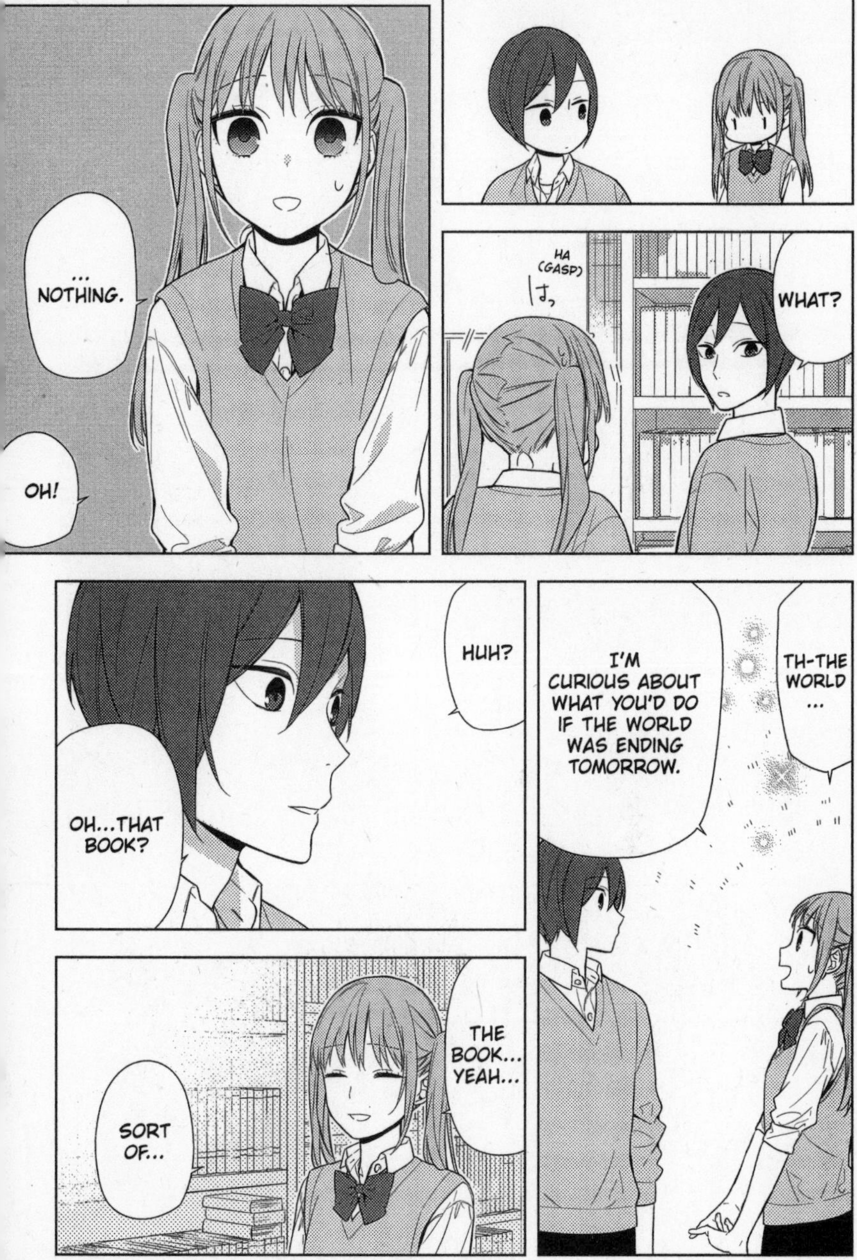
WHAT?
HA (GASP)
はっ
... NOTHING.
OH!
TH-THE WORLD ...
I'M CURIOUS ABOUT WHAT YOU'D DO IF THE WORLD WAS ENDING TOMORROW.
HUH?
OH...THAT BOOK?
THE BOOK... YEAH...
SORT OF...

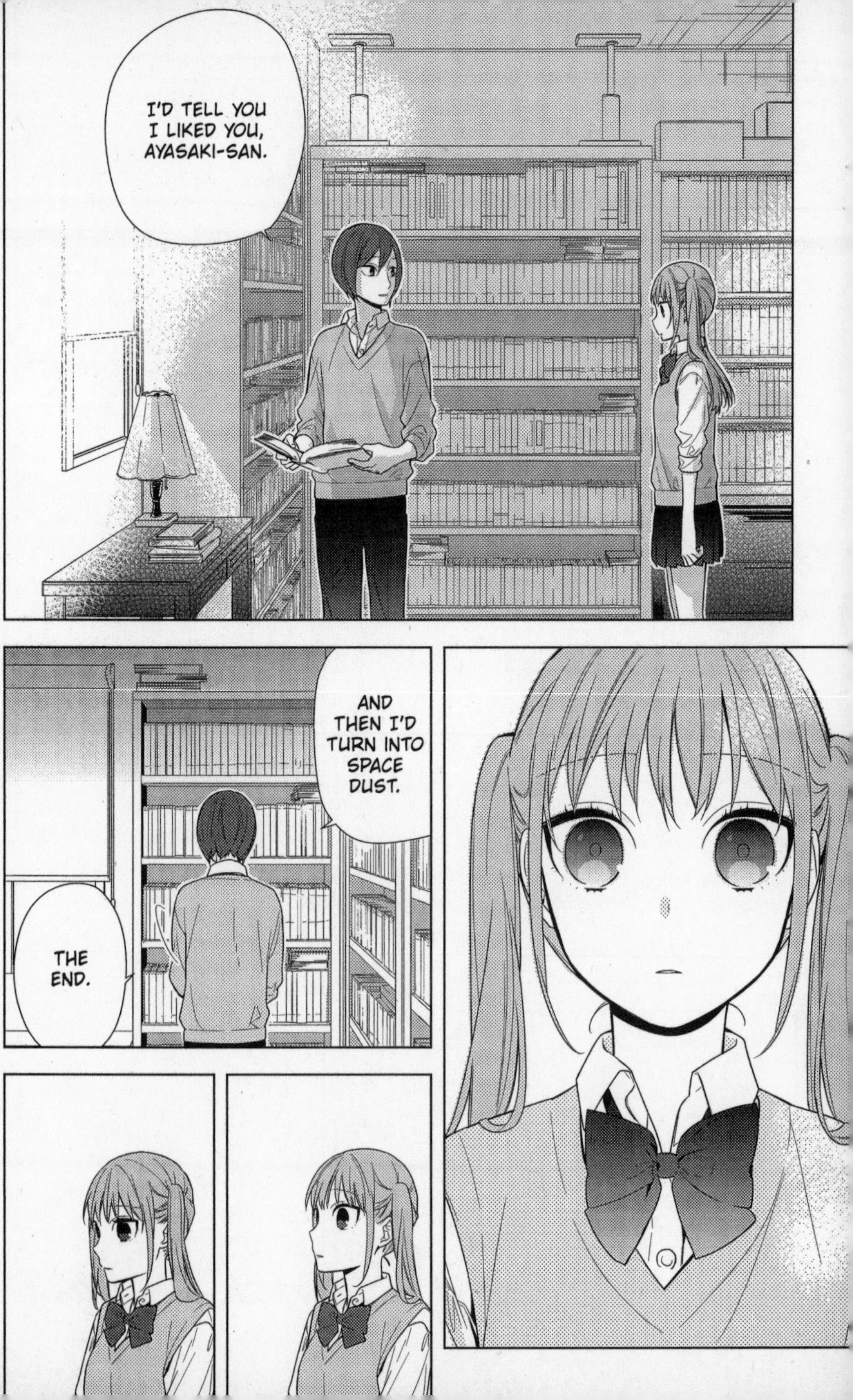
I'D TELL YOU I LIKED YOU, AYASAKI-SAN.
AND THEN I'D TURN INTO SPACE DUST.
THE END.

ARE YOU TEASING ME?

NO.

...NO.

ACTU-ALLY...

...I'M SORRY.

FORGET I SAID...

KUSHA (CRINKLE)

OH.

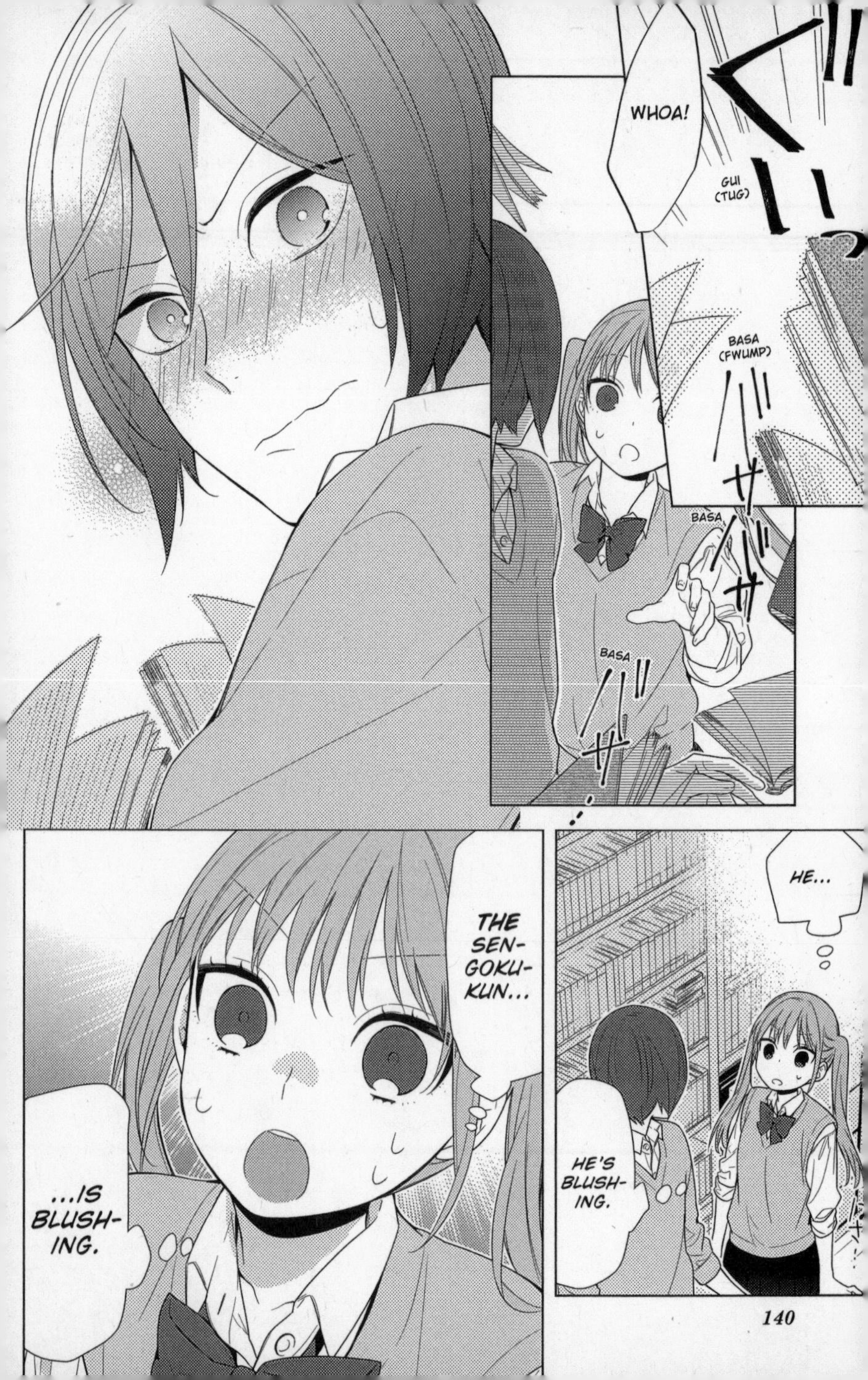
WHOA!
GUI (TUG)
BASA (FWUMP)
BASA
BASA
HE...
HE'S BLUSH-ING.
THE SEN-GOKU-KUN...
...IS BLUSH-ING.

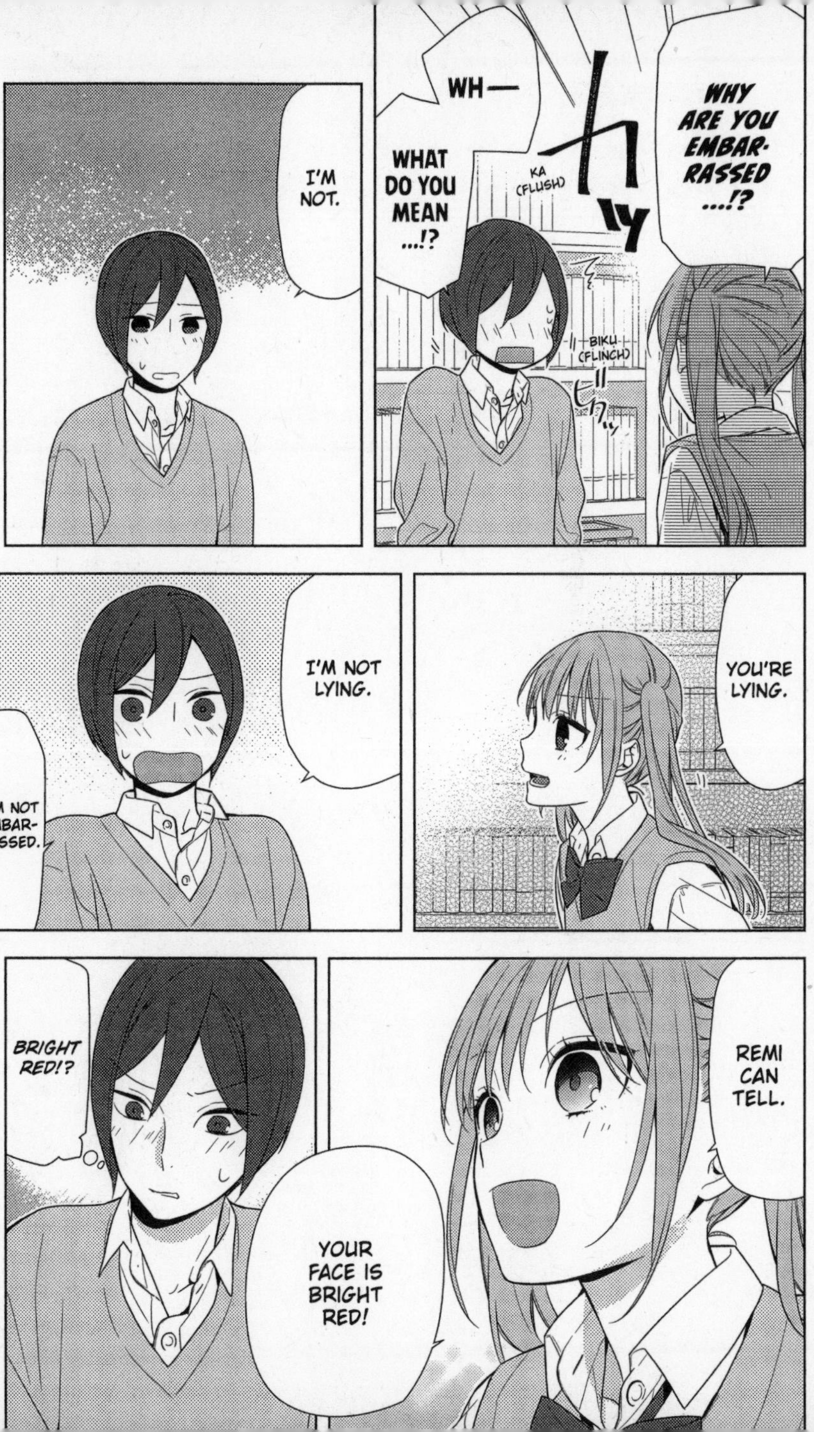
WHY ARE YOU EMBARRASSED....!?
WH—
KA (FLUSH)
WHAT DO YOU MEAN ...!?
BIKU (FLINCH)
I'M NOT.
YOU'RE LYING.
I'M NOT LYING.
I'M NOT EMBARRASSED.
REMI CAN TELL.
YOUR FACE IS BRIGHT RED!
BRIGHT RED!?

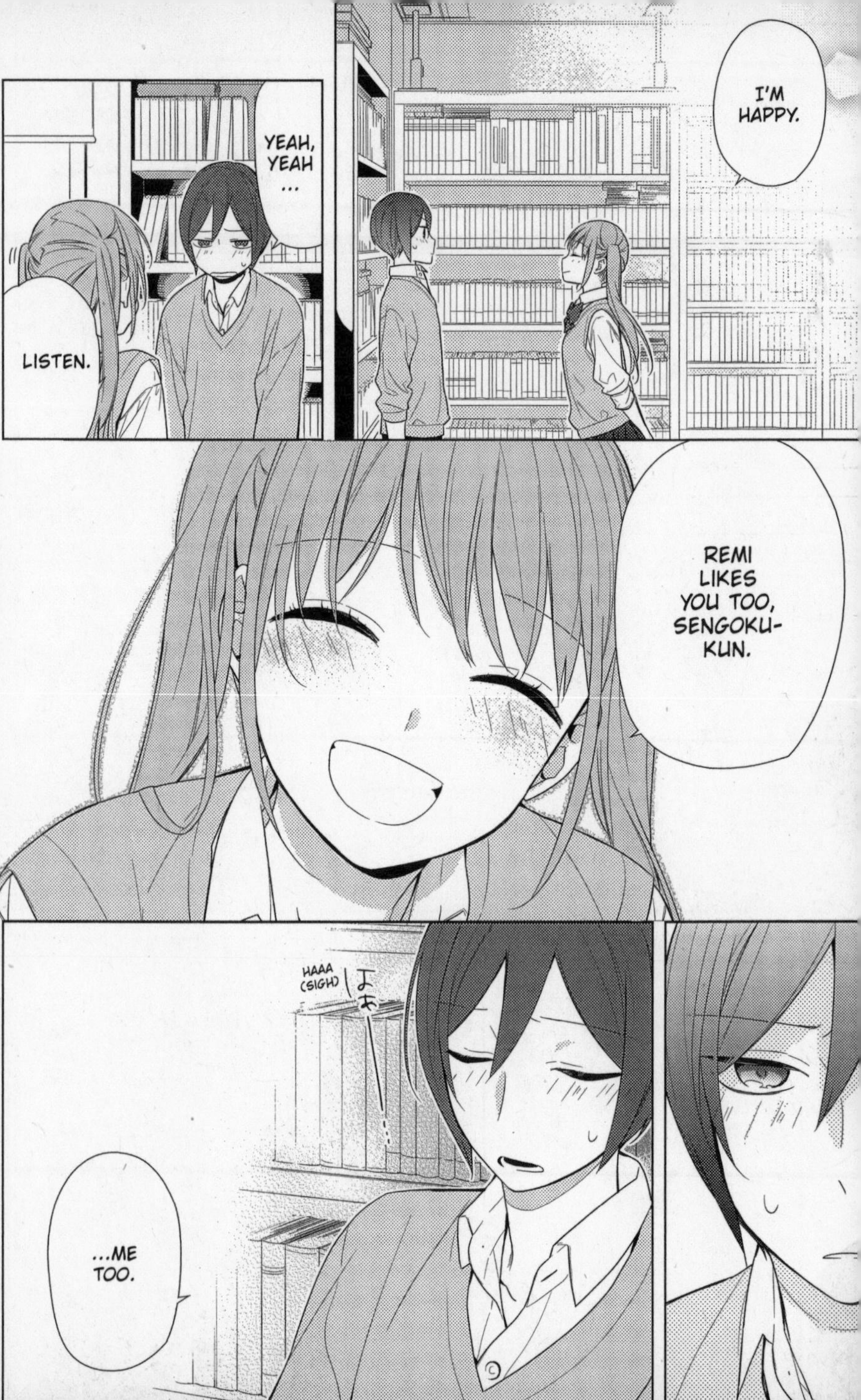
I'M HAPPY.
YEAH, YEAH ...
LISTEN.
REMI LIKES YOU TOO, SENGOKU-KUN.
HAAA (SIGH)
...ME TOO.

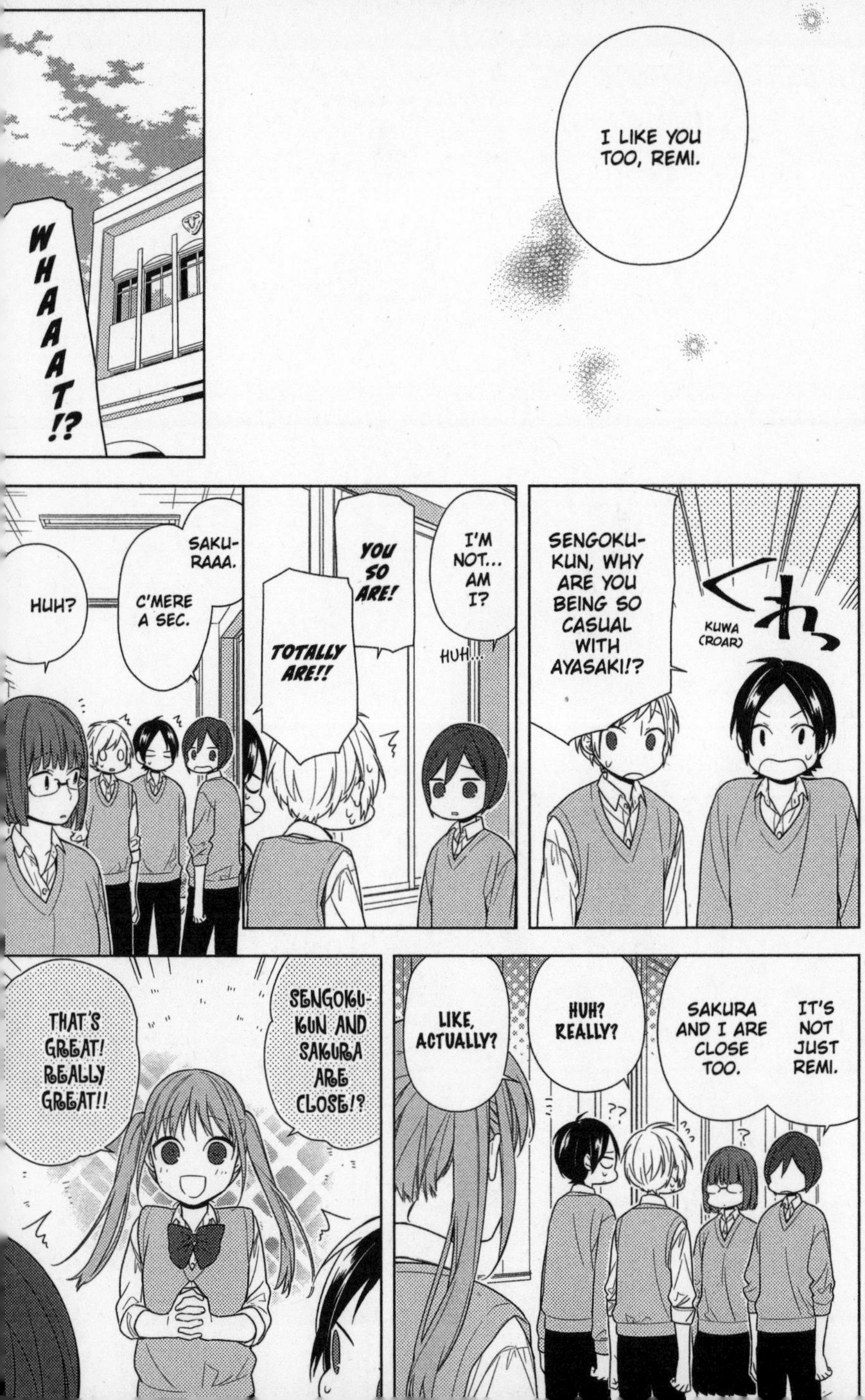
I LIKE YOU TOO, REMI.
WHAAAAT!?
SENGOKU-KUN, WHY ARE YOU BEING SO CASUAL WITH AYASAKI!?
くわ
KUWA (ROAR)
I'M NOT... AM I?
YOU SO ARE!
TOTALLY ARE!!
HUH...
SAKU-RAAA.
C'MERE A SEC.
HUH?
IT'S NOT JUST REMI.
SAKURA AND I ARE CLOSE TOO.
HUH? REALLY?
LIKE, ACTUALLY?
SENGOKU-KUN AND SAKURA ARE CLOSE!?
THAT'S GREAT! REALLY GREAT!!

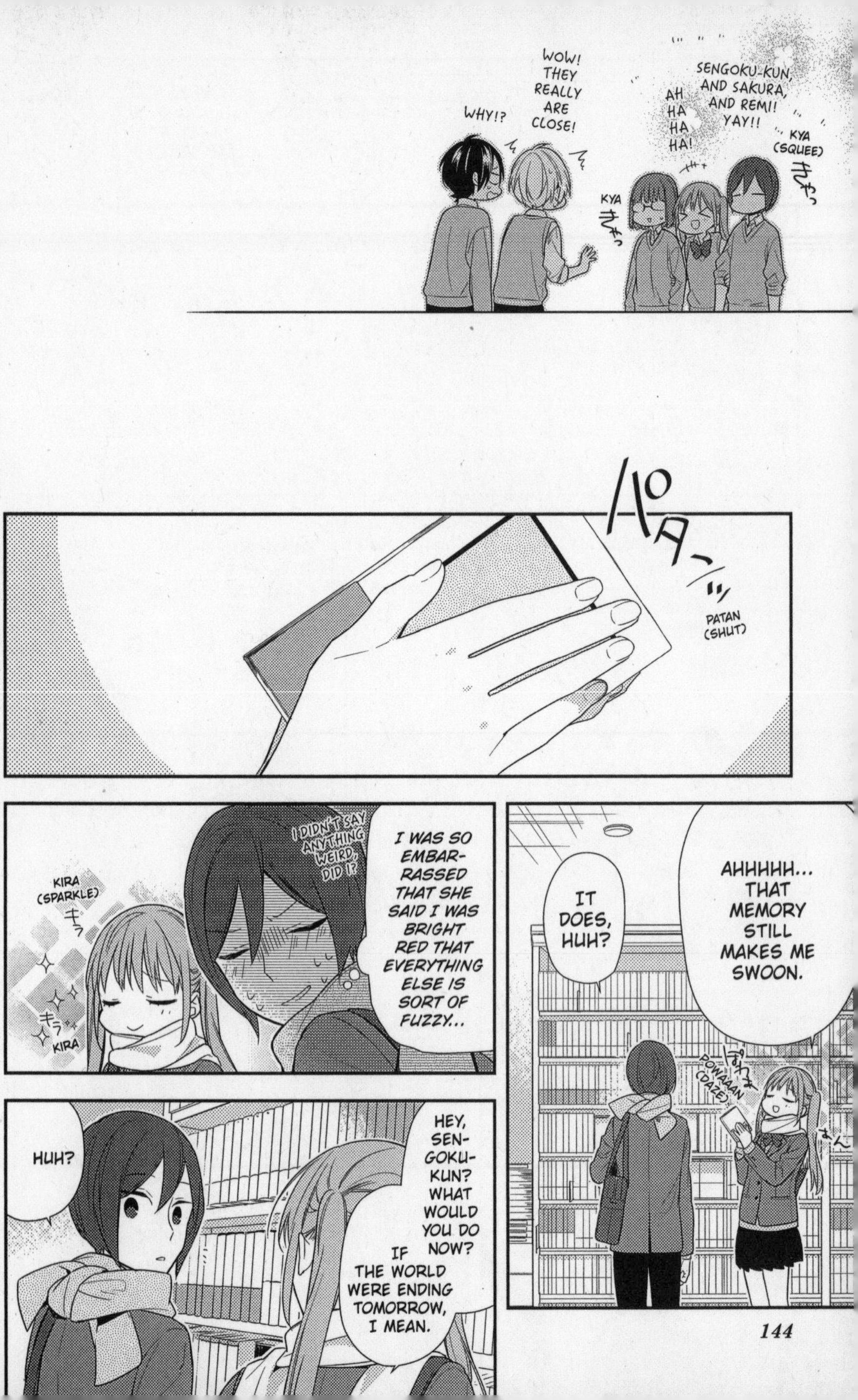
SENGOKU-KUN, AND SAKURA, AND REMI! YAY!!
KYA (SQUEE)
AH HA HA HA!
KYA
WOW! THEY REALLY ARE CLOSE!
WHY!?
PATAN (SHUT)
AHHHHH... THAT MEMORY STILL MAKES ME SWOON.
IT DOES, HUH?
POWAAAN (DAZE)
I WAS SO EMBARRASSED THAT SHE SAID I WAS BRIGHT RED THAT EVERYTHING ELSE IS SORT OF FUZZY...
I DIDN'T SAY ANYTHING WEIRD, DID I?
KIRA (SPARKLE)
KIRA
HEY, SENGOKU-KUN? WHAT WOULD YOU DO NOW?
IF THE WORLD WERE ENDING TOMORROW, I MEAN.
HUH?

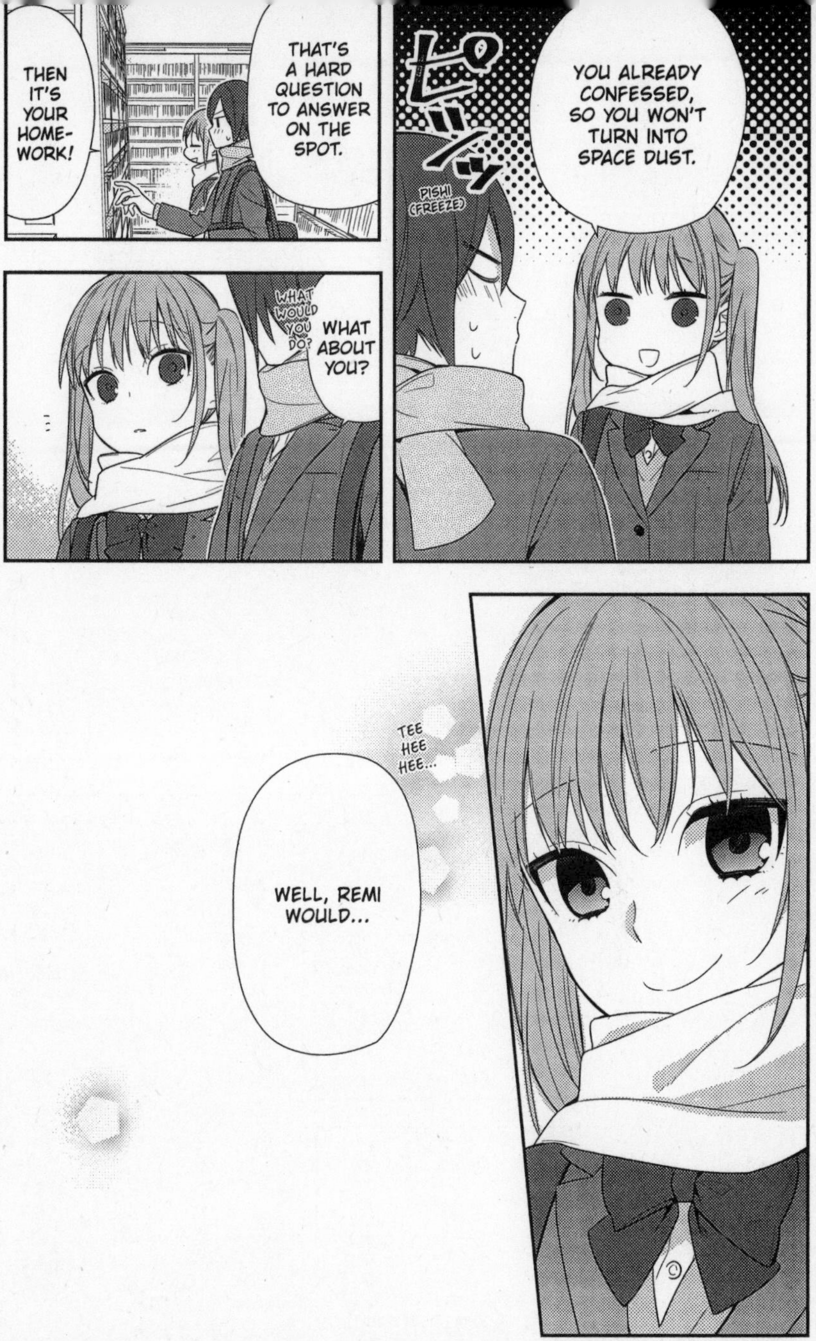
YOU ALREADY CONFESSED, SO YOU WON'T TURN INTO SPACE DUST.
PISHI (FREEZE)
THAT'S A HARD QUESTION TO ANSWER ON THE SPOT.
THEN IT'S YOUR HOME-WORK!
WHAT ABOUT YOU?
WHAT WOULD YOU DO?
TEE HEE HEE...
WELL, REMI WOULD...

HORIMIYA

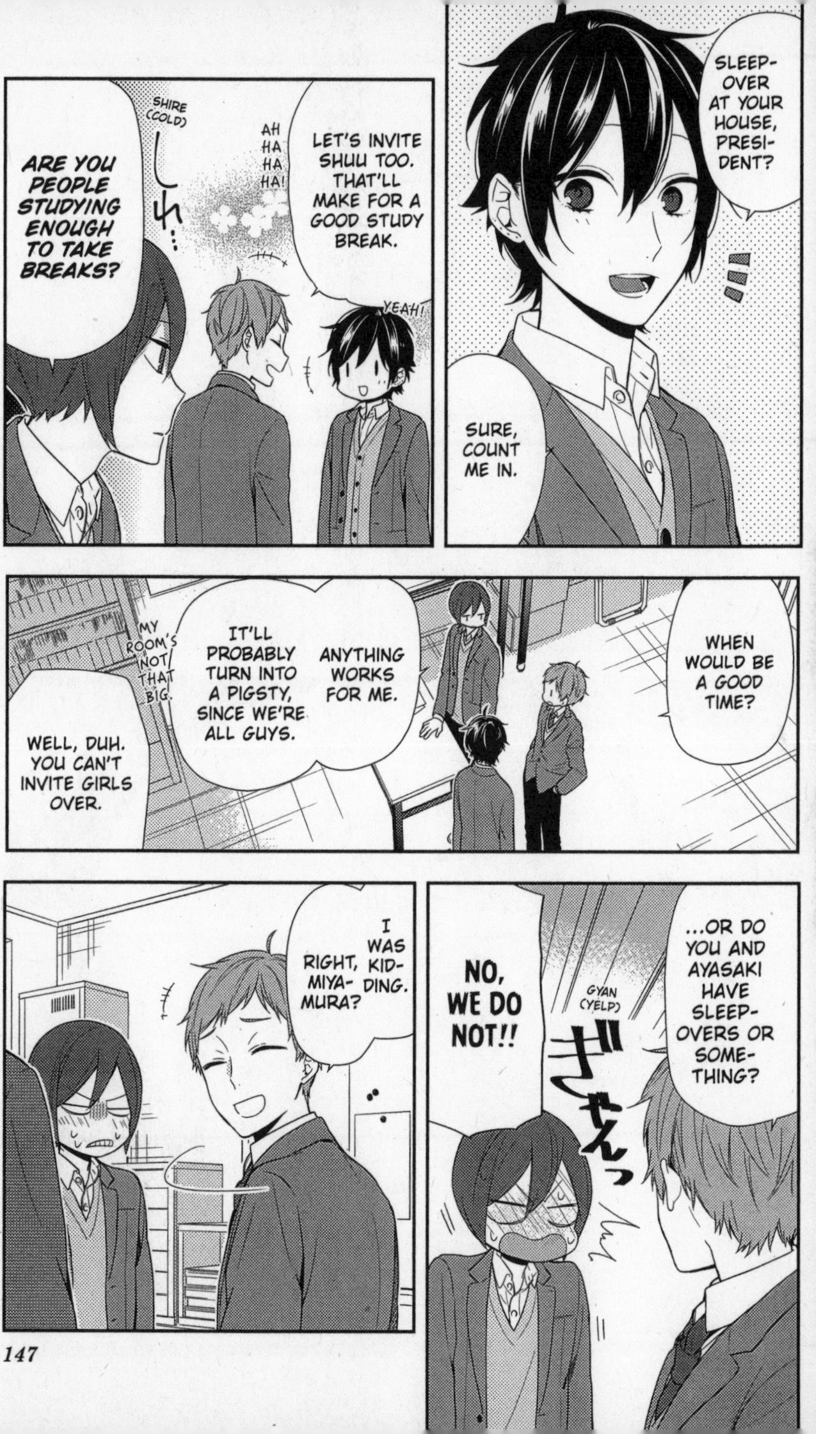
SLEEP-OVER AT YOUR HOUSE, PRESIDENT?
SURE, COUNT ME IN.
LET'S INVITE SHUU TOO. THAT'LL MAKE FOR A GOOD STUDY BREAK.
AH HA HA HA!
YEAH!
SHIRE (COLD)
ARE YOU PEOPLE STUDYING ENOUGH TO TAKE BREAKS?
WHEN WOULD BE A GOOD TIME?
ANYTHING WORKS FOR ME.
IT'LL PROBABLY TURN INTO A PIGSTY, SINCE WE'RE ALL GUYS.
MY ROOM'S NOT THAT BIG.
WELL, DUH. YOU CAN'T INVITE GIRLS OVER.
...OR DO YOU AND AYASAKI HAVE SLEEP-OVERS OR SOME-THING?
GYAN (YELP)
NO, WE DO NOT!!
I WAS KID-DING.
RIGHT, MIYA-MURA?

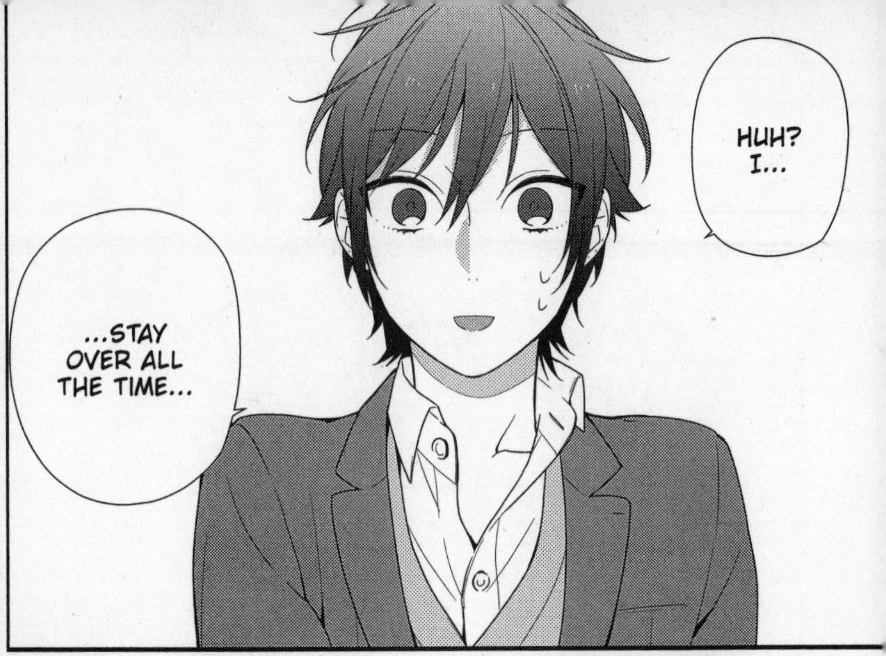
HUH? I...
...STAY OVER ALL THE TIME...
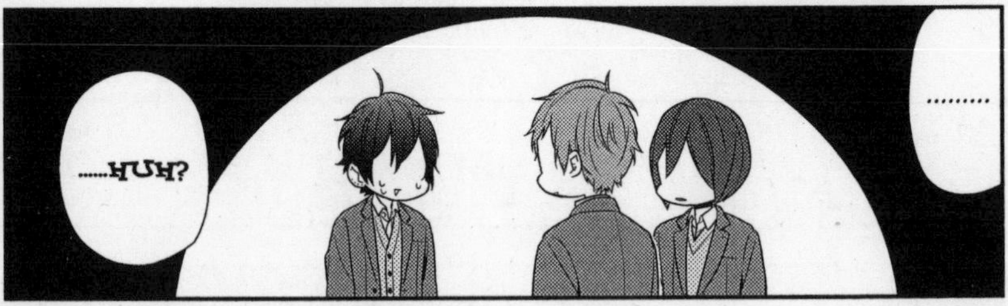
....
......HUH?
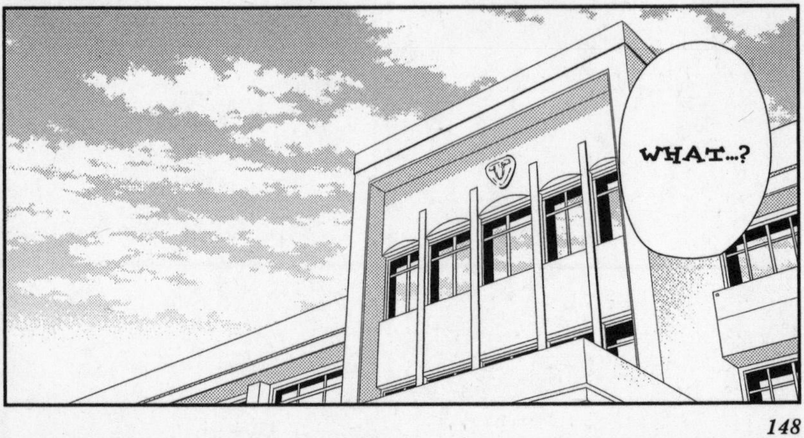
WHAT...?

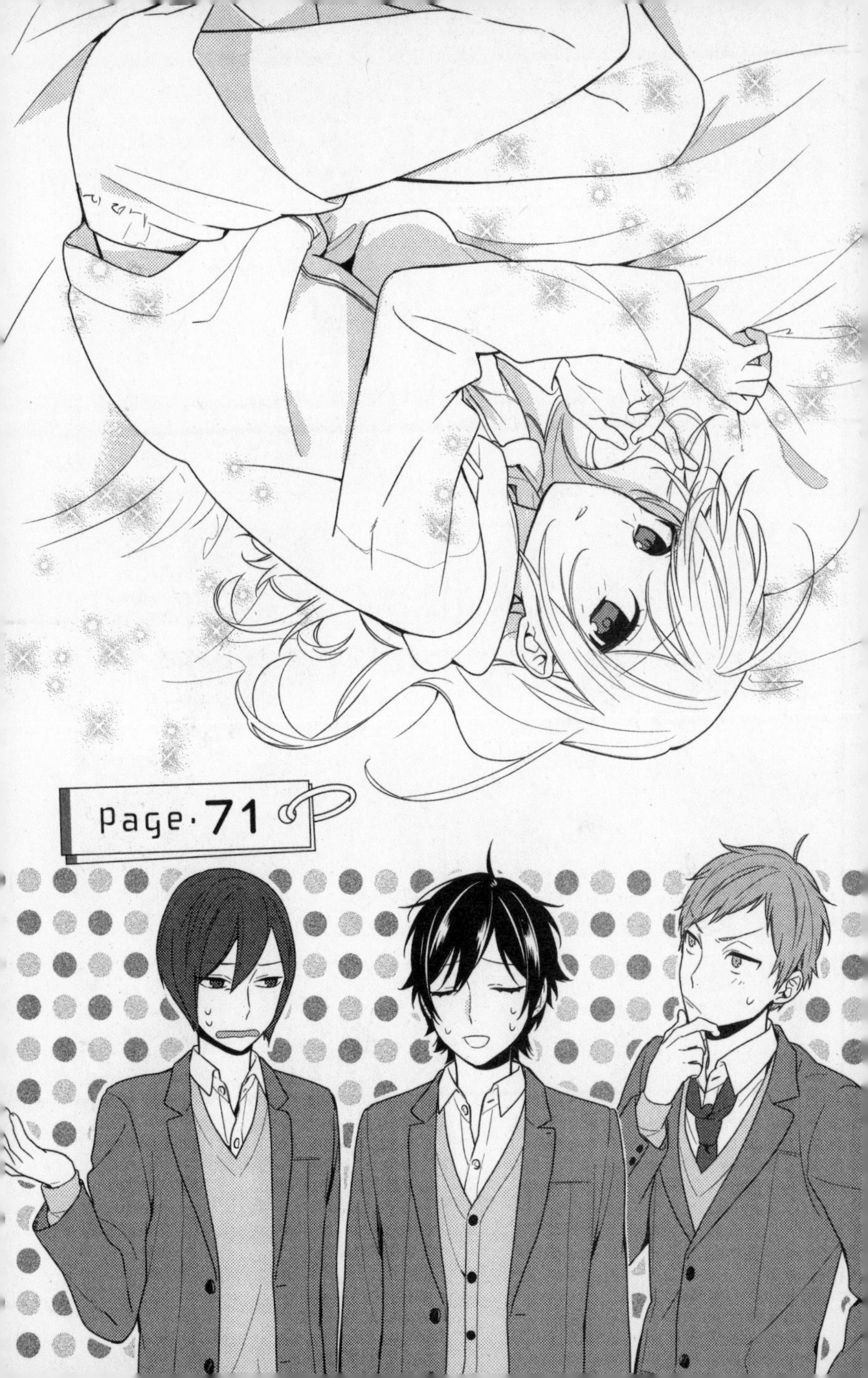
page.71

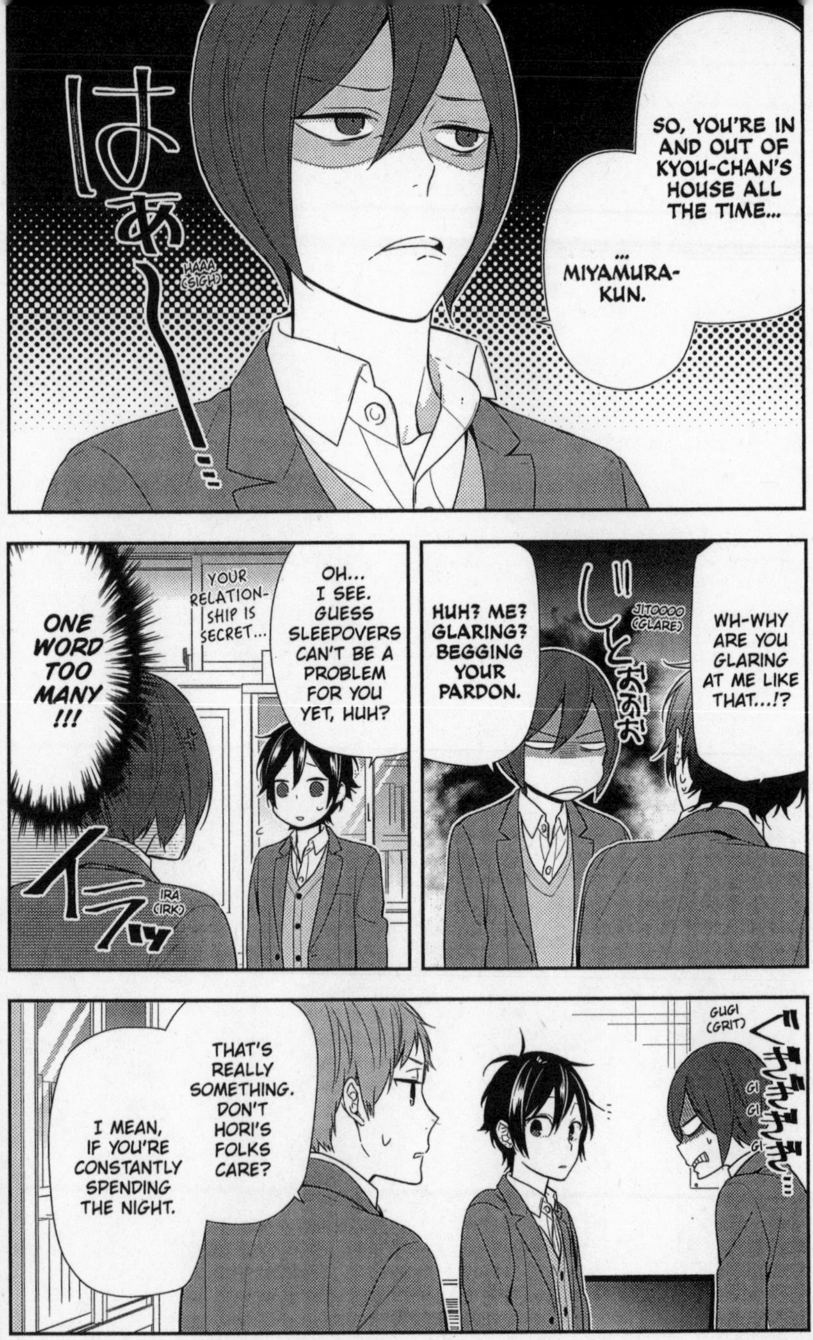
SO, YOU'RE IN AND OUT OF KYOU-CHAN'S HOUSE ALL THE TIME...
... MIYAMURA-KUN.
はあ〜…
HAAA (SIGH)
WH-WHY ARE YOU GLARING AT ME LIKE THAT...!?
JITOOOO (GLARE)
HUH? ME? GLARING? BEGGING YOUR PARDON.
OH... I SEE. GUESS SLEEPOVERS CAN'T BE A PROBLEM FOR YOU YET, HUH?
YOUR RELATION-SHIP IS SECRET...
ONE WORD TOO MANY !!!
イラッ
IRA (IRK)
GUGI (GRIT)
GI GI GI
THAT'S REALLY SOMETHING. DON'T HORI'S FOLKS CARE?
I MEAN, IF YOU'RE CONSTANTLY SPENDING THE NIGHT.

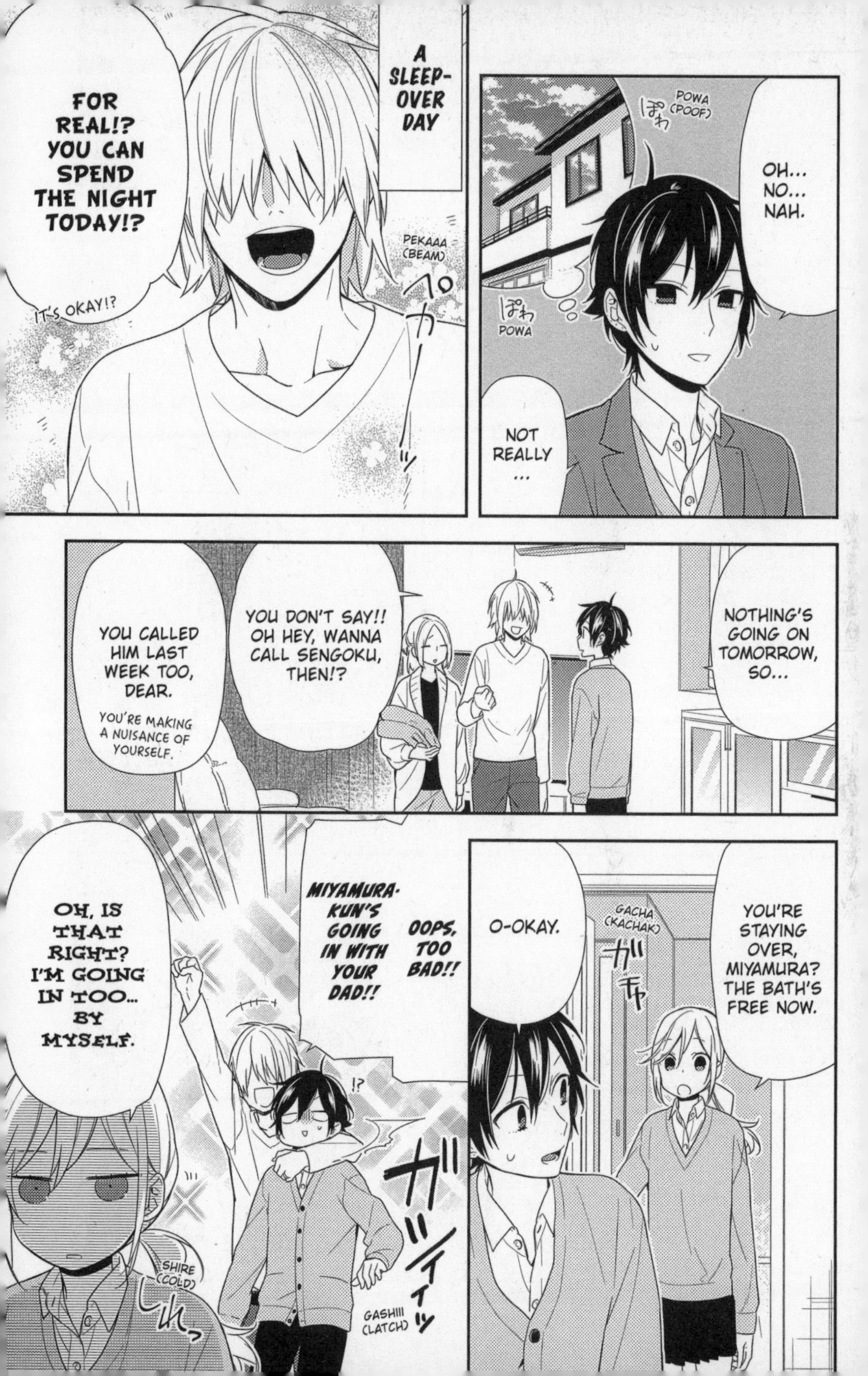
POWA ぽわ (POOF)
OH... NO... NAH.
ぽわ POWA
NOT REALLY ...
A SLEEP-OVER DAY
FOR REAL!? YOU CAN SPEND THE NIGHT TODAY!?
PEKAAA (BEAM)
IT'S OKAY!?
NOTHING'S GOING ON TOMORROW, SO...
YOU DON'T SAY!! OH HEY, WANNA CALL SENGOKU, THEN!?
YOU CALLED HIM LAST WEEK TOO, DEAR.
YOU'RE MAKING A NUISANCE OF YOURSELF.
YOU'RE STAYING OVER, MIYAMURA? THE BATH'S FREE NOW.
GACHA (KACHAK)
O-OKAY.
OOPS, TOO BAD!!
MIYAMURA-KUN'S GOING IN WITH YOUR DAD!!
!?
GASHIII (LATCH)
OH, IS THAT RIGHT? I'M GOING IN TOO... BY MYSELF.
SHIRE (COLD)

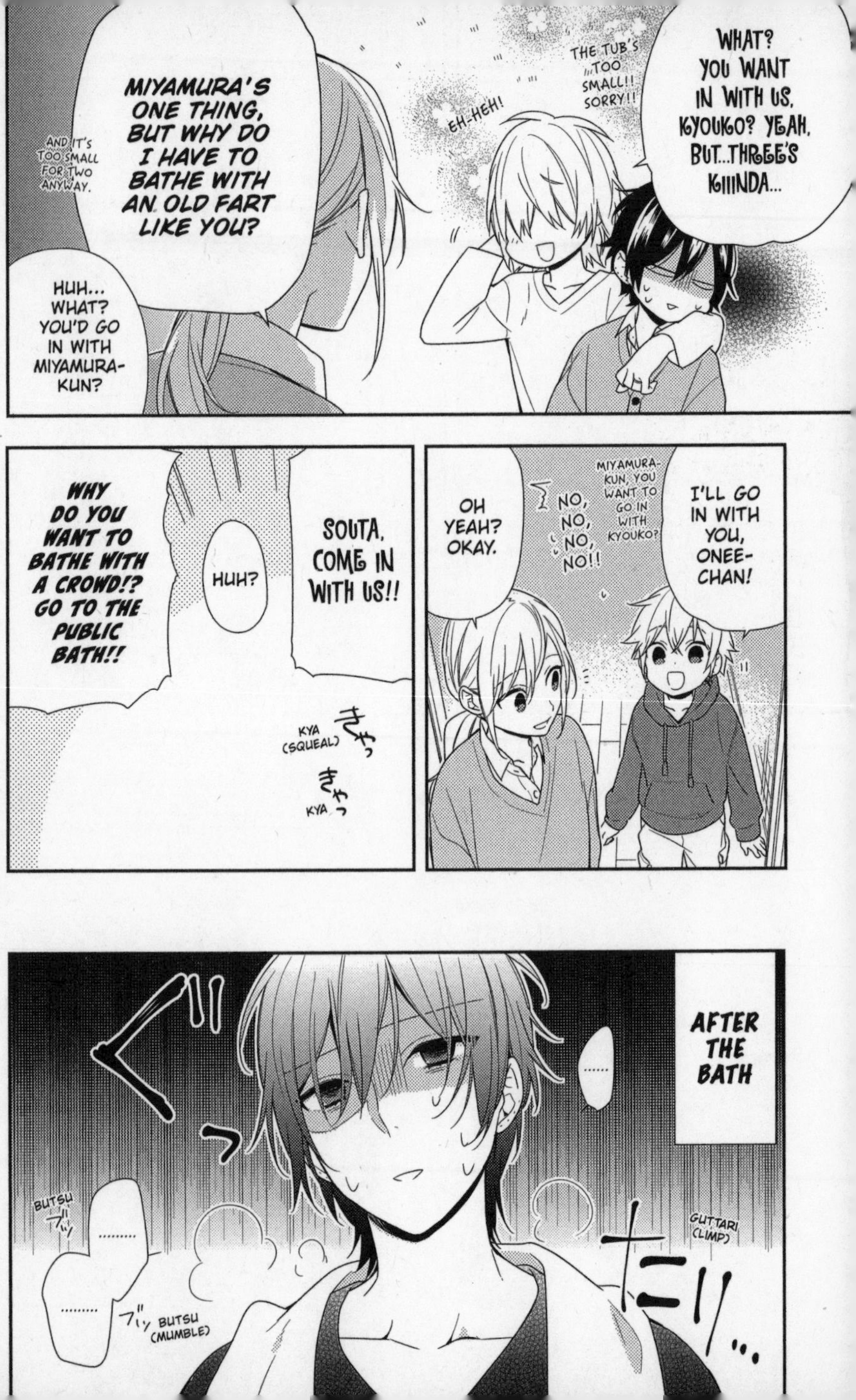
WHAT? YOU WANT IN WITH US, KYOUKO? YEAH, BUT...THREE'S KIIINDA...
THE TUB'S TOO SMALL!! SORRY!!
EH-HEH!
MIYAMURA'S ONE THING, BUT WHY DO I HAVE TO BATHE WITH AN OLD FART LIKE YOU?
AND IT'S TOO SMALL FOR TWO ANYWAY.
HUH... WHAT? YOU'D GO IN WITH MIYAMURA-KUN?
I'LL GO IN WITH YOU, ONEE-CHAN!
MIYAMURA-KUN, YOU WANT TO GO IN WITH KYOUKO?
NO, NO, NO, NO!!
OH YEAH? OKAY.
SOUTA, COME IN WITH US!!
HUH?
WHY DO YOU WANT TO BATHE WITH A CROWD!? GO TO THE PUBLIC BATH!!
きゃっ KYA (SQUEAL)
きゃっ KYA
AFTER THE BATH
GUTTARI (LIMP)
......
BUTSU
....
....
BUTSU (MUMBLE)

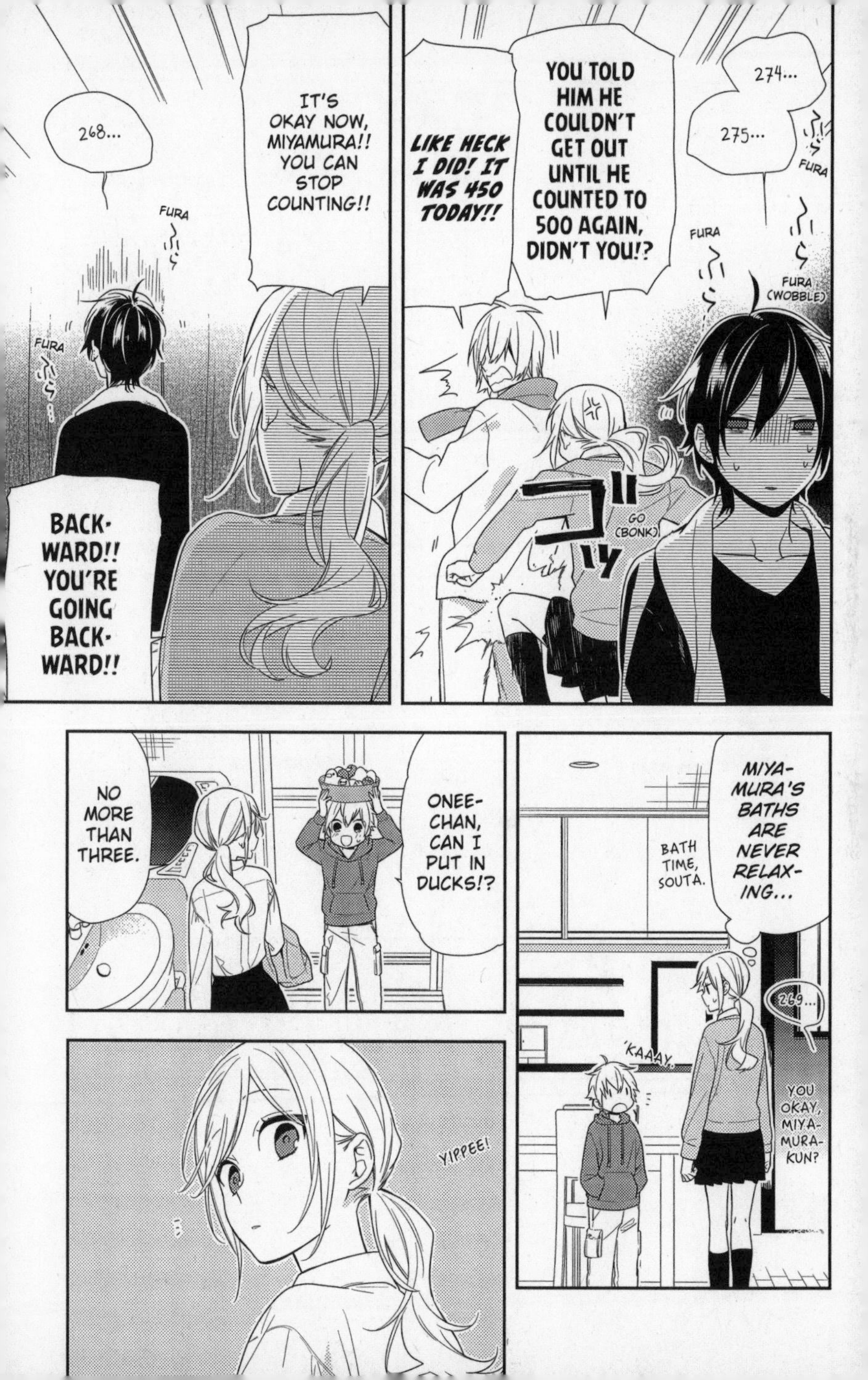
274...
275...
FURA
FURA
FURA (WOBBLE)
YOU TOLD HIM HE COULDN'T GET OUT UNTIL HE COUNTED TO 500 AGAIN, DIDN'T YOU!?
LIKE HECK I DID! IT WAS 450 TODAY!!
GO (BONK)
IT'S OKAY NOW, MIYAMURA!! YOU CAN STOP COUNTING!!
268...
FURA
FURA
BACKWARD!! YOU'RE GOING BACKWARD!!
MIYAMURA'S BATHS ARE NEVER RELAXING...
BATH TIME, SOUTA.
269...
'KAAAY.
YOU OKAY, MIYAMURA-KUN?
ONEE-CHAN, CAN I PUT IN DUCKS!?
NO MORE THAN THREE.
YIPPEE!
...

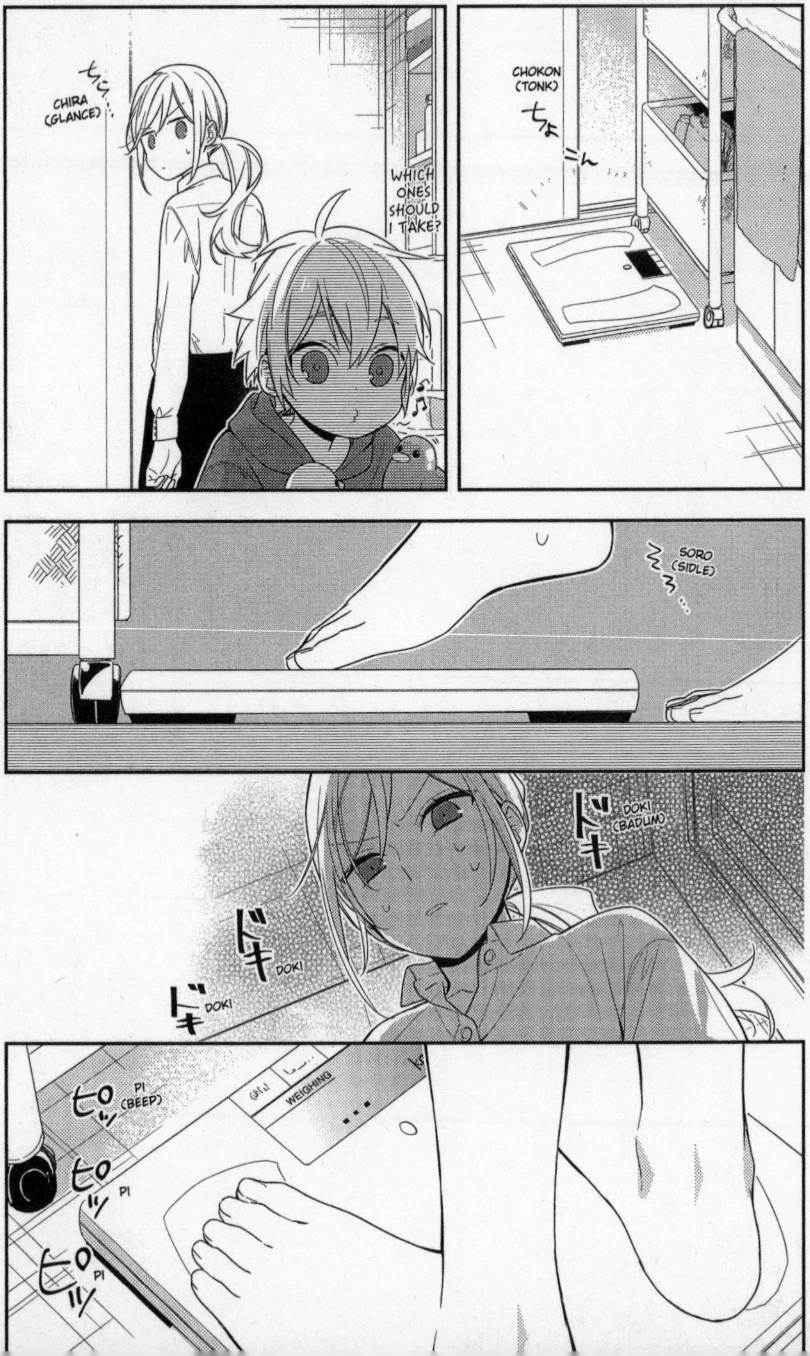
CHOKON (TONK)
ちょこん
CHIRA (GLANCE)
ちら…
WHICH ONES SHOULD I TAKE?
SORO (SIDLE)
そろ…
ドキ
DOKI (BADUM)
ドキ
DOKI
ドキ
DOKI
ピッ
PI (BEEP)
ピッ
PI
ピッ
PI
WEIGHING

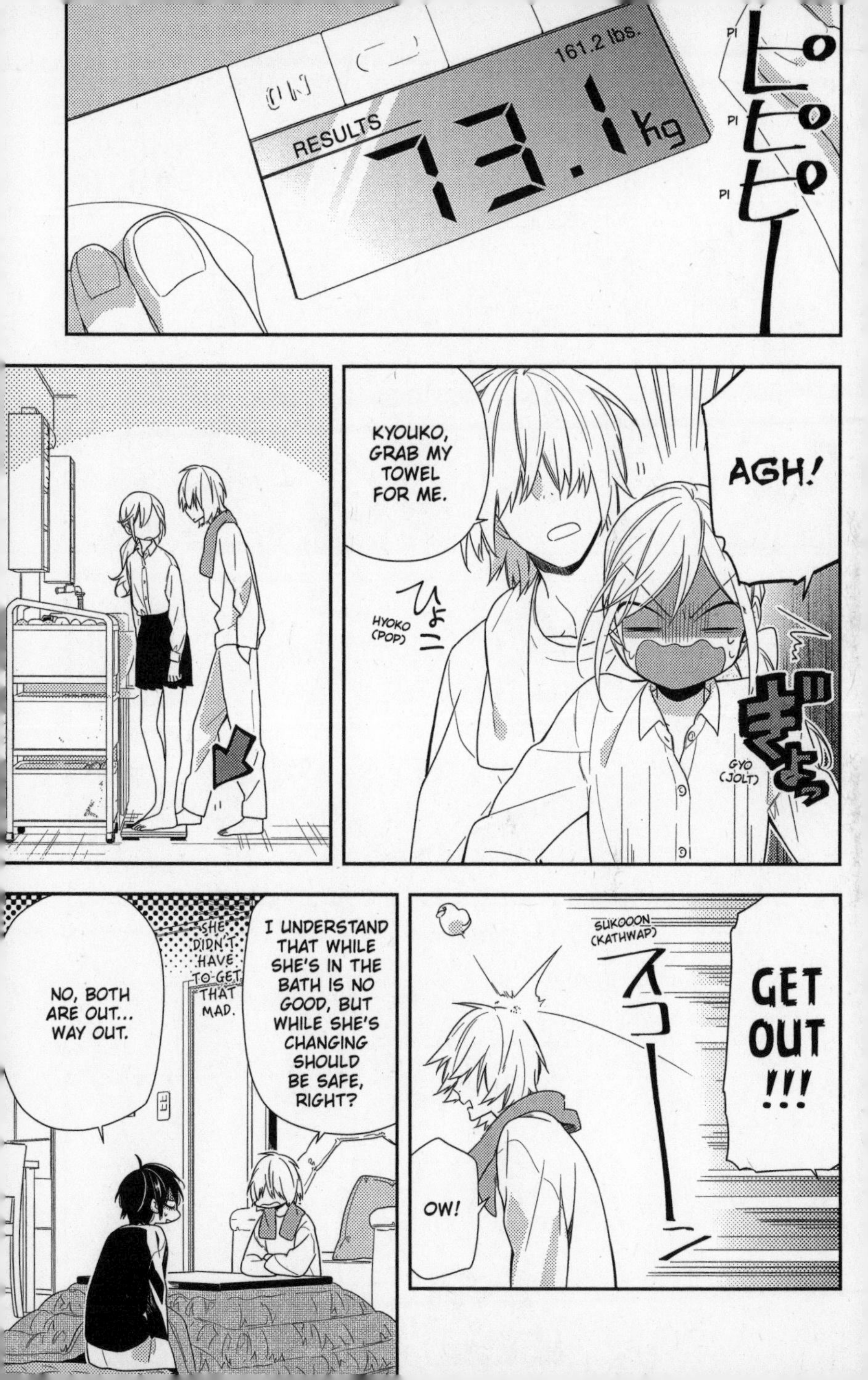
161.2 lbs.
RESULTS
73.1 kg
ピピピー
PI
PI
PI
KYOUKO, GRAB MY TOWEL FOR ME.
ひょこ
HYOKO (POP)
AGH!
ぎょっ
GYO (JOLT)
GET OUT!!!
スコーーン
SUKOOON (KATHWAP)
OW!
I UNDERSTAND THAT WHILE SHE'S IN THE BATH IS NO GOOD, BUT WHILE SHE'S CHANGING SHOULD BE SAFE, RIGHT?
SHE DIDN'T HAVE TO GET THAT MAD.
NO, BOTH ARE OUT... WAY OUT.

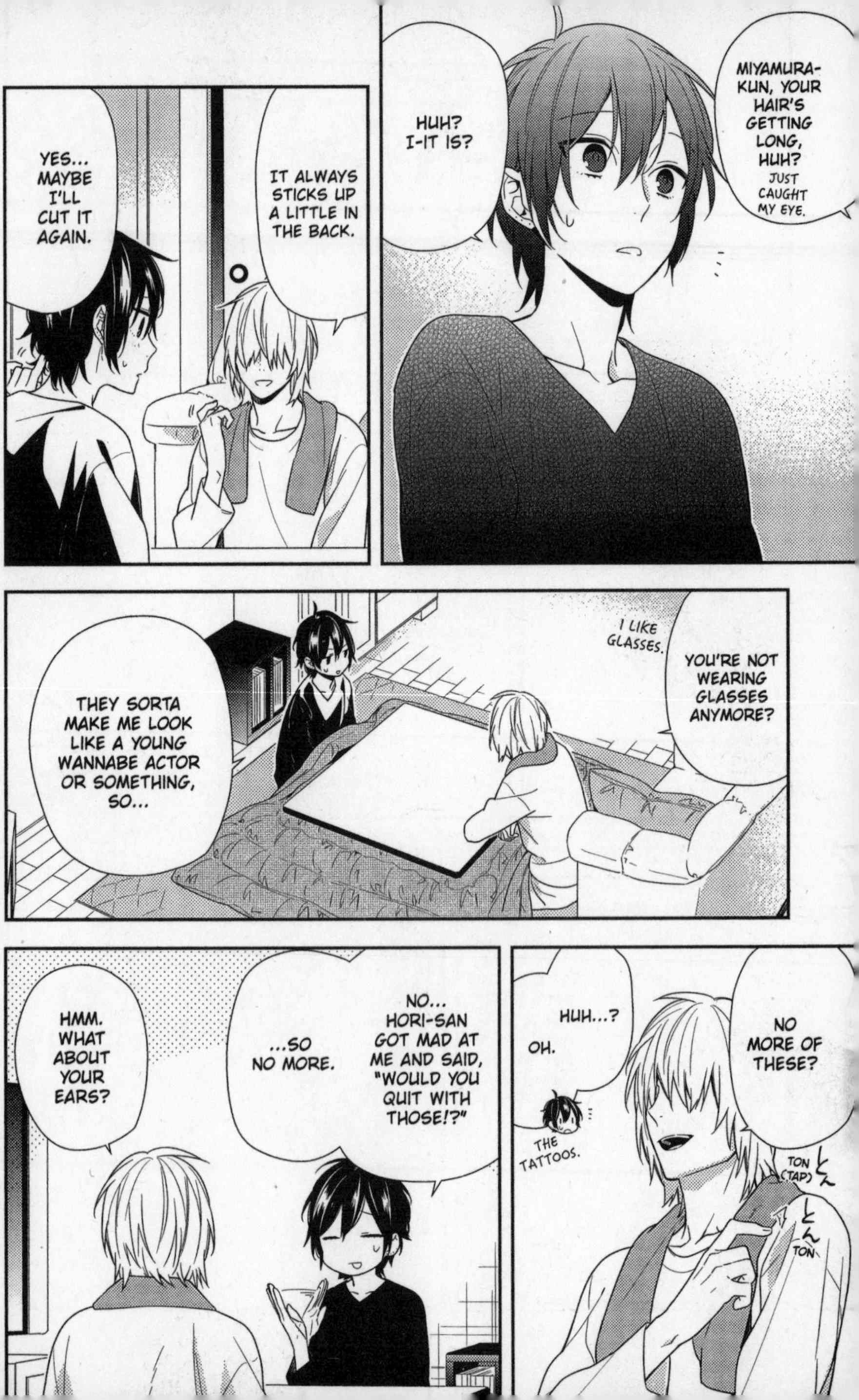
MIYAMURA-KUN, YOUR HAIR'S GETTING LONG, HUH?
JUST CAUGHT MY EYE.
HUH? I-IT IS?
IT ALWAYS STICKS UP A LITTLE IN THE BACK.
YES... MAYBE I'LL CUT IT AGAIN.
YOU'RE NOT WEARING GLASSES ANYMORE?
I LIKE GLASSES.
THEY SORTA MAKE ME LOOK LIKE A YOUNG WANNABE ACTOR OR SOMETHING, SO...
NO MORE OF THESE?
TON (TAP) とん
とん TON
HUH...?
OH.
THE TATTOOS.
NO... HORI-SAN GOT MAD AT ME AND SAID, "WOULD YOU QUIT WITH THOSE!?"
...SO NO MORE.
HMM. WHAT ABOUT YOUR EARS?

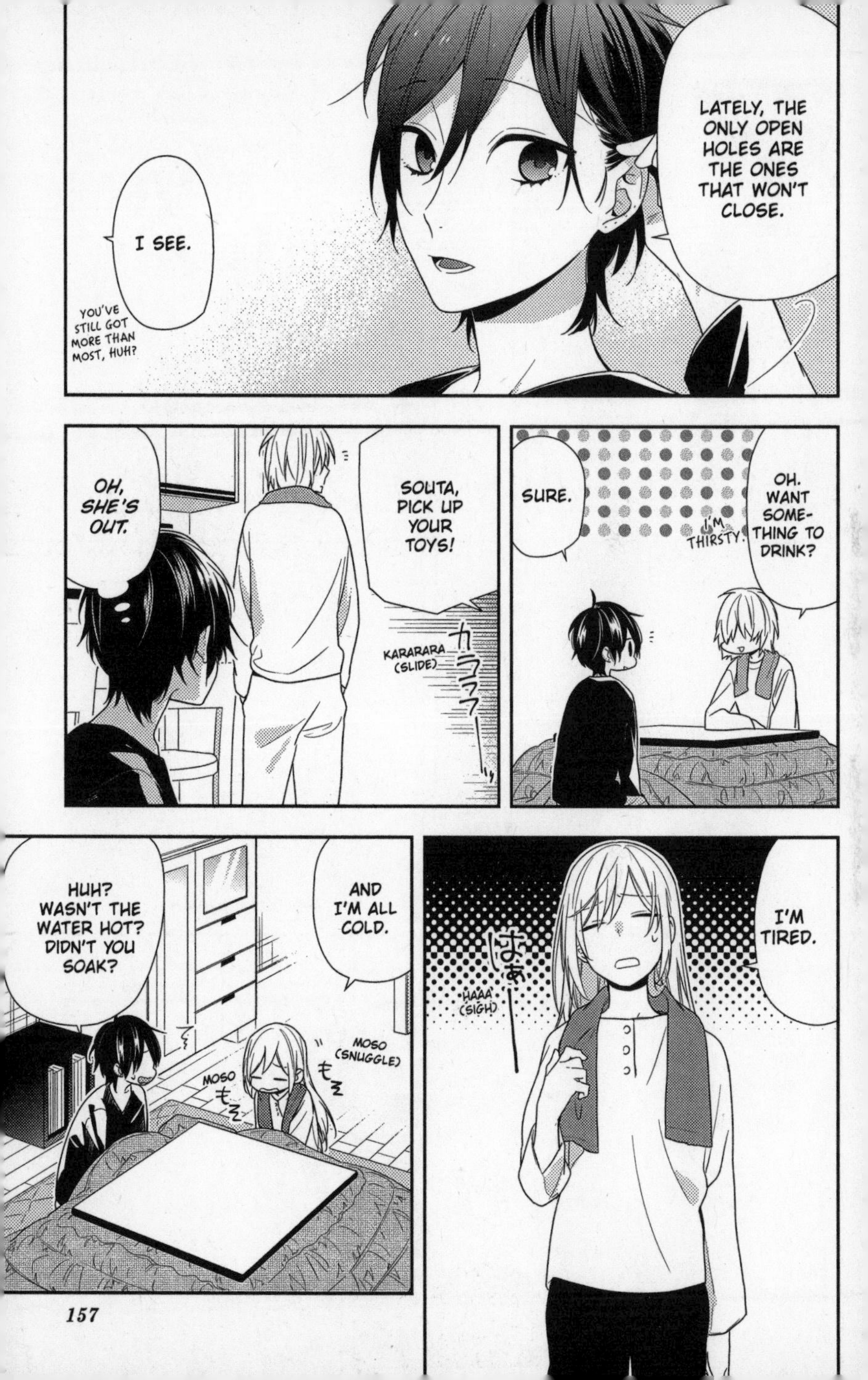
LATELY, THE ONLY OPEN HOLES ARE THE ONES THAT WON'T CLOSE.
I SEE.
YOU'VE STILL GOT MORE THAN MOST, HUH?
OH. WANT SOME-THING TO DRINK?
I'M THIRSTY.
SURE.
SOUTA, PICK UP YOUR TOYS!
KARARARA (SLIDE)
OH, SHE'S OUT.
I'M TIRED.
HAAA (SIGH)
AND I'M ALL COLD.
MOSO (SNUGGLE)
MOSO
HUH? WASN'T THE WATER HOT? DIDN'T YOU SOAK?

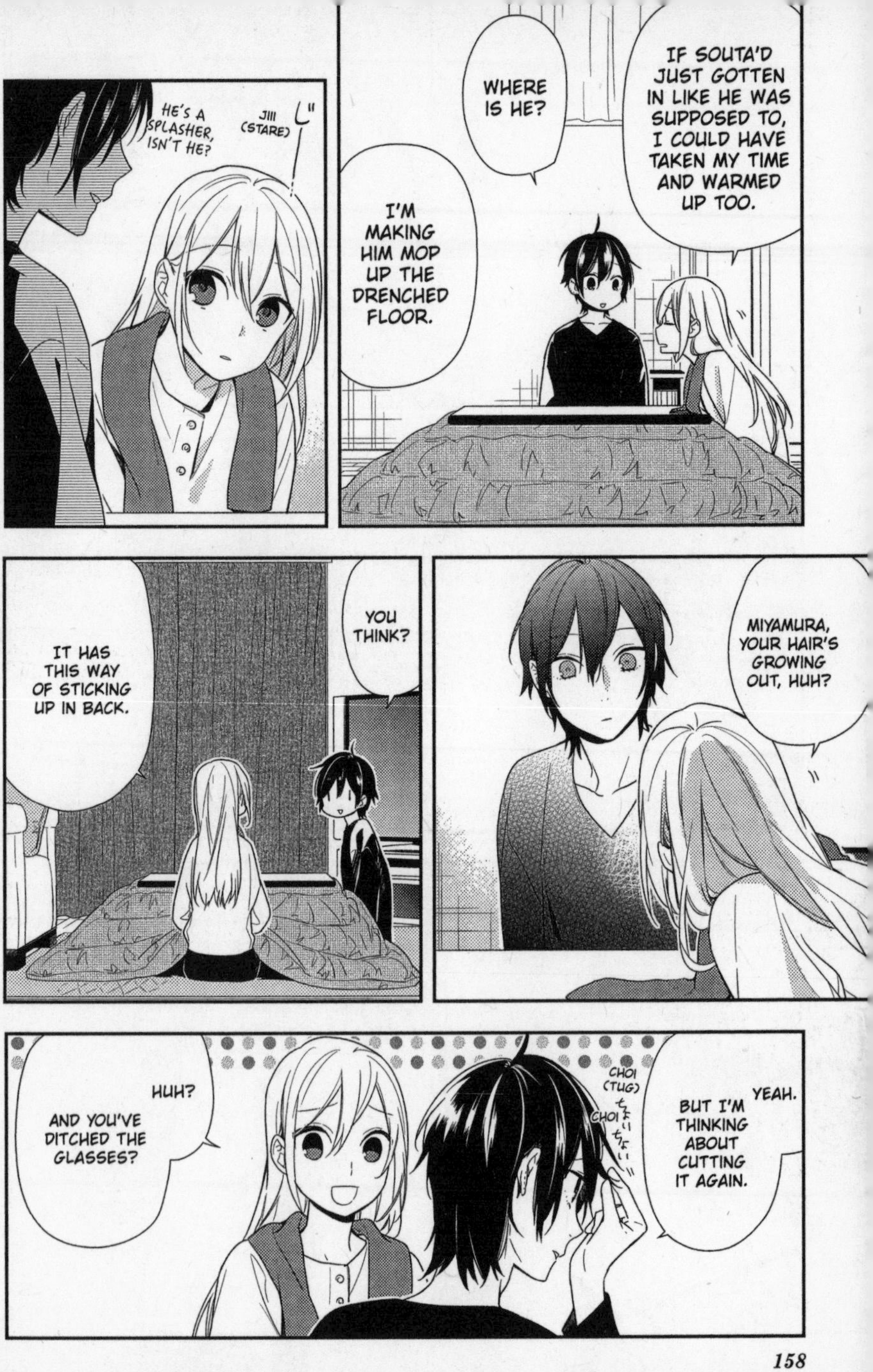
IF SOUTA'D JUST GOTTEN IN LIKE HE WAS SUPPOSED TO, I COULD HAVE TAKEN MY TIME AND WARMED UP TOO.
WHERE IS HE?
I'M MAKING HIM MOP UP THE DRENCHED FLOOR.
JIII (STARE)
HE'S A SPLASHER, ISN'T HE?
MIYAMURA, YOUR HAIR'S GROWING OUT, HUH?
YOU THINK?
IT HAS THIS WAY OF STICKING UP IN BACK.
YEAH.
BUT I'M THINKING ABOUT CUTTING IT AGAIN.
CHOI (TUG)
CHOI
HUH?
AND YOU'VE DITCHED THE GLASSES?

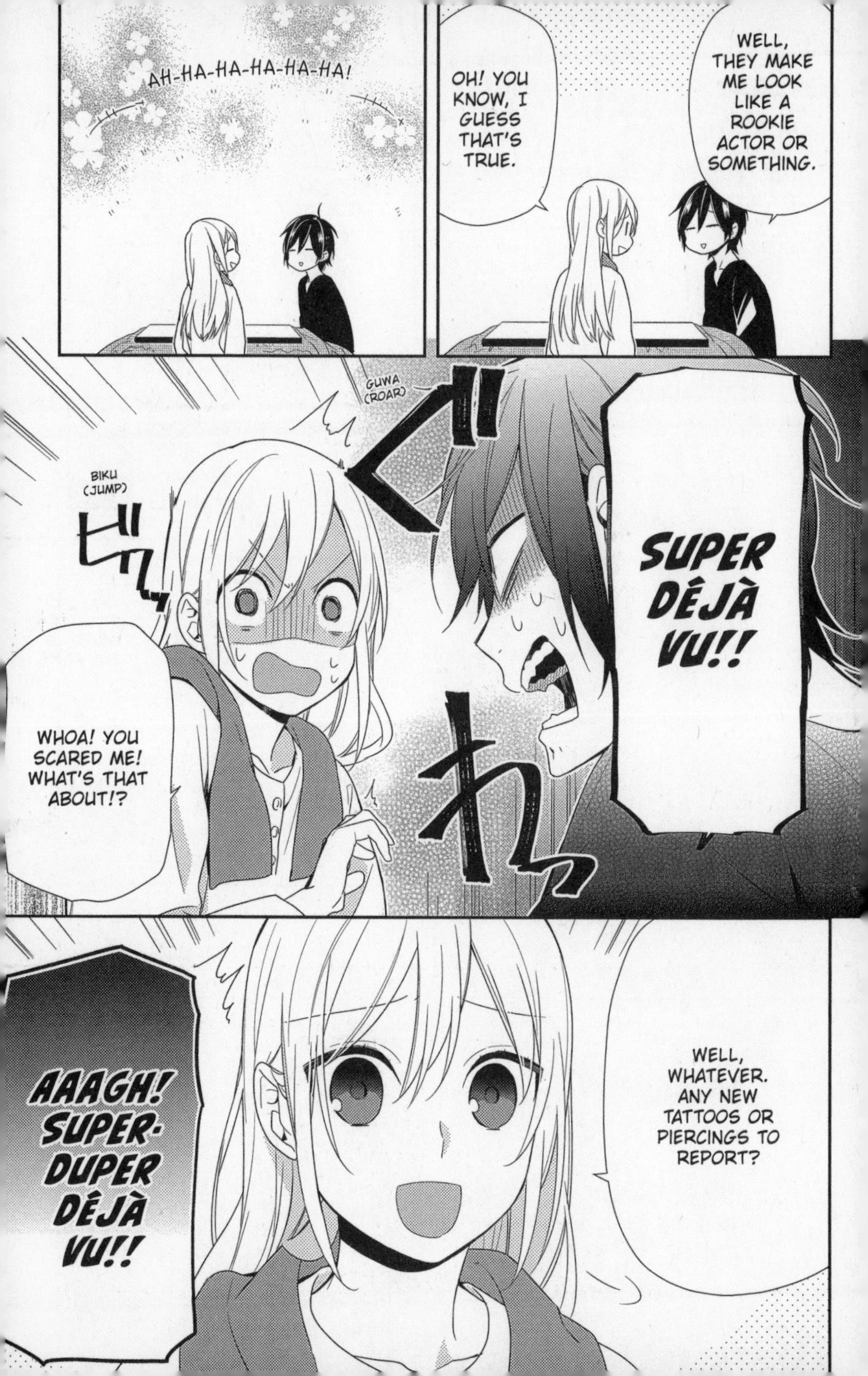
WELL, THEY MAKE ME LOOK LIKE A ROOKIE ACTOR OR SOMETHING.
OH! YOU KNOW, I GUESS THAT'S TRUE.
AH-HA-HA-HA-HA-HA!
GUWA (ROAR)
SUPER DÊJÀ VU!!
BIKU (JUMP)
WHOA! YOU SCARED ME! WHAT'S THAT ABOUT!?
WELL, WHATEVER. ANY NEW TATTOOS OR PIERCINGS TO REPORT?
AAAGH! SUPER-DUPER DÊJÀ VU!!

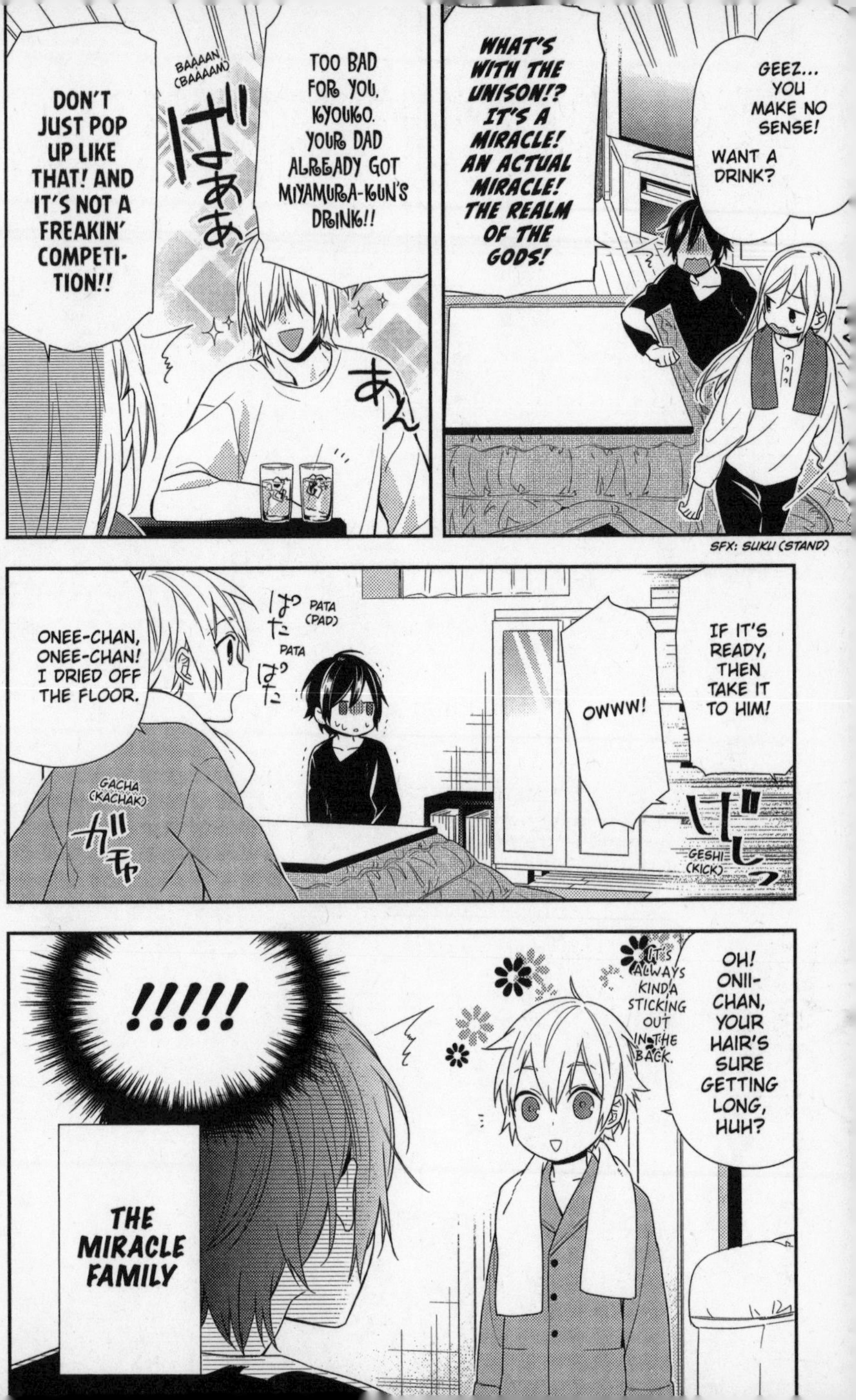
GEEZ... YOU MAKE NO SENSE!
WANT A DRINK?
SFX: SUKU (STAND)
WHAT'S WITH THE UNISON!? IT'S A MIRACLE! AN ACTUAL MIRACLE! THE REALM OF THE GODS!
TOO BAD FOR YOU, KYOUKO. YOUR DAD ALREADY GOT MIYAMURA-KUN'S DRINK!!
BAAAAN (BAAAAM)
ばあぁ
あん
DON'T JUST POP UP LIKE THAT! AND IT'S NOT A FREAKIN' COMPETITION!!
IF IT'S READY, THEN TAKE IT TO HIM!
OWWW!
GESHI (KICK)
げしっ
PATA (PAD) PATA
ぱたぱた
ONEE-CHAN, ONEE-CHAN! I DRIED OFF THE FLOOR.
GACHA (KACHAK)
ガチャ
OH! ONII-CHAN, YOUR HAIR'S SURE GETTING LONG, HUH?
IT'S ALWAYS KINDA STICKING OUT IN THE BACK.
!!!!!
THE MIRACLE FAMILY

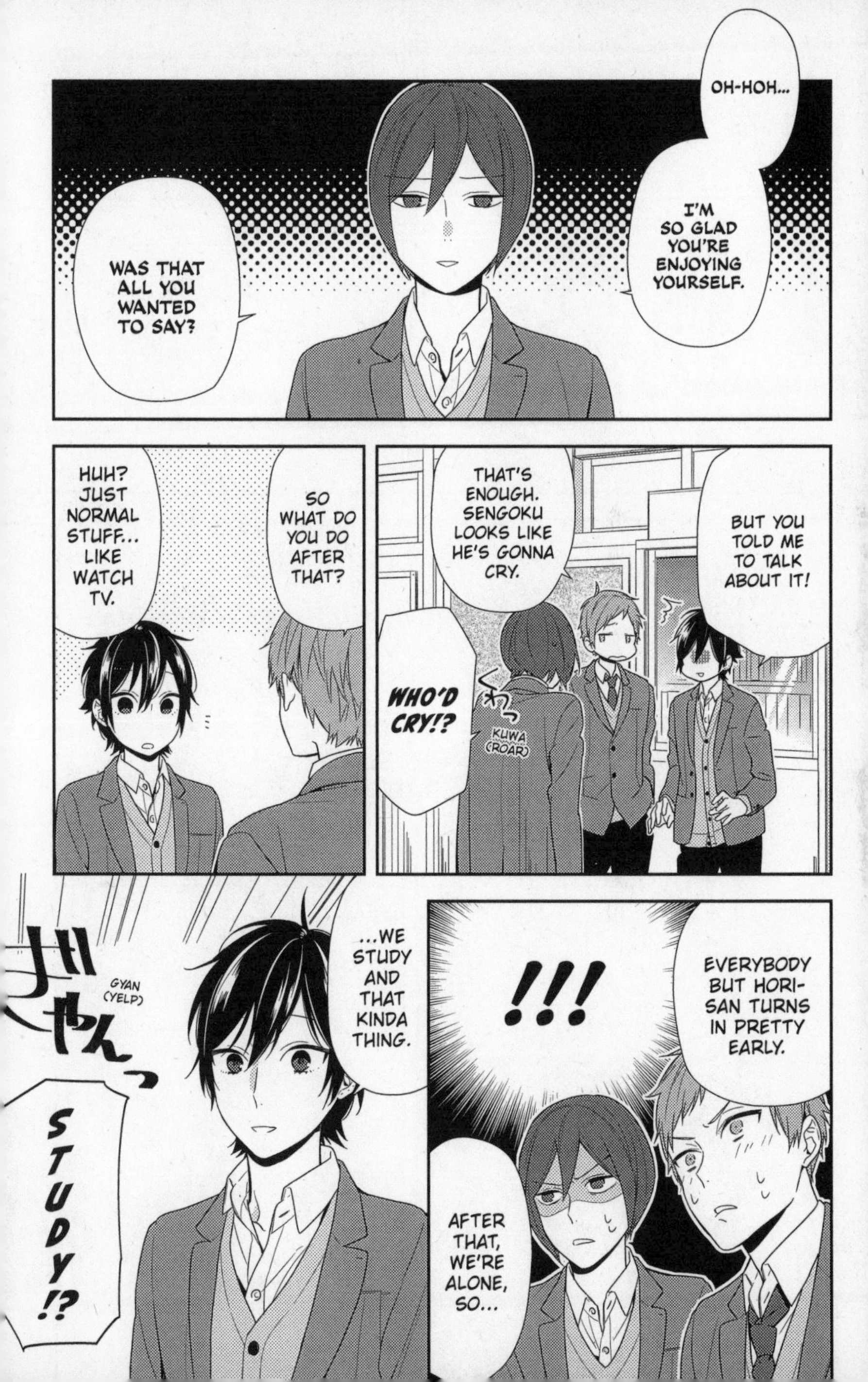
OH-HOH...
I'M SO GLAD YOU'RE ENJOYING YOURSELF.
WAS THAT ALL YOU WANTED TO SAY?
BUT YOU TOLD ME TO TALK ABOUT IT!
THAT'S ENOUGH. SENGOKU LOOKS LIKE HE'S GONNA CRY.
WHO'D CRY!?
KUWA (ROAR)
SO WHAT DO YOU DO AFTER THAT?
HUH? JUST NORMAL STUFF... LIKE WATCH TV.
EVERYBODY BUT HORI-SAN TURNS IN PRETTY EARLY.
!!!
AFTER THAT, WE'RE ALONE, SO...
...WE STUDY AND THAT KINDA THING.
GYAN (YELP)
STUDY!?

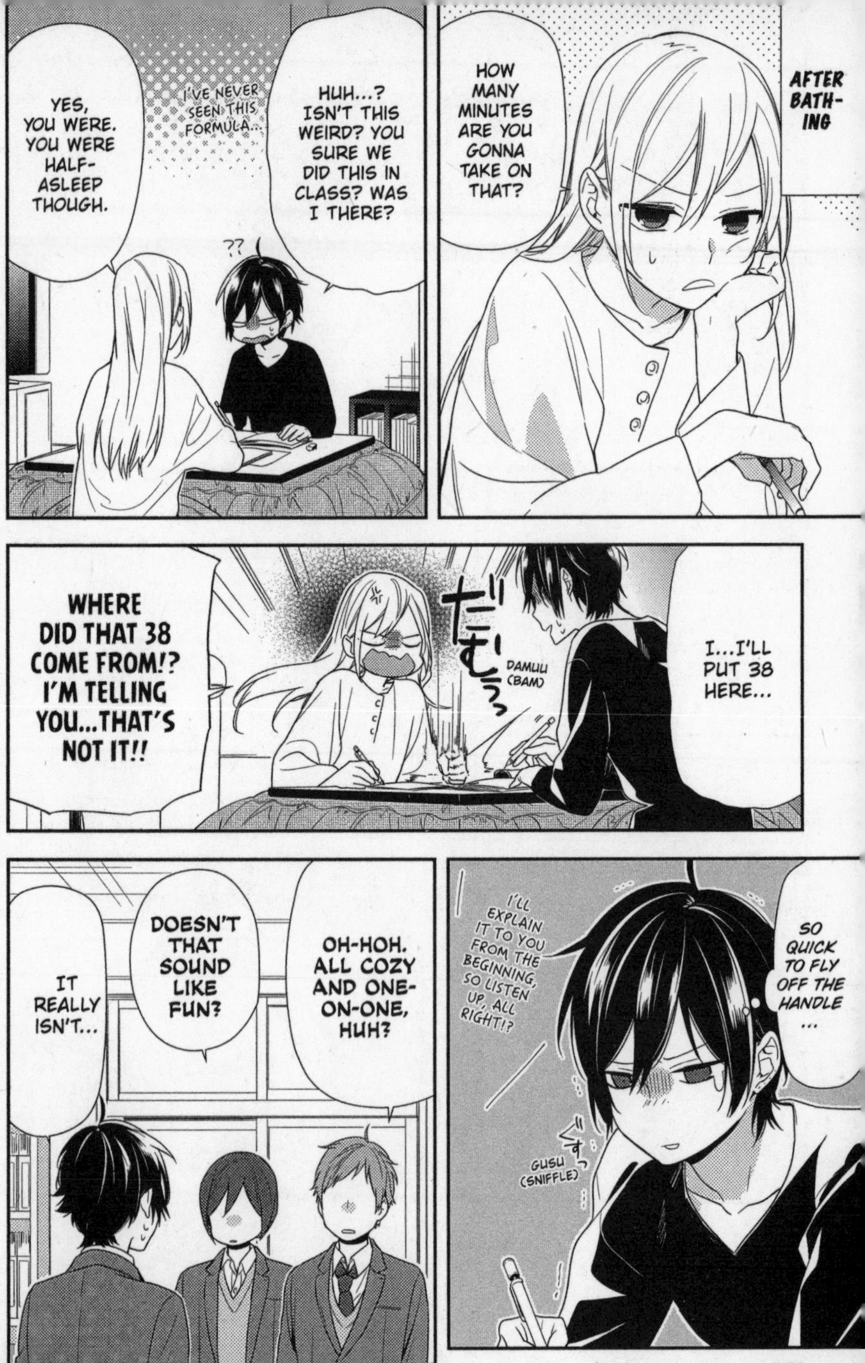
AFTER BATHING
HOW MANY MINUTES ARE YOU GONNA TAKE ON THAT?
HUH...? ISN'T THIS WEIRD? YOU SURE WE DID THIS IN CLASS? WAS I THERE?
I'VE NEVER SEEN THIS FORMULA...
??
YES, YOU WERE. YOU WERE HALF-ASLEEP THOUGH.
I...I'LL PUT 38 HERE...
DAMUU (BAM)
WHERE DID THAT 38 COME FROM!? I'M TELLING YOU...THAT'S NOT IT!!
SO QUICK TO FLY OFF THE HANDLE...
I'LL EXPLAIN IT TO YOU FROM THE BEGINNING, SO LISTEN UP, ALL RIGHT!?
GUSU (SNIFFLE)
OH-HOH. ALL COZY AND ONE-ON-ONE, HUH?
DOESN'T THAT SOUND LIKE FUN?
IT REALLY ISN'T...

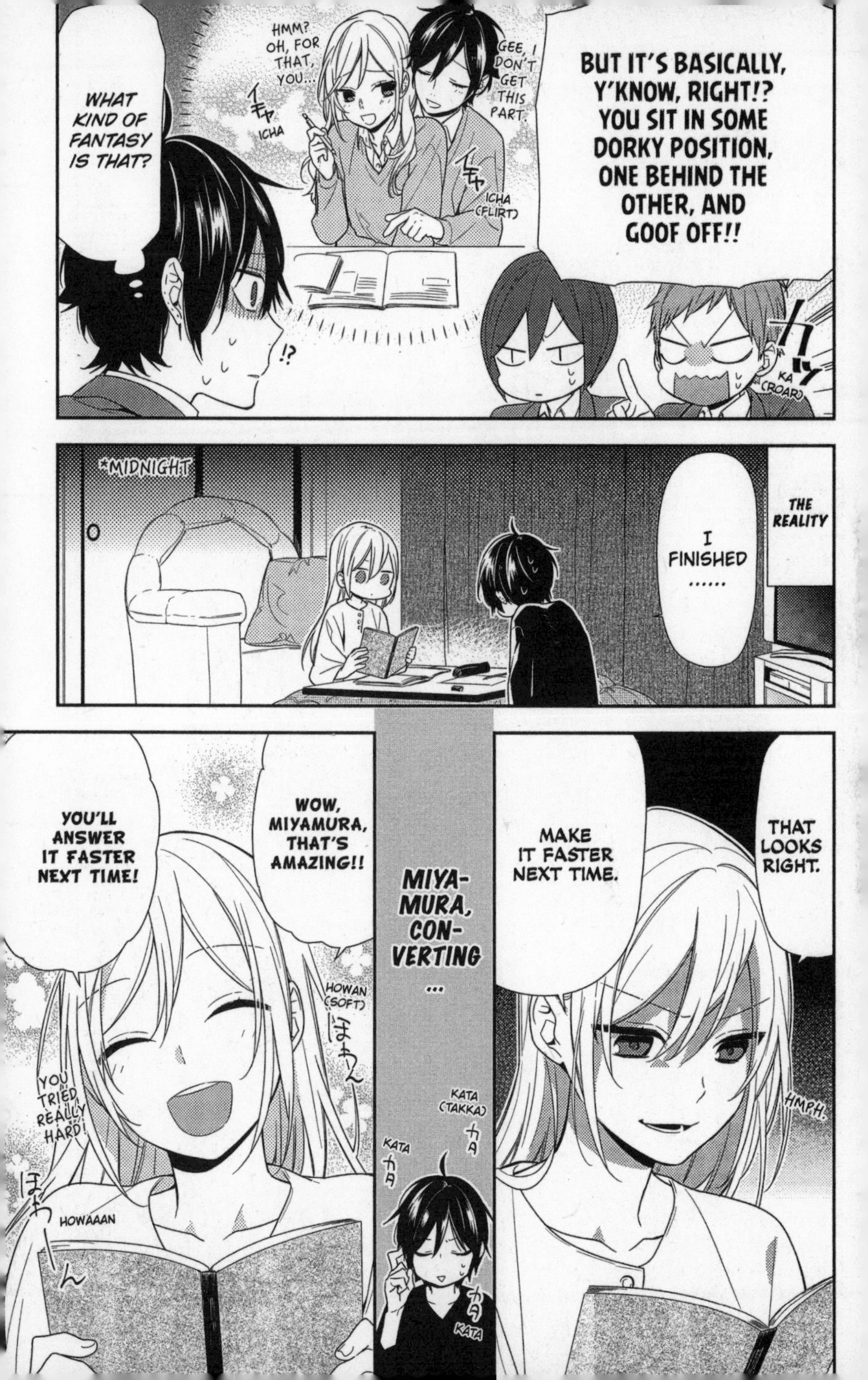
BUT IT'S BASICALLY, Y'KNOW, RIGHT!? YOU SIT IN SOME DORKY POSITION, ONE BEHIND THE OTHER, AND GOOF OFF!!
GEE, I DON'T GET THIS PART.
HMM? OH, FOR THAT, YOU...
ICHA (FLIRT)
ICHA
WHAT KIND OF FANTASY IS THAT?
!?
KA (ROAR)
THE REALITY
I FINISHED ......
*MIDNIGHT
THAT LOOKS RIGHT.
MAKE IT FASTER NEXT TIME.
HMPH.
MIYA-MURA, CON-VERTING ...
KATA (TAKKA)
KATA
KATA
WOW, MIYAMURA, THAT'S AMAZING!!
YOU'LL ANSWER IT FASTER NEXT TIME!
HOWAN (SOFT)
YOU TRIED REALLY HARD!
HOWAAAN

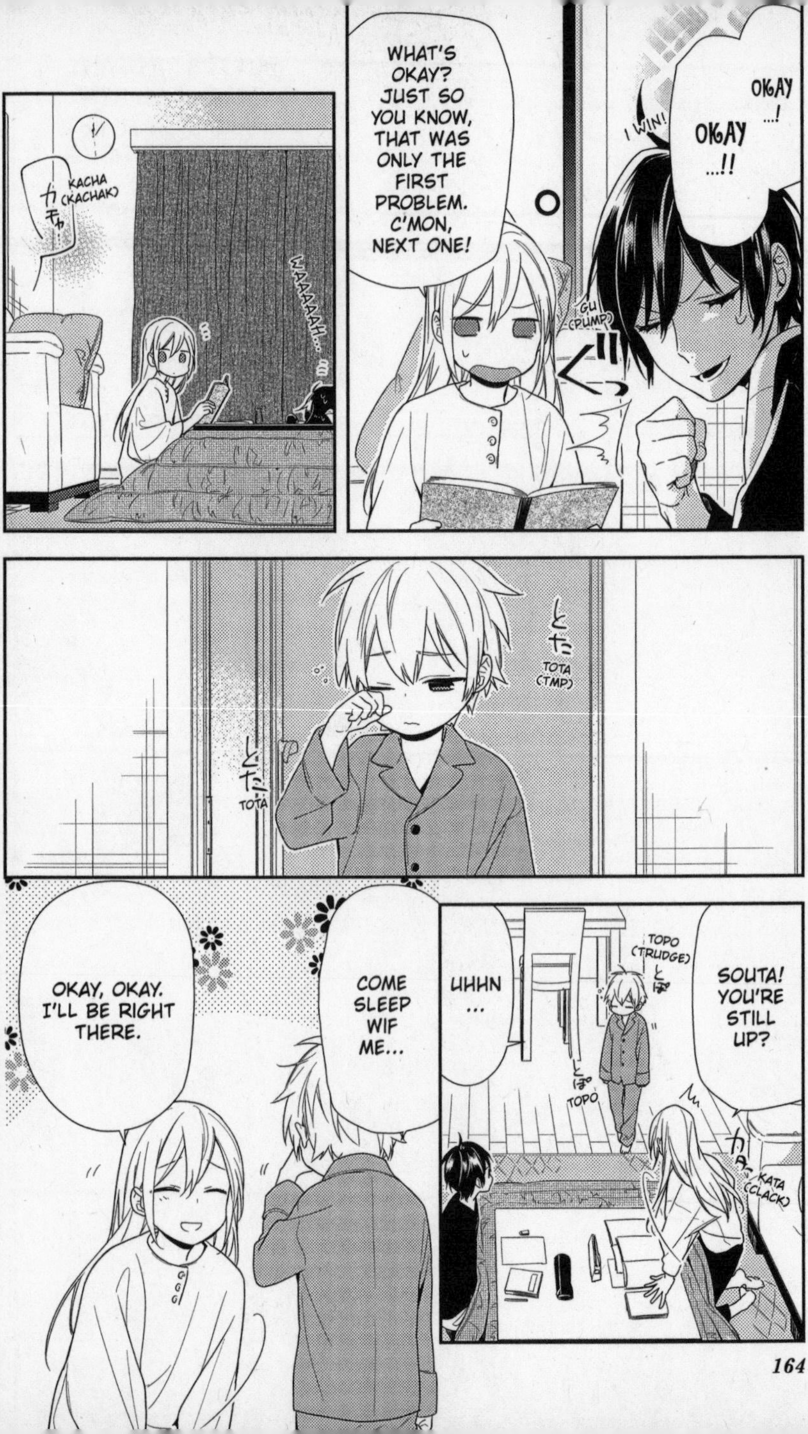
OKAY ...!
OKAY ...!!
I WIN!
GU (PUMP)
WHAT'S OKAY? JUST SO YOU KNOW, THAT WAS ONLY THE FIRST PROBLEM. C'MON, NEXT ONE!
KACHA (KACHAK)
WAAAAAH...
TOTA (TMP)
TOTA
SOUTA! YOU'RE STILL UP?
KATA (CLACK)
TOPO (TRUDGE)
TOPO
UHHN ...
COME SLEEP WIF ME...
OKAY, OKAY. I'LL BE RIGHT THERE.

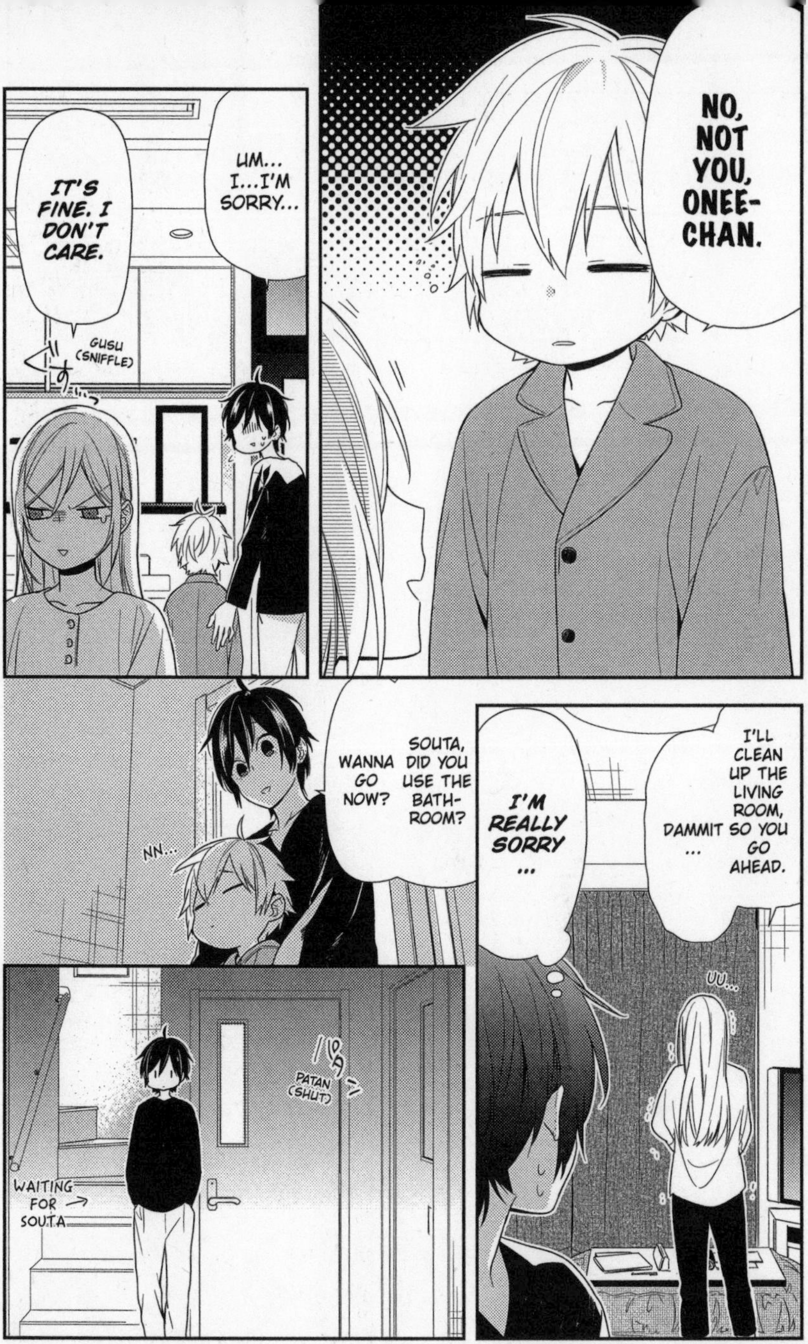
NO, NOT YOU, ONEE-CHAN.
UM... I...I'M SORRY...
IT'S FINE. I DON'T CARE.
GUSU (SNIFFLE)
I'LL CLEAN UP THE LIVING ROOM, SO YOU GO AHEAD.
DAMMIT ...
I'M REALLY SORRY ...
UU...
SOUTA, DID YOU USE THE BATHROOM?
WANNA GO NOW?
NN...
PATAN (SHUT)
WAITING FOR SOUTA

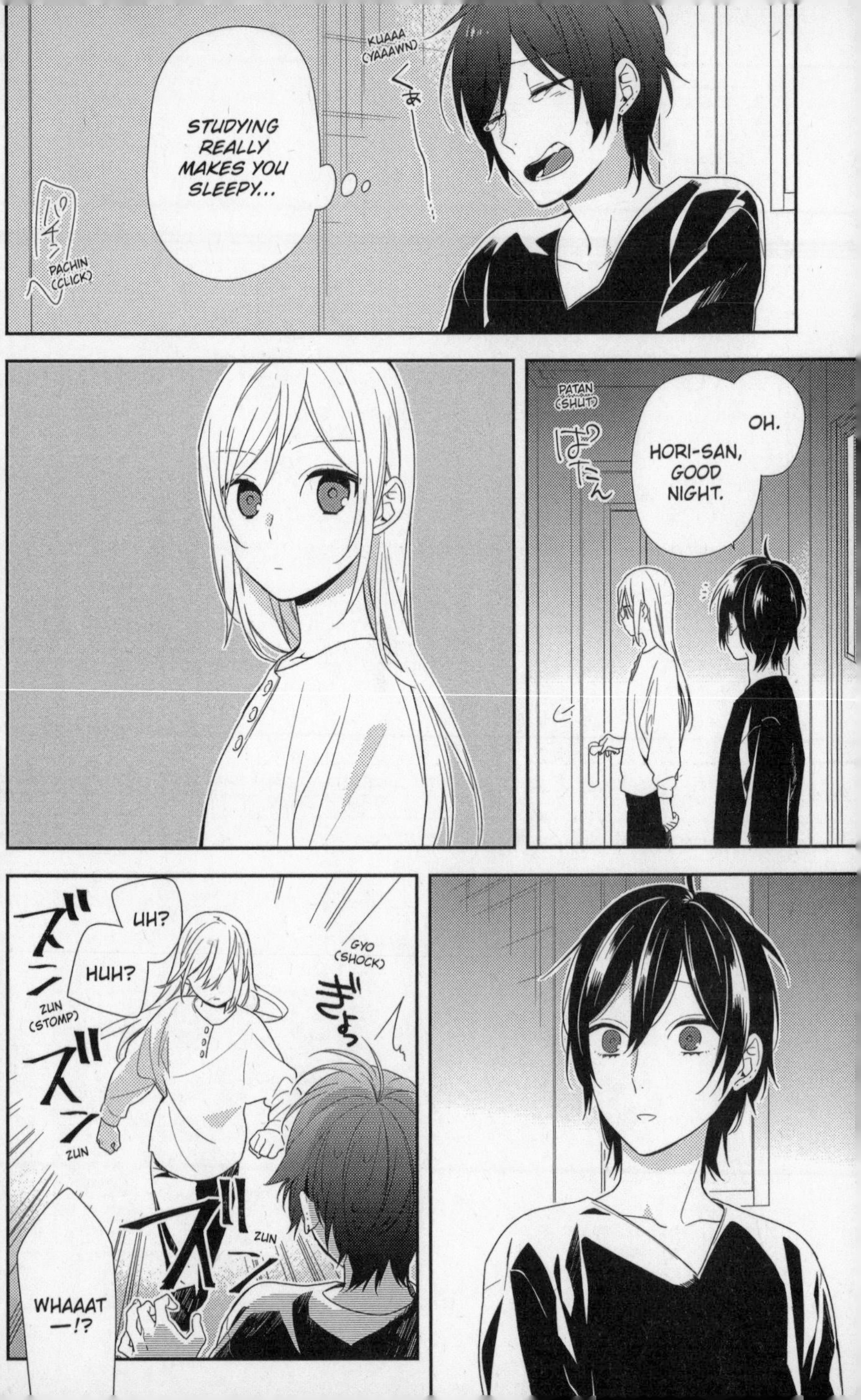
KUAAA (YAAAWN)
くあ〜
STUDYING REALLY MAKES YOU SLEEPY...
パチン
PACHIN (CLICK)
PATAN (SHUT)
ぱたん
OH.
HORI-SAN, GOOD NIGHT.
UH?
HUH?
GYO (SHOCK)
ぎょ
ズン
ZUN (STOMP)
ズン
ZUN
ズン
ZUN
WHAAAT—!?

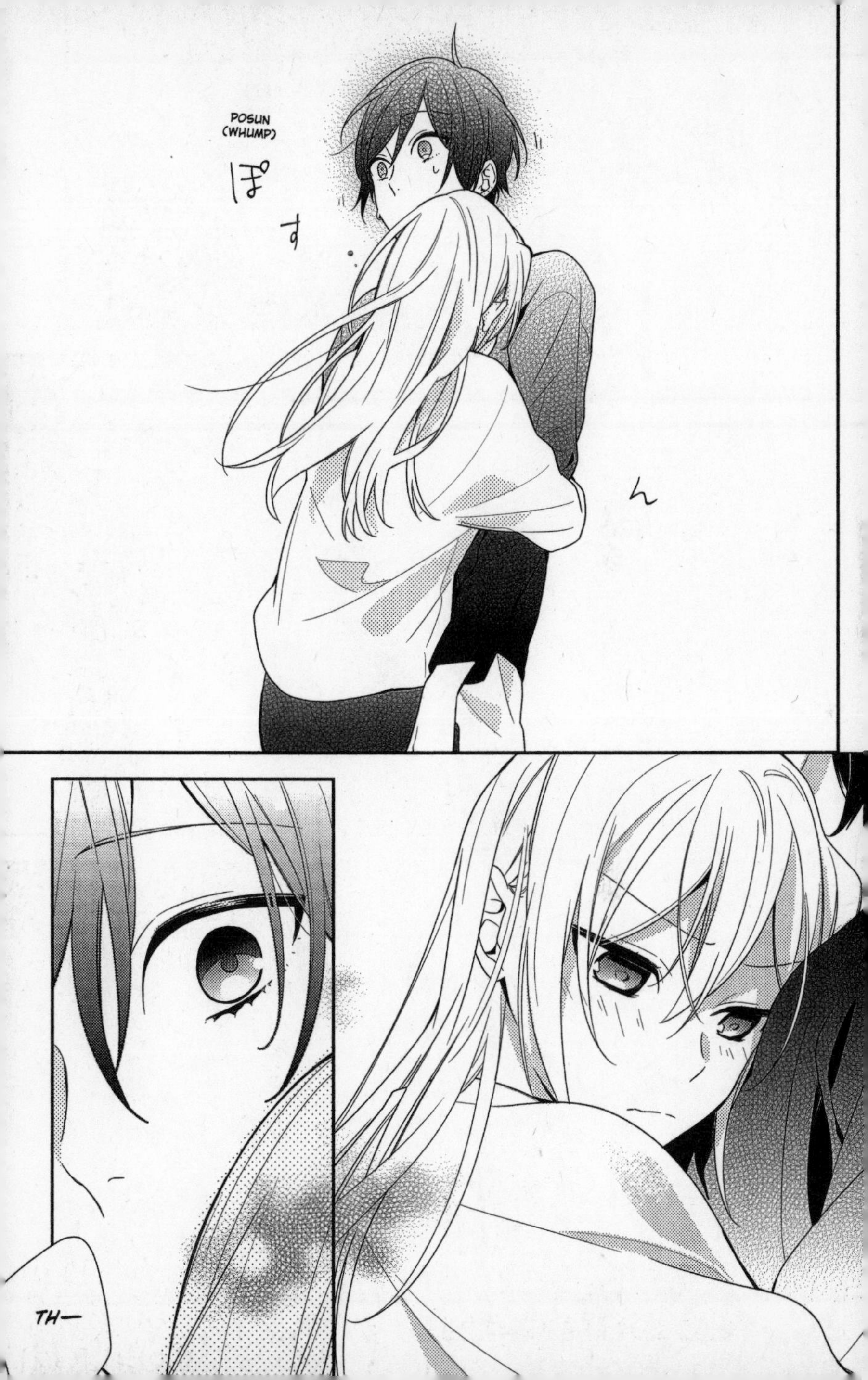
POSUN (WHUMP)
ぽす
ん
TH—

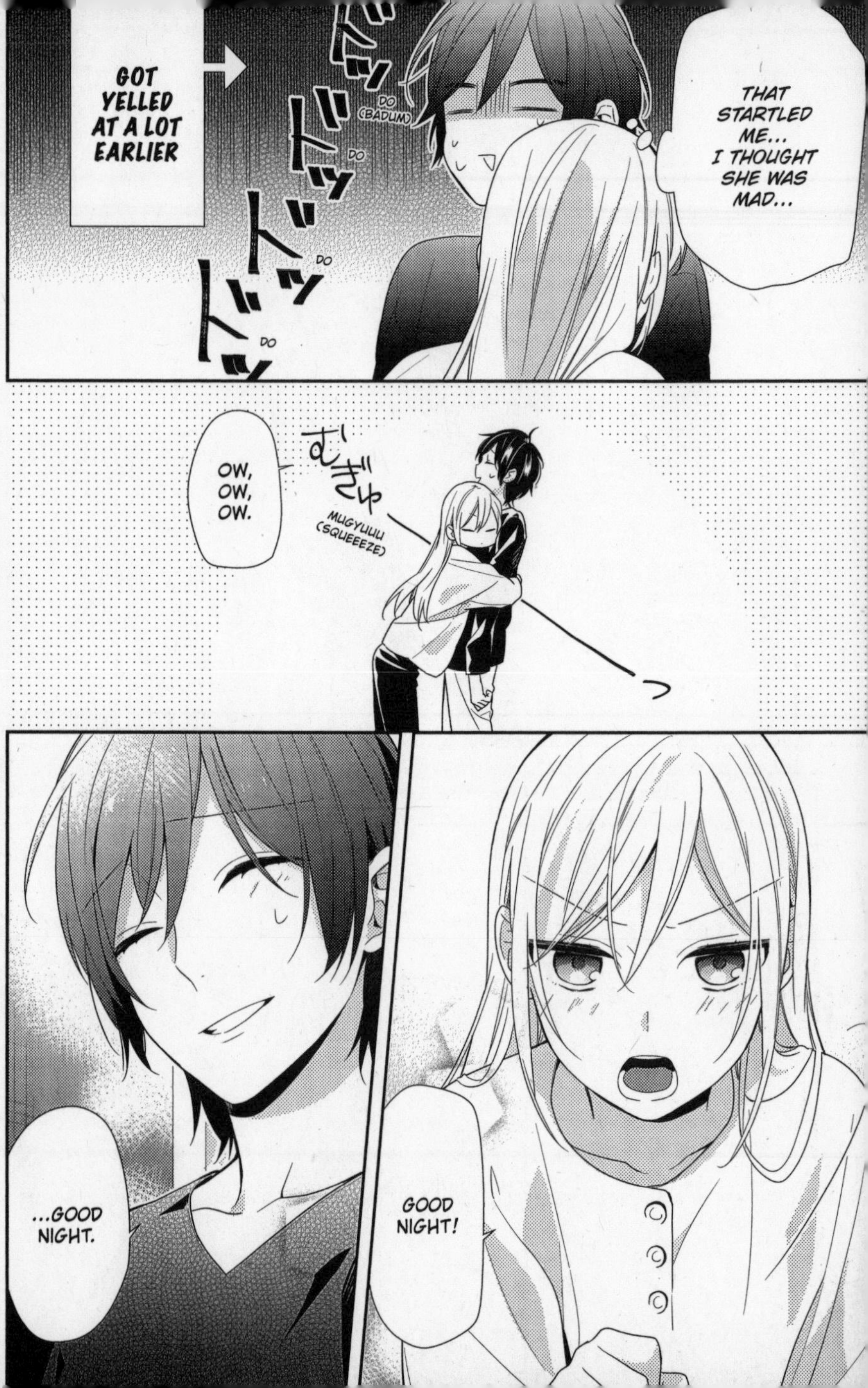
THAT STARTLED ME... I THOUGHT SHE WAS MAD...
ドッ DO (BADUM)
ドッ DO
ドッ DO
ドッ DO
GOT YELLED AT A LOT EARLIER
むぎゅ MUGYUUU (SQUEEZE)
OW, OW, OW.
GOOD NIGHT!
...GOOD NIGHT.

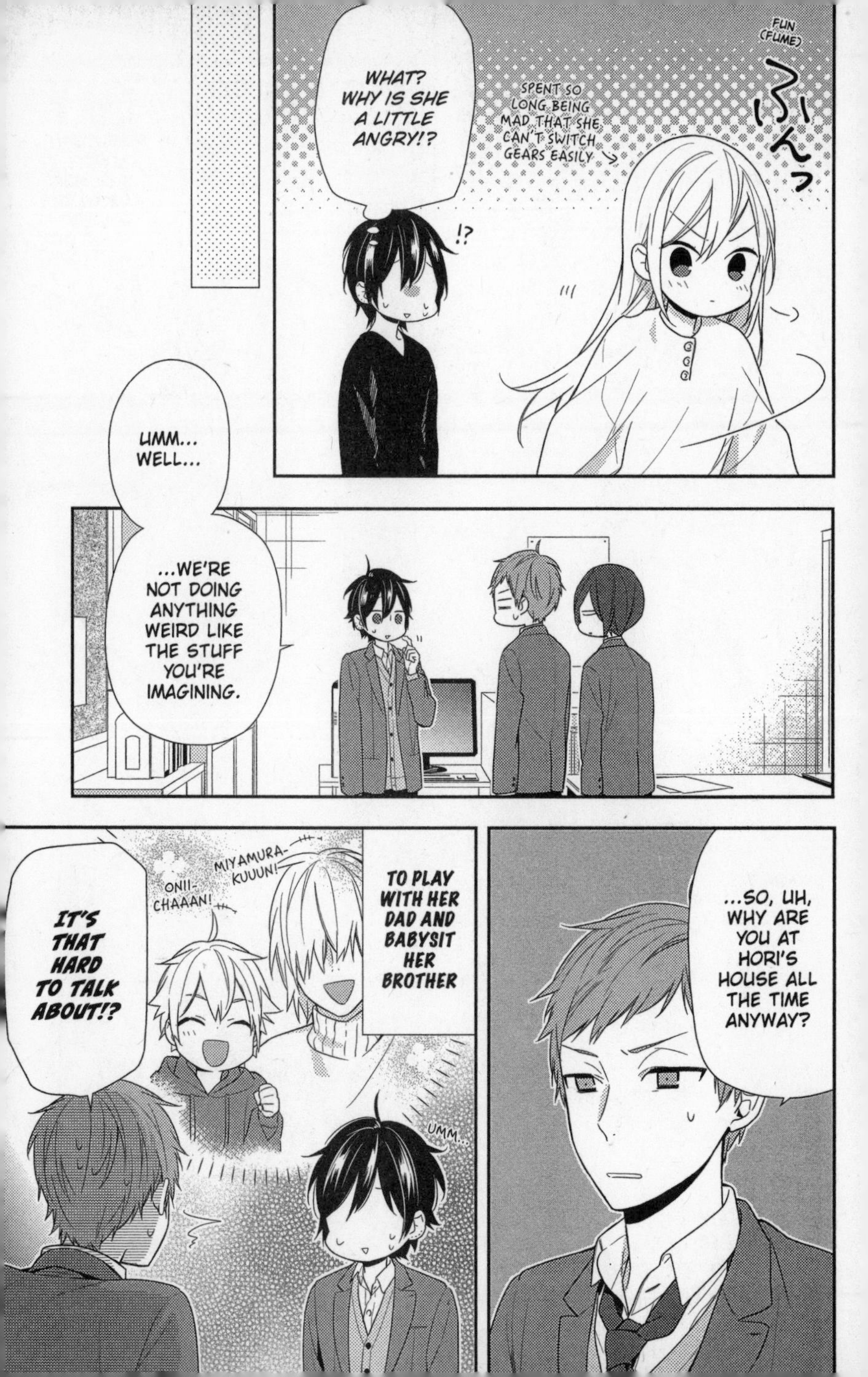
FUN (FUME)
ふんっ
SPENT SO LONG BEING MAD THAT SHE CAN'T SWITCH GEARS EASILY
WHAT? WHY IS SHE A LITTLE ANGRY!?
!?
UMM... WELL...
...WE'RE NOT DOING ANYTHING WEIRD LIKE THE STUFF YOU'RE IMAGINING.
...SO, UH, WHY ARE YOU AT HORI'S HOUSE ALL THE TIME ANYWAY?
TO PLAY WITH HER DAD AND BABYSIT HER BROTHER
MIYAMURA-KUUUN!
ONII-CHAAAN!
UMM...
IT'S THAT HARD TO TALK ABOUT!?

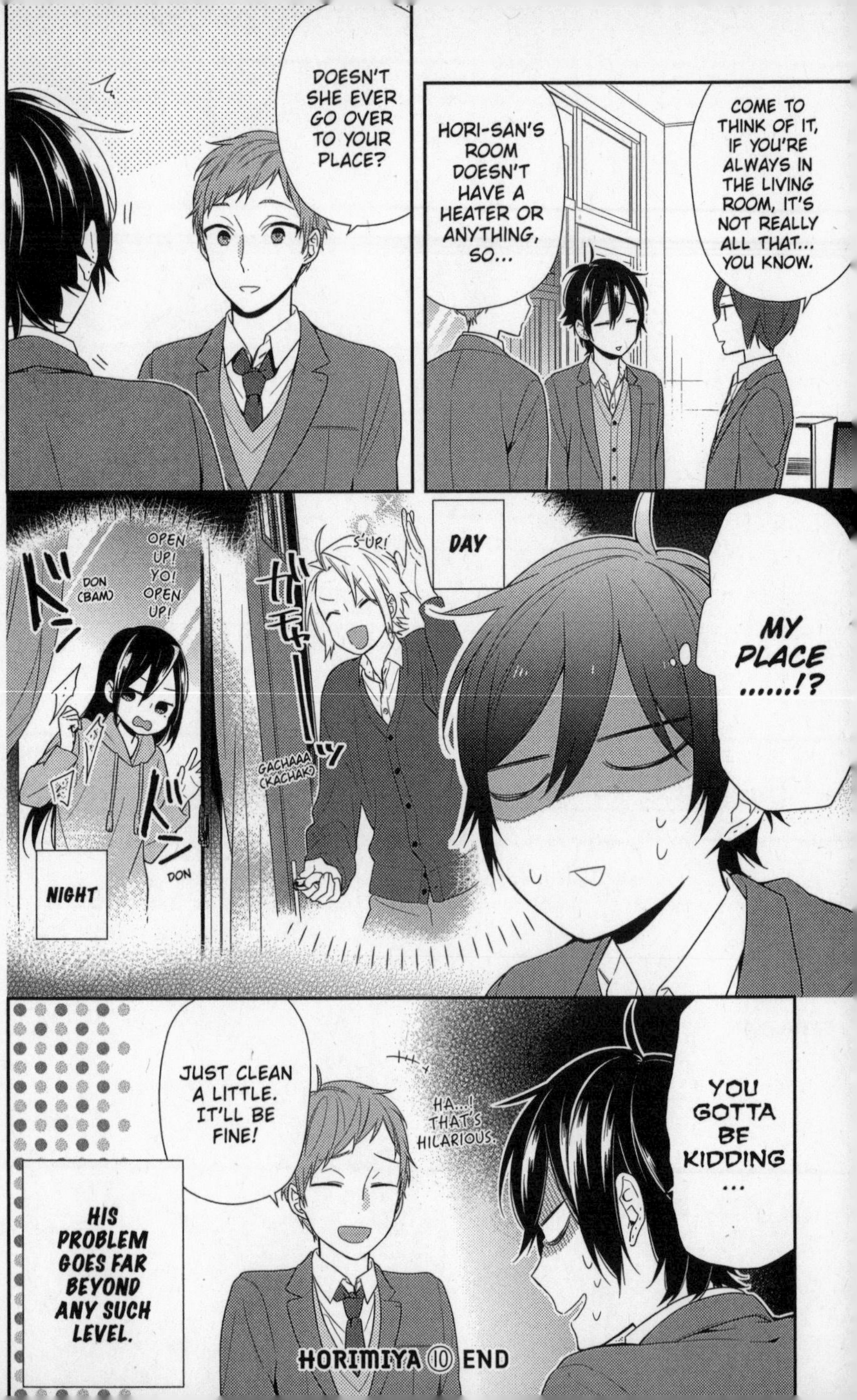
COME TO THINK OF IT, IF YOU'RE ALWAYS IN THE LIVING ROOM, IT'S NOT REALLY ALL THAT... YOU KNOW.
HORI-SAN'S ROOM DOESN'T HAVE A HEATER OR ANYTHING, SO...
DOESN'T SHE EVER GO OVER TO YOUR PLACE?
MY PLACE ......!?
DAY
S-UR!
GACHAAA (KACHAK)
OPEN UP! YO! OPEN UP!
DON (BAM)
DON
NIGHT
YOU GOTTA BE KIDDING ...
HA...! THAT'S HILARIOUS.
JUST CLEAN A LITTLE. IT'LL BE FINE!
HIS PROBLEM GOES FAR BEYOND ANY SUCH LEVEL.
HORIMIYA ⑩ END

To Be Continued...

Translation Notes

Page 19 – Ringing in the New Year at the shrine
Going to the shrine first thing in the New Year is a well-known Japanese tradition (*hatsumoude*). But going to the shrine on New Year's Eve and staying to ring in the New Year is called *ninenmairi* ("two-year visit"), which is what Hori and Miyamura are doing here.

Page 28 – *Amazake*
This sweet beverage, the name of which means "sweet sake," is made from fermented rice, but it's generally either low in alcohol or non-alcoholic.

Page 66 – Living ghost
In Japanese folklore, a living ghost is said to be the wandering soul of a person who is only asleep or very sick and who generally isn't aware that their soul has gone elsewhere. Living ghosts are usually fueled by strong negative emotions such as rage or jealousy, and they can be just as dangerous as regular ghosts.

Page 74 – The season for ghost stories
Summer is the season for ghost stories in Japan.

Page 89 – Tamanori Snack
Tamanori is the term for the balancing-ball circus trick the squirrel-like critter is doing.

Page 121 – Goethe
Johann Wolfgang von Goethe (1749–1832) was a German writer and Renaissance man arguably best known for his books *Faust* and *The Sorrows of Young Werther*. His works tend to connote a romantic streak in their readers when they appear in Japanese pop culture.

Page 173 – First dream of the New Year
Japanese superstition says that whatever one dreams about on the first night of the year foretells one's luck for that year.

Page 173 – "New ears?"
The most common way to wish someone a happy New Year in Japanese is *akemashite omedetou gozaimasu*, which is literally "Congratulations on the beginning (of the year)." The verb *akeru*, which means "to open," is the part that Miyamura recognizes, so in the original edition, he asks, "Open? What are we opening?"

BONUS MANGA: MYAMURA ⑧

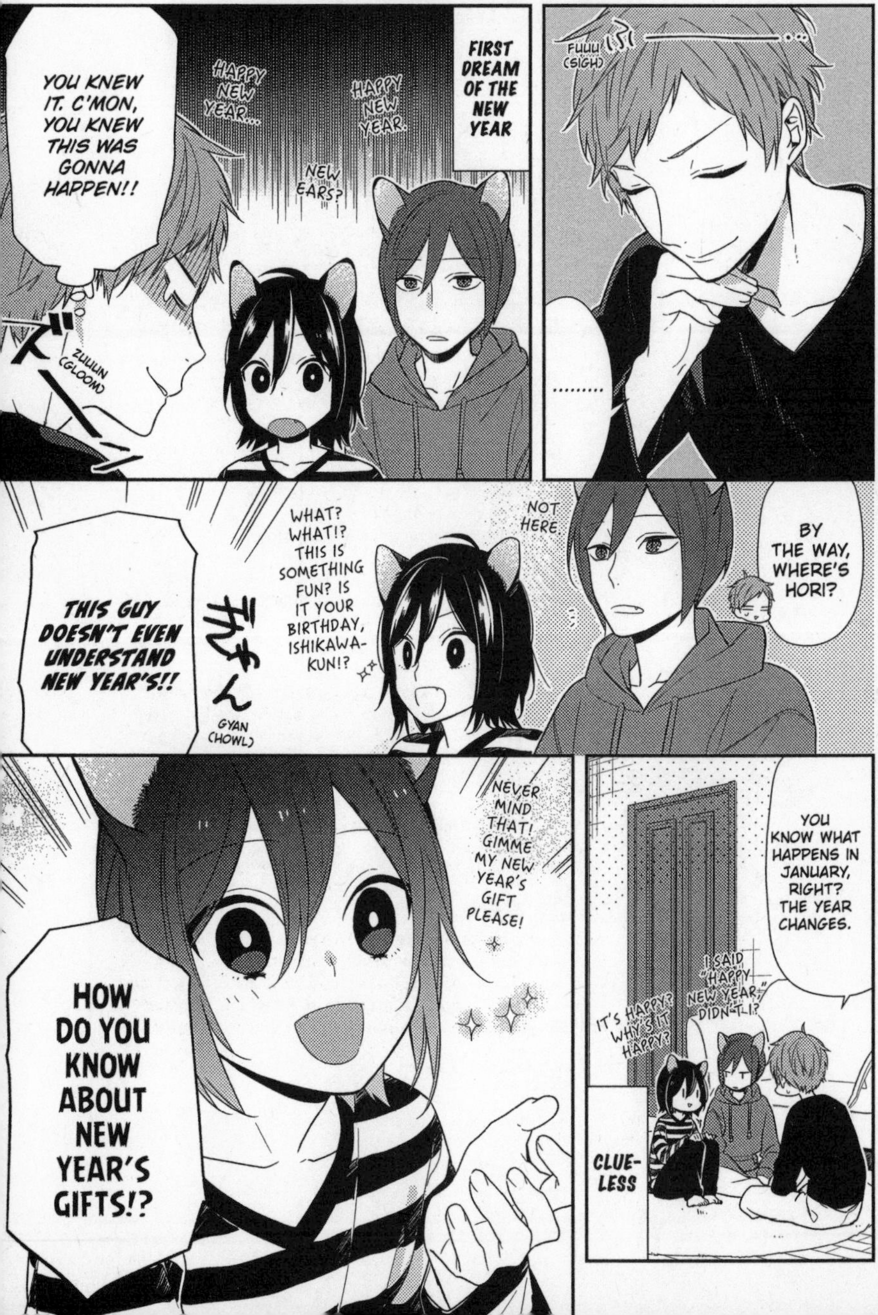

FUUU (SIGH)
....
FIRST DREAM OF THE NEW YEAR
HAPPY NEW YEAR.
HAPPY NEW YEAR...
NEW EARS?
YOU KNEW IT. C'MON, YOU KNEW THIS WAS GONNA HAPPEN!!
ZUUUN (GLOOM)
BY THE WAY, WHERE'S HORI?
NOT HERE.
WHAT? WHAT!? THIS IS SOMETHING FUN? IS IT YOUR BIRTHDAY, ISHIKAWA-KUN!?
GYAN (HOWL)
THIS GUY DOESN'T EVEN UNDERSTAND NEW YEAR'S!!
YOU KNOW WHAT HAPPENS IN JANUARY, RIGHT? THE YEAR CHANGES.
I SAID "HAPPY NEW YEAR," DIDN'T I?
IT'S HAPPY? WHY'S IT HAPPY?
CLUE-LESS
NEVER MIND THAT! GIMME MY NEW YEAR'S GIFT PLEASE!
HOW DO YOU KNOW ABOUT NEW YEAR'S GIFTS!?

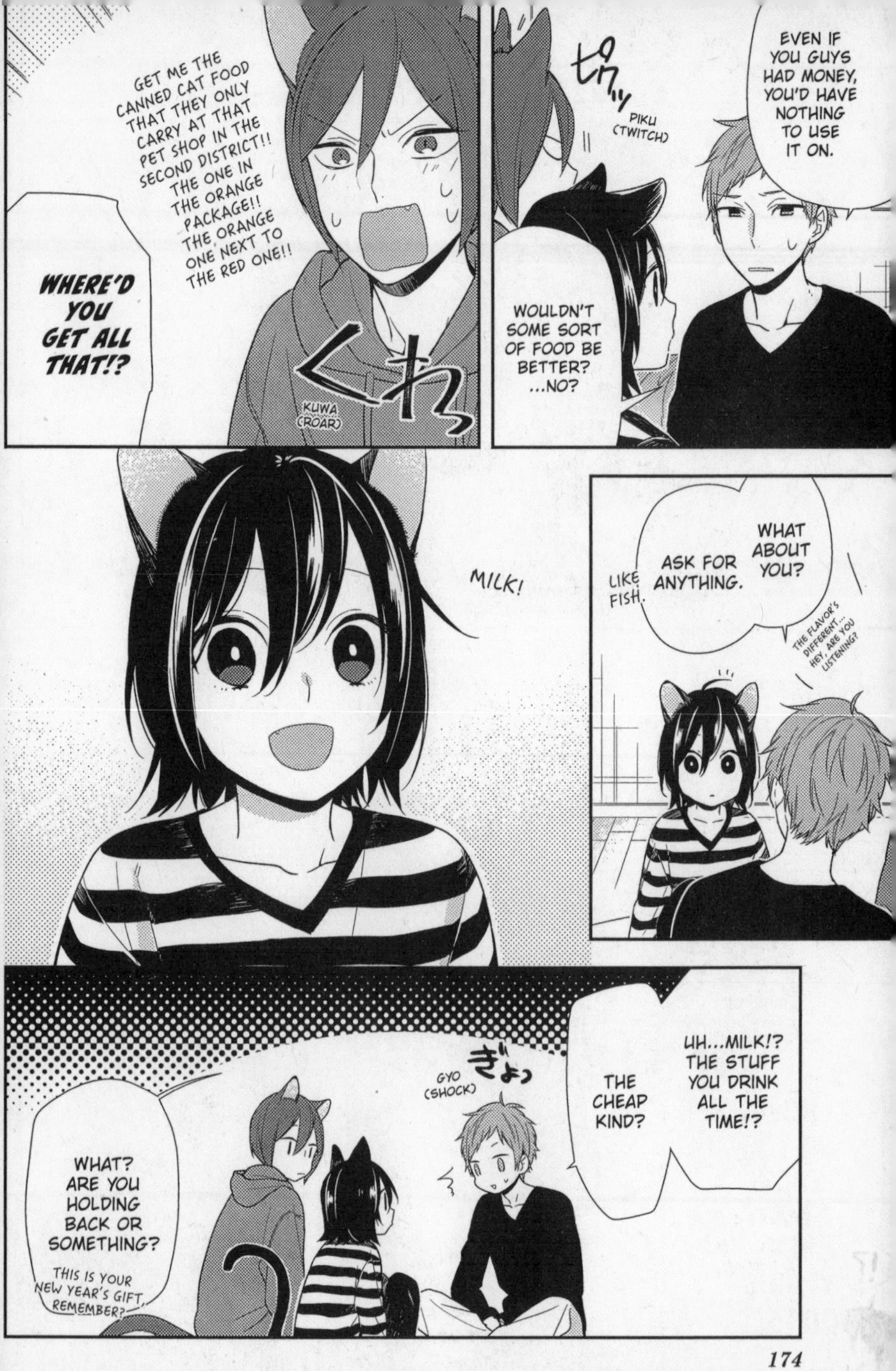
EVEN IF YOU GUYS HAD MONEY, YOU'D HAVE NOTHING TO USE IT ON.
ピクッ
PIKU (TWITCH)
WOULDN'T SOME SORT OF FOOD BE BETTER? ...NO?
GET ME THE CANNED CAT FOOD THAT THEY ONLY CARRY AT THAT PET SHOP IN THE SECOND DISTRICT!! THE ONE IN THE ORANGE PACKAGE!! THE ORANGE ONE NEXT TO THE RED ONE!!
WHERE'D YOU GET ALL THAT!?
くわ
KUWA (ROAR)
WHAT ABOUT YOU?
ASK FOR ANYTHING.
LIKE FISH.
THE FLAVOR'S DIFFERENT... HEY, ARE YOU LISTENING?
MILK!
UH...MILK!? THE STUFF YOU DRINK ALL THE TIME!?
THE CHEAP KIND?
ぎょっ
GYO (SHOCK)
WHAT? ARE YOU HOLDING BACK OR SOMETHING?
THIS IS YOUR NEW YEAR'S GIFT, REMEMBER?

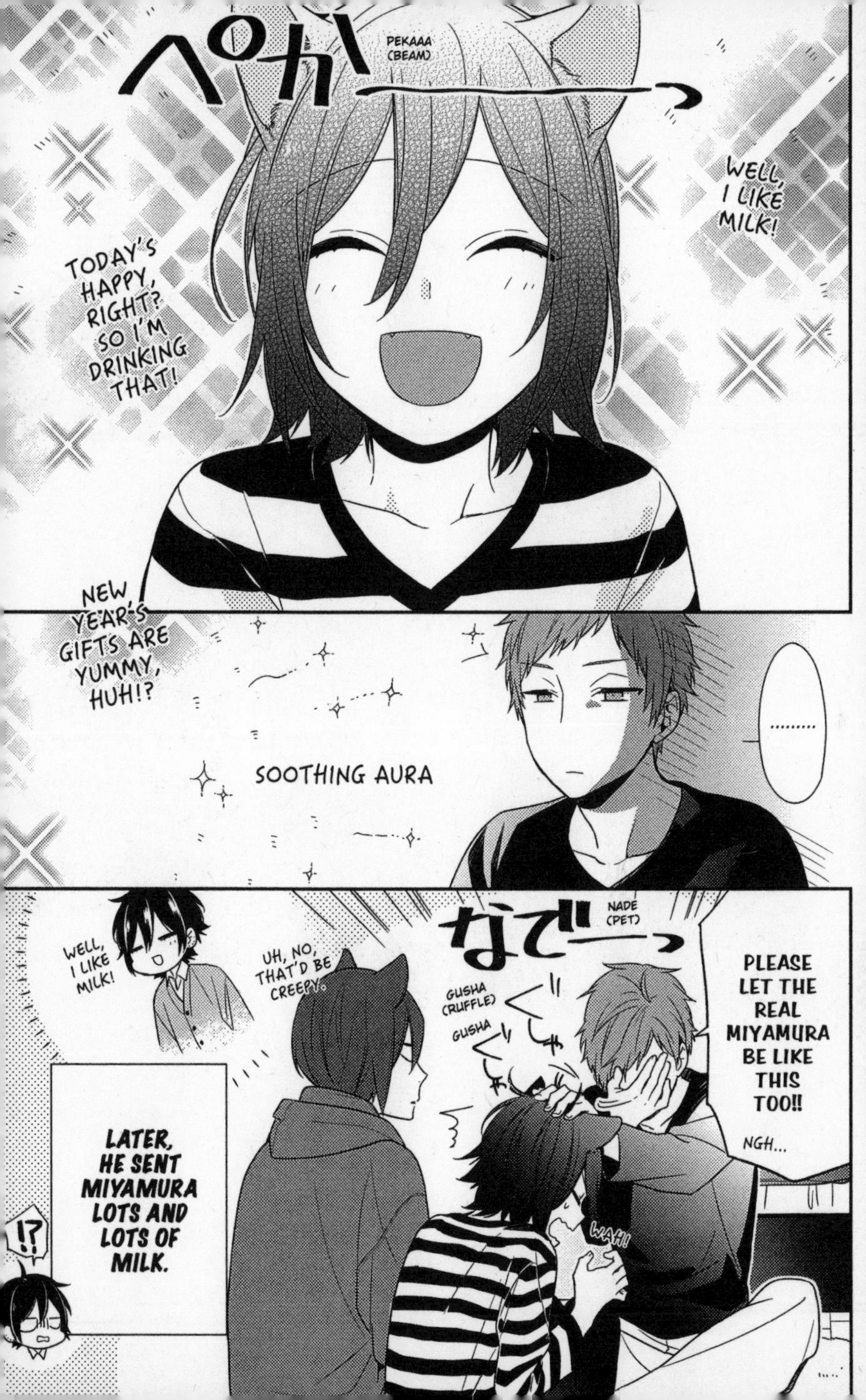
ぺかー
PEKAAA (BEAM)
WELL, I LIKE MILK!
TODAY'S HAPPY, RIGHT? SO I'M DRINKING THAT!
....
SOOTHING AURA
NEW YEAR'S GIFTS ARE YUMMY, HUH!?
PLEASE LET THE REAL MIYAMURA BE LIKE THIS TOO!!
NGH...
なでー
NADE (PET)
GUSHA (RUFFLE)
GUSHA
WAH!
UH, NO, THAT'D BE CREEPY.
WELL, I LIKE MILK!
LATER, HE SENT MIYAMURA LOTS AND LOTS OF MILK.
!?
....

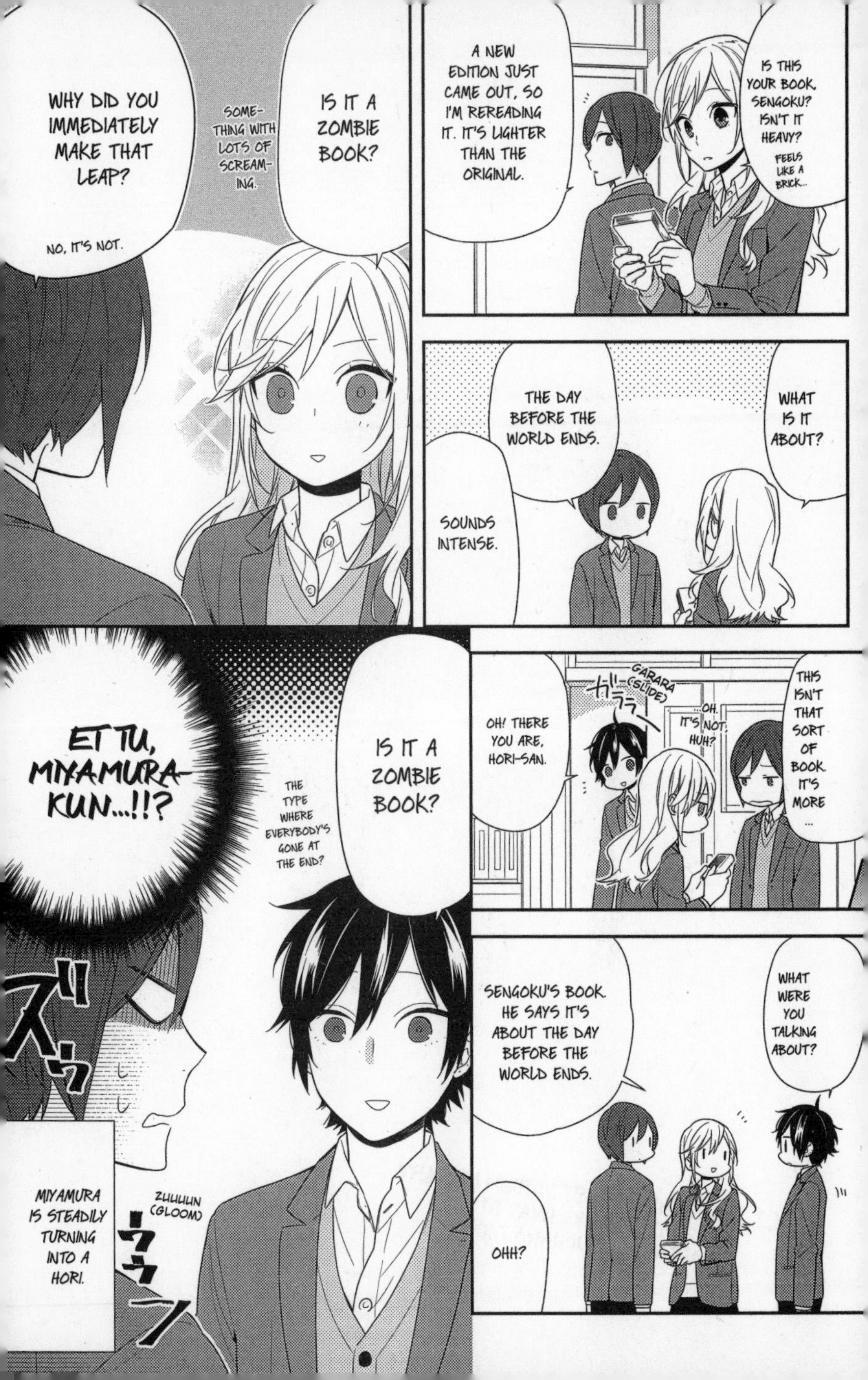
IS THIS YOUR BOOK, SENGOKU? ISN'T IT HEAVY?
FEELS LIKE A BRICK...
A NEW EDITION JUST CAME OUT, SO I'M REREADING IT. IT'S LIGHTER THAN THE ORIGINAL.
WHAT IS IT ABOUT?
THE DAY BEFORE THE WORLD ENDS.
SOUNDS INTENSE.
IS IT A ZOMBIE BOOK?
SOME-THING WITH LOTS OF SCREAM-ING.
WHY DID YOU IMMEDIATELY MAKE THAT LEAP?
NO, IT'S NOT.
THIS ISN'T THAT SORT OF BOOK. IT'S MORE ...
GARARA (SLIDE)
...OH. IT'S NOT, HUH?
OH! THERE YOU ARE, HORI-SAN.
WHAT WERE YOU TALKING ABOUT?
SENGOKU'S BOOK. HE SAYS IT'S ABOUT THE DAY BEFORE THE WORLD ENDS.
OHH?
IS IT A ZOMBIE BOOK?
THE TYPE WHERE EVERYBODY'S GONE AT THE END?
ET TU, MIYAMURA-KUN...!!?
ZUUUUN (GLOOM)
MIYAMURA IS STEADILY TURNING INTO A HORI.

HORIMIYA

HERO × Daisuke Hagiwara

Translation: Taylor Engel
Lettering: Alexis Eckerman

This book is a work of fiction. Names, characters, places, and incidents are the
product of the author's imagination or are used fictitiously. Any resemblance
to actual events, locales, or persons, living or dead, is coincidental.

HORIMIYA vol. 10
© HERO · OOZ
© 2016 Daisuke Hagiwara / SQUARE ENIX CO., LTD. First published in Japan
in 2016 by SQUARE ENIX CO., LTD. English translation rights arranged with
SQUARE ENIX CO., LTD. and Yen Press, LLC through Tuttle-Mori Agency, Inc.

English translation © 2018 by SQUARE ENIX CO., LTD.

Yen Press
1290 Avenue of the Americas
New York, NY 10104

Visit us at yenpress.com · facebook.com/yenpress ·
twitter.com/yenpress · yenpress.tumblr.com ·
instagram.com/yenpress

First Yen Press Edition: February 2018

Yen Press is an imprint of Yen Press, LLC.
The Yen Press name and logo are trademarks
of Yen Press, LLC.

The publisher is not responsible for websites
(or their content) that are not owned by the
publisher.

Library of Congress Control Number:
2015960115

ISBNs: 978-0-316-41605-4 (paperback)
        978-0-316-41633-7 (ebook)

10 9 8 7 6 5 4 3 2 1

BVG

Printed in the United States of America